Communications in Computer and Information Science 456

Mohammad S. Obaidat · Joaquim Filipe (Eds.)

E-Business and Telecommunications

International Joint Conference, ICETE 2013
Reykjavik, Iceland, July 29–31, 2013
Revised Selected Papers

 Springer

Editors
Mohammad S. Obaidat
Department of Computer Science
Monmouth University
West Long Branch, NJ
USA

Joaquim Filipe
Polytechnic Institute of Setúbal, INSTICC
Setúbal
Portugal

ISSN 1865-0929   ISSN 1865-0937 (electronic)
ISBN 978-3-662-44787-1   ISBN 978-3-662-44788-8 (eBook)
DOI 10.1007/978-3-662-44788-8

Library of Congress Control Number: 2014950810

Springer Heidelberg New York Dordrecht London

Printed on acid-free paper

Springer is part of Springer Science+Business Media (www.springer.com)

Preface

The present book includes extended and revised versions of a set of selected best papers from the 10th International Joint Conference on e-Business and Telecommunications (ICETE), which was held in July 2013, in Reykjávik, Iceland. This conference reflects a continuing effort to increase the dissemination of recent research results among professionals who work in the areas of e-business and telecommunications. ICETE is a joint international conference integrating four major areas of knowledge that are divided into six corresponding conferences: DCNET (Int'l Conf. on Data Communication Networking), ICE-B (Int'l Conf. on e-Business), OPTICS (Int'l Conf. on Optical Communication Systems), SECRYPT (Int'l Conf. on Security and Cryptography), WINSYS (Int'l Conf. on Wireless Information Systems) and SIGMAP (Int'l Conf. on Signal Processing and Multimedia).

The program of this joint conference included several outstanding keynote lectures presented by internationally renowned distinguished researchers who are experts in the various ICETE areas. Their keynote speeches have contributed to heighten the overall quality of the program and significance of the theme of the conference.

The conference topic areas define a broad spectrum in the key areas of e-business and telecommunications. This wide view reporting made ICETE appealing to a global audience of engineers, scientists, business practitioners, ICT managers, and policy experts. The papers accepted and presented at the conference demonstrated a number of new and innovative solutions for e-business and telecommunication networks and systems, showing that the technical problems in these closely related fields are challenging and worthwhile approaching in an interdisciplinary perspective such as that promoted by ICETE.

ICETE 2013 received 341 papers in total, with contributions from 56 different countries, in all continents, which demonstrate its success and global dimension. To evaluate each submission, a double-blind paper evaluation method was used: each paper was blindly reviewed by at least two experts from the International Program Committee. In fact, most papers had 3 reviews or more. The selection process followed strict criteria in all tracks. As a result only 44 papers were accepted and orally presented at ICETE as full papers (13 % of submissions) and 58 as short papers (17 % of submissions). Additionally, 75 papers were accepted for poster presentation. With these acceptance ratios, ICETE 2013 continues the tradition of previous ICETE conferences as a distinguished and high-quality conference.

We hope that you will find this collection of the best ICETE 2013 papers an excellent source of inspiration as well as a helpful reference for research in the aforementioned areas.

December 2013

Mohammad S. Obaidat
Joaquim Filipe

Organization

Conference Chair

Mohammad S. Obaidat   Monmouth University, USA

Program Co-chairs

DCNET

Mohammad S. Obaidat   Monmouth University, USA
José Luis Sevillano   University of Seville, Spain
Zhaoyang Zhang   Zhejiang University, China

ICE-B

David Marca   University of Phoenix, USA
Marten van Sinderen   University of Twente, The Netherlands

OPTICS

Panagiotis Sarigiannidis   University of Western Macedonia, Greece
Piero Castoldi   Scuola Superiore Sant'Anna, Italy
Víctor Torres-Padrosa   Universitat de Girona, Spain

SECRYPT

Pierangela Samarati   Università degli Studi di Milano, Italy

SIGMAP

Enrique Cabello   Universidad Rey Juan Carlos, Spain
Maria Virvou   University of Piraeus, Greece

WINSYS

Mohammad S. Obaidat   Monmouth University, USA
Hong Ji   Beijing University of Post and
                                   Telecommunications (BUPT), China

| Petros Nicopolitidis | Aristotle University, Greece |
| Dimitrios D. Vergados | University of Piraeus, Greece |

Organizing Committee

Marina Carvalho	INSTICC, Portugal
Helder Coelhas	INSTICC, Portugal
Bruno Encarnação	INSTICC, Portugal
Ana Guerreiro	INSTICC, Portugal
André Lista	INSTICC, Portugal
Filipe Mariano	INSTICC, Portugal
Andreia Moita	INSTICC, Portugal
Raquel Pedrosa	INSTICC, Portugal
Vitor Pedrosa	INSTICC, Portugal
Cláudia Pinto	INSTICC, Portugal
Cátia Pires	INSTICC, Portugal
Susana Ribeiro	INSTICC, Portugal
Rui Rodrigues	INSTICC, Portugal
Sara Santiago	INSTICC, Portugal
André Santos	INSTICC, Portugal
Mónica Saramago	INSTICC, Portugal
Mara Silva	INSTICC, Portugal
José Varela	INSTICC, Portugal
Pedro Varela	INSTICC, Portugal

DCNET Program Committee

Baber Aslam, Pakistan
Boris Bellalta, Spain
Christos Bouras, Greece
Christian Callegari, Italy
Fernando Cerdan, Spain
Paskorn Champrasert, Thailand
Min-Xiou Chen, Taiwan
Josep Domenech, Spain
Pingyi Fan, China
Hiroaki Fukuda, Japan
Francois Gagnon, Canada
Sebastià Galmés, Spain
Jose Daniel Garcia, Spain
Katja Gilly, Spain
Carlos Guerrero, Spain
Jinhua Guo, USA
Aun Haider, Pakistan

Antonio Izquierdo-Manzanares, USA
Carlos Juiz, Spain
Dimitris Kanellopoulos, Greece
Randi Karlsen, Norway
Philip Koopman, USA
Michael Kounavis, USA
Isaac Lera, Spain
Der Ming Liou, Taiwan
Pascal Lorenz, France
S. Kami Makki, USA
Wojciech Mazurczyk, Poland
Pascale Minet, France
Petros Nicopolitidis, Greece
Ibrahim Onyuksel, USA
Antonio Pescape', Italy
Ramon Puigjaner, Spain
Francisco J. Ros, Spain

Hangguan Shan, China
Arun K. Somani, USA
Junichi Suzuki, USA
Kenji Suzuki, USA
Dirk Trossen, UK
Pere Vilà, Spain
Luis Javier Garcia Villalba, Spain
Hiroshi Wada, Australia

Ping Wang, USA
Bernd E. Wolfinger, Germany
Józef Wozniak, Poland
Christos Xenakis, Greece
Jianbin Xiong, China
Laurance T. Yang, Canada
Cliff C. Zou, USA

DCNET Auxiliary Reviewers

Javier Fernandez, Spain
Beatriz Gomez, Spain

ICE-B Program Committee

Andreas Ahrens, Germany
Giuseppe Andronico, Italy
Anteneh Ayanso, Canada
Elarbi Badidi, UAE
Joseph Barjis, The Netherlands
Morad Benyoucef, Canada
Ross Brown, Australia
Rebecca Bulander, Germany
Wojciech Cellary, Poland
Soon Chun, USA
Anton Civit, Spain
Michele Colajanni, Italy
Rafael Corchuelo, Spain
Ioanna Dionysiou, Cyprus
Damiano Distante, Italy
Habiba Drias, Algeria
Yanqing Duan, UK
Erwin Fielt, Australia
Erwin Folmer, The Netherlands
Geoffrey Charles Fox, USA
Rafael Z. Frantz, Brazil
José María García, Austria
Sam Guinea, Italy
Inma Hernández, Spain
Andreas Holzinger, Austria
Ela Hunt, Switzerland
Arun Iyengar, USA
Hurevren Kilic, Turkey

Yung-Ming Li, Taiwan
Rungtai Lin, Taiwan
David Marca, USA
Gavin McArdle, Ireland
Gianluca Carlo Misuraca, Spain
Nicole Mitsche, UK
Adrian Mocan, Germany
Wai Yin Mok, USA
Ali Reza Montazemi, Canada
Maurice Mulvenna, UK
Daniel O'Leary, USA
Wilma Penzo, Italy
Krassie Petrova, New Zealand
Willy Picard, Poland
Charmaine Du Plessis, South Africa
Pak-Lok Poon, China
Philippos Pouyioutas, Cyprus
Bijan Raahemi, Canada
Sofia Reino, Spain
Manuel Resinas, Spain
Carlos Rivero, Spain
Erik Rolland, USA
Niall Rooney, UK
Fabricia Roos, Brazil
Gustavo Rossi, Argentina
Jarogniew Rykowski, Poland
Amit Sawant, USA
Bettina Schauer, Austria

Hassan A. Sleiman, Spain
Riccardo Spinelli, Italy
Zhaohao Sun, Australia
Pierre Tiako, USA
Laurentiu Vasiliu, Ireland

Yiannis Verginadis, Greece
Michael Weiss, Canada
Moe Thandar Wynn, Australia
Edzus Zeiris, Latvia
Lina Zhou, USA

ICE-B Auxiliary Reviewers

Marwa Djeffal, Algeria
Gretel Fernández, Spain
Meriem Laifa, Algeria

Amir Meshkat, The Netherlands
Nagarajan Venkatachalam, Australia

OPTICS Program Committee

Gaetano Assanto, Italy
Luis Cancela, Portugal
Adolfo Cartaxo, Portugal
Piero Castoldi, Italy
Jiajia Chen, Sweden
Marco Genovese, Italy
Ahmed Kamal, USA
Burak Kantarci, Canada
Hoon Kim, Singapore
Miroslaw Klinkowski, Poland
Christos Liaskos, Greece
Malamati Louta, Greece
Michael McGarry, USA
Amalia Miliou, Greece
Paolo Monti, Sweden
Maria Morant, Spain
Michela Svaluto Moreolo, Spain
Nabil Naas, Canada

Petros Nicopolitidis, Greece
Satoru Okamoto, Japan
Jordi Perelló, Spain
Periklis Petropoulos, UK
Marco Presi, Italy
João Rebola, Portugal
Enrique Rodriguez-Colina, Mexico
Panagiotis Sarigiannidis, Greece
Mehdi Shadaram, USA
Surinder Singh, India
Wolfgang Sohler, Germany
Fernando Solano, Poland
Marc Sorel, UK
Salvatore Spadaro, Spain
António Teixeira, Portugal
Víctor Torres-Padrosa, Spain
Naoya Wada, Japan
Yixin Wang, Singapore

OPTICS Auxiliary Reviewers

Abdulkadir Celik, USA
George Vasileiou, Greece

SECRYPT Program Committee

Alessandro Armando, Italy
Carlo Blundo, Italy
Andrey Bogdanov, Denmark
Michael Brenner, Germany
Carlos Blanco Bueno, Spain
David Chadwick, UK
Frederic Cuppens, France
Nora Cuppens-Boulahia, France
Reza Curtmola, USA
Tassos Dimitriou, Greece
Josep Domingo-Ferrer, Spain
Eduardo B. Fernandez, USA
Alberto Ferrante, Switzerland
Josep-Lluis Ferrer-Gomila, Spain
William Fitzgerald, Ireland
Sara Foresti, Italy
Steven Furnell, UK
Joaquin Garcia-Alfaro, France
Mark Gondree, USA
Dimitris Gritzalis, Greece
Stefanos Gritzalis, Greece
Yong Guan, USA
Sokratis Katsikas, Greece
Shinsaku Kiyomoto, Japan
Ruggero Donida Labati, Italy
Costas Lambrinoudakis, Greece
Bo Lang, China
Adam J. Lee, USA
Patrick P.C. Lee, Hong Kong
Albert Levi, Turkey
Jiguo Li, China
Ming Li, USA
Antonio Lioy, Italy
Giovanni Livraga, Italy
Javier Lopez, Spain
Haibing Lu, USA
Emil Lupu, UK

Olivier Markowitch, Belgium
Vashek Matyas, Czech Republic
Carlos Maziero, Brazil
Wojciech Mazurczyk, Poland
Alessandro Mei, Italy
Chris Mitchell, UK
Atsuko Miyaji, Japan
Marco Casassa Mont, UK
David Naccache, France
Eiji Okamoto, Japan
Rolf Oppliger, Switzerland
Stefano Paraboschi, Italy
Joon Park, USA
Günther Pernul, Germany
Roberto Di Pietro, Italy
Joachim Posegga, Germany
Silvio Ranise, Italy
Kui Ren, USA
David G. Rosado, Spain
Pierangela Samarati, Italy
Nicolas Sklavos, Greece
Willy Susilo, Australia
Juan Tapiador, Spain
Vicenc Torra, Spain
Jaideep Vaidya, USA
Luca Viganò, Italy
Sabrina de Capitani di Vimercati, Italy
Cong Wang, Hong Kong
Haining Wang, USA
Lingyu Wang, Canada
Ping Wang, USA
Xinyuan (Frank) Wang, USA
Alec Yasinsac, USA
Meng Yu, USA
Lei Zhang, USA
Jianying Zhou, Singapore

SECRYPT Auxiliary Reviewers

Marcel Ambroze, UK
Clara Bertolissi, France
Jorge Blasco, Spain
Christina Boura, Denmark
Roberto Carbone, Italy
Aldar Chan, Singapore
Andreas Dittrich, Switzerland
Nicholas Farnan, USA
William Garrison, USA
Matt Henricksen, Singapore
Javier Herranz, Spain
Stefan Heyse, Afghanistan
Duygu Karaoglan, Turkey
Frédéric Lafitte, Belgium
Efthymios Lalas, Greece

Yang Lu, China
Alessio Merlo, Italy
Jelena Milosevic, Switzerland
Moussa Ouedraogo, Luxembourg
Henning Perl, Germany
Nikos Pitropakis, Greece
Panos Rizomiliotis, Greece
Rodrigo Roman, Singapore
Merve Sahin, Turkey
Kyoji Shibutani, Japan
Alessandro Sorniotti, Switzerland
Ingo Stengel, UK
Elmar Tischhauser, Belgium
Zhongmei Wan, China

SIGMAP Program Committee

Harry Agius, UK
Zahid Akthar, Italy
João Ascenso, Portugal
Pradeep K. Atrey, Canada
Ramazan Aygun, USA
Alejandro Linares Barranco, Spain
Adrian Bors, UK
Enrique Cabello, Spain
Kasim Candan, USA
Wai-Kuen Cham, China
Chin-Chen Chang, Taiwan
Shu-Ching Chen, USA
Zhixin Chen, USA
Wei Cheng, Singapore
Cristina Conde, Spain
Rob Evans, Australia
William Grosky, USA
Malka Halgamuge, Australia
Hermann Hellwagner, Austria
Wolfgang Hürst, The Netherlands
Razib Iqbal, Canada
Mohan Kankanhalli, Singapore
Sokratis Katsikas, Greece
Brigitte Kerherve, Canada
Constantine Kotropoulos, Greece

Jing Li, China
Ilias Maglogiannis, Greece
Hong Man, USA
Daniela Moctezuma, Spain
Chamin Morikawa, Japan
Alejandro Murua, Canada
Maria Paula Queluz, Portugal
Rudolf Rabenstein, Germany
Pedro Real, Spain
Gerardo Reyes, Mexico
Luis Alberto Morales Rosales, Mexico
Massimo De Santo, Italy
Mei-Ling Shyu, USA
Oscar S. Siordia, Spain
Akshya Swain, New Zealand
George Tsihrintzis, Greece
Andreas Uhl, Austria
Zhiyong Wang, Australia
Michael Weber, Germany
Nicolas Wicker, France
Sanjeewa Witharana, Germany
Lei Wu, USA
Chengcui Zhang, USA
Yongxin Zhang, USA

SIGMAP Auxiliary Reviewers

Roberto Ángel Meléndez Armenta, Mexico
Mariana Lobato Baez, Mexico
Hoang Van Xiem, Portugal

WINSYS Program Committee

Taufik Abrão, Brazil
Vicente Alarcon-Aquino, Mexico
Josephina Antoniou, Cyprus
Francisco Barcelo Arroyo, Spain
Abdelmalik Bachir, UK
Bert-Jan van Beijnum, The Netherlands
Luis Bernardo, Portugal
Chien-Liang Chen, Taiwan
Yen-Da Chen, Taiwan
Sungrae Cho, Korea
Hsi-Tseng Chou, Taiwan
Iñigo Cuiñas, Spain
Luis Rizo Dominguez, Mexico
Christos Douligeris, Greece
Amit Dvir, Hungary
Val Dyadyuk, Australia
Jocelyne Elias, France
Marco Di Felice, Italy
Gianluigi Ferrari, Italy
Panayotis Fouliras, Greece
Damianos Gavalas, Greece
Annarita Giani, USA
Stefanos Gritzalis, Greece
Jinhua Guo, USA
Jeroen Hoebeke, Belgium
Daesik Hong, Korea
Ali Abu-el Humos, USA
Athanassios C. Iossifides, Greece
Jehn-Ruey Jiang, Taiwan
Georgios Kambourakis, Greece
Akimitsu Kanzaki, Japan
Majid Khabbazian, Canada
Abdelmajid Khelil, Germany

Charalampos Konstantopoulos, Greece
Gurhan Kucuk, Turkey
Günes Karabulut Kurt, Turkey
Wei Li, Australia
Ju Liu, China
Hsi-pin Ma, Taiwan
Michele Magno, Italy
S. Kami Makki, USA
Pietro Manzoni, Spain
Panagiotis Melidis, Greece
Luis Mendes, Portugal
Nathalie Mitton, France
Petros Nicopolitidis, Greece
Grammati Pantziou, Greece
Al-Sakib Khan Pathan, Malaysia
Dennis Pfisterer, Germany
António Rodrigues, Portugal
Enrique Rodriguez-Colina, Mexico
Francisco J. Ros, Spain
Jörg Roth, Germany
Manuel García Sánchez, Spain
Christian Schindelhauer, Germany
Miguel Sepulcre, Spain
Kuei-Ping Shih, Taiwan
Razvan Stanica, France
Leonardo Soto Sumuano, Mexico
Claude Tadonki, France
Shensheng Tang, USA
Cesar Vargas-Rosales, Mexico
Guiyi Wei, China
Georg Wittenburg, Germany
Dimirios Zorbas, France

WINSYS Auxiliary Reviewers

Zhuo Chen, Australia
Xiaojing Huang, Australia
Oleg Starostenko, Mexico

Invited Speakers

Laurence T. Yang	Huazhong University of Science and Technology, China and St Francis Xavier University, Canada
Pascal Lorenz	University of Haute Alsace, France
Donal O'Mahony	Trinity College Dublin, Ireland
David Naccache	Ecole Normale Superieure, France

Contents

Optical Communication Systems

Security and Cryptography

Signal Processing and Multimedia Applications

Wireless Information Networks and Systems

Invited Speakers

QoS and QoE in the Next Generation Networks and Wireless Networks

Pascal Lorenz[✉]

University of Haute Alsace, 34, rue du Grillenbreit, 68008 Colmar, France
lorenz@ieee.org

Abstract. With the development of new multimedia applications, telecommunication networks should be developed to offer real QoS. Different protocols such as MPLS, IntServ and DiffServ introduce new mechanisms which can be used to offer QoS in high speed Next Generation Networks (NGN). This paper is focused essentially on QoS and QoE mechanisms in wired and wireless networks through the presentation of communication architectures and protocols.

1 Introduction

To offer Quality of Service (QoS) there are a lot of parameters that should be taken into account, such as bandwidth, latency, jitter, packet loss, packet delay. A given application does not take into account all parameters with the same priority. For video applications, the most important QoS parameter is based on the bandwidth. For Voice over IP (VoIP) applications, the most important QoS parameter is based on latency with end to end delay no larger than 200 ms.

The QoS can be linked to the:

- Network level: in this case the QoS depend of the network policy and of the used mechanisms such as filters, rerouting in the core of the network, control access at the corners of the network.
- Application level: in this case it is the application which improve the QoS and there is no link with the network infrastructure.

The Classes of Service (CoS) classify the services in different classes and manage each type of traffic with a particular way. ETSI (European Telecommunications Standards Institute) has introduced four CoS: Class 1 for Best Effort until Class 4 for QoS guaranteed. Many SLA (Service Level Agreement) offers three CoS: Premium (for 15 % of network resources), Olympic (for 80 % of network resources) and Best Effort. QoE (Quality of Experience) is a subjective measure of a customer's for a supplied service [7, 8].

Internet is increasing exponentially and the bandwidth doubles every 18 months. In 2001, there were 180 million users and today there is more than 2 billion users. 90 % of the Internet traffic is based on TCP and 10 % on UDP protocol (75 % for WWW applications, 3 % for the Emails, 4 % for FTP and 7 % for the News).

© Springer-Verlag Berlin Heidelberg 2014
M.S. Obaidat and J. Filipe (Eds.): ICETE 2013, CCIS 456, pp. 3–16, 2014.
DOI: 10.1007/978-3-662-44788-8_1

2 QoS Mechanisms

There are many QoS mechanisms that can be used to offer QoS in the network. In the last years, we have observed a growth of the networks capacity with the development of Wavelength Division Multiplexing (WDM) technologies.

The different types of QoS mechanisms [1] can:

- Provide a fair service with Best Effort algorithms.
- Maximize the bandwidth allocation to the source receiving the smallest allocation (max-min allocation of bandwidth). This algorithm allows decreasing the bandwidth allocated to other source.
- Drop the packets if congestion occurs in routers when the buffer is full (tail drop algorithm) or when the buffer occupancy increases too much (RED: Random Early Detection algorithm).
- Use congestion control mechanisms in end systems to inform the source about network congestion with ICMP or tagged packets with ECN (Explicit Congestion Notification) protocols. In this case, all routers should implement the congestion control mechanisms.
- Divide the output buffers in N queues and introduce a scheduler (processor sharing or round robin algorithms).
- Classify the IP flows at different layers: the edge routers perform classification/ marking and the backbone routers rely on marking.
- Support n drop priorities to offer a minimum bandwidth service with n RED algorithms running in parallel (weighted RED algorithm).
- Introduce a weight to each queue (Generalized Processor Sharing/Weighted Round Robin algorithms).

The new communication networks must offer QoS and mobility. The two major possibilities are:

- QoS mechanisms based on signalization and routers. It is the solution used by the telecommunication world or
- Overprovisioning the network for new applications such as TV on demand, telephony IP. Overprovisioning is not a global solution but is an asset for traffic engineering and for QoS in Internet networks.

In the core of the network, the architectures can be based on these two following models:

- With signalization (such as the SS7, X25/ATM, Internet/Telecom networks). These networks offer good QoS but theses solutions are expensive: an UMTS access point costs about 15000 $.
- without signalization (such as the Arpanet, 1st and 2nd Internet generation networks). These networks offer no QoS but these solutions are cheap: a WiFi access point costs about 100 $.

Initially ATM (Asynchronous Transfer Mode) was the best and unique network to offer QoS, but now ATM is less and less used. Therefore we can observe in the evolution of network architectures based on full ATM, on IP over ATM and now on full IP.

The different network architectures can be represented as follows (Fig. 1):

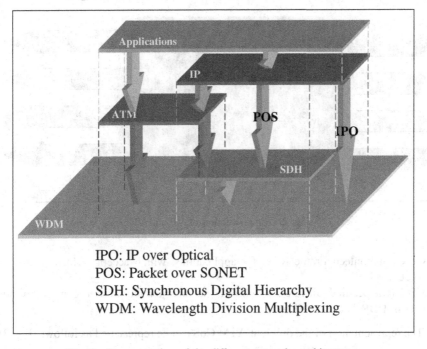

IPO: IP over Optical
POS: Packet over SONET
SDH: Synchronous Digital Hierarchy
WDM: Wavelength Division Multiplexing

Fig. 1. Representation of the different networks architectures.

We will now present the ATM protocol that is the first protocol which offers QoS.

3 ATM Protocol

ATM is a connection-oriented protocol, which offers real QoS guaranties. The QoS is negotiated during the establishment of the connection and depends of the available resources.

ATM is based on VC (Virtual Channels) and on VP (Virtual Paths). VP and the VC can be represented as follow (Fig. 2):

In ATM networks, there are six CoS:

- CBR (Constant Bit Rate), which guarantees a constant bit rate for applications such as videoconferencing, telephony.
- RT-VBR (Real-Time Variable Bit Rate) for transmissions with a variable rate for applications requiring real-time constraints, such as MPEG transmissions.
- NRT-VBR (Non-Real-Time Variable Bit Rate) for transmissions with a variable rate for applications requiring no real-time constraints, such as multimedia transfers.
- ABR (Available Bit Rate) for transmissions of traffic using the remaining bandwidth or based on bursty traffic. ABR guaranties always a minimum rate.

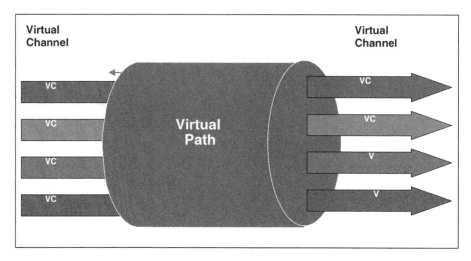

Fig. 2. Representation of VP and VC.

- GFR (Guaranteed Frame Rate) for applications, which accept to loose sometime some services.
- UBR (Unspecified Bit rate), which offer no rate guaranty and no congestion indication. UBR is a Best Effort CoS.

The representation of the different ATM CoS can be represented as follows (Fig. 3):

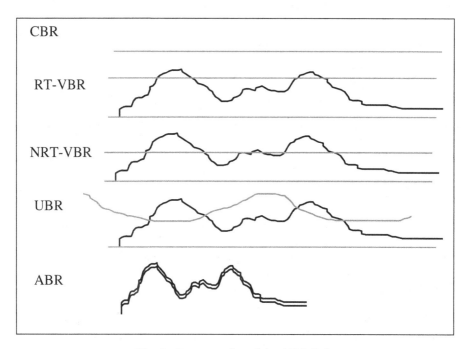

Fig. 3. Representation of the ATM CoS.

For theses CoS, different AAL (ATM Adaptation layer) have been defined:

- AAL1: for oriented connection and real-time traffic (CBR)
- AAL2: for variable real time traffic (VBR)
- AAL3/4: for variable real-time traffic (ABR, GFR)
- AAL5: for reliable or non-reliable services and unicast or multicast traffic (UBR).

In ATM networks, QoS is provided by the signalization and stream controls mechanisms. The major QoS parameters used by ATM networks are:

- CTD: Cell Transfer Delay
- CMR Cell Misinsertion Ratio
- CLR: Cell Loss Ratio
- CER: Cell Error Ratio
- PCR: Peak Cell Rate
- MCR: Minimum Cell Rate
- CVDT: Cell variation Delay Tolerance
- SCR: Sustainable Cell Rate
- BT: Burst Tolerance
- CDV: Cell Delay Variation

The ATM stream control mechanisms are based on:

- CAC (Connection Admission Control) that determines if a connection can be accepted or not.
- Usage Parameter Control/Network Parameter Control (UPC/NPC) that controls the traffic and the conformity of a connection.
- The Resource Management mechanisms that optimize the traffic.

An example of an ATM control mechanism can be represented as follows (Fig. 4):

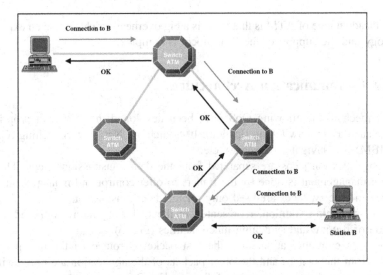

Fig. 4. ATM control mechanism.

There are three major protocols used to manage IP over ATM: LAN Emulation (LANE), Classical IP and Multi Protocol Over ATM (MPOA).

MPOA is used in wide area network and avoids the router bottleneck problems thanks to the introduction of a route server for the ATM address resolution. MPOA can be considered as a virtual router, which divides data transmission from data computation functions.

A MPOA architecture can be represented as follows (Fig. 5):

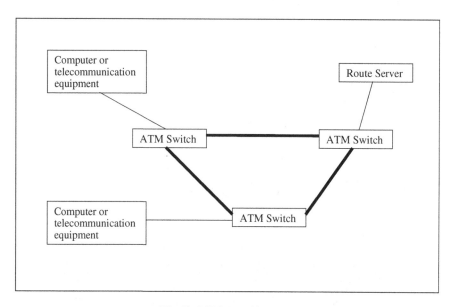

Fig. 5. MPOA architecture.

The disadvantage of ATM is that there is a big overhead. ATM is also an expensive technology and the support of the IP protocol is complex.

4 New Communication Architectures

The first mechanisms allowing QoS have been developed in 1996 with proprietary solutions such as Tag Switching (Ipsilon), IP Switching, Net Flow Switching (Cisco), ARIS (IBM), IP Navigator (Cascade), etc.

The signalization steps are separated from the data transmissions steps. The signalization management is done by the routers to offer control and management functionalities and the switches are used only for the data transmission.

The IP switching solution, represented in the following figure, is based on the separation of routing and switching functionalities (Fig. 6):

In a given communication, only the first packet is routed (if the first packet is unknown from the switch) and the other packets of the application are only switched and no more routed as represented in following Fig. 7:

IP protocol is used for routing, signaling and for the switching tables management that represent 20 % of the traffic. Layer 2 protocols such as ATM or Ethernet protocols are only used the fast forwarding that represent 80 % of the traffic.

The different QoS mechanisms for an IP network (such as MPLS, DiffServ, IntServ, RSVP) can be represented in an OSI architecture as follows (Fig. 8):

We will now describe the different IP QoS protocols MPLS, RSVP, IntServ and DiffServ.

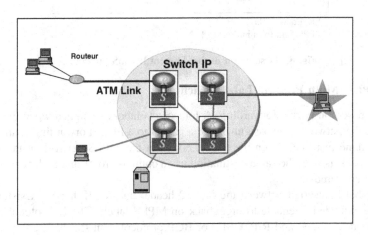

Fig. 6. IP switching architecture.

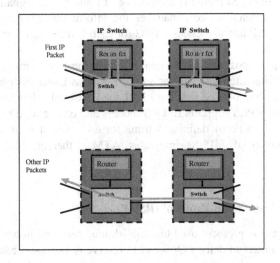

Fig. 7. Representation of IP switch mechanisms.

Transport Layer	IntServ, RSVP, DiffServ
Network Layer (IP)	MPLS
Data Link Layer (Ethernet, FR, ATM, PPP)	
Physical Layer (Sonet/SDH, optical fiber, 802.17: Resilient Packet Ring)	

FR: Frame Relay
PPP: Point-to-Point Protocol

Fig. 8. Description of the different IP QoS protocols.

4.1 MPLS (Multi Protocol Label Switching)

MPLS is based on packet forwarding. A four octets label is assigned when the packet enter into the network. The assignment of a packet to a FEC (Forwarding Equivalence Class) is done just once when the packet enters in the MPLS network at the ingress node. All packets with the same destination use a common route and at the egress node the labels are removed.

The label is inserted between the layer 2 header and the IP header. Existing protocols are extended to enable to piggyback on MPLS labels. The IP protocol is switched instead of routed and RIP, OSPF or BGP protocols can still be used.

MPLS nodes (called LSR or Label Switching Router) forward the packets based on the label value. MPLS combines L3 routing (IP) and L2 forwarding. The LSR can implement DiffServ, with a DiffServ over MPLS architecture.

A LSP (Label Switched Paths) is a sequence of routers. The signalization protocol LDP (Label Distribution Protocol) manages the information exchange between the LSR to establish a LSP and associates a FEC for each LSP. A LSR sent periodically a LDP Hello Message.

With MPLS it is possible to introduce a path protection/restoration with the introduction of an alternate route and the use of RSVP as Label Distribution Protocol. With CR-LDP (Constraint-based Routing LDP), the LSR establishes LSPs satisfying to a set of constraints. MPLS supports IP QoS models and can be used to build VPNs. It supports all types of traffic by defining a trunk for each pair of ingress/egress router.

GMPLS (Generalized MPLS) integrates ATM, Ethernet, FR, TDM, optical networks.

4.2 Ressource Reservation Protocol (RSVP)

RSVP is a signalization protocol used to establish unidirectional flows in IP networks. RSVP is used by routers to deliver QoS and to reserve resources in each node along a path. RSVP sends periodic refresh messages to maintain a state along a reserved path. A bandwidth is reserved for a given flow and requires resources reservation and releasing at regular intervals.

The establishment/maintain of unidirectional flows in IP networks is done through the PATH and RESV messages. The RSVP messages are encapsulated inside IP packets. RSVP supports MPLS, multicast and unicast traffics.

4.3 Integrated Services (Intserv)

IntServ is based on traffic control mechanisms and on the signalization protocol RSVP. The reservation is done at the router level. The problem is that:

- There is a poor scalability because the amount of state increases proportionally with the number of flows,
- All routers must implement RSVP,
- There is no policy for reservation control,
- Stations must support signalization.

Therefore, RSVP is only for small networks. The three CoS for IntServ are:

- Guaranteed Service (Premium service), for applications requiring fixed delay bound (CBR, RT-VBR).
- Controlled-Load Service (Olympic service) for applications requiring reliable and enhanced best-effort service (NRT-VBR, GFR, ABR).
- Null service, when there is no need of time constraints, but only a better best-effort service (UBR).

4.4 Differentiated Services (Diffserv)

DiffServ is a relative-priority scheme in which the IP packets are classified and marked at the network ingress to create several packet classes. The selected type of service is indicated inside each IP packet. DiffServ scalability comes from the traffic aggregation with the use of aggregate classification state in the core of the network. To share the bandwidth, DiffServ offers a hierarchy of different flows and is similar to MPLS, but more adapted for MAN.

Complex mechanisms depend of the number of services implemented in boundary nodes. SLA can be used between the client and the provider to specify for each service the amount of traffic that can be sent. The three CoS for DiffServ are:

- Expedited Forwarding (Premium service) for fixed bit rate between the source and the destination (CBR, RT-VBR).
- Assured Forwarding (Olympic service) for bursty services. There is no QoS guaranteed but only a low loss probability (ABR, GFR, nrt-VBR).
- Bulk Handling for applications requiring no QoS such as file transfer or mail (UBR).

4.5   Conclusion

The integration of QoS mechanisms is easier in small networks, because large networks ingrate a lot of heterogeneous domains.

DiffServ is less complex and easier to be implemented than IntServ, but it gives less accurately and less QoS flow differentiation. DiffServ is located in the core of the network between the routers and IntServ at the periphery of the networks.

IntServ works on micro-flows, it is a complex technology based on a "hard" approach of QoS. In DiffServ the load control is done at aggregate level by the network and not at flow level by TCP. MPLS is another evolution of IP service: it is a generic connection orientation that increases of routing functionalities.

To summarize, in the LANs it is IntServ offers the best approach, in MANs it is DiffServ (or IntServ) and in the WANs it is MPLS.

5   Qos in Wireless Networks

There are many different types of wireless networks: cellular networks, mobile networks, data transmission networks and satellites networks [2, 4, 5, 6].

For example, the wave radio-electrical networks penetrate the buildings and can be used for large distances. The wave infrared networks are used for small distance and do not penetrate the buildings. The micro-wave frequency networks do not penetrate the buildings and are used for networks no larger than 80 km. Light wave networks are based on lasers that are quickly absorbed by the rain or the snow.

In wireless terminals, some problems begin to be solved to offer a better management of the duration of the batteries (via hydrogen and supercondensator batteries), the screens (via OLED-Flexible Organic Light Emitting Diode screens) and keyboard (via laser keyboard). These different solutions are represented in the Fig. 9:

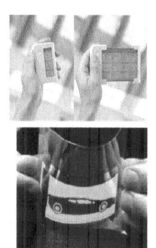

Fig. 9. OLED and laser keyboard.

There are multiple access techniques: FDMA (Frequency Division Multiple Access) developed for analogical networks, TDMA (Time Division Multiple Access) developed for numerical networks, CDMA (Code Division Multiple Access) developed for third generation networks and OFDM (Orthogonal Frequency Division Multiplexing) developed for the four generation networks.

5.1 Satellites

There are three types of satellites:

- LEO (Low Earth Orbit),
- MEO (Medium Earth Orbit),
- GEO (Geostationary Earth Orbit).

The frequencies used by the satellites use:

- Ku band (10 GHz to 18 GHz),
- C band (4 GHz to 6 GHz) for the connections between terrestrial stations and satellites,
- Ka band (20 GHz to 30 GHz).
- V band (40 GHz to 50 GHz) for future applications.

The LEO satellites are located between 500 and 2000 km. The communication delays are 0.01 s and the maximum rate is 155 Mbit/s. To cover the world 50 satellites are necessary and one satellite covers the skyline during 15 min. LEO based on 800 MHz, offer a 300 kbit/s rate and can be used for localization such as the GPS (Global Positioning System) system. LEO based on 2 GHz, offer a 10 kbit/s rate are used essentially for telephony applications. LEO based on 20 GHz to 30 GHz, offer 155 Mbit/s rate for multimedia applications.

MEO satellites are located at an altitude between 5000 km and 20000 km for communication delays of 0.1 s. A communication can remain one hour and 12 satellites are necessary to cover the earth.

GEO satellites are located at an altitude of 36600 km with communication delays of 0.27 s. The duration of GEO satellites are between 15 and 20 years and three satellites can cover the world.

Today, we can observe the development of pico-satellite (1 kilo) located at an altitude of 340 km and of HAPs (High Altitude Platforms).

5.2 2G to 4G Networks

In this section, we will present quickly the second generation (2G) and the third generation (3G) wireless networks.

The pico-cells are used for distances between 5 and 50 m, the micro-cells for distances between 50 and 500 m and the macro-cells for distances between 0.5 and 10 km.

In wireless networks, the Public Land Mobile Network (PLMN) is composed by the:

– Base Station Subsystem (BSS) that manage radio resources with the:

- Mobile Station,
- Base Transceiver Station (BTS),
- Base Station Controller (BSC).

– Network and Switching Subsystem (NSS) that manage network resources with the:

- Visitor Location Register (VLR) for mobiles localization,
- Home Location Register (HLR) that contain subscription information,
- Mobile Switching Center (MSC).

– Operation Sub-System (OSS) for the administration and management of the network.

The BSC establishes the communications with the Mobile services Switching Center (MSC). When the best BTS is selected, the mobile asks for a logical signaling channel to the BSC, which manages the communications synchronization.

The 2G are based on 900, 1800 and 1900 MHz frequencies and offer a 10 kbit/s transmission rate.

GPRS (General Packet Radio Service) is a 2.5G network that offers a maximum rate of 48 kbit/s. It is based on packet switching; the cost of the communication depends only of the amount of data and not the duration of the communication. The evolution of a 2G network to a 2.5G network can be done without modification of the BSS, because 2.5G networks use the same frequency and can reuse the BTSs and the BSCs.

In GPRS networks, there is a need of two additional routers: SGSN (Serving GPRS Support Node) for the resources, sessions, taxation and mobility management and GGSN (Gateway GPRS Service Node) for IP networks interconnections.

EDGE (Enhanced Data rate for GSM Evolution) is a 2.75G network that will offer a 150 kbit/s rate. E-GPRS (Enhanced GPRS) apply EDGE to GPRS to offer similar services than UMTS (Universal Mobile Telecommunication System).

IMT2000 (International Mobile Telecommunication 2000) is essentially composed by UMTS and CDMA2000 systems. UMTS (Universal Mobile Telecommunication System) is based on 3GPP (Third Generation Partnership Project). CDMA 2000 is an American evolution of the IS-95 standard.

3G networks integrate in a same network, cellular network, wireless network, data transmission network, intelligent terminals and multimedia services such as bandwidth on demand. 3G networks are based on 1885 MHz to 2200 MHz frequencies and offer a 384 kbit/s transmission rate.

3,5G networks are based on HSDPA (High Speed Downlink Packet Access) which offers a 1 Mbit/s transmission rate.

3,75G networks are based on HSUPA (High-Speed Uplink Packet Access) which offers a 4 Mb/s transmission rate.

4G networks is based on the 30 GHz frequency and offer 300 Mb/s transmission rate.

5.3 Wireless Personal Area Networks (Wpan) - Ieee 802.15

WPAN networks are composed by a lot of different versions of IEEE 802.15. The majors IEEE 802.15 standards are:

- IEEE 802.15.1: Bluetooth WPAN has a rate of 1 Mbit/s and use the 2400 MHz frequency in a 10 meters diameter around the access point.
- IEEE 802.15.3: Ultra WideBand (UWB) is a wireless technology for transmitting digital data over a wide spectrum of frequency with very low power and with a 400 Mbit/s transmission rate.
- IEEE 802.15.4: standard developed for the communications between toys and sensors (ZigBee) with a 200 kbit/s transmission rate.

5.4 Wireless Lan (Wlan) - Ieee 802.11

WLAN networks are composed by different versions of IEEE 802.11 standards. The majors IEEE 802.11 standards are:

- IEEE 802.11b (WiFi – Wireless Fidelity): frequency of 2.4 GHz, transmission rate of 11 Mbit/s over 100 m. This protocol is based on CDMA/CA.
- IEEE 802.11g: frequency of 2.4 GHz and a transmission rate of 54 Mbit/s.
- IEEE 802.11a (WiFi 5): frequency of 5 Ghz and a transmission rate of 54 Mbit/s.
- IEEE 802.11i: developed to manage security aspects via EAP, WEP, TKIP, WPA.
- IEEE 802.11e: developed to manage QoS aspects.
- IEEE 802.11f: developed to manage handover aspects.
- IEEE 802.11n: based on power control offer a transmission rate of 400 Mbit/s.

WiGig (Wireless Gigabit Alliance) based on 57/66 GHz frequencies will offer a transmission rate of 6 Gbit/s with the IEEE 802.11ad protocol.

5.5 Wman (Wireless Metropolitan Area Network) Ieee 802.16

The major protocol WiMax is based on 10/66 Ghz frequencies and offer a transmission rate of 120 Mbit/s over 50 km. WiMax-Mobile (IEEE 802) is based on the 3,5 Ghz frequency can offer a transmission rate of 1 Mbit/s for mobile station moving at a speed of 250 km/h [3].

The others IEEE 802.16 standards are LMDS (Local Multi-point Distribution Service) and MMDS (Multi-channel Multi-point Distribution Service).

6 Conclusion

There are a lot of networks, each network offer different types of QoS based on a specific protocol. The required QoS and the price of the communication should be taken into account to decide what the best wireless network at the given location. For example, if the cheaper network WiFi is not available or does not offer enough QoS, we can to try to connect to WiMax. And if WiMax is not available, another more expansive solution can be to choose 3G or 4G networks.

The 2G GSM standard was initially based on ISDN, GPRS standard on Frame Relay and UMTS standard on ATM/AAL2 protocol. Now, the second generation of UMTS and CDMA2000 standards are based on IP protocol, which is the now the major protocol to offer QoS in wired and wireless networks.

Future works will be based on the development of the virtualization techniques, green networks and on the cloud. All these new networks should be able to offer real QoS at the best price and in a green context.

References

1. Vicente, A.M., Apostolopoulos, G., Alfaro, F.J., Sánchez, J.L., Duato, J.: Efficient deadline-based QoS algorithms for high-performance networks. IEEE Trans. Comput. **57**, 928–939 (2008)
2. Al-Manthari, B., Hassanein, H., Abu Ali, N., Nasser, N.: Fair class-based downlink scheduling with revenue considerations in next generation broadband wireless access systems. IEEE Trans. Mob. Comput. **8**, 721–734 (2009)
3. Park, E.C.: Efficient uplink bandwidth request with delay regulation for real-time service in mobile wimax networks. IEEE Trans. Mob. Comput. **8**, 1235–1249 (2009)
4. Le, L., Hossain, E.: Tandem queue models with applications to QoS routing, multihop wireless networks. IEEE Trans. Mob. Comput. **7**, 1025–1040 (2008)
5. Park, S., Jeong, S.H.: Mobile IPTV: approaches, challenges, standards, and QoS support. IEEE Internet Comput. **13**, 23–31 (2009)
6. Singh, S., Shrimpton, T.: Verifying delivered QoS in multihop wireless networks. IEEE Trans. Mob. Comput. **6**, 1370–1383 (2007)
7. Kim, A., Jeong, S.H.: A QoS/QoE control architecture for multimedia communications. In: International Conference on Information Networking, pp. 346–349, February 2012
8. Laghari, K.R., Pham, T.T., Nguyen, H., Crespi, N.: QoM: a new quality of experience framework for multimedia services. In: IEEE Symposium on Computers and Communications (ISCC), pp. 851–856, July 2012

Practical Instantaneous Frequency Analysis Experiments

Roman Korkikian[1,2], David Naccache[2,3]([✉]), Guilherme Ozari de Almeida[1,2], and Rodrigo Portella do Canto[1,2]

[1] Altis Semiconductor, 224, Bd. John Kennedy, 91105 Corbeil Essonnes, France
{roman.korkikian,guilherme.ozari-de-almeida}@altissemiconductor.com,
{roman.korkikian,guilherme.ozari-de-almeida}@etudiants.u-paris2.fr
[2] Sorbonne Universités – Université Paris II,
12 Place du Panthéon, 75231 Paris, France
david.naccache@u-paris2.fr, david.naccache@ens.fr
[3] Département d'Informatique, École Normale Supérieure,
45, rue d'Ulm, 75230 Paris Cedex 05, France

Abstract. This paper investigated the use of instantaneous frequency (IF) instead of power amplitude and power spectrum in side-channel analysis. By opposition to the constant frequency used in Fourier Transform, instantaneous frequency reflects local phase differences and allows detecting frequency variations. These variations reflect the processed binary data and are hence cryptanalytically useful. IF exploits the fact that after higher power drops more time is required to restore power back to its nominal value. Whilst our experiments reveal IF does not bring specific benefits over usual power attacks when applied to unprotected designs, IF allows to obtain much better results in the presence of amplitude modification countermeasures.

Keywords: AES · CPA · CSBA · Instantaneous frequency · Side-channel attacks

1 Introduction

The physical interpretation of data processing (a discipline named the *physics of computational systems* [20]) draws fundamental comparisons between computing technologies and provides physical lower bounds on the area, time and energy required for computation [5,14]. In this framework, a corollary of the second law of thermodynamics states that in order to perform a transition between states, energy must be lost irreversibly. A system that conserves energy cannot make a transition to a definite state and thus cannot make a decision (compute) ([20], 9.5).

At any given point in the evolution of a technology, the smallest logic devices must have a definite physical extent, require a certain minimum time to perform their function and dissipate a minimal switching energy when transiting from one state to another.

© Springer-Verlag Berlin Heidelberg 2014
M.S. Obaidat and J. Filipe (Eds.): ICETE 2013, CCIS 456, pp. 17–34, 2014.
DOI: 10.1007/978-3-662-44788-8_2

Because CMOS state transition energy is essentially proportional to the number of switched bits, transition energy leakage is the most popular side-channel attack vector. Because commuting also requires time, transition time and processed data might be also related.

Historically, timing attacks were developed to extract secrets from software algorithms [15] while hardware algorithms were usually assumed to run in constant time and hence be immune to timing attacks. The constant hardware execution time assumption is supported by the fact that usual block-cipher hardware implementations require an identical number of clock cycles to process any data. This article shows that this intuition is not always true, *i.e.* two different inputs may require distinct processing time and can hence be distinguishable.

Energy consumed during each clock cycle creates a waveform in the power domain. A duty cycle, *i.e.* the time during which the power wave is not equal to its nominal value, can be considered as the execution time of a hardware implemented algorithm. As shown later the duty cycle may depend on the processed data. Fourier transform can not determine local duty cycles since frequency is defined for the sine or cosine function spanning the whole data length with constant period and amplitude. However, recent techniques described in this paper that can detect local frequencies and hence determine wave duty cycle.

In 2005 it was observed that not only signal amplitude, but also power spectrum, can leak secret information [8]. Following the introduction of Differential Frequency Analysis (DFA) [9], power analysis on frequency domain was investigated on a series of papers [18,19,21,22]. DFA applies Fourier transform to map a time-series into the frequency domain. Since each Fourier point is a linear combination of all other sample points, a spectrum is a direct function of the initial signal amplitude and hence, power spectra can also be used in side-channel attacks.

Reference [18] rightly noted that the term Differential Spectral Based Analysis (DSBA) is semantically preferable because DFA does not exploit variations in frequencies, but *differences in spectra*. As the matter of fact all time-domain power models and distinguishers remain in principle fully applicable in the frequency domain.

Dynamic Voltage Scrambling (DVS) is a particular side-channel countermeasure that triggers random power supply changes aiming to decorrelate the signal's amplitude from the processed data [2,17]. While DVS degrades DPA's and DSBA's performances, nothing prevents the existence of more subtle side-channel attacks exploiting DVS-resistant die-hard information present in the signal. This paper successfully exhibits and exploits such DVS-resistant information.

Our Contribution. We show that, in addition to the signal's amplitude and spectrum, traditionally used for side-channel analysis, instantaneous frequency variations may also leak secret data. To the authors' best knowledge, "pure" frequency leakage has not been considered as a side-channel vector so far. Hence a re-assessment of several countermeasures, especially, these based on amplitude alterations, seems in order. As an example this paper examines DVS, which makes AES implementation impervious to power and spectrum attacks while leaving it vulnerable to Correlation Instantaneous Frequency Analysis (CIFA), a new attack described in this paper.

Organization. This paper is organized as follows. Section 2 turns a signal processing algorithm called *Hilbert Huang Transform* (HHT) into an attack process. Section 3 illustrates an HHT performed on a real power signal and motivates the exploration of instantaneous frequency as a side-channel carrier. Section 4 compares the cryptanalytic effectiveness of Correlation Instantaneous Frequency Analysis, Correlation Power Analysis and Correlation Spectrum Based Analysis on an unprotected AES FPGA implementation and on AES FPGA power traces with a simulated DVS. Section 5 concludes the paper.

2   Preliminaries

The notion of *instantaneous frequency*, computable by the HHT, was introduced in [12]. During the last decade, HHT has found many practical applications including oceanographic exploration and medical research [11]. This section recalls HHT's main mathematical features and describes the hardware setup used for evaluating the attacks introduced in this paper.

2.1   Hilbert Huang Transform

The HHT represents the analysed signal in the time-frequency domain by combining the *Empirical Mode Decomposition* (EMD) with the *Discrete Hilbert Transform* (DHT).

DHT is a classical linear operator that transforms a signal $u(1), \ldots, u(N)$ into a time series $H_u(1), \ldots, H_u(N)$ as follows:

$$H_u(t) = \frac{2}{\pi} \sum_{k \neq t \bmod 2} \frac{u(k)}{t - k} \tag{1}$$

DHT can be used to derive an *analytical representation* $u_a(1), \ldots, u_a(N)$ of the real-valued signal $u(t)$:

$$u_a(t) = u(t) + iH_u(t) \text{ for } 1 \leq t \leq N \tag{2}$$

Equation (2) can be rewritten in polar coordinates as

$$u_a(t) = a(t)e^{i\phi(t)} \tag{3}$$

where

$$a(t) = \sqrt{(u^2(t) + H_u^2(t))} \text{ and } \phi(t) = \arctan\left(\frac{H_u(t)}{u(t)}\right) \tag{4}$$

represent the *instantaneous amplitude* and the *instantaneous phase* of the analytical signal, respectively.

The *phase change rate* $w(t)$ defined in Eq. (5) can be interpreted as an *instantaneous frequency* (IF):

$$w(t) = \phi'(t) = \frac{d}{dt}\phi(t) \tag{5}$$

For a real-valued time-series the definition of $w(t)$ becomes:

$$w(t) = \phi(t) - \phi(t-1) \tag{6}$$

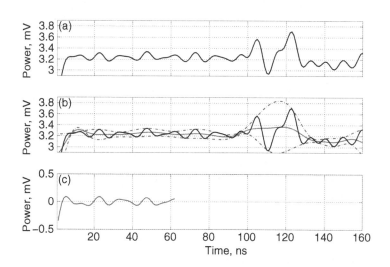

Fig. 1. Illustration of the EMD: (a) is the original signal $u(t)$; (b) $u(t)$ in thin solid black line, upper and lower envelopes are dot-dashed with their mean $m_{i,j}$ in thick solid red line; (c) shows the difference between $u(t)$ and the envelope's mean (Color figure online).

The derivative must be well defined since physically there can be only one instantaneous frequency value $w(t)$ at any given time t. This is insured by the *narrow band condition*: the signal's frequency must be uniform [13]. Further, the physical meaningfulness of DHT's output is closely related to the input's fitness into a narrow frequency band [6]. However, we wish to work with non-stationary signals having more than one frequency. This is achieved by de-composing these signals into several components, called *Intrinsic Mode Functions*, such that each component has nearly the same frequency.

Definition 1 (Intrinsic Mode Function). *An Intrinsic Mode Function (IMF) is a function satisfying the following conditions:*

1. *the number of extrema and the number of zero crossings in the considered data set must be either equal or differ by at most one;*
2. *the mean value of the curve specified as a sum of the envelope defined by the local maxima and the envelope defined by the local minima is zero.*

First Step: Empirical Mode Decomposition (EMD). EMD, the HHT's first step, is a systematic way of extracting IMFs from a signal. EMD involves approximation with splines. By Definition 1, EMD uses local maxima and minima separately. All the local signal's maxima are connected by a cubic spline to define an upper envelope. The same procedure is repeated for the local minima to yield a lower envelope. The first EMD component $h_{1,0}(t)$ is obtained by subtraction from $u(t)$ the envelopes' mean $m_{1,0}(t)$ (see Fig. 1):

$$h_{1,0}(t) = u(t) - m_{1,0}(t) \tag{7}$$

Ideally, $h_{1,0}(t)$ should be an IMF. In reality this is not always the case and EMD has to be applied to $h_{1,0}(t)$ as well:

$$h_{1,1}(t) = h_{1,0}(t) - m_{1,1}(t) \tag{8}$$

EMD is iterated k times, until an IMF $h_{1,k}(t)$ is reached, that is

$$h_{1,k}(t) = h_{1,k-1}(t) - m_{1,k}(t) \tag{9}$$

Then, $h_{1,k}(t)$ is defined as the first IMF component $c_1(t)$.

$$c_1(t) \stackrel{\text{def}}{=} h_{1,k}(t) \tag{10}$$

Next, the IMF component $c_1(t)$ is removed from $u(t)$

$$r_1(t) = u(t) - c_1(t) \tag{11}$$

and the procedure is iterated on all the subsequent residues, until the residue $r_n(t)$ becomes a monotonic function from which no further IMFs can be extracted.

$$\begin{cases} r_2(t) = r_1(t) - c_2(t) \\ \dots \\ r_n(t) = r_{n-1}(t) - c_n(t) \end{cases} \tag{12}$$

Finally, the initial signal $u(t)$ is re-written as a sum:

$$u(t) = \sum_{j=1}^{n} c_j(t) + r_n(t), \quad \text{for} \quad 1 \le t \le N \tag{13}$$

where, $c_j(t)$ are IMFs and $r_n(t)$ is a constant or a monotonic residue.

Second Step: Representation. The second HHT step is the representation of the initial signal in the time-frequency domain. All components $c_j(t)$, $j \in [1, n]$ obtained during the first step are transformed into analytical functions $c_j(t) + iH_{c_j}(t)$, allowing the computation of instantaneous frequencies by formula (6). The final transform $U(t, w)$ of $u(t)$ is:

$$U(t, w) = \sum_{j=1}^{n} a_j(t) \exp\left(i \sum_{\ell=1}^{t} w_j(\ell) \right) \tag{14}$$

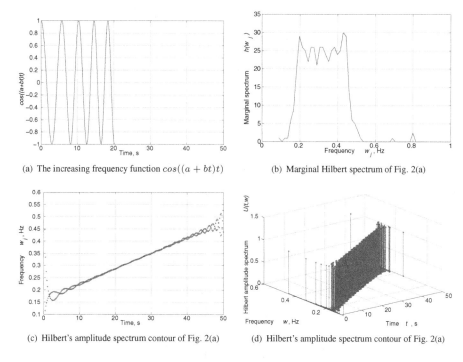

(a) The increasing frequency function $cos((a + bt)t)$

(b) Marginal Hilbert spectrum of Fig. 2(a)

(c) Hilbert's amplitude spectrum contour of Fig. 2(a)

(d) Hilbert's amplitude spectrum contour of Fig. 2(a)

Fig. 2. Analysis of the function $cos((a + bt)t)$.

where $j \in [1, n]$ is indexing components, $t \in [1, N]$ represents time and:

$$a_j(t) = \sqrt{c_j^2(t) + H_{c_j}^2(t)} \qquad \text{is the } \textit{instantaneous amplitude};$$

$$w_j(t) = \arctan\left(\frac{H_{c_j}(t+1)}{c_j(t+1)}\right) - \arctan\left(\frac{H_{c_j}(t)}{c_j(t)}\right) \text{ is the } \textit{instantaneous frequency};$$

Equation (14) represents the amplitude and the instantaneous frequency as a function of time in a three-dimensional plot, in which amplitude can be contoured on the frequency-time plane. This frequency-time amplitude distribution is called the *Hilbert amplitude spectrum* $U(t, w)$, or simply the *Hilbert spectrum* [12]. In addition to the Hilbert spectrum, we define the *marginal spectrum* or *HTT power spectral density* $h(w)$, as

$$h(w_j) = \sum_{t=1}^{T} U(t, w_j) \qquad (15)$$

The marginal spectrum measures the total amplitude (or energy) contributed by each frequency value. To illustrate HHT decomposition consider the function $u(t) = \cos(t(a + bt))$. In Fig. 2(a) parameters a and b were arbitrarily set to $a = 1$ and $b = 0.02$. Figure 2(a) shows that the cosine's frequency increases progressively. Figure 2(b) presents the Hilbert marginal spectrum of the signal

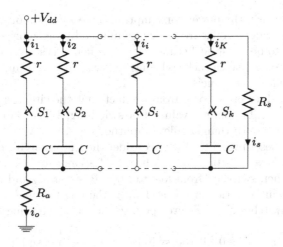

Fig. 3. Inverters switch simulation.

$u(t) = \cos((1 + 0.02t)t)$. Figure 2(c) shows the contour of Hilbert's amplitude spectrum, *i.e.* frequency evolution in time, and this evolution is indeed nearly linear. The 3D Hilbert amplitude spectrum is illustrated in Fig. 2(d).

2.2 AES Hardware Implementation

The AES-128 implementation used for our experiments runs on an Altera Cyclone II FPGA development board clocked by an external 50 MHz oscillator. The AES architecture uses a 128-bit datapath. Each AES round is completed in one clock cycle and key schedule is performed during encryption. The substitution box is described as a VHDL table mapped into combinational logic after FPGA synthesis. Encryption is triggered by a high `start` signal. After completing the rounds the device halts and drives a `done` signal high.

The implementation has no side-channel countermeasures. To simulate DVS, 200,000 physically acquired power consumption traces were processed by Algorithm 1. Algorithm 1 splits a time-series into segments and adds a uniformly distributed random voltage offset to each segment.

The rationale for simulating a DVS by processing a real signal (rather than adding a simple DVS module to the FPGA) is the desire to work with a rigorously modelled signal, free of the power consumption artefacts created by the DVS module itself.

3 Hilbert Huang Transform and Frequency Leakage

3.1 Why Should Instantaneous Frequency Variations Leak Information?

Most of the power consumed by a digital circuit is dissipated during rising or falling clock edges when registers are rewritten with new values. This activity is typically reflected in the power consumption trace as spikes occurring exactly during clock rising edges. Spike frequency, computed by the Fourier transform, is usually assumed to be constant because clock frequency is stable. In reality, this assumption is incorrect since each spike has its own duty cycle and consequently its own assortment of frequencies.

Differences in duty cycle come from the fact that the circuit's power supply must be restored to its nominal value after switching. Bigger amplitude spikes take more time to resorb than smaller amplitude ones.

To illustrate these spike differences, consider the simple circuit in Fig. 3. Each parallel branch has a resistor r, a switch S_i and a capacitor C that simulate a single inverter when switched from low to high. Resistor R_s and the current i_s represent the circuit's static current and R_a is the resistor used for acquisition. Initially all the switches $S_1 \dots S_k$ are open, so the current flowing through R_a is simply i_s.

Assume that at $t_0 = 0$ all the switches $S_1 \dots S_k$ are suddenly closed. All capacitors start charging and current flowing through R_a rises according to the following equation:

$$i_o(t) = i_s + k \left(\frac{V_{dd}}{r} e^{-\frac{t}{rC}} \right) \tag{16}$$

Equation (16) shows that current amplitude depends on the number of closed switches. However, there is one more parameter in the equation, namely the time t that characterizes the switching spike. The current i_o needs some time to "practically" reach an asymptotic nominal value i_s and this time depends on the number of closed switches k. Consider the time T_k required by $i_o(t)$ to reach $\Gamma\%$ of its asymptotic value, i.e. $\frac{\Gamma}{100} i_s$:

$$i_o(T_k) = i_s - k \left(\frac{V_{dd}}{r} e^{-\frac{T_k}{rC}} \right) = \frac{\Gamma}{100} i_s \tag{17}$$

This is equivalent to:

$$T_k = rC \ln \left(\frac{100}{100 - \Gamma} \frac{V_{dd}}{i_s r} \right) + rC \ln (k) = \alpha + \beta \ln(k) \tag{18}$$

Equation (18) shows that convergence time has a constant part α and a variable part $\beta \ln(k)$ that depends on the number of closed switches k. Equation (18) shows that both spike period and spike frequency depend on the processed data and could hence in principle be used as side-channel carriers. Nevertheless, power consumption is a non-stationary signal, which justifies the use of HHT.

The dependency between the number of switches and spike period in Eq. (18) is non-linear and hard to formalize as a simple formula for a real circuit. Section 3.2 shows that the standard Hamming distance model can be used in conjunction with instantaneous frequency.

3.2 Power Consumption of One AES Round

The relationship between processed data and power amplitude is a well understood phenomenon [1,7,10,16]. However, to the best of our knowledge the dependency

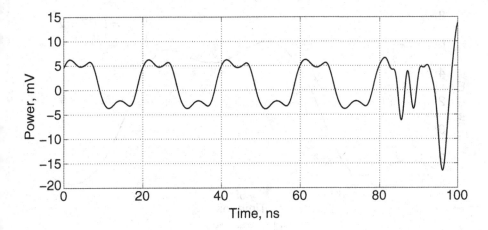

Fig. 4. Four AES last rounds.

of instantaneous frequency on processed data has not been explored so far. This may be partially explained by the fact that Fourier Transform, previously used in some papers, is not inherently adapted to non-stationary and non-linear signals. Fourier analysis cannot extract frequency variations from a signal because frequency is defined as a constant parameter of the underlying sine function spanning the whole data-set $u(t)$. By opposition, HHT allows extracting instantaneous frequencies and exploiting them for subsequent cryptanalytic purposes.

To illustrate information leakage through frequency variation, the AES last rounds' power consumption was measured using a Picoscope 3207 A with 250 MHz bandwidth at 10 G/s equivalent time sampling rate. Every signal had 1,000 samples and 100,000 traces were acquired for various input plaintexts. A power consumption example of the 4 last rounds is shown on the Fig. 4.

The AES last round was extracted from each power trace as shown on Fig. 5(a). The number of bits switches in the AES last round was computed with the known key. Afterwards the traces with the same number of bits switches were averaged.

In classic side-channel models [7], flipping more bits would consume more energy. Figure 5 shows that such is indeed the case for power consumption of 55, 65 and 75 bit flips where $v_{75} > v_{65} > v_{55}$. As per our assumption, the *frequency signatures of these three operations are also different*.

To show that HHT can detect frequency differences consider the power spectral density (PSD) of signals during 55, 65 and 75 bits switchings (Fig. 5(c)). The maximal spectral amplitude of the 55 bit change is located at 51.18 MHz (point f_{55}), that of the 65 bit change is at 51.12 MHz (point f_{65}) and that of the 75 bit change is at 50.73 MHz (point f_{75}) which is supportive of the hypothesis that HHT can distinguish frequency variations even in non-stationary signals because $f_{55} > f_{65} > f_{75}$.

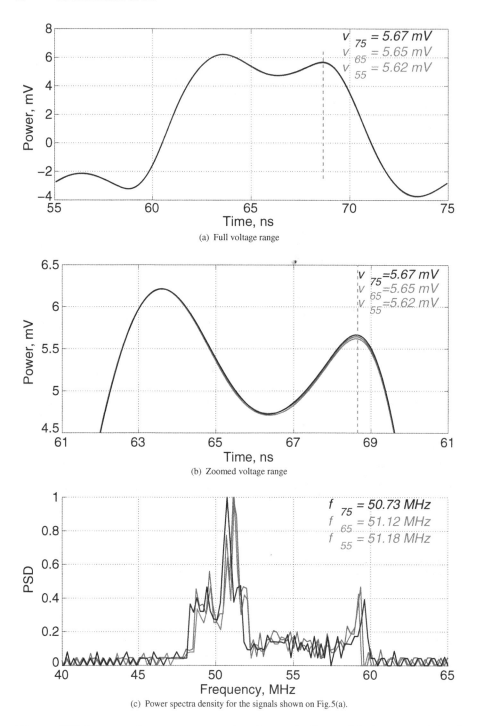

Fig. 5. AES last round power consumption for 55 (red), 65 (blue) and 75 (black) register's flip-flops (Color figure online).

This shows that not only amplitude but also frequency varies during register switch. Logically, power consumption increases as more bits are flipped. However, HHT was previously applied only for one AES round and HHT's applicability for the entire AES power traces must be verified. That is why the next section carefully examines the effect of register alteration on IF when AES FPGA implementation is sampled at a smaller rate.

3.3   Hilbert Huang Transform of an AES Power Consumption Signal

We start by performing a Hilbert Huang decomposition of a real signal. The analysis was performed on the power trace of the previously described AES-128 implementation. The acquisition was performed 1 G/s real time rate with 1 GHz differential probe. Signals were averaged 10 times and had 1,000 samples (Fig. 6(a)).

EMD decomposed the power trace to five IMFs and a residue, shown in Fig. 6(b). After decomposition, each IMF was Hilbert Transformed to derive the power signal's time-frequency representation.

Figure 6(c) is an IF distribution of Fig. 6(a).

Amplitude combination over frequency gave the power spectral density plot shown in blue on Fig. 7. An important observation in Fig. 7 is that HHT spectrum shows the distribution of a periodic variable over the main peak frequencies. Notably, the peak near 50 MHz that corresponds to the board's oscillator is not represented by a single point, but by a set of points. This data scatter can be explained by the fact that the IF of AES rounds varies, and HHT distinguishes this variation.

The main difference between HHT and FFT spectra (see plot shown in red on Fig. 7) is that HHT defines frequency as the speed of phase change and can hence detect intra-time-series deviations from the carrier's oscillation, whereas FFT frequency stems from the sine function, which is independent of the signals' shape.

So far, it was shown that IF varies for different rounds even within a given trace. However, an attack is only possible when IF depends on the data's Hamming weight.

The dependency is apparent in Fig. 8 showing the relationship between Hamming distance of the 9-th and 10-th AES round states and IF, taken from the first IMF component at the beginning of the 10-th round. Figure 8 was drawn using 200,000 HHT-processed power traces. The thin solid line in Fig. 8 represents the mean IF value, obtained from the first IMF component, as a function of Hamming distance.

The principal trend is the ascending line. Figure 8 corresponds well to the simulation of a register's power consumption since frequency is decreasing due to the increase in Hamming distance. The relationship in Fig. 8 between Hamming distance and IF looks linear and therefore the Pearson correlation coefficient can be used as an SCA distinguisher.

IF adoption for side-channel attacks presents some particularities. The disadvantage of the method is that data scatter is higher than in usual DPA and hence

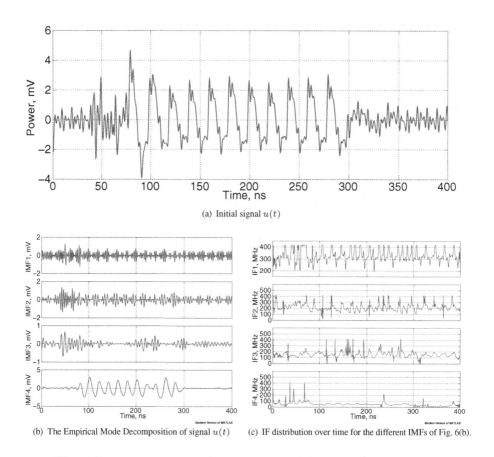

(a) Initial signal $u(t)$

(b) The Empirical Mode Decomposition of signal $u(t)$ (c) IF distribution over time for the different IMFs of Fig. 6(b).

Fig. 6. Power consumption of our experimental AES-128 implementation.

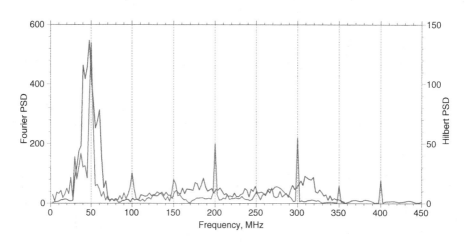

Fig. 7. Fourier and Hilbert power spectrum density of Fig. 6(a).

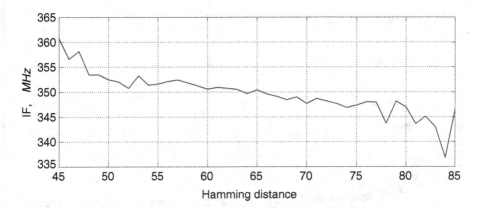

Fig. 8. Dependency between the Hamming distance of 9-th and 10-th AES round states and the IF of the first IMF component at time 276 ns (corresponding to the beginning of the last AES round).

the attack requires more power traces. Another issue is that each time-series will be decomposed into a set of IMFs, hence every sample will be wrapped-up with a set of IFs virtually multiplying the amount of data to be processed. However, the advantage is that because frequency based analysis is independent of local amplitude, CIFA can still be attempted in the presence of certain countermeasures.

4   Correlation Instantaneous Frequency Analysis

This section introduces Correlation Instantaneous Frequency Analysis (CIFA) and compares its performance with Correlation Power Analysis (CPA) and to Correlation Spectral Based Analysis (CSBA).

4.1   Correlation Instantaneous Frequency Analysis on Unprotected Hardware

During the acquisition step 200,000 power traces were acquired at a sampling rate of 2.5 GS/s. Each power signal was averaged 10 times to reduce noise. All traces were HHT-processed using the Matlab HHT code of [3,4]. Most traces were decomposed into 6 components, but 5 and 7 IMFs occurred as well. To reduce the amount of processed information only the first four IMFs were used.

Generally, each higher rank IMF carries information present in smaller instantaneous frequencies (Fig. 6(c)), this is why IMFs from different power traces were aligned index-wise, i.e. all first IMFs from every encryption were analyzed first, then all second IMFs and so on.

We chose the Hamming distance model and Pearson's correlation coefficient to investigate CIFA's properties and compare CIFA with other attacks.

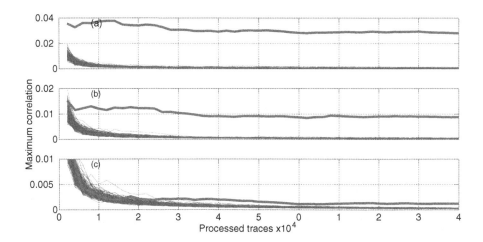

Fig. 9. Maximum correlation coefficients for a byte of the last round AES key in an unprotected implementation. Although the three attacks eventually succeed CPA>CSBA>CIFA. (a) CPA (b) CSBA (c) CIFA.

CPA. CPA applied to power traces produces Fig. 9(a). Clearly, CPA outperforms CIFA. CIFA's poorer performance can be partially attributed to the power model, because IF is not linearly dependent on the Hamming distance.

CSBA. Figure 9(b) presents CSBA applied against Fourier power trace spectra with the same power model and distinguisher. The correct key byte can be distinguished from 2000 power traces and on.

CIFA. The application of the selected power model and of the distinguisher to IFs yields Fig. 9(c) where the correct key byte emerges from 16,000 power traces and on.

The three experiments seem to suggest that CSBA is superior to CIFA but inferior to CPA. That is CIFA < CSBA < CPA.

While it appears that CPA and CSBA outperform CIFA in the absence of countermeasures, we will now see that CIFA survives countermeasures that derail CPA and CSBA.

4.2   Correlation Instantaneous Frequency Analysis in the Presence of DVS

As mentioned previously DVS alters power supply to reduce dependency between data and consumed power. According to [2,17] DVS is cheap in terms of area overhead since only a voltage controller and a random number generator must be added to the protected design.

To simulate DVS all the traces of the unprotected AES were modified by Algorithm 1. Each power trace was partitioned into γ segments of normally distributed lengths covering the whole dataset.[1] Each segment was lifted by a uniformly distributed random offset ℓ that did not exceed a predetermined value D set to $D = 12\,\mathrm{mV}$.

Algorithm 1. Dynamic Voltage Scrambling (DVS) Simulator.

Input:
  A power trace $u(1), \ldots, u(N)$;
  γ : the number of segments;
  m : mean value of segment length $m \stackrel{\text{def}}{=} N/\gamma$;
  σ : standard deviation of segment length;
  D : maximum offset for segment lifting;
Output:
  a DVS-protected power trace $u'(1), \ldots, u'(N)$;

  ▷ *Split a trace to a set of segments of normally distributed random length chunks*
  $\tau_0 \leftarrow 1$
  $\tau_\gamma \leftarrow N$
  for $i = 1$ **to** $\gamma - 1$ **do**
    $\tau_i \leftarrow \tau_{i-1} + \mathcal{N}(m, \sigma)$
  end for

  ▷ *Lift each segment by a uniformilly distributed random offset ℓ*
  for $s = 1$ **to** γ **do**
    $\ell_s \in_R [0, D]$
    for $t = \tau_{s-1}$ **to** τ_s **do**
      $u'(t) \leftarrow u(t) + \ell_s$
    end for
  end for

A trace modification example is presented in Fig. 10, in which the trace of Fig. 6(a) was processed by Algorithm 1.

Logically, DVS decreases power analysis performance by reducing the attacker's SNR. We disposed of 200,000 DVS-modified power traces. All of which were used to mount power analysis attacks under the same conditions as before, i.e., using Pearson's correlation coefficient and the Hamming distance model.

The same final round key byte used for attacks against the unprotected implementation was targeted. CPA and CSBA failed to detect the correct key byte even with 150,000 traces (Fig. 11(a), (b)). This confirms the intuition that DVS has a beneficial effect on the required number of power traces.

However CIFA was able to recover the byte from 60,000 traces and on (Fig. 11(c)). This illustrates that whilst CIFA is usually outperformed by CPA and CSBA, CIFA is much more resilient to DVS, to which CPA and CSBA are very sensitive.

---

[1] The mean m and the standard deviation σ were arbitrary set to $m = 40\,\mathrm{ns}$ and $\sigma = 5\,\mathrm{ns}$ in our experiment.

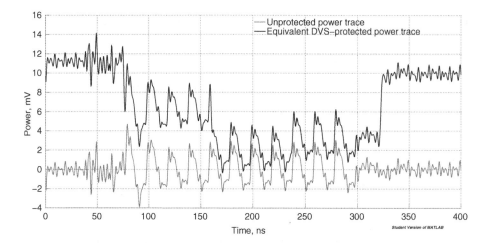

Fig. 10. Power traces of the FPGA AES implementation. The unprotected signal is shown in red. The DVS-protected signal is shown in black (Color figure online).

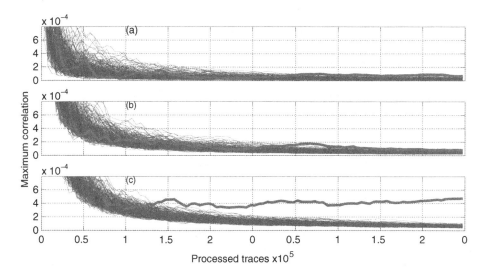

Fig. 11. Maximum correlation coefficient for a byte of the last round AES key with simulated DVS. (a) CPA (b) CSBA (c) CIFA.

5   Conclusions and Further Research

This paper investigated the use of instantaneous frequency instead of power amplitude and power spectrum in side-channel analysis. By opposition to the constant frequency used in Fourier Transform, instantaneous frequency reflects local phase differences and allows to detect frequency variations. These variations depend on the processed binary data and are hence cryptanalitically useful.

The relationship stems from the fact that after higher power drops more time is required to restore power back to its nominal value.

IF analysis does not bring specific benefits when applied to unprotected designs on which CPA and CSBA yield better results. However, CIFA allows to discard the effect of amplitude modification countermeasures, e.g. DVS, because CIFA extracts from signal features not exploited so far.

Acknowledgments. The authors thank Natacha Laniado for editing and proofreading this work.

References

1. Agrawal, D., Archambeault, B., Rao, J.R., Rohatg, P.: The EM Side-Channel(s). In: Kaliski, B.S., Koç, Ç.K., Paar, C. (eds.) CHES 2002. LNCS, vol. 2523, pp. 29–45. Springer, Heidelberg (2003)
2. Baddam, K., Zwolinski, M.: Evaluation of dynamic voltage and frequency scaling as a differential power analysis countermeasure. In: Proceedings of the 20-th International Conference on VLSI Design Held Jointly with 6-th International Conference: Embedded Systems, VLSID '07, pp. 854–862. IEEE Computer Society (2007)
3. Battista, B., Knapp, C., McGee, T., Goebel, V.: Application of the empirical mode decomposition and Hilbert-Huang transform to seismic reflection data. In: Geophysics, vol. 72, pp. H29–H37. SEG (2007)
4. Battista, B., Knapp, C., McGee, T., Goebel, V.: Matlab program demonstrating performing the empirical mode decomposition and Hilbert-Huang transform on seismic reflection data, August 2012. http://software.seg.org/2007/0003/mat/emd. zip
5. Bennett, C.: Logical reversibility of computation. IBM J. Res. Dev. **17**, 525–532 (1973). IBM Corp.
6. Boashash, B.: Estimating and interpreting the instantaneous frequency of a signal. I. fundamentals. Proc. IEEE **80**, 520–538 (1992)
7. Brier, E., Clavier, C., Olivier, F.: Correlation power analysis with a leakage model. In: Joye, M., Quisquater, J.-J. (eds.) CHES 2004. LNCS, vol. 3156, pp. 16–29. Springer, Heidelberg (2004)
8. Gebotys, C.H., Ho, S., Tiu, C.C.: EM analysis of Rijndael and ECC on a wireless Java-based PDA. In: Rao, J.R., Sunar, B. (eds.) CHES 2005. LNCS, vol. 3659, pp. 250–264. Springer, Heidelberg (2005)
9. Gebotys, C., Tiu, C., Chen, X.: A countermeasure for EM attack of a wireless PDA. In: International Conference on Information Technology: Coding and Computing, 2005, ITCC 2005, vol. 1, pp. 544–549, April 2005
10. Gierlichs, B., Batina, L., Tuyls, P., Preneel, B.: Mutual Information Analysis - A Generic Side-Channel Distinguisher. In: Oswald, E., Rohatgi, P. (eds.) CHES 2008. LNCS, vol. 5154, pp. 426–442. Springer, Heidelberg (2008)
11. Huang, N., Shen, S.: The Hilbert-Huang Transform and its Applications. World Scientific Publishing Company, Singapore (2005)
12. Huang, N., Shen, Z., Long, S., Wu, M., Shih, S., Zheng, Q., Tung, C., Liu, H.: The empirical mode decomposition and the Hilbert spectrum for nonlinear and non-stationary time series analysis. Proc. R. Soc. Lond. Ser. A: Math. Phys. Eng. Sci. **454**, 903–995 (1998)

13. Kaslovsky, D., Meyer, F.: Noise Corruption of Empirical Mode Decomposition and Its Effect on Instantaneous Frequency. ArXiv e-prints, August 2010. http://arxiv.org/pdf/1008.4176v1
14. Keyes, R.: Physical limits in digital electronics. IEEE Proc. **63**, 740–767 (1975)
15. Kocher, P.C.: Timing Attacks on Implementations of Diffie-Hellman, RSA, DSS, and Other Systems. In: Koblitz, N. (ed.) CRYPTO 1996. LNCS, vol. 1109, pp. 104–113. Springer, Heidelberg (1996)
16. Kocher, P.C., Jaffe, J., Jun, B.: Differential power analysis. In: Wiener, M. (ed.) CRYPTO 1999. LNCS, vol. 1666, pp. 388–397. Springer, Heidelberg (1999)
17. Krieg, A., Grinschgl, J., Steger, C., Weiss, R., Haid, J.: A side channel attack countermeasure using system-on-chip power profile scrambling. In: IEEE International On-Line Testing Symposium, pp. 222–227. IEEE Computer Society (2011)
18. Luo, Q.: Enhance multi-bit spectral analysis on hiding in temporal dimension. In: Gollmann, D., Lanet, J.-L., Iguchi-Cartigny, J. (eds.) CARDIS 2010. LNCS, vol. 6035, pp. 13–23. Springer, Heidelberg (2010)
19. Mateos, E., Gebotys, C.: Side channel analysis using giant magneto-resistive (GMR) sensors. In: 2-nd International Workshop on Constructive Side-Channel Analysis and Secure Design - COSADE 2011, pp. 42–49, Feburary 2011
20. Mead, C., Conway, L.: Introduction to VLSI Systems. Addison-Wesley, Reading (1980)
21. Peng, Z., Gaoming, D., Qiang, Z., Kaiyan, C.: EM frequency domain correlation analysis on cipher chips. In: 2009 1-st International Conference on Information Science and Engineering (ICISE), pp. 1729–1732, December 2009
22. Schimmel, O., Duplys, P., Boehl, E., Hayek, J., Bosch, R., Rosenstiel, W.: Correlation power analysis in frequency domain. In: First International Workshop on Constructive Side-Channel Analysis and Secure Design - COSADE 2010, pp. 1–3 (2010)

Data Communication Networking

The Impact of Initial Delays in OSPF Routing

Anne Bouillard[1], Claude Jard[2], and Aurore Junier[3][(✉)]

[1] ENS/INRIA, Paris, France
[2] LINA, University of Nantes, Nantes, France
[3] INRIA, Rennes, France
Aurore.Junier@inria.fr

Abstract. Routing protocols, as illustrated by the OSPF protocol, generally have a periodic behavior to continuously update the information on the network topology. This behavior is a consequence of the parallel activity of a program loop installed on each router. These loops may be more or less synchronized in accordance with a shift of the initial phase. This article explores the question of the values of these delays and their impact on the accumulation of messages in the input buffers of routers. The studies are conducted using a simulated Petri net model. A heuristic for determining initial delays is proposed. And a core network in Germany serves as illustration.

Keywords: OSPF routing · Synchronization · Simulation · Time Petri Nets

1 Introduction

Routing protocols generally work in a dynamic environment where they have to constantly monitor changes. This function is implemented locally in routers by a programming loop that generates regular behaviors. Open Shortest Path First (OSPF) protocol [9] is an interesting example, widely used in networks. OSPF is a link-state protocol that performs internal IP routing. This protocol regularly fills the network with messages "hello" to monitor the changes of network topology and messages "link state advertisements" (LSA) to update the table of shortest paths in each router.

A lot of work [1,2] has been devoted to stability issues. The stability is required if there is a change in the network state (e.g., a link goes down), all the nodes in the network are guaranteed to converge to the new network topology in finite time (in the absence of any other events). The question is difficult when the change is determined as a result of a bottleneck in a router (as possible in the OPSF-TE [5]). If the response to a congestion is the exchange of additional messages, the situation may become critical. But it has been proved [1] that OSPF-TE is rather robust in that matter.

In this article we look at a related problem which is to focus on the possibilities of congestion of the input buffers of routers due to LSA traffic.

© Springer-Verlag Berlin Heidelberg 2014
M.S. Obaidat and J. Filipe (Eds.): ICETE 2013, CCIS 456, pp. 37–57, 2014.
DOI: 10.1007/978-3-662-44788-8_3

Indeed, we believe that there are situations where the cyclical behavior of routers may cause harmful timings in which incoming messages collide in a very short time in front of routers.

In current implementations, the refresh cycle is very slow and congestion is unlikely in view of the routers' response time. Nevertheless, we address the question to increase the refresh rate to ensure better responsiveness to changes. This article shows a possibility of divergence, and discusses the possibilities of avoiding harmful synchronization by adjusting the phase shift of cyclical behavior.

The approach is as follows. We modeled LSAs exchanges using Time Petri Nets (in a fairly abstract representation). This model was simulated for a topology of 17 nodes representing the heart of an existing network in Germany (data provided by Alcatel). We then demonstrated the possibility of accumulation of messages for well-chosen parameter values. Accumulation is due to a possible overlap of refresh phases in terms of messages. To validate this model, and thus the reality of the observed phenomenon, we reproduced it on a network emulator available from Alcatel. Curves could indeed be replicated. Parameter values were different, but it was difficult to believe that the model scaled with respect to the rough abstraction performed. Once the problem identified, the question is then to try to solve it by computing optimum initial delays. Such a computation can be performed using linear integer programming on a simplified graphical model. We will show using simulation that the computed values are relevant to avoid message accumulation in front of routers.

The rest of the paper is organized as follows: we first present in Sect. 2 the modeling of the LSA flooding process and its validation. In Sect. 3, simulation shows a possible overload of buffers depending on the refresh period. Then, in Sect. 4, we study a possible adjustment of the initial delays, which aims at minimizing the overload. We show how to compute these delays. The impact is then demonstrated using simulation.

2   TPN Modeling of the LSA Flooding Process

2.1   LSA Flooding Process

The network is represented by a directed graph $G = (V, E)$, where V is a finite set of n vertices (the routers) and E is a binary relation on V to represent the links. The ith router is denoted by R_i. The set $\mathcal{V}(R_i)$ denotes the set of neighbors of R_i, of cardinality $|\mathcal{V}(R_i)|$. To help the reader Table 1 gives the list of the main notations introduced in this paper.

The LSA flooding occurs periodically every T_r seconds (30 min in the standard). Thus, the LSA flooding process starts at time kT_r, $\forall k \in \mathbb{N}$.

The LSA of a router R_i records the content of its database. Then, R_i shares this LSA (denoted LSA_i) with its neighbors to communicate its view of the network at the beginning of each period. The router R_i sends LSA_i after an *initial delay* d_i. More precisely, R_i sends LSA_i at $d_i + kT_r$, $\forall k \in \mathbb{N}$. Suppose that a router R_j receives LSA_i and that it starts processing it at time t. Then, R_j ended the processing of LSA_i at time $t + T_p$, where T_p is the time needed by any router to process an LSA or an acknowledgment (Ack). During this processing, R_j updates its database and sends a new LSA to its other neighbors if some new information is learned. Consequently, R_j could send a new LSA at time $t + T_p$, and its neighbors will receive it at time $t + T_p + T_t$, where T_t represents the time to send a message.

Note that any information received by R_j can be taken into account if some properties are satisfied. The most important one is the age of the LSA. An LSA that is too old is simply ignored. In all cases, at time $t + T_p$, R_j sends an Ack to R_i. The objective is to inform R_i that LSA_i has been correctly received. In parallel, R_i waits for an Ack from all of its neighbors before a given time. If an Ack is not received before the end of this time, R_i sends LSA_i again until an Ack is properly received.

The LSA flooding process ends when every router has synchronized to the same database.

2.2   The Simulation Model

Time Petri Net (TPN) [4] is an efficient tool to model discrete-event systems and to capture the inherent concurrency of complex systems. In the classical definition, transitions are fired over an interval of time. Here, transitions are fired at a fixed time. This assumption is justified by observations of actual OSPF traces whose data processing time does not vary that much. In our case, the formal definition of TPN is the following:

Definition 21 (Time Petri Net). A Time Petri Net (TPN) is a tuple (P,T, B,F,M_0,φ) where

- P is a finite non-empty set of places;
- T is a finite non-empty set of transitions;
- $B : P \times T \to \mathbb{N}$ is the backward incidence function;
- $F : T \times P \to \mathbb{N}$ is the forward incidence function;
- $M_0 : P \to \mathbb{N}$ is the initial marking function;
- $\varphi : T \to \mathbb{N}$ is the temporal mapping of transitions.

The remainder of this part is devoted to the construction of the TPN that models message exchanges of the LSA flooding process. The objective is to model and observe the dynamic behavior of a given network.

Router Modeling. The TPN that models the behavior of the LSA flooding process in a router R_i needs three timers: d_i, T_r and T_p. Their functions are: creating LSA_i, managing a message received and retransmitting a received LSA when needed. Messages are processed one by one. The following paragraphs present each functional part of the TPN that models a router.

- *Place Processor.* Initially this place contains one token, representing the processing resource of a router that is used to process LSAs and Acks. This place mimics the queuing mechanism of R_i and guaranties that only one message is processed at once. For each different kind of messages (LSA_i and Ack)

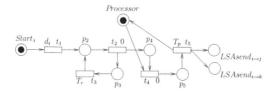

Fig. 1. Part of TPN that creates the LSA of a router R_i.

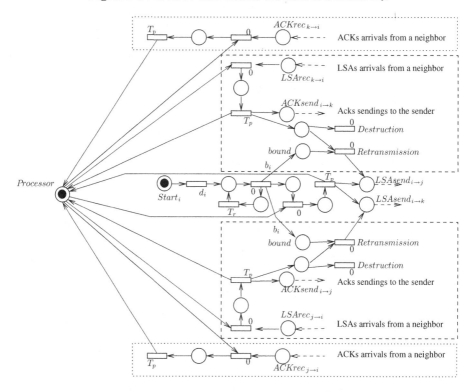

Fig. 2. TPN of a router R_i that has two neighbors, R_j and R_k.

the processing mechanism is the following: an instantaneous transition is fired, to reserve the resource of R_i. Note that it can only be fired if a message is waiting. Then the successor transition with timing T_p can be fired, modeling the processing time of the router, and *Processor* becomes marked again, enabling the processing of a new message.

- *Creation of LSA.* Figure 1 represents the part of the TPN that creates LSA_is at time $d_i + kT_r$, for $k \in \mathbb{N}$ in router R_i. Initially $Start_i$ contains one token, t_1 fires at time d_i and a token appears in p_2 at time d_i for the first time. Afterward, the cycle p_2, t_2, p_3, t_3 generates a token in p_4 at times $d_i + kT_r$, $k \in \mathbb{N}$. Those token will be processed using the mechanism described above, generating tokens in places $LSAsend_{i \to j}$, $R_j \in \mathcal{V}(R_i)$.

- *Reception of an Ack* (dotted rectangles on Fig. 2). A token in $ACKrec_{j \to i}$ represents this event. It is processed using the mechanism described above and does not generate any new message.
- *Reception of an LSA from a neighbor* (dashed rectangles in Fig. 2). A token in place $LSArec_{j \to i}$ represents this event. It is processed using the mechanism described above and generate an Ack, that is sent to the sender. It can also possibly generate an LSA message that will be retransmitted to its other neighbors (transition *Retransmission*). Otherwise, the token is destroyed (transition *Destruction*). In the flooding mechanism, an LSA_j is retransmitted only if it is received for the first time during one flooding period. That way, the LSA flooding process ensures that every router converges to the same database before the end of every period. To model this, we bound the number of retransmissions per period (for R_i, the number of retransmissions of an LSA received from R_j is b_i, that is modeled by placing b_i tokens in each place *bound* of R_i at the beginning of each period). The tokens are inserted in these places by weighted arcs between t_2 and each place *bound*.
- *Global TPN*. Figure 2 represents the behavior for one router. Such a net is built for each router. Finally, place $LSAsend_{i \to j}$ (resp. $ACKsend_{i \to j}$) is connected to place $LSArec_{i \to j}$ (resp. $ACKrec_{i \to j}$) by inserting a transition $LSA_{i \to j}$ (resp. $ACK_{i \to j}$) with firing time T_t between them.

2.3   Model Validation

We performed our experimentations on the 17-node German telecommunication network represented in Fig. 3. This article focuses on the study of router R_8 that has the largest number of neighbors ($|\mathcal{V}(R_8)| = 6$).

The arrivals of LSAs and Acks in the actual network are captured by an emulation using the Quagga Routing Software Suite [3], where each node is set from an Ubuntu Linux machine that hosts a running instance of the Quagga Routing Software Suite. Figure 4 represents the arrival of messages in R_8 by the emulation of the LSA flooding on the German topology during 8000 s with $T_r = 1800$ s.

During the emulation, the processors of routers are parametrized with a 900 MHz CPU, and the mean size of an LSA (resp. an Ack) is 96 bytes (resp. 63 bytes). The processing time of an LSA (resp. an Ack) is approximately 0.8 μs (resp. 0.5 μs). The transmission time of an LSA (resp. an Ack) in 96 ms (resp. 64 ms).

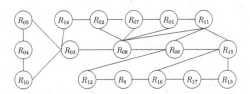

Fig. 3. German telecommunication network.

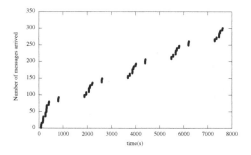

Fig. 4. Emulation of the arrivals to R_8.

Unfortunately, these parameters can not be used directly to parametrize the TPN, as the TPN only represents the behavior of the LSA flooding process. However, an actual router is much more loaded. Thus, T_p and T_t must be adjusted to include the whole load of the router.

The simulations presented in this article are produced by the software Renew (see [6]) which can simulate Time Petri Nets. Note that the TPN are automatically generated (the TPN that models the German Telecommunication network is not represented here due to its size). Figure 5 represents the simulation of message arrivals using the TPN where $T_r = 1800$ s, $T_p = 15$ s, $T_t = 30$ s. To correspond to the sendings emulated in Fig. 4 the number of LSAs retransmitted per neighbour during a period is $b_i = \lceil \frac{(n-1)}{4|\mathcal{V}(R_i)|} \rceil$.

One can observe that Figs. 4 and 5 are quite similar: the parameters chosen as above are defined to represent the actual behavior of an LSA flooding process. The two curves are both composed of periods that last 1800 s. They show on each period a burst of message arrivals that lasts approximately 800 s, then message arrivals stop until the next period. We therefore conclude that our abstract model correctly captures the phenomenon of LSA flooding.

From now on we fix the parameters $((b_i)_{i \in \{1,...,n\}}, T_p, T_t$ and $T_r)$ as defined above.

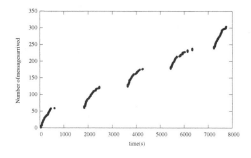

Fig. 5. Message arrivals to R_8 with $T_r = 1800$ s.

3   Study of Period Length

We study here the effect of the period length T_r on both message arrivals and queue length. We first discuss the normal case where $T_r = 1800\,\text{s}$. Then, we present a congested case where $T_r = 514\,\text{s}$. Finally, we observe a limit case where $T_r = 1000\,\text{s}$.

3.1   Low Traffic Case

Figure 6 represents the simulated queue length of R_8 during $10^5\,\text{s}$ (approx. 1 day), where $T_r = 1800\,\text{s}$. One can observe a lot of fluctuations. At the beginning of each period R_8 receives and processes messages. However, the number of messages that are received is much larger than those which are processed. Consequently, the queue length increases. Afterward, the sendings stop, and R_i keeps processing messages. The queue length decreases.

3.2   Congested Case

Figure 7 represents the message arrivals in R_8 during $8000\,\text{s}$, and Fig. 8 the queue length of R_8 during $10^5\,\text{s}$, where $T_r = 514\,\text{s}$. One can observe that messages arrive continuously on router R_8. Then, R_8 is never idle and never empties its queue. Consequently the queue length permanently increases.

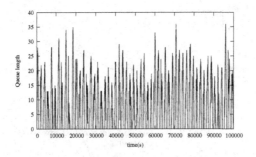

Fig. 6. Buffer length of R_8 with $T_r = 1800\,\text{s}$.

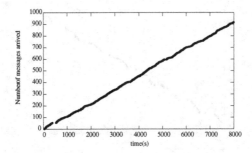

Fig. 7. Message arrivals to R_8 with $T_r = 514\,\text{s}$.

3.3   Limit Case

Figure 9 represents the message arrivals in R_8 during 8000 s, and Fig. 10 shows the queue length of router R_8 during 10^5 s, where $T_r = 1000$ s. This time, the sendings of a period are not merged with the sendings of the next period. Then, each period is long enough so that R_8 can process messages from its queue before the beginning of the next one. Figure 10 shows the fluctuations of the queue length that correspond to this. However the queue length is not empty at the end of each period. Consequently, the stability of this router is not ensured.

3.4   Sufficient Condition for Congestion

Suppose being in the worst case where each router learns some new information from each router and let us now focus on the quantity of messages received during a period.

Theorem 31. Let $n(j)$ be the number of messages received by a router R_j during a flooding period T_r. Then

$$n(j) \geqslant n(|\mathcal{V}(R_j)|).$$

Proof. Let us first focus on the case of networks with a tree topology. In this case, we show that the above inequality is in fact an equality. Two kinds of messages

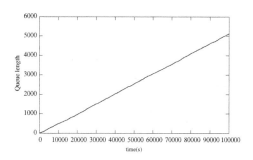

Fig. 8. Buffer size of R_8 with $T_r = 514$ s.

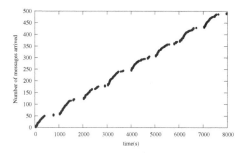

Fig. 9. Message arrivals to R_8 with $T_r = 1000$ s.

can be received: LSAs and Acks. Let us first count the number of messages received by router R_j concerning the flooding from router R_i. Consider R_i as the root of the tree, R_j can receive LSA_i from its father only: R_j will receive one and only once LSA_i. Afterward R_j sends LSA_i to its children and will receive an Ack (as illustrated in Fig. 11). As a consequence, the number of messages received for the flooding of LSA_i is the number of neighbors of R_j. Consider the flooding of LSA_j. The router R_j sends the LSA to its neighbors and will receive an Ack from them. Globally, R_j will then receive exactly $n(|\mathcal{V}(R_j)|)$ messages.

For networks with a general topology, one can observe that the flooding of LSA_i defines a spanning tree of the graph: (R_j, R_k) is an edge of the spanning tree if R_k first received LSA_i from R_j. Then for the flooding of LSA_i, R_j receives at least the messages it would received if the topology were the spanning tree, which gives the desired inequality.

The number of messages processed by router R_j during a flooding period is $1 + n(j)$: it processes the received messages plus LSA_j. Define $N(j)$ the number of messages processed during a flooding period by R_j, we have

$$N(j) = n(|\mathcal{V}(R_j)|) + 1.$$

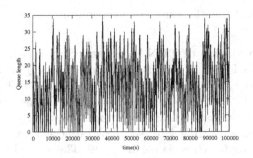

Fig. 10. Buffer length of R_8 with $T_r = 1000\,\text{s}$.

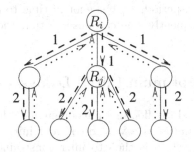

$\dashrightarrow^{j}$ send of LSA_i at step j

$\cdots\!\!\rightarrow$ ack sent in response to LSA_i received

Fig. 11. Flooding of LSA_i: LSA and ACKs transmissions in a tree topology.

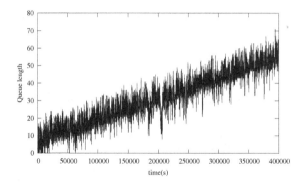

Fig. 12. Queue length of R_3 with $T_r = 554\,$s of tree topology.

If a router can not process every message of its buffer before the end of each period a congestion occurs. Also, given the minimal bound of Theorem 31 the congestion is ensured by the following threshold on T_r.

Lemma 32. If $T_r < T_p N(j)$ then the queue length of R_j tends to infinity.

Proof. The proof is straightforward from Theorem 31.

Example 33 (Simulation of TPN by Renew Software). Consider the tree topology network of Fig. 11. Theorem 31 ensures that the number of messages received by R_j ($|\mathcal{V}(R_j)| = 4$) is $N(j) = 9 \times 4 + 1 = 37$. Therefore, if T_p is set to 15 s in the TPN, if $T_r < 15 \times 37 = 555$ s the network is congested. Simulation of the TPN, representing this topology, with $T_p = 15\,$s, $T_r = 554\,$s, $T_t = 30\,$s has been made during 4.10^5 s to illustrate this result. The evolution of the queue length of router R_j is shown in Fig. 12. The queue length of R_j clearly increases during the simulation, showing that the network is congested. Finally, as the simulation has been made with the largest period length that ensures congestion, during each period, R_j has enough time to process many messages from his queue. Consequently, one can observe that the queue length varies a lot.

4   Computing Optimum Initial Delays

In Sect. 2.2, we emulated the flooding phenomenon of the OSFP protocol using Time Petri nets. The initial idea was to consider initial delays for each router as parameters. The question is then to infer constraints on these parameters that ensure a minimum size of the input buffers. Even if this kind of question can be theoretically solved using symbolic model-checking [8], the computation complexity is high. The state of the art of the current existing tools did not allow us to automatically produce such symbolic constraints.

In order to compute initial delays, we adopt the following method. We only take into account the message contributing to the flooding mechanism: when an LSA message concerning router R_j is received at router R_i, it is forwarded only if it is received for the first time. Then, we will model neither the LSA messages that are not the first to be received at a node, nor the Acknowledgments.

4.1 Constraints Modeling

Our goal is to perform the floodings as closed as possible while interacting as little as possible. We say that two floodings do not interact if, for each router, the first LSA received from those two floodings in that router are not queued at the same time.

More formally, we consider a graph $G = (V, E)$, where $V = \{R_1, \ldots, R_n\}$ is the set of routers and $E \subseteq V \times V$ is the set of links between the routers. If $(R_i, R_j) \in E$, then $\tau_{i,j}$ denotes the transmission time between R_i and R_j, and $\tau_{i,j} = \infty$ if $(R_i, R_j) \notin E$. The sojourn time of a message in R_i, between its reception and its forwarding, belongs to the interval $[\delta_i, \Delta_i[$. This time also holds for the source of messages.

Let us first compute the intervals of time $I_{i,j}$ when the first LSA originating from R_i is received in R_j if the flooding starts at time 0. If $i = j$, then $I_{i,i} = [0, 0]$, and otherwise, we have $I_{i,j} = [\alpha_{i,j}, \beta_{i,j}[$ where $\alpha_{i,j} = \min_{k \in \{1,\ldots,n\}} \alpha_{i,k} + \delta_k + \tau_{k,j}$ and $\beta_{i,j} = \min_{k \in \{1,\ldots,n\}} \beta_{i,k} + \Delta_k + \tau_{k,j}$.

The quantities $\alpha_{i,k} + \delta_k$ and $\beta_{i,k} + \Delta_k$ respectively represent the minimal and the maximal departure times from R_k.

For the computation of both $\alpha_{i,j}$ and $\beta_{i,j}$, we recognize the computation of a shortest path in a graph with respective edge lengths $(\delta_i + \tau_{i,j})$ and $(\Delta_i + \tau_{i,j})$. Let $\alpha = (\alpha_{i,j})$ and $\beta = (\beta_{i,j})$ the matrices of the shortest-paths. They can, for example, be computed using the Floyd-Warshall algorithm. Now, the messages originating from R_i are present in R_j during an interval of time included in $[\alpha_{i,j}, \beta_{i,j} + \Delta_j[= [\alpha_{i,j}, \gamma_{i,j}[$. We denote by $D_{i,j}$ this interval and D the matrix of these intervals.

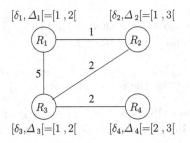

Fig. 13. Example of a toy topology.

Example 41 (Sojourn Times in the Routers). Figure 13 represents a toy topology with 4 vertices. Matrix D is then:

$$D = \begin{pmatrix} [0,2[& [2,6[& [5,9[& [8,14[\\ [2,6[& [0,3[& [3,7[& [6,12[\\ [5,9[& [3,7[& [0,2[& [3,7[\\ [9,14[& [7,12[& [4,7[& [0,3[\end{pmatrix}.$$

Now, if the flooding from server R_i starts at time d_i, its first LSA received by R_j is present in that server at most in the interval $d_i + D_{i,j} = [d_i + \alpha_{i,j}, d_i + \gamma_{i,j}]$.

Then, in order to have no interference between the floodings in router R_j, the family of intervals $(d_i + D_{i,j})_{i \in \{1,\ldots,n\}}$ must be two-by-two disjoint, and to have no interference at all, the following condition must hold:

$$\forall i, j, k \in \{1, \ldots, n\}, \ i \neq k \Rightarrow d_i + D_{i,j} \cap d_k + D_{k,j} = \emptyset,$$

that is,

$$\forall i, j, k \in \{1, \ldots, n\}, \ i \neq k \Rightarrow \begin{cases} d_i + \gamma_{i,j} \leq d_k + \alpha_{k,j} & \text{or} \\ d_k + \gamma_{k,j} \leq d_i + \alpha_{i,j}. \end{cases}$$

For each triple (i, j, k), the two constraints above are exclusive: as $\gamma_{i,j} > \alpha_{i,j}$, if one holds, necessarily, the other one does not hold.

Now, if we don't consider the first flooding from each router only, we have to study the interferences between the first and second flooding from each router (if there is no interference between those two sets of flooding, then there will be no interference at all).

If the flooding period is T, then the constraints must then be transform in

$$\forall i, j, k \in \{1, \ldots, n\}, \quad \begin{aligned} d_i + \gamma_{i,j} &\leq d_k + \alpha_{k,j} & \text{or} \\ d_k + \gamma_{k,j} &\leq d_i + \alpha_{i,j} & \text{and} \\ d_k + \gamma_{k,j} &\leq d_i + T + \alpha_{i,j} & \text{and} \\ d_i + \gamma_{i,j} &\leq d_k + T + \alpha_{k,j} \end{aligned} \quad (1)$$

The two cases are illustrated on Fig. 14. Note that, depending on which of the two first constraint is satisfied, one of the two last inequalities is trivially satisfied.

The problem we want to solve is then to find $(d_i)_{i \in \{1,\ldots,n\}}$ such that all the constraints are satisfied and T is minimized.

Theorem 42. Given $(\alpha_{i,j})_{i,j \in \{1,\ldots,n\}}$, $(\gamma_{i,j})_{i,j \in \{1,\ldots,n\}}$ and T, the problem of finding $(d_i)_{i \in \{1,\ldots,n\}}$ satisfying the constraints of Eq. (1) is NP-complete.

Proof. The problem is trivially in NP as for any assignment of (d_i) and period T, it is possible to check in polynomial time if the constraints are satisfied (there are $O(n^3)$ constraints).

Now, to show that the problem is NP-hard, we reduce the salesman problem with triangular inequality to that problem.

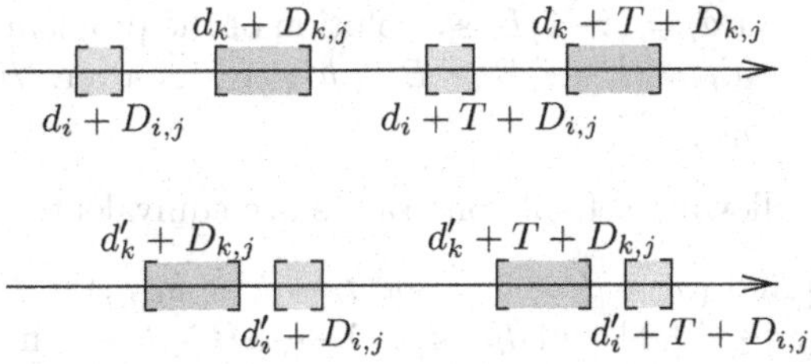

Fig. 14. Different possibilities for the constraints. In the first case, $d_i + D_{i,j}$ is before $d_k + D_{k,j}$ and in the second case, $d'_k + D_{k,j}$ is before $d'_i + D_{i,j}$, but in both cases, $d_k + D_{k,j}$ is before $d_i + T + D_{i,j}$ and $d_i + D_{i,j}$ is before $d_k + T + D_{k,j}$.

Suppose a complete weighted graph, with positive weights of the edges $w(u,v)$, satisfying the triangular inequality: for all vertices u, v, x, $w(u,x) + w(x,v) \leq w(u,v)$. Set $\gamma_{i,j} = \max_{k \in \{1,\ldots,n\}} w(k,i)$ and $\alpha_{i,j} = \gamma_{k,j} - w(i,k)$.

This assignment of the variables is made in such a way that if for some j, $d_i - d_k \geq \gamma_{k,j} - \alpha_{i,j}$, then this holds for all j, as $\gamma_{k,j} - \alpha_{i,j} = w_{i,k}$.

Now, let (d_i) and T be a solution of our problem. There is a Hamiltonian cycle of weight $W \leq T$ in the graph: suppose, without loss of generality that $d_1 \leq d_2 \leq \cdots \leq d_n$.

Then, $w(1,2) + w(2,3) + \cdots + w(n,1) \leq (d_2 - d_1) + (d_3 - d_2) + \cdots + (d_1 - d_n + T) = T$.

Conversely, suppose that there is a Hamiltonian cycle of weight W, corresponding without loss of generality to the cycle $1, 2, \ldots, n$. Set $d_1 = 0$ and $d_i = d_{i-1} + w(i-1, i)$. We have for all i, j d_i every constraint is satisfied and $T = W$ is a possible period: if $k > i$, $d_k - d_i = w(i, i+1) + \cdots + w(k-1, k) \geq w(i,k)$. Moreover, $(d_i + W) - d_k = w(k, k+1) + \cdots + w(n, i) + \cdots + w(i-1, i) \geq w(k,i)$.

Hence, we have a Hamiltonian path of length at most T if and only if we can find a solution to our problem with period at most T: the problem is NP-hard.

4.2   Exact Solution with Linear Programming

This problem can be solved with a linear program using both integer and non-integer variables. The trick is to encode the constraints

$$d_i + \gamma_{i,k} \leq d_k + \alpha_{k,j} \text{ or}$$
$$d_k + \gamma_{k,j} \leq d_i + \alpha_{i,j}$$

into a linear program, and this is why we introduce integer variables.

First, this set of constraints can be rewritten in

$$d_k - d_i \geq b_{i,k,j} \text{ or } d_i - d_k \geq b_{k,i,j}$$

with $b_{i,k,j} = \gamma_{i,j} - \alpha_{k,j}$. Set $B = \max_{i,j,k} b_{i,k,j}$.

Lemma 43. There is a solution of this problem where for all $i \in \{1, \ldots, n\}$, $d_i \in [0, nB]$.

Proof. The assignment $d_i = (i-1)B$ is a solution of the problem. Indeed, $\forall i < k$, $\forall j \in \{1, \ldots, n\}$, $d_k - d_i = (k-i)B \geq B \geq b_{i,k,j}$. Moreover, $\forall i, k, j$, $d_k - d_i = (n-k+i)B \geq B \geq b_{i,k,j}$.

Lemma 44. The following sets of constraints are equivalent.

(i) $d_i, d_k \in [0, nB]$ and $(d_k - d_i \geq b_{i,k,j}$ or $d_i - d_k \geq b_{k,i,j})$
(ii) $d_i, d_k \in [0, nB]$, $q \in \{0, 1\}$ and $d_k - d_i + (1-q)nB \geq b_{i,k,j}$ and $d_i - d_k + qnB \geq b_{k,i,j}$.

Proof. Suppose that the constraints (i) are satisfied. Either $d_k - d_i \geq b_{i,j,k}$ and the constraints in (ii) with $q = 1$ are satisfied (we have the two constraints $d_k - d_i \geq b_{i,j,k}$ and $d_i - d_k + nB \geq nB \geq b_{k,i,j}$); or $d_i - d_k > b_{k,i,j}$ and similarly, the constraints in (ii) with $q = 0$ are satisfied.

Suppose now that the constraints (ii) are satisfied. If $q = 1$, then, trivially, $d_k - d_i \geq b_{i,j,k}$ and if $q = 0$, then $d_i - d_k \geq b_{k,i,j}$.

Consequently, the linear program is

$$\text{Minimize } T \text{ under the constraints}$$

$$\forall i, j, k \in \{1, \ldots, n\}, \ i \neq k,$$
$$0 \leq d_i \leq nB$$
$$\begin{cases} q_{i,k,j} \in \{0, 1\} \\ d_k - d_i + (1 - q_{i,j,k})nB \geq b_{i,k,j} \\ d_i - d_k + q_{i,j,k}nB \geq b_{k,i,j} \\ d_k - d_i \leq T - \max_{j \in \mathbb{N}_n} b_{k,i,j} \end{cases}$$

Example 45. The toy example above gives $T = 28$, with $d_1 = 0$, $d_2 = 21$, $d_3 = 14$ and $d_4 = 5$.

Computing this exact solution is possible but has two drawbacks. First, as the problem is NP-complete, computing the initial delays in larger networks may be untractable. Second, this solution does not exhibit monotony properties. For example, if the linear program lead to a period T and the target period is $T' > T$, it might be better to stretch the values $d_i - d_k$ to $(d_i - d_k)T'/T$. It is unfortunately not ensured with the solution found. In the next paragraph, we show how to compute a solution complying with this additional constraint.

4.3 Heuristic Using a Greedy Algorithm

To simplify the problem we only use strongest constraints: with $c_{i,k} = \max_{k \in \mathbb{N}_n} b_{i,k,j}$,

$$c_{i,k} \leq d_k - d_i \leq T - c_{k,i} \quad \text{or} \quad c_{k,i} \leq d_i - d_k \leq T - c_{i,k}. \tag{2}$$

Lemma 46. If $(d_i)_{i \in \{1,\ldots,n\}}$ is a solution to the constraints of Eq. (2) with a period T, then for $T' > T$, $(\frac{T'}{T}d_i)$ is a solution for the same constraints with period T'.

Proof. If $c_{i,k} \leq d_k - d_i \leq T - c_{k,i}$, then as $\frac{T'}{T} \geq 1$, $\frac{T'}{T}(d_k - d_i) \geq d_k - d_i \geq c_{i,k}$. Second, $\frac{T'}{T}(d_k - d_i) = \frac{T'}{T}(T - c_{k,i}) = T' - \frac{T'}{T}c_{k,i} \leq T' - c_{i,k}$.

Solving these constraints is still a NP-complete problem. In fact the proof of Theorem 42 is valid in this case.

Now, in order to assign the values, we can use the greedy algorithm presented in Algorithm 1. At each step, the algorithm assigns one initial delay, that is chosen to be the smallest as possible, given the initial delays already assigned, while satisfying the constraints set by them.

Lemma 47. At each step of the algorithm, the constraints (2) such that $i, k \in D$ are satisfied.

Proof. We show the result by induction. When $D = \emptyset$ or $|D| = 1$, then this is obviously true as no constraints are involved. Suppose this is true for D and let s the next element that is added to D in the algorithm. From line 8, we know that $d_s \geq \max_{i \in D} d_i + c_{i,s}$. Then, for all $i \in D$, $d_s - d_i \geq c_{i,s}$. Now, from line 9, for all $i \in D$, $T \geq d_s - d_i + c_{s,i}$, so $d_s - d_i \leq T - c_{s,i}$. So, the constraints involving s are satisfied. Now, if the constraints between i and j, $i, j \in D$ are satisfied at one step of the algorithm, they will remain satisfied during the following steps, as T can only increase.

Example 48 (Application of Algorithm 1). With our toy example, we have

$$C = (c_{i,j}) = \begin{pmatrix} 0 & 8 & 11 & 14 \\ 6 & 0 & 9 & 12 \\ 9 & 7 & 0 & 7 \\ 14 & 12 & 9 & 0 \end{pmatrix}.$$

Algorithm 1. Initial delays computation.

> **Data:** $c_{i,j}$.
> **Result:** $d_1, \ldots, d_n, T$.
> 1 **begin**
> 2 $D \leftarrow \emptyset$;
> 3 $S \leftarrow \{1, \ldots, n\}$;
> 4   **foreach** $i \in S$ **do** $d_i \leftarrow 0$;
> 5   **while** $S \neq \emptyset$ **do**
> 6 $s \leftarrow \mathrm{Argmin}_{i \in S} d_i$;
> 7 $S \leftarrow S \setminus \{s\}$;
> 8   **foreach** $i \in S$ **do** $d_i \leftarrow \max(d_i, d_s + c_{s,i})$;
> 9   **foreach** $i \in D$ **do** $T \leftarrow \max(T, d_s - d_i + c_{s,i})$;
> 10 $D \leftarrow D \cup \{s\}$;

If 1 is chosen first ($d_i = 0$ $\forall i \in \{1, 2, 3, 4\}$), the values are updates to $d_1 = 0$, $d_2 = \max(0, d_1 + c_{1,2}) = 8$, $d_3 = 11$ and $d_4 = 14$; $T = 0$. Then, 2 is chosen and we get $d_3 = \max(d_3, d_2 + c_{2,3}) = 17$ and $d_4 = 20$; $T = \max(T, d_2 - d_1 + c_{2,1}) = 14$. Finally, we have $d_1 = 0$, $d_2 = 8$, $d_3 = 17$, $d_4 = 24$ and $T = 38$.

Note that this problem could also have been solved using a linear program (with integer variables), by replacing the variables $q_{i,k,j}$ in the linear program of the previous paragraph by $q_{i,k}$: forgetting the parameter j, exactly leads to the same constraints of Eq. (2). In this case, we find $T = 36$, with $d_1 = 0$, $d_2 = 30$, $d_3 = 11$ and $d_4 = 18$. Our heuristic is near this optimal.

In the next lemma, we assume that our target period is $T' < T$, that is, we are not able to find a solution so that there is at most one message in the queues of the routers. We assume here that the sojourn time of a message does not depend on the queue length.

Lemma 49. Let (d_i) be a solution for the initial delays with period T. The same assignment with period $T' < T$ ensures that in each router, there are never more than $\lceil \frac{T}{T'} \rceil$ messages simultaneously.

Proof. Set $\lceil \frac{T}{T'} \rceil = q$. We number the messages: m_i^j is the j-th message originating from router i. For $\ell \in \{0, \dots, q-1\}$, in each server, simultaneously, there cannot be several messages among $(m_i^{kq+\ell})_{k \in \mathbb{N}, i \in \mathbb{N}_n}$, because $qT' \geq T$. As a consequence, there cannot be more than q messages in a router.

4.4   Simulation Results with Initial Delays

In this section, we present simulations of the TPN modeling of the German telecommunication network with initial delays defined by Algorithm 1, in the stable case ($T_r = 1800\,\mathrm{s}$) and in the limit case ($T_r = 1000\,\mathrm{s}$).

We first need to define the transmission and sojourn times used by the algorithm:

- the transmission time has already been defined to $\tau_{ij} = T_t = 30\,\mathrm{s}$, for all the links of the network;
- for each router R_i, the sojourn time is at least equal to the processing time $\delta_i = T_p = 15\,\mathrm{s}$, the time to process the message where the queue is empty. The maximum sojourn time is extracted from the simulation of the TPN of Sect. 2 (with no initial delays). During the simulation, the maximum queue length is Q_i in router R_i. Then, we take $\Delta_i = Q_i T_p$.

Note that doing this enables to take into account all the messages from the LSA flooding mechanism, and not only the first LSA message in each router.

The Low Traffic Case. Let's first consider the low traffic case, where $T_r = 1800\,\mathrm{s}$. The maximal queue length of each router is extracted from a simulation of the TPN during approximately 3.5 days ($3.10^5\,\mathrm{s}$). Here is the list of each maximal queue length: $Q = (7, 8, 13, 2, 2, 17, 8, 37, 4, 5, 13, 2, 2, 3, 13, 6, 2)$. Then, Algorithm 1 returns the following initial delays:

$$d = (0, 105, 1200, 810, 75, 255, 420, 1335, 1035, 1080, 1155, 1530, 630, 330, 780, 330, 1680).$$

Furthermore, Algorithm 1 computes $T_{rMax} = 16695\,\mathrm{s}$.

Figure 15 represents the result of the TPN simulation with the initial delays listed above when $T_r = 1800$ s. The maximum queue length of router R_8 during a simulation of 3.10^5 s is now $Max_8 = 25$, which gives a significant improvement: it was $Max_8 = 37$ without the computation of initial delays. Moreover, the queue length is below 10 for most of the time.

The Limit Case. Now, let us discuss the efficiency of our method on the limit case introduced in Sect. 3.3, where the most loaded router, R_8, processes messages continuously $(T_r = 1000\,\text{s})$. The list of maximal queues

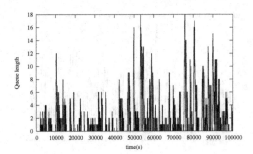

Fig. 15. Buffer length of R_8 with $T_r = 1800$ s and initial delays.

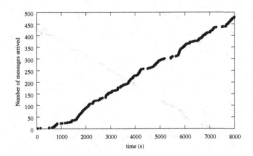

Fig. 16. Buffer length of R_8 with $T_r = 1800$ s and initial delays.

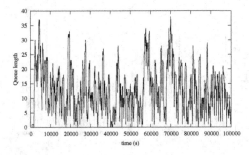

Fig. 17. Buffer length of R_8 with $T_r = 1000$ s and initial delays.

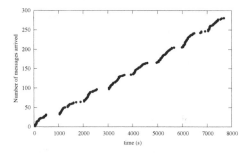

Fig. 18. Message arrivals to R_6 with $T_r = 1000\,$s without initial delays.

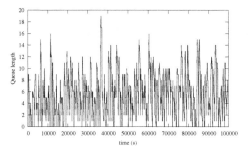

Fig. 19. Buffer length of R_6 with $T_r = 1000\,$s without initial delays.

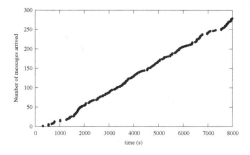

Fig. 20. Message arrivals to R_6 with $T_r = 1000\,$s and initial delays.

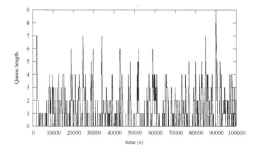

Fig. 21. Buffer length of R_6 with $T_r = 1000\,$s and initial delays.

length, extracted again from a long simulation of approximately 3.5 days, is:
$Q = (9, 8, 13, 3, 2, 18, 8, 44, 4, 6, 15, 2, 3, 3, 14, 10, 2)$. Using this matrix, Algorithm 1 computes $T_{rMax} = 18795$ s and the following initial delays:

$$d = (0, 115, 470, 955, 155, 465, 595, 655, 135, 280, 635, 715, 720, 465, 900, 365, 875).$$

Figure 16 (resp. Fig. 17) represents the message arrivals to R_8 (resp. the queue length of R_8) simulated with the TPN when $T_r = 1000$ s and using the previous definition of d.

One can observe that defining the initial delays implies some improvements. Indeed, the message arrivals are efficiently spread over the periods. In addition, the queue length is often below 15 when it was 20 previously (see Fig. 10). The maximal length, however, reached on the full simulation of 3.10^5 s is $Max_8 = 58$. It was unfortunately $Max_8 = 44$, when all initial delays were set to 0. Thus, our method worsens the load of R_8 for some periods.

In this case, as R_8 works without any interruption from a period to another, it seems natural that delaying messages does not significantly improve the queue length of this router. Consequently, we now evaluate the impact of our method on the queue length of the other routers.

Router R_6 is the most loaded router of the German telecommunication network, after R_8. Figures 18 and 19 (resp. Figs. 20 and 21) represent the message arrivals and the queue length of this router when $T_r = 1000$ s and initial delays are set to 0 (resp. defined by Algorithm 1).

Message arrivals are still efficiently spread over the periods. Also, $Max_6 = 13$ with the initial delays when it is $Max_6 = 21$ otherwise. Observing Figs. 19 and 21, one can notice an overall reduction during the simulation time represented.

In fact, this improvement is observed on each router (except R_8). The list of maximal queue lengths obtained when the defined initial delays is: $Q = (6, 6, 7, 1, 1, 13, 5, 58, 2, 2, 11, 1, 2, 1, 11, 3, 1)$.

5   Conclusions

This article presents a method usable for the OSPF protocol and cyclic protocols that use delay parameters. This method aims at increasing the reactivity of the network to topology changes, and at minimizing the queue length of routers. Algorithm 1 provides an efficient way to spread messages over the whole period. Furthermore, it shows to be a good tool to reduce queue lengths.

Currently the risk of OSPF instability remains low. However, this is not the case for all periodical protocols. One can cite the example of the routing protocol between autonomous systems: BGP (Border Gateway Protocol [10]). Indeed, the instability issues of this protocol are still intensively studied today [7]. In particular, we know that configuration mistakes or some frequent variations of the network topology can prevent the convergence of the protocol and can overuse the network resources. Consequently, it would be interesting to observe the result of the introduced method on this protocol's instabilities.

Appendix

Table 1. List of main notations.

Notation	Full name
$G = (V, E)$	Directed graph representing the network
n	Number of routers
R_i	i^{th} router in the network
$\mathcal{V}(R_i)$	Set of neighbors of R_i
$\|\mathcal{V}(R_i)\|$	Cardinality of $\mathcal{V}(R_i)$
d_i	Initial delay of R_i
b_i	Number of retransmission of an LSA received from a neighbor of R_i
LSA_i	Link state advertisement message of R_i
Ack	Acknowledgment message
T_r (or T)	Period length of the LSA flooding process
T_p	Processing time of messages
T_t	Time to send a message
(P,T,B,F,M_0,φ)	A Time Petri Net (TPN)
$Start_i$	Initial place of TPN to create LSA_is
$LSAsend_{i \to j}$	Place to send LSA_i to R_j
$ACKsend_{i \to j}$	Place to send an Ack from R_i to R_j
$LSArec_{j \to i}$	Place to receive LSA_j in R_i
$ACKrec_{j \to i}$	Place to receive an Ack from R_j in R_i
$Processor$	Place to guaranty that one message is processed at a time
$bound$	Place to bound the number of retransmission from a neighbor
$Retransmission$	Place to retransmit a received LSA
$Destruction$	Place to destroy a received LSA
$n(j)$ (resp. $N(j)$)	Number of messages received (resp. processed) by R_j during T_r
$\tau_{i,j}$	Transmission time between R_i and R_j
$[\delta_i, \Delta_i[$	Sojourn time of a message in R_i
$I_{i,j} = [\alpha_{i,j}, \beta_{i,j}[$	Time of first LSA_i received in R_j
$\alpha = (\alpha_{i,j})$	Matrix of values $\alpha_{i,j}$
$\beta = (\beta_{i,j})$	Matrix of values $\beta_{i,j}$
$D = (D_{i,j})$	$D_{i,j} = [\alpha_{i,j}, \gamma_{i,j}[$ with $\gamma_{i,j} = \beta_{i,j} + \Delta_j$
$Q = (Q_i)$	Maximal queue length of R_i
$b_{i,k,j}$ and B	$b_{i,k,j} = \gamma_{i,j} - \alpha_{k,j}$ and $B = \max_{i,k,j} b_{i,k,j}$
$C = (c_{i,k})$	$c_{i,k} = \max_{k \in \mathbb{N}_n} b_{i,k,j}$

References

1. Basu, A., Riecke, J.: Stability issues in OSPF routing. In: Proceedings of the 2001 Conference on Applications, Technologies, Architectures, and Protocols for Computer Communications, (SIGCOMM'01), pp. 225–236. ACM, New York (2001)
2. Francois, P., Filsfils, C., Evans, J., Bonaventure, O.: Achieving sub-second IGP convergence in large IP networks. (SIGCOMM'05) Comput. Commun. Rev. **35**(3), 35–44 (2005)
3. Ishiguro, K.: Quagga, a routing software package for TCP/IP networks (2012). http://www.nongnu.org/quagga/
4. Jard, C., Roux, O.H.: Communicating Embedded Systems, Software and Design, Formal Methods. ISTE and Wiley, London and Hoboken (2010)
5. Katz, D., Kompella, K., Yeung, D.: Traffic Engineering (TE) Extensions to OSPF Version 2. Updated by RFC 4203 (2003)
6. Kummer, O., Wienberg, F., Duvigneau, M., Kohler, M., Moldt, D., Rolke, H.: Renew the reference net workshop. In: 24th International Conference on Application and Theory of Petri Nets (ATPN'03) (2003)
7. Labovitz, C., Malan, G.R., Jahanian, F.: Origins of internet routing instability. In: Proceedings of the International Conference on Computer Communications (INFOCOM'99), pp. 218–226. IEEE, New York (1999)
8. Lime, D., Roux, O.H., Seidner, C., Traonouez, L.-M.: Romeo: a parametric model-checker for Petri Nets with stopwatches. In: Kowalewski, S., Philippou, A. (eds.) TACAS 2009. LNCS, vol. 5505, pp. 54–57. Springer, Heidelberg (2009)
9. Moy, J.: RFC 2328 OSPF v2. Technical report (1998)
10. Rekhter, Y., Li, T.: RFC 1771 A Border Gateway Protocol 4 (BGP-4) (1995)

Managing Virtual Entities in MMOGs: A Voronoi-Based Approach

Laura Ricci$^{(\boxtimes)}$, Luca Genovali, and Barbara Guidi

Department of Computer Science, University of Pisa, Pisa, Italy
{ricci,guidi}@di.unipi.it, luke.sky.1973@gmail.com

Abstract. The definition of a distributed architecture for Massively Multiplayer Online Game raises several research challenges. Among these, the problem of managing the virtual entities of the MMOG and of maintaining their persistence is one of the most relevant ones. The management of the entities cannot be simply delegated to the peers, because the load assigned to a single peer may be high. Furthermore, a centralized server is needed to manage the state of the entities when all the peers leave the game. This paper proposes an integrated server/P2P architecture for MMOG and focus on the problem of the assignment of the virtual entities to the server/peers. We propose to define this assignment through a Voronoi Tessellation which is defined by exploiting the position of the peers. Each peer manages the entities located in the intersection of a superset of its Area of Interest and of its Voronoi region, while the entities located outside these areas are assigned to the server. A set of experimental results proving the effectiveness of our approach are presented.

Keywords: MMOG · Voronoi · Peer to Peer · Load balancing · Distributed algorithms

1 Introduction

Massively Multiplayer Online Games (MMOGs) [1–6] enable geographically distant users to communicate, interact and collaborate within a virtual environment. In particular, online gaming entertainment has acquired lots of popularity in the last years from both industry and research communities. The market size of online gaming has received a 5 billion evaluation in 2010, while the number of total users have reached around 20 million worldwide.

Currently, most MMOGs rely on a client server architecture which supports a straightforward management of the main functionalities of the MMOG, such as user identification, management of the state of the virtual world, synchronization between players, and billing. However the most important drawback of these architectures is their limited scalability which prevent a satisfactory playability when huge amounts of concurrent users are playing simultaneously.

© Springer-Verlag Berlin Heidelberg 2014
M.S. Obaidat and J. Filipe (Eds.): ICETE 2013, CCIS 456, pp. 58–73, 2014.
DOI: 10.1007/978-3-662-44788-8_4

Recently several solutions based on P2P based MMOG have been presented. The main advantage of these solutions is that they are inherently scalable because when the amount of users grows, more resources are added to the infrastructure. However, a pure P2P-based approach is barely feasible. As a matter of fact, the lack of a centralized authority makes it complex to enforce security, consistency of concurrent updates to the state of the virtual world and persistence of its state when a few players are present in the virtual world.

An interesting alternative exploiting the advantages of both the client/server and of the P2P architecture is to define an hybrid solution which properly distributes the functionalities of the MMOG among the server and the peers. For instance, the state of the virtual world may be partitioned and distributed to the server and to the peers by exploiting the locality property characterizing most MMOGs. As a matter of fact, an avatar generally interacts with other entities (avatars and passive entities) located in its proximity, i.e. in its *Area of Interest, AOI*. A simple solution is to define a partition of the state of the MMOG where a peer manages the entities in its AOI, while the server manages entities located in areas not covered by the AOI of any peer. This solution is simple, however it does not resolve the problem of the ownership of the entities which are located in the intersection of the AOI of a set of peers.

In this paper we propose *HyVVE, Hybrid Voronoi-based Virtual Environment*, an hybrid architecture based on a Voronoi Tessellation [7] of the virtual world which exploits the locality of MMOGs.

Given *n sites* in an Euclidean space, a *Voronoi Tessellation* partitions the virtual world into *n areas* such that the area corresponding to a site *n* includes all the points which *are closer* to *n* with respect to any other site.

In a *Voronoi-based* MMOG, the position of each peer in the virtual world is exploited to define the *Voronoi Tessellation* of the world which is exploited to assign entities to the peers/server. In *HyVVE* the entities assigned to a peer are those belonging to the intersection of its *CCAOI*, a circular area representing a super-set of its *AOI*, and of its Voronoi area. We consider a superset of the *AOI* of a peer to implement a prefetching of the entities close to the border of the *AOI* of the peer. The server manages all the entities belonging to areas not covered by the *CCAOI* of any peer. The solution where a peer manages all the entities in its Voronoi area is not feasible, because when a few peers are present in the virtual world, the number of entities assigned to a peer would be huge, and the peer would not be able to support such a load, especially if its computational capability is not high. *HyVVE* supports a load distribution mechanism which scale in a natural way. When the world is scarcely populated, most entities are mapped to the server. However, the server load is not high in this case, because a few entities are accessed and modified by the peers. When the number of the peers increases, the amount of entities assigned to the peers increases proportionally so that the load is distributed between the peers. In a crowding scenario, i.e. when a huge amount of peers gather in the same region of the world, the entities located in that region are managed by these peers, while the server manages entities belonging to inhabited regions of the virtual world.

In this scenario, where peers are close to each other and their *AOIs* intersect, the ownership of the entities is defined by considering the Voronoi regions of the peers. When a conflict occurs because an entity is located in the *CCAOI* of a set of peers, the Voronoi Tessellation is exploited to determine the owner of the entity. Since each point of the space is mapped to a unique Voronoi Area, each entity of the virtual world is assigned to a unique node peer.

The paper is organized as follows. Section 2 discusses the state of art in the area of Voronoi based virtual worlds. Section 3 introduces the mathematical notions which are the basis of our approach, while Sect. 4 discusses how Voronoi Tessellation can be exploited for the definition of virtual environments. Section 5 describes the architecture of *HyVVE*. A set of experimental results are presented in Sect. 6, while Sect. 7 reports some conclusion and discusses future works.

2   Related Works

Voronoi diagrams and Delaunay-based overlays are a well know solution to maintain network topology for P2P virtual environments.

One of the first works along this line is VON [8–10]. VON exploits a Voronoi division of the MMOG in order to manage event dissemination in a scalable manner. VON defines an overlay such that each peer maintains a direct connection with all the peers within its AOI. In order to maintain overlay connectivity, each peer also has a direct link with peers that may also be outside of the AOI. To reduce bandwidth consumption, VON has been further upgraded with an enhanced event dissemination system [10] and state management [9].

VoroGame [11–13], proposes an hybrid architecture for the management of passive entities. Their architecture combines a Voronoi-based network and a Distributed Hash Table (DHT). Two different peers, one for each overlay, are responsible for each entity in the MMOG. Voronoi nodes are responsible and maintain a copy for any of the entities that are in their Voronoi area. They also maintain, for each of these entities, a list of peers that have to be notified for a state change of the given entity. This list is periodically sent to the corresponding DHT node, whose task is to broadcast state updates.

The work in [14] proposes a solution to deal with cluster of players in Delaunay-based topologies. They employ a flooding messaging strategy to spread notification inside the AOI. However, when a peer detects the message rate to exceed its maximum capacity, it triggers a procedure for cluster management. This procedure logically collapses the cluster to a single point, allowing communications to temporarily skip many small neighbouring Voronoi regions, which helps reduce the communication overhead. The approach has been proved effective with realistic movement traces from Second Life.

The definition of a P2P overlay for *MMOG* based upon *Voronoi Diagrams* has been investigated in [8,10,15–22]. Some recent proposals [8,14,22] have discussed the benefits of defining an overlay where the P2P connections correspond to the links of a Delaunay Triangulation generated by considering the locations of avatars of the MMOG [23]. According to this proposal, each peer is paired with a site of a Voronoi diagram defined on the virtual space and the position of the peer is exploited to define the space partition. In this way, the area corresponding to a peer P includes all the points of the MMOG which *are closer* to P with respect to any other. The *Delaunay Triangulation* corresponding to the *Voronoi tessellation* defines the *P2P* overlay connecting the peers. In a *MMOG* any event generated by a peer should be notified to any other peer in its *AOI*. This notification may be implemented through a *AOI-cast* mechanism [24], i.e. an application level multicast constrained within the boundary of the area of interest. *Flooding* the heartbeat through the *Voronoi links* generates a large amount of redundant messages and presents evident scalability problems. A more refined approach dynamically computes a *spanning tree* on the *Voronoi links* including all the peers of the *AOI* and exploits this tree to notify the heartbeat. Both solutions are based on *forwarding*, i.e. any heartbeat is routed to the peers in the *AOI* through a sequence of intermediate peers. An obvious drawback of these solutions is the high latency in the delivery of an event, especially in *crowding scenarios*, i.e. when a set of peers lie close to each other in the *virtual world* and their *AOI* overlap. In this case *several routing hops* may be required to notify an event due to the large amount of peers located in the *AOI*. The resulting *latency* may be not tolerable in *MMOG* and may compromise the interactivity of the application. On the other hand, since the number of *Voronoi neighbours* is 6 on average [7], in this solutions a peer manages a small number of connections. An alternative solution [8] defines *direct links* between a peer and any other one in its *AOI*. The resulting overlay includes these links besides the Voronoi ones, which have to be maintained to guarantee the connectivity of the overlay. This solution minimizes the latency, but increases the number of connections of each peer. In a crowding scenario like the one previously described, a peer should manage a large number of connections, since a large amount of peers are located in its *AOI*.

The problem of maintaining the *Voronoi* structure of the overlay in a dynamic *P2P* environment, like a *MMOG*, where the positions of the peers change continuously and no centralized coordination entity does exist, is a challenging issue. It is worth noticing that several distributed algorithm for the management of the Voronoi overlay have been recently proposed.

References [1, 21, 25, 26] propose protocols to build and maintain Delaunay triangulation-based overlay networks. In [27] Liebeherr *et. al.* proposed the first protocol to build a distributed Delaunay triangulation, which is exploitable as a multicast application layer. Their protocol is based on the locally equiangular property [27] of Delaunay triangulations. Periodically, each node checks whether it respects this property and whether its neighbors do too. Whenever a violation is detected, the node creates new triangles to maintain a correct structure. This protocol has been exploited in HyperCast [27], a P2P framework for managing communication between nodes within an overlay, in which the peers can organize themselves into a virtual network and exchange data with other peers in the overlay. Reference [27] exploits *Compass Routing* to define a Spanning Tree supporting an application layer multicast. This algorithm can be used to notify an event to all the peers in the AOI of a given peer.

The approach present in [25] is based on a gossip approach which results particularly suitable in a dynamic environment like a MMOG.

3   Voronoi Diagrams and Delaunay Triangulations

This section introduces the basic mathematical concepts we have exploited for the definition of HyVVE.

A *Voronoi diagram*, [7] also referred as *Voronoi tessellation*, is a special kind of decomposition of a metric space determined by the distances of the points of the spaces to a specified discrete set of entities in the space, i.e. the *sites*.

Let us denote the Euclidean distance between two points p and q by $dist(p,q)$.

Definition 1. *Let $S = \{s_1, s_2, ..., s_n\}$ be a set of n distinct points in the plane, i.e. the sites. The Voronoi Diagram of S is a partition of the plane into n cells, one for each site in S, such that the point q belongs to the cell corresponding to a site s_i if and only if $dist(q, s_i) < dist(q, s_j) \forall s_j \in S, i \neq j$.*

Fig. 1. A voronoi tessellation.

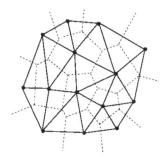

Fig. 2. A delaunay triangulation.

In the following, we will denote the Voronoi Diagram of S by $Vor(S)$ and the cell corresponding to a site s_i by $V(s_i)$. Figure 1 shows the Voronoi Tessellation defined by the set of sites represented by black dots. Each colored region represents $V(s_i)$, where s_i is the site corresponding to the black dot belonging to the region.

A *Delaunay Triangulation* is a mathematical structure dual with respect to the *Voronoi Tessellation*.

A *Delaunay triangulation $Dt(P)$* for a set P of sites in the plane is a triangulation, i.e. a partition of the plane into a set of triangles, such that the circumcircle of any triangle in $Dt(P)$ is empty, i.e. it does not include any other point in P.

Given a set of n sites $S = \{s_1, s_2, ..., s_n\}$ of the plane, the *Delaunay triangulation* is the *dual structure* of the Voronoi diagram, where the sites correspond to the vertexes of the triangles, and an edge of a triangle connects two vertexes

s_1, s_2 if and only if $V(s_1)$ and $V(s_2)$ share a common edge, i.e. s_1 and s_2 are Voronoi neighbours.

Figure 2 shows a *Delaunay Triangulation* on the top of s *Voronoi diagram*, where the borders of the Voronoi regions are shown by dotted lines and the corresponding *Delaunay Triangulation* links are shown by continuous lines.

4   Exploiting Voronoi Diagrams in P2P MMOGs

In a *Voronoi-based* approach, the position of each peer in the virtual world is exploited to define a *Voronoi tessellation* of the virtual world. Given n *sites* corresponding to the peers, a *Voronoi tessellation* partitions the virtual world into n *areas* such that the area corresponding to a site n includes all the points which *are closer* to n with respect to any other site. Two sites are *Voronoi neighbours* iff the borders of their areas overlap. The connected graph defined by linking neighbour sites corresponds to the *Delaunay Triangulation* associated to the *Voronoi tessellation*. A *P2P* overlay is defined by connecting peers whose sites are Voronoi neighbours. In the following, the links of this overlay will be referred as *Voronoi links*.

The adoption of this solution presents relevant advantages:

- *Mapping of Entities to the Peers:* a straightforward *mapping of entities to the peers* assigns each entity to the peer which manages the Voronoi region where the entity is located.
- *Bandwidth Saving:* since each site of a Voronoi tessellation has on the average 6 neighbours [7], each peer manages a bounded number of connections with other peers, i.e. those corresponding to the Delaunay links.
- *Overlay Connectivity:* the connections corresponding to the Delaunay links guarantee that the overlay is connected. Even if a peer is located in an uninhabited region of the virtual world, it remains connected with the rest of the MMOG through the Delaunay connections.
- *Existence of Routing Algorithms for Delaunay Networks:* compass routing is based on a fast-to-compute angle argument which exploits the mathematical properties of geometric networks and has been proved to be cycle free for Delaunay networks. The algorithm can be exploited to define efficient AOI-cast mechanisms.

5   HyVVE: The Architecture

Even if the definition of a pure P2P network for $MMOG$ is a challenging alternative to the classical *client/server* solution, several problems should still be solved for the definition of a comprehensive solution. One of the main problems still to be solved concerns the management of the $MMOG$ state when the number of peers is very low or zero. The main problem when a low number of peers belong to the $MMOG$ is related to the high load assigned to each peer. A further problem is the maintenance of the state of the $MMOG$ when all the peers have left it, because this state should be restored later when some peer joins the $MMOG$.

To manage the problem of state persistence, we propose *HyVVE*, an *hybrid architecture* including a small number of "classical" servers controlling the state of the $MMOG$ and a huge amount of interacting peers. Note that this solution differs from a solution based on the definition of Super-Peer based architecture, because the set of servers is *statically defined*, while the Super-Peers are dynamically elected, they participate to the $MMOG$ as normal peers and support the further task of routing the event notification for the peers they manage. In HyVVE, the server controls the join of peers to the $MMOG$, their authentication and manages a portion of the $MMOG$ state. For the sake of simplicity, we consider a system where a single server S is defined. The server is a supervisor which does not belong to the P2P overlay and is connected to all the peers. When a peer enters the $MMOG$ or updates its position, it notifies this event to the server so that the server continuously has a vision of the whole $MMOG$ and is able to compute a Voronoi tessellation including all the peers of the $MMOG$. In this way, it is able to exploit the tessellation to distribute portions of the state of the $MMOG$ to the joining peers. On the other way round, *HyVVE* differs from client/server architectures because a distributed protocol is exploited to exchange events like positional and object updates directly between the peers, without any intervention by the server. This avoid that the server becomes, like in classical client/server solutions, a bottleneck for the entire system. The server is involved at a peer bootstrap and then it receives the positional updates of the peer, but these are not forwarded to other peers, instead they are exploited by the server to decide if it must give up entities to the peers or acquire entities from them. To implement the distributed protocol supporting events exchange, in *HyVVE* the peers are connected by a Delaunay overlay which is built and maintained through *GoDel*, a gossip-based protocol proposed in [25]. *Godel* is based on the definition of a stack of gossip protocols. The first one is a random peer sampling protocol which guarantees that each peer has a view including a set of other peers chosen at random. This level is introduced to guarantee the connectivity of the overlay. The second level is a gossip protocol where each peer chooses its neighbours by applying the *equiangular property* of the Delaunay triangulations [7]. In [25] we have shown that the local views of the peers may be temporarily inconsistent, but the protocol guarantees the convergence to a state where each peer has the exact knowledge of its Delaunay neighbours. Based on this knowledge, each peer may define the Voronoi tessellation including itself and its neighbours.

Let us consider now the *Voronoi-based tessellation* enabling a natural mapping of the entities of the $MMOG$ to the peers. Each entity is mapped to the peer whose Voronoi region includes it so that each entity is managed by a single peer of the $MMOG$. The problem of this approach is that, when the $MMOG$ includes a small number of peers, a large number of entities may be associated to a single peer which may be not able to manage all them. As a matter of fact, when a few peers are present in the $MMOG$ all entities are partitioned between them and a single peer may *result overloaded*. To avoid peer overloading, we associate with each peer a new circular area, the *CCAOI, Centered Coordination AOI,*

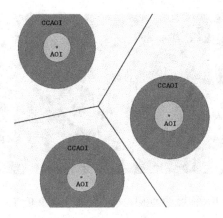

Fig. 3. AOI and CCAOI.

whose center is the position of the peer and whose radius is larger than of the AOI. The goal of the $CCAOI$ is to reduce the number of entities assigned to a peer when its Voronoi Area is too large. As a matter of fact, in this solution each peer manages the entities located inside the *Intersection Area, IA*, i.e. the area corresponding to the *intersection* between *Voronoi Area* and its $CCAOI$, while the entities located outside the *Intersection Area* of any peer are assigned to the server. Both these areas change dynamically when the peer moves like its AOI.

As Fig. 3 shows, the area managed by the peer is only the blue one while the yellow area does not belong to any *Interaction Area* and the entities located in this area are managed by the server.

The server initially owns the state of the whole $MMOG$. When a peer joins the $MMOG$, it first contacts S for the *authentication*, then it receives from S, and from its Delaunay neighbours the set of entities belonging to its Intersection Area.

It is important to note that when the $CCAOI$ is totally included in the Voronoi area of the peer, the IA overlaps the $CCAOI$. On the other way round, if the $CCAOI$ is a super-set of the Voronoi Area, the IA overlaps the Voronoi Area of the peer. In a third scenario the IA is the portion of the $CCAOI$ overlapping the Voronoi area of the peer.

The first case corresponds to a scenario where a very small number of peers are present in the $MMOG$. Note that in this case the *Voronoi Area* is much larger than the $CCAOI$. In this scenario, the introduction of the *Interaction Area* enables each peer to take care only of the coordination of the closer entities, i.e. the entities located inside its IA while the server manage the entities located within its Voronoi Area, but not belonging to its Intersection Area, i.e. the entities located far from it.

Note that in this scenario the server does not become a bottleneck for the system, even if a large number of entities are mapped to it because of the presence

Fig. 4. Each entity is managed by a peer.

of a few peers. As a matter of fact, the probability that the peers update the entities mapped to the regions managed by the server, i.e. the yellow regions in Fig. 3, is low, because these entities are located far away the peers. Note that as the number of peers decreases, the entities are assigned back to the server that, in a natural way, acquires the total control of the system, when the last peer leaves the $MMOG$. In this case the server acts as a *backup server* for the $MMOG$ state, and when each peer exits the $MMOG$, the state of the $MMOG$ will be stored by the server to be restored later. Furthermore, in this way the load of the peers is reduced.

When the number of peers increases, the number of entities owned by the server decreases, because it delegates the management of the entities to the joining peers. In this scenario, as in a crowding situation, the *Interaction Area* of each peer may overlap its Voronoi region and the management of the state of the $MMOG$ may be delegated entirely to the peers, as shown in Fig. 4, where the management of the $MMOG$ is totally delegated to the peers and the server owns no entity. In this scenario the only task of the server is to control and authenticate the peer joining the network since all the entities are managed by the peers.

Consider now a crowding scenario, for instance one where peers fight against each other and a large number of peers is concentrated in a small portion of the virtual space, as showed in Fig. 5. In this case, the Voronoi Area of each peer is included in its $CCAOI$, hence the IA of the peer overlaps its Voronoi Area and, despite the large number of peers, the area that the server must manage is very large. Even in this situation, the server does not become a bottleneck, because it does not receive updates for the entities it owns since they are located far away from the peers. Again its task is to store the state of the entities and to decrease the load of the peer.

In our solution, the server itself becomes, compared to the classical client/ server model, both a *backup* and a *load distribution* mechanism.

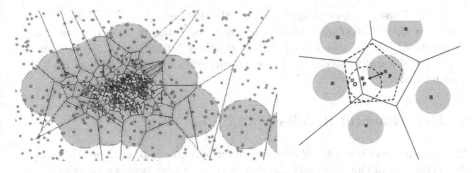

Fig. 5. A crowding scenario.

Fig. 6. Entity delegation to server.

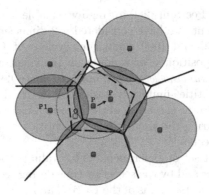

Fig. 7. Entity delegation between peers.

5.1 Entities Delegation

When a new peer enters the $MMOG$ or the overlay is modified due to the movement of the peers, the server checks if some entity it owns falls within the IA of a peer and, in this case, it sends the entity to this peer.

The peers instead have a limited knowledge of the $MMOG$ because of the local information obtained by the direct connections with peers that fall in their AOI and with their Delaunay neighbours. When a peer P receives information from a neighbour V about either a position update or a new neighbour notification, P updates its local Delaunay Triangulation with the new neighbours positions and check whether any of the entities owned fall in the IA of its neighbours or in the server area. In both cases, P is no longer the owner of the entity and sends the entity to the new owner.

For instance, in Fig. 6, the peer P moves from left to right and the entity O, first included in the $IA(P)$ managed by P, because of the shift of P, enters the area under server competence. If we observe the movement of P, from left to right, the entity O would be assigned to the server.

In Fig. 7 we see the exchange of an entity between peer P and P_1. Dotted lines show the $CCAOI$ and the Voronoi region of P before its movement, when the entity O just falls in $IA(P)$. When P moves following the arrow, then O enters $IA(P_1)$ and P_1 becomes the new owner of O by receiving from P all the information.

6   Experimental Results

This section describes a set of experiments whose goal is to evaluate the load of the server and of the peers and the number of transfers between the server and the peers for management of the entities. The experiments have been conducted by varying the number of peers, the radius of the $CCAOI$ and the speed of the peers.

We have exploited PeerSim [28], an highly scalable simulator for P2P networks. In the experiments we have considered a 2-dimensional virtual environment of size 600×800 and 1000 simulation cycles. At the start up of each simulation, peers are positioned at random on the map, afterwards the peers move according to the *random way-point mobility model* [29].

We consider 1000 entities uniformly positioned in the virtual world. Initially, all the entities belong to the server, then the server transfers subset of entities to the interested peers during the simulation. The entities may be then exchanged directly between the peers.

The goal of the first set of experiments is to evaluate the average number of entities owned by a peer and by the server by considering scenarios characterized by different number of peers, radius of the $CCAOI$ and avatars' speed. The speed is the number of pixels covered by a single movement of a peer. We fix the number of entities to 1000, while the number of peers varies in the range $[1 \ldots 1000]$ with a step of 100. We consider two values for the $CCAOI$ radius, i.e. 50 and 10 pixels, while the speed of the avatars varies in the range $[1 \ldots 2, 5]$ with a step of 0.5.

Figure 8 shows the average number of entities owned by the server, while the average number of entities owned by each peer is shown in Fig. 9. Note that, when the radius of the $CCAOI$ is fixed at 50 or at 10, the behaviour of the function is the same for different avatars' speeds. For this reason, the lines corresponding to different speed are completely overlapped. First of all, we observe that the server load decreases when the number of peers increases, because a larger set of peers contributes to the management of the entities.

It is interesting to note that the server does not own any entity when the radius of the $CCAOI$ is equal to 50 and the number of peers is larger than 300 because, in this case, the IA of the peers covers the whole virtual environment, no entity is managed by the server and the partition of the entities among the peers is determined by the Voronoi partition of the virtual world. Also the load of the peers decreases when the number of peers increases, but, while the reduction is remarkable when the radius of the $CCAOI$ is 50, it is negligible when the radius is 10. As a matter of fact, in the latter scenario, the size of the $CCAOI$ is very small and each region of the virtual world is covered by a single peer. On the

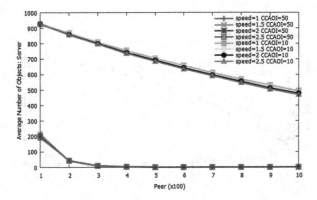

Fig. 8. Average number of entities of the server with 1000 objects.

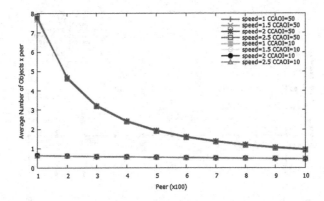

Fig. 9. Average number of entities for each peer with 1000 objects.

other side, when the size of the *CCAOI* is larger, some portions of the virtual world are covered by a set of peers, and this implies a reduction of the average load of a peer.

Figure 11 shows the average number of entity transfers initiated by a peer and Fig. 10 those initiated by the server, at each simulation cycle. First of all, note that the number of transfers is influenced by the avatars' speed. As a matter of fact, the difference between the *IA* of a peer before and after its movement is larger when the speed increases and this implies a larger number of entities to acquire.

The probability that the *IA* of a peer is a subset of its Voronoi area is higher when the radius of the *CCAOI* is small, even when the number of peers increases. In this case, a peer must acquire entities from the server at each movement. As a matter of fact note that the number of transfers from the server is larger when the size of the *CCAOI* is 10 with respect to 50. When the radius of the *CCAOI* is 50 and the number of peers is larger than 300 no transfer between the server and the peers occurs since, as observed before, the server does not manage any entity.

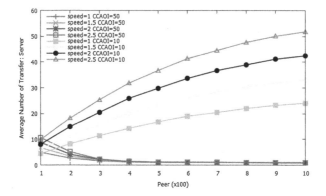

Fig. 10. Average transfers of the server with 1000 objects.

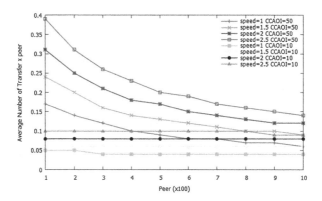

Fig. 11. Average transfer of a peer with 1000 objects.

As far as concerns the transfers initiated by the peers, the average number of transfers for each peer does not depend from their number when the size of the *CCAOI* is small, because, as observed before, the number of entities managed by each peer is nearly constant. When the *CCAOI* is large, the average number of transfers of a peer at each cycle decreases proportionally to the number of peers, because when the number of peers is high, no entity is transferred between peers and the server.

The last set of experiments evaluates the average number of transfers initiated by the server/by the peers by considering different radius of the *CCAOI*. Note in Fig. 12 that, when the radius of the *CCAOI* is equal to 20, the average transfers initiated by a the server increases until the radius of the *AOI* is 400, then it decreases. As a matter of fact, the *IA* of each peer is included in its Voronoi Area, when the number of peers is lower than 400 and the number of transfers increases with the number of peers. When the number of peer is larger than 400, the peers starts to exchange entities so that the number of transfers with the

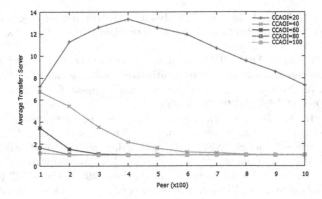

Fig. 12. Average number of entities for the server: variable CCAOI.

server decreases. This phenomenon occurs for smaller number of peers when the radius of the *CCAOI* is larger.

7 Conclusions

This paper presents an hybrid architecture for MMOGs based on a Voronoi Tessellation of the virtual world. Our approach allows a dynamical distribution of the load for the management of the entities among the server and the peers. We have introduced the concept of CCAOI to avoid peer overloading. Objects which are not close to any peer are managed by the server which delegates the ownership of an object to a peer P when the object becomes close to P, due the peers' movement. In the following we plan to evaluate our approach in more realistic scenarios and to extend it in several directions. For instance, we plan to consider both further realistic mobility models and also traces taken from real MMOG. Further, we are considering several distributed algorithms for the management of the consistency of the entities managed by the peers. These algorithms are required, for instance, when an object is concurrently accessed by a set of peers. We are also fully integrating our architecture with Godel, a gossip-based suite of protocols able to dynamically maintain in an efficient way a Delaunay triangulation (and the corresponding Voronoi Tessellation).

Acknowledgments. The authors thank Katia Monni for her support in developing the experiments.

References

1. Ohnishi, M., Nishide, R., Ueshima, S.: Incremental construction of delaunay overlaid network for virtual collaborative space. In: 3rd International Conference on Creating, Connecting and Collaborating through Computing, C5 '05, pp. 75–82 (2005)

2. Bharambe, A., Pang, J., Seshan, S.: Colyseus: a distributed architecture for online multiplayer games. In: 3rd Conference on Networked Systems Design & Implementation, vol. 3

3. Yu, A.P., Vuong, S.T.: MOPAR: a mobile peer-to-peer overlay architecture for interest management of massively multiplayer online games. In: International Workshop on Network and Operating Systems Support for Digital Audio and Video, NOSSDAV '05, pp. 99–104 (2005)

4. Knutsson, B., Lu, H., Xu, W., Hopkins, B.: Peer-to-peer support for massively multiplayer games. In: 23rd Annual Joint Conference of the IEEE Computer and Communications Societies, INFOCOM 2004, vol. 1, pp. 96–107. IEEE (2004)

5. Carlini, E., Ricci, L., Coppola, M.: Flexible load distribution for hybrid distributed virtual environments. Future Gener. Comput. Syst. **29**(6), 1561–1572 (2013)

6. Carlini, E., Coppola, M., Ricci, L.: Integration of P2P and clouds to support massively multiuser virtual environments. In: 9th Annual Workshop on Network and Systems Support for Games (NetGames), pp. 1–6. IEEE (2010)

7. Aurenhammer, F.: Voronoi diagrams - a survey of a fundamental geometric data structure. ACM Comput. Surv. **23**(3), 345–405 (1991)

8. Hu, S.Y., Chen, J.F., Chen, T.H.: VON: a scalable peer-to-peer network for virtual environments. Netwrk. Mag. Global Internetwkg. **20**(4), 22–31 (2006)

9. Hu, S., Chang, S., Jiang, J.: Voronoi state management for peer-to-peer massively multiplayer online games. In: 5th IEEE Consumer Communications and Networking Conference, CCNC 2008, pp. 1134–1138. IEEE (2008)

10. Jiang, J., Huang, Y., Hu, S.: Scalable AOI-cast for peer-to-peer networked virtual environments. In: ICDCSW the 28th International Conference on Distributed Computing Systems Workshops (2008)

11. Buyukkaya, E., Abdallah, M.: Efficient triangulation for P2P networked virtual environments. In: Proceedings of the 7th ACM SIGCOMM Workshop on Network and System Support for Games, NetGames '08, pp. 34–39. ACM (2008)

12. Cavagna, R., Abdallah, M., Buyukkaya, E., Bouville, C.: A framework for scalable virtual worlds using spatially organized P2P networks. In: ICPADS Workshop on Peer-to-Peer Network Virtual Environment, P2P-NVE. IEEE, December 2008

13. Cavagna, R., Abdallah, M., Buyukkaya, E., Bouville, C.: VoroGame: a hybrid P2P architecture for massively multiplayer games. In: 2009 6th Consumer Communications and Networking Conference. IEEE, January 2009

14. Varvello, M., Biersack, E., Diot, C.: Dynamic clustering in delaunay-based P2P networked virtual environments. In: 6th SIGCOMM Workshop on Network and System Support for Games, NetGames '07, pp. 105–110. ACM (2007)

15. Bonotti, A., Genovali, L., Ricci, L.: A publish subscribe support for networked multiplayer games. In: Third European Conference on Internet and Multimedia Systems and Applications, EurolMSA '07, pp. 236–241 (2007)

16. Ricci, L., Salvadori, A.: Nomad: virtual environments on P2P voronoi overlays. In: Meersman, R., Tari, Z. (eds.) OTM-WS 2007, Part II. LNCS, vol. 4806, pp. 911–920. Springer, Heidelberg (2007)

17. Genovali, L., Ricci, L.: AOI-cast strategies for P2P massively multiplayer online games. In: 6th Conference on Consumer Communications and Networking, CCNC'09, pp. 1317–1321. IEEE (2009)

18. Genovali, L., Ricci, L.: JaDE: a JXTA support for distributed virtual environments. In: 13th Symposium on Computers and Communications Program, ISCC, Marrakesh, Morocco. IEEE (2008)

19. Genovali, L., Ricci, L.: Voronoi models for distributed environments. In: CoNEXT Student Workshop, Madrid, Spain. ACM (2008)

20. Ricci, L., Genovali, L., Carlini, E., Coppola, M.: AOI-cast by compass routing in delaunay based DVE overlays. In: International Conference on High Performance Computing and Simulation, HPCS 2011, Istanbul, Turkey. IEEE, July 2011
21. Lee, D., Lam, S.: Efficient and accurate protocols for distributed delaunay triangulation under churn. In: ICNP (2008)
22. Ohnishi, M., Nishide, R., Ueshima, S.: Incremental construction of delaunay overlay network for virtual collaborative space. In: Third International Conference on Creating, Connecting and Collaborating through Computing (2005)
23. Ghaffari, M., Hariri, B., Shirmohammadi, S.: A Delaunay triangulation architecture supporting churn and user mobility in MMVEs. In: 18th International Workshop on Network and Operating Systems Support for Digital Audio and Video, NOSSDAV '09, pp. 61–66 (2009)
24. Albano, M., Quartulli, A., Ricci, L., Genovali, L.: AOI cast by tolerance based compass routing in distributed virtual environments. In: 8th Annual Workshop on Network and Systems Support for Games, NetGames '09, pp. 13:1–13:2. ACM (2009)
25. Baraglia, R., Dazzi, P., Guidi, B., Ricci, L.: GoDel: delaunay overlays in P2P networks via Gossip. In: International Conference on P2P Computing, P2P '12, pp. 1–12. IEEE (2012)
26. Kato, H., Eguchi, T., Ohnishi, M., Ueshima, S.: Autonomous generation of spherical p2p delaunay network for global internet applications. In: The Fourth International Conference on Creating, Connecting and Collaborating through Computing, C5'06, pp. 184–191. IEEE (2006)
27. Liebeherr, J., Nahas, M.: Application layer multicast with delaunay triangulations. IEEE J. Sel. Areas Commun. 40(8) (2002)
28. Montresor, A., Jelasity, M.: PeerSim: a scalable P2P simulator. In: 9th International Conference on Peer-to-Peer (P2P'09). IEEE (2009)
29. Bettstetter, C., Hartenstein, H., Pérez-Costa, X.: Stochastic properties of the random waypoint mobility model. Wireless Netw. **10**, 555–567 (2004)

Host Identity Detection in IPv6 Networks

Libor Polčák[✉], Martin Holkovič, and Petr Matoušek

Faculty of Information Technology, Brno University of Technology,
Božetěchova 2, 612 66 Brno, Czech Republic
{ipolcak,matousp}@fit.vutbr.cz, xholko00@stud.fit.vutbr.cz

Abstract. It is important to keep networks secure and reliable. In order to backtrack security incidents, provide accounting for offered services etc., it is necessary to know the identity of network users. With various methods for IPv6 address assignments, user identification in IPv6 networks is challenging. This paper proposes a new approach for user identity tracking in LANs. The approach is based on network control traffic that is already present in IPv6 networks. In contrast to current methods, the proposed approach does not bring any extensive workload to active network devices and works in networks with Multicast Listener Discovery snooping. In addition, the approach is able to detect that an address is no longer used. The proposed approach is passive to end devices. In order to make the approach reliable, we studied the behaviour of current operating systems during IPv6 address assignments. We implemented a tool called *ndtrack* based on the proposed approach and tested it in a real network.

Keywords: Computer network security · Host identity · IPv6 monitoring · SLAAC · Neighbor Discovery

1 Introduction

In order to maintain a reliable network, its administrators need to monitor the network and its weak points, detect misuse of the network, backtrack security incidents, provide accountings for the offered services etc. The knowledge of the identity of computers and their users in the managed network is essential to achieve these tasks. The imminent exhaustion of IPv4 address space and the transition to IPv6 [1] requires keeping track of IPv6 addresses used in the managed network.

The IPv6 architecture guarantees at least 2^{64} addresses allocated to each LAN [2]. There are several mechanisms that manage the allocation of addresses. For example, Stateless Address Autoconfiguration (SLAAC) [3] allows an end device to generate as many IPv6 addresses as it needs, e.g. for privacy concerns [4,5], as long as the addresses are not already used by another device in the network. Note that the addresses are not handled centrally but generated by end devices. Moreover, the network operator is not able to influence the address

© Springer-Verlag Berlin Heidelberg 2014
M.S. Obaidat and J. Filipe (Eds.): ICETE 2013, CCIS 456, pp. 74–89, 2014.
DOI: 10.1007/978-3-662-44788-8_5

generation process. In addition, there is not a node in the network that keeps track of IPv6 addresses being used by devices connected to the network. Even more, a host does not send any specific message when an address is no longer used by the host.

One possibility of user identity tracking is through authentication. For example, RADIUS authenticates a user and MAC address of his or her device connected to a network. In some networks, such as the campus network at our university, users have to register their MAC address before they are allowed to access the Internet and services offered in the network. However, unlike network layer addresses, MAC addresses are not propagated outside of LANs. Hence, the knowledge of bindings between network layer addresses and MAC addresses is crucial for network management, security, and accounting.

In this paper, we propose a new approach for the problem of the user identification in IPv6 networks accessed by users with devices that are not under direct control of the network operators, i.e. the problem of learning the MAC and IPv6 address pairing. In order to achieve this, we studied the implementation of IPv6 in current operating systems (OSes). As a result, the approach is suitable for campus-wide networks, networks of companies that allow their staff or customers to connect their own devices to the network ("bring your own device" policy), Wi-Fi and Ethernet hot spots, and hotel networks.

One of the contributions of this paper is the identification of the differences in the behaviour of current OSes and their violations of RFCs concerning IPv6 address assignments. The main contribution of this paper is the proposal of a new approach for user identification in IPv6 networks, which is based on monitoring control messages that are already present in the network.

The proposed approach does not influence or modify IPv6 in any way. Since the method is completely transparent for network hosts, it does not require any additional changes in the network hardware or software. Moreover, the privacy of the users in the network, with respect to the outside world, is not affected by the proposed mechanism. The approach was successfully tested in a real network. In contrast to previously published methods, the proposed approach does not need any significant additional load on network devices, it can detect the exact time of address assignment even if the address is not used for communication, and the approach detects that an IPv6 address is no longer used.

This paper is organized as follows. Section 2 overviews the address assignment mechanisms in IPv6. The results of the study of the behaviour of current OSes during IPv6 address assignments are presented in Sect. 3. Section 4 outlines the proposed approach for user identity tracking in LANs. Section 5 discusses the related work and discuss alternative approaches. Our experiments are summarised in Sect. 6. Section 7 concludes the paper.

2 Preliminaries

This section reviews the basics of *Duplicate address detection* (DAD), a part of *Neighbor Discovery* (ND), and overviews common methods for IPv6 address assignments.

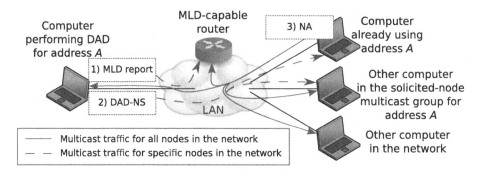

Fig. 1. Messages exchanged during DAD. As another computer is already using address *A*, the computer performing DAD cannot use the address.

2.1 Duplicate Address Detection

When a new IPv6 address is about to be used by a device, the device needs to test that the address is not already used in the network [3,6]. Until the new address is proven to be unique, it is called *tentative*. In order to prove that the tentative address is unique, the device has to perform the following steps (depicted in Fig. 1):

1. The device joins the solicited-node multicast group [2] whose address is derived from the tentative IPv6 address using *Multicast Listener Discovery* (MLD) protocol [7]. The request (MLD report) is sent to a multicast group of all MLD-capable routers – ff02::16.
2. The device issues a *Neighbor Solicitation* (NS) request to the solicited-node multicast group whose address is derived from the tentative address. In this paper, NS requests issued during DAD are denoted as *DAD-NS*.
3. If the tentative address is already used by another device, the other device should reply with a *Neighbor Advertisement* (NA) to the multicast group for all nodes in the network (ff02::1). Only if no NA is received before a timeout, the new address can be used.

To avoid race conditions in address assignments, RFC 4862 requires [3] that each host has to join the solicited-node multicast group before it sends the DAD-NS, i.e. step (1) has to be performed before step (2). Note that requests sent during step (1) and (2) are delivered only to the network hosts that are members of the respective multicast groups in network with enabled *MLD snooping* (i.e. multicast does not behave as broadcast).

As a result, there is no central point in the network that gathers all active addresses; the knowledge is spread over the network and is available through the solicited-node multicast groups.

2.2 Multicast Group Management

In general, in order to detect empty multicast groups, a dedicated router (or a group of routers) may be configured as an *MLD querier*. The MLD querier periodically queries multicast groups to verify that some hosts are still part of each multicast group. If there is at least one host in a multicast group, the MLD querier receives a reply that the multicast group is still active in the network.

MLD querying is also performed for solicited-node multicast groups. If no address corresponding to the queried solicited-node multicast address is used, there is no reply in the multicast group. However, if more than one IPv6 address in the network coincide into one solicited-node multicast group, only one of the hosts replies. Such coincidence are rare due to the addressing scheme used for solicited-node multicast groups, which was specifically designed to reduce such coincidences.

2.3 Methods for Address Assignment

SLAAC [3] is a basic method for address assignments in IPv6. In contrast to DHCP, dominant in IPv4, SLAAC is not based on leases. Instead, a device itself generates its addresses. First, the device learns the network (higher) part of IPv6 address from a *Router Advertisement* (RA), a message periodically send by gateways in the network. Then, the device generates the lower part of the IPv6 address called *interface identifier* (IID) [2]. The original method for selecting an IID uses modified EUI-64 IID [2]. Later, privacy extensions [5] introduced completely random IIDs which may change during time. Besides privacy extensions, Windows machines use random IIDs [8,9]. In all cases, the uniqueness of the selected IPv6 address has to be proven by DAD.

Although there is a variant of DHCP called stateful DHCPv6 [10], it does not provide the same information as DHCP since DHCPv6 assigns IPv6 address according to *DHCP Unique Identifier* (DUID). DUID is generated by each host, mostly during OS installation. As a consequence, DUID is changed when a host is rebooted to another OS. Therefore, the MAC and IP address pairings are not stored in DHCPv6 logs. On the other hand, the assigned address has to be confirmed by DAD.

Finally, it is possible to assign a static address. Whenever a new static IPv6 address is entered on a host, it has to be validated by DAD.

As mentioned above, DAD, or more generally ND, is a part of each mechanism for address assignments. Hence, we choose ND as a basis for the proposed network monitoring approach. However, as discussed in Sect. 3, ND is not implemented in the same way among current OSes. Based on this study, Sect. 4 proposes a new method for monitoring IPv6 addresses in a network without knowledge of OSes installed on the hosts in the network.

3 Study of Operating System Behaviour During ND

This section describes implementation of ND in current OSes. We studied [11] the exact sequences of messages that are issued during DAD after an address is assigned or automatically generated. The main goal was to validate that OSes follow the sequence ordered by RFC 4862 [3] (discussed in Sect. 2). However, the results are not positive and some OSes diverge.

Table 1. Operating systems tested for compliance with RFCs specifying ND.

OS family	Tested variants
Windows	XP SP3, Vista, Vista SP3, Server 2008 R2, 7, 7 SP1, and 8
Linux	various distributions including Red Hat, CentOS, Debian, and Ubuntu (kernels 2.4.27–3.2)
Mac OS X	10.6.2 (kernel 10.2)
Unix	FreeBSD 9.0, OpenBSD 5.0, and Solaris 5.11

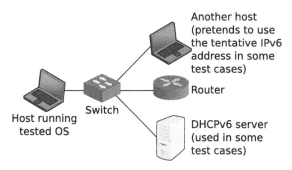

Fig. 2. The network topology used for OS behaviour study. DHCPv6 server and the another host were active only in specific test cases.

Firstly, we selected OSes (see Table 1) that we believe are the most common in current LANs. Then, we connected hosts running these OSes into our laboratory network (see Fig. 2) and captured all packets that were sent or received by each host in all test cases.

Several experiments (test cases) were performed during the study:

– In test cases focused on SLAAC, the router in the network (see Fig. 2) sent an RA. Consequently, the tested host generated link-local IPv6 address and one or more IPv6 address from the scope advertised by the router. We analyzed the messages issued by the tested host during DAD for the generated addresses.
– Next set of test cases focused on DHCPv6. DHCPv6 server in the network (see Fig. 2) was activated and the tested hosts were configured to use it. One of the goal of this test was to confirm that OSes perform DAD for IPv6 addresses obtained from a DHCPv6 server.
– Next set of tests aimed at DAD during static address assignments.
– In order to test the behaviour of hosts in the presence of different hosts having the same IPv6 address, a different host was connected to the network (see Fig. 2). A specialized program that is able to spoof NAs was running on the added host. Consequently, the computer was able to simulate a collision of all IPv6 addresses; including randomly generated RFC 4941 addresses. The goal was to validate that the examined host does not use any address that is claimed to be used in the network.

The evaluation of the packet traces [11] gathered from the test cases revealed following anomalies:

1. Windows Vista and later (for all IPv6 addresses) and FreeBSD (for static and EUI-64 IPv6 addresses) ignore DAD-NS if the other host has the same MAC address.
2. Windows Vista and later use a tentative link local address to join multicast groups before they start DAD for the address.
3. Solaris (for all addresses), FreeBSD (for static addresses), and Windows Server 2008 R2, Windows 7 and later (for link local addresses) diverge from the recommended sequence of actions during DAD because they send DAD-NS before they join the solicited-node multicast group derived from the tentative address.
4. Windows 8, Solaris, and Mac OS X send NAs during DAD that are not mandatory. These NAs are destined to the all-nodes-in-the-network multicast group (ff02::1).
5. OpenBSD does not join solicited-node multicast groups at all.
6. All selected OSes that register to multicast groups reply to MLD queries. However, we discovered that some OSes do not meet the maximal timeout specified in an RA. Although the RA announced maximal timeout of 0.1 s, some acknowledgements were received after 0.7–0.8 s.

The results of the study show that there are various differences in behaviour of current operating systems. The behaviour of FreeBSD is even not consistent and depends on the type of the IPv6 address that was generated.

4   Proposed Approach for Address Assignment Detection

The study of the behaviour of current operating systems presented in Sect. 3 allowed us to propose a new approach for address assignment detection in IPv6 networks [12]. The life-cycle of an IPv6 address A can be tracked by the extended Mealy FSM depicted in Fig. 3. Network control traffic is used as the input of the FSM, the output is the information that the address started or ceased to be used. The FSM is extended with a variable to store the MAC address of the interface that uses the tracked IPv6 address.

4.1   Inputs of the FSM

The FSM tracks ND messages to detect address assignments. MLD queries and responses are used to detect that the address is no longer used. Hence, we recommend to enable MLD querying on a router in the network.

In addition, if MLD snooping is active in the network (multicast traffic is not broadcasted), it is necessary to provide DAD-NSes and NA replies to the network host running the proposed FSM.

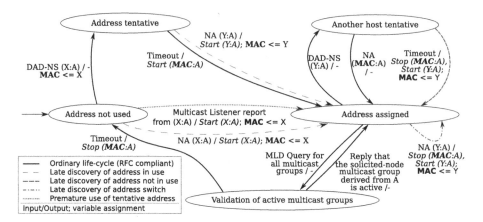

Fig. 3. The life-cycle of an IPv6 address A can be monitored by the Mealy FSM extended by the variable **MAC** to store the MAC address of the interface that currently uses A. Binding between MAC address X and A is denoted as (X:A).

- In case that OpenFlow switches [13] are available in the monitored network, we recommend simulating the FSM on the OpenFlow collector(s) and configuring OpenFlow switches to redirect (or copy) all DAD-NSes, NAs, and MLD queries to the collector(s);
- otherwise, the computer simulating the FSM should
  1. join the multicast group for *all nodes* (ff02::1) and *all MLDv2-capable routers* (ff02::16),
  2. detect all requests to join solicited-node multicast groups,
  3. join the detected groups.

Additionally, if a frame with source or destination address A is seen on the collector in OpenFlow-based networks, the FSM can treat them in the same way as if NA for given MAC/IPv6 address pair was received.

4.2   States and Shifting Logic of the FSM

The initial state of the FSM is the *Address not used*. When a host generates the address A, it issues DAD-NS, and the FSM shifts to *Address tentative*.

If everything worked according to RFCs, the only trigger for transition from *Address tentative* would be the timeout as the address would not be used in the network. However, Solaris, some versions of Windows, and FreeBSD do not join the solicited-node multicast groups before issuing the DAD-NS. As a consequence, in networks with MLD snooping, some address assignments may have been unnoticed earlier and the address can already be used. Therefore, it is possible to receive an NA from another host. In both cases the FSM detects the MAC address that is bound to the IPv6 address and shifts to *Address assigned*.

Similarly to the NA received after DAD-NS, the FSM may detect an NA for the address A in the initial state (e.g. non-mandatory NA during DAD).

Consequently, the FSM shifts directly to *Address assigned*. Additionally, the FSM shifts between these two states in case of Windows using a tentative link local address as the source address to join multicast groups.

In order to detect that the address was dropped by the host, *Validation of active multicast groups* is reached after an MLD query is received. In case that the solicited-node multicast group derived from address A is acknowledged, the address is most likely being used as the solicited-node multicast groups were designed so that two hosts are not likely to be in one solicited-node multicast group. If the MLD query expires, the address is definitely not used any more, and the FSM returns to the initial state.

While the FSM is in *Address assigned*, another host might try to use the address. When DAD-NS is received, the FSM shifts to *Another host tentative*. Ordinarily, the address is still in use and the NA follows. If the address was no longer used but it had not been detected (e.g. because the MLD query was not issued, yet), the NA would not be sent. In such case, the FSM also shifts back to *Address assigned*, however, the detected MAC address changes. In a rare occasion when an NA from another MAC address is seen in *Address assigned*, the FSM loops in this state and the MAC addresses are swapped. This loop is present in the FSM only for safety reason as the study of OS behaviour does not suggest that it is needed.

5 Alternative Approaches

This section discusses related work and alternative approaches for the detection of pairings between IPv6 addresses and MAC addresses. Later, these methods are compared to the detection approach proposed in Sect. 4 and advantages and disadvantages are identified.

5.1 Related Work

Several attempts have been made to study IPv6 IIDs. Groat et al. [4] proposed to use *ping* or *traceroute* to monitor a location of a node that uses a static interface identifier of any sort. Dunlop et al. [9] list an example of Windows using random, yet static networks IIDs. However, both papers aimed at global tracking of a movement of a specific user. In contrast, we want to monitor only the local network. In addition, both Groat et al. and Dunlop et al. need to know the address in advance. Our research is concerned with unknown IPv6 addresses. Another difference is that we want to learn all addresses that belong to every device connected to a network. Moreover, the proposed approach is passive to end devices.

Similarly to our goal, Grégr et al. [14] are also interested in learning the IPv6 addresses that were used by a host with a specific MAC address. They presented a campus network monitoring system which gathers data from the *neighbor cache* (NC) of the routers in the network using SNMP. However, two conflicting requirements needs to be balanced. In order to have sound information about the IPv6 addresses in the network, they need to poll routers sufficiently often. Since routers are critical devices and the polling results in additional workload, the polling cannot be too frequent. As a consequence, a new address selected by a device in the network is learned with a delay. During a security incident, an attacker can use an address for a limited time. Consequently, the monitoring system can miss that the IPv6 address was used in case the expiration timeout of NC records is shorter than the polling interval.

Groat et al. [15] studied the possibility of using DHCPv6 for monitoring the identity of users in the network. The proposed approach is more general as it is not restricted to DHCPv6.

A tool called *addrwatch* [16] can monitor ND messages in the network. However, we identified several weaknesses of the tool. Firstly, *addrwatch* just reports ND messages. They are not put in any context. Secondly, *addrwatch* completely ignores multicast messages, therefore, it cannot detect address assignments in a network with MLD snooping (multicast is not broadcasted). Finally, *addrwatch* does not detect that an address is no longer used.

Asati and Wing [17] deal with the same problem as we do. However, their solution involves changes in routers behaviour. The proposed approach does not need any change on any critical network device.

5.2 Discussion

Although we have not found a reference, we expect that some administrators use port mirroring and parse the mirrored traffic with a sniffer to learn the MAC and IP address bindings. The proposed approach does not depend on processing all network traffic and consequently it is more efficient. In addition, the bandwidth of the mirroring port could be insufficient for all traffic traversing the mirroring switch or even one full-duplex port. Moreover, in case of mirroring the port connected to the router in the network, the learned MAC and IP address pairings are more or less the same to these stored in the NC of the router.

The amount of traffic for processing can be reduced in networks with Open-Flow switches [13]. In addition to ordinary traffic processing, OpenFlow switches send a copy of the first packet of each new flow to a central point in the network – a controller. The controller is a programmable device and therefore can be instructed to collect information about detected usage of IP addresses by devices connected to the network. However, this simple approach only reveals the address if it is actively used. To track the correct time of address assignments and address drops, we recommend following the instructions in Sect. 4.

Table 2 summarizes the identified methods for detection of IPv6 assignments. Two methods gather information from NC. The method proposed by Asati and Wing [17] failed in IETF standardization process and as it requires changes in the router behaviour, it cannot be used in practice. Neighbor cache polling (NCP) detects both address assignments and address drops with a delay. Detection delay depends on the frequency of polling while the detection of inactivity depends on the NC record expiration time. As NC is not available on switches, both methods cannot detect addresses used for internal communication.

Table 2. Methods for monitoring of usage of IP addresses.

Source of informations	Methods
Neighbor cache	Neighbor cache polling (NCP) [14], Asati and Wing [17]
Network control traffic	Proposed approach, *addrwatch* [16]
Network traffic	Parsing of mirrored traffic, Simple OpenFlow-based monitoring

The proposed approach is based on very similar principles to addrwatch. The main advantage of the proposed approach is that the FSM correlates the detected messages. In addition, the proposed approach joins the multicast groups (in networks without OpenFlow switches) and therefore works in networks with MLD snooping, except OpenBSD and static addresses in FreeBSD (see Sect. 6 for more details). As the detection of address assignments in networks with MLD snooping depends on joining solicited-node multicast groups, the approach may fail in larger networks where delays prevent the monitoring device from joining the solicited-node multicast group in time. Nevertheless, the proposed approach never yields worse information than *addrwatch*. In combination with OpenFlow switches, the proposed approach detects all address assignments, even in networks with MLD snooping (see Sect. 6).

As the parsing of mirrored traffic results more or less in similar information to the information gathered by NCP, it is not practical. Simple monitoring using OpenFlow (i.e. without information from control traffic) has several advantages in comparison to NCP: (1) the additional traffic load on the data plane is negligible as OpenFlow switches are optimised for copying traffic and passing it to the controller, (2) the controller detects active addresses immediately, and (3) it is possible to detect that an IP address is no longer used for active communication by setting OpenFlow timeouts for active flows. Nevertheless, OpenFlow monitoring combined with the proposed approach detects the exact time of address assignments and it can detect if an address was already dropped or if it is not used for active communication and thus, the address can be used for communication in the future.

6 Experiments

This section describes the experiments with *ndtrack* [18], a tool that follows the proposed approach for IPv6 address assignments that is sketched in Sect. 4 (specifically the approach tracking multicast groups).

The first experiment aimed at real network monitoring. As most of the devices were not under our control, we could not confirm that *ndtrack* detected all devices. However, we checked that all our devices were detected. The other three experiments were performed in a laboratory network; they focused on the quality of the monitoring approach.

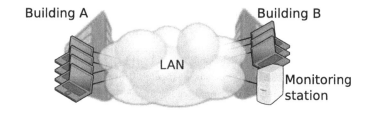

Fig. 4. The network topology of the real network monitoring. Some of the computers were not under our control.

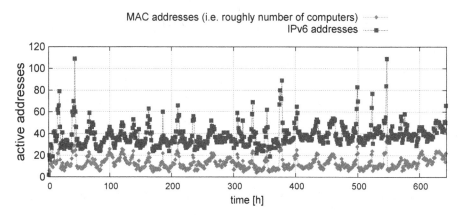

Fig. 5. Statistics of the real network monitoring. IPv6 addresses were successfully detected to be used (the number of known addresses rises during working hours) and dropped (the number of IPv6 addresses lowers at night).

6.1   Real Network Deployment

The first experiment aimed at long-term monitoring (almost a month) of SLAAC in a network with MLD querying enabled. The network spans two buildings and is available for all employees of the faculty (see Fig. 4).

We successfully validated that *ndtrack* detected IPv6 addresses of devices under our control among other devices of our colleagues that were being used in the network. Then we validated that the addresses are correctly identified as no longer assigned after the hosts disconnect or stop using the addresses (see Fig. 5 for the statistics).

In order to make the experiment more convincing, we connected a device to the network in a different building than the one in which the monitoring station was located. All addresses assigned to the device were correctly identified and later dropped when we disconnected the device.

6.2   Network with MLD Snooping

We validated the behaviour of *ndtrack* in the presence of MLD snooping in our laboratory. A monitoring station running *ndtrack* and a testing computer were

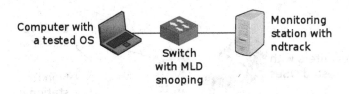

Fig. 6. The network topology for the experiments in a network with active MLD snooping.

Table 3. Effectivity of the proposed approach (✓ = Detected) in networks with active MLD snooping — without (⊖) and with (⊕) joining the solicited-node multicast group. In addition, the table shows expected effectiveness in OpenFlow-based networks (⊙).

OS	Static addresses			SLAAC addresses		
	⊖	⊕	⊙	⊖	⊕	⊙
Windows 7 and earlier	-	✓	✓	-	✓	✓
Windows 8	✓	✓	✓	✓	✓	✓
Linux	-	✓	✓	-	✓	✓
Mac OS X	✓	✓	✓	✓	✓	✓
FreeBSD	-	-	✓	-	✓	✓
OpenBSD	-	-	✓	-	-	✓
Solaris	✓	✓	✓	✓	✓	✓

connected to a switch with MLD snooping enabled as depicted in Fig. 6. In the first set of experiments, *ndtrack* did not follow the advice given in Sect. 4 and did not join the appropriate multicast groups. In the second set of experiments *ndtrack* joined the multicast groups as recommended in Sect. 4. Several OSes were tested during each set of experiments.

The results of the experiment are summarised in Table 3. When *ndtrack* did not join the multicast groups, DAD-NS were not propagated by the switch in the network. Consequently, *ndtrack* was not able to learn the identity of computers that follows the recommended sequence of messages during DAD. Windows 8, Mac OS X, and Solaris send additional NAs (as discussed in Sect. 3) which allowed *ndtrack* to learn their identity without joining the multicast groups. When *ndtrack* was a member of the specified multicast groups during DAD performed by the tested computer, *ndtrack* successfully detected all OSes except OpenBSD and static addresses in FreeBSD.

OpenBSD does not join the solicited-node multicast groups derived from the tentative address. Consequently, *ndtrack* did not know that it should join the solicited-node multicast group. As a result, the switch with activated MLD snooping did not propagate the DAD-NS to the monitoring station.

As already stated in Sect. 3, FreeBSD sends DAD-NS for a static address before it joins the solicited-node multicast groups derived from the tentative address. Therefore, *ndtrack* joined the solicited-node multicast groups derived

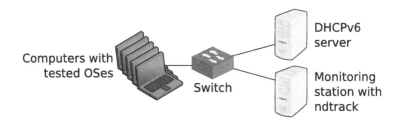

Fig. 7. The network topology for the experiments in a network with stateful DHCPv6.

from the tentative address after the DAD-NS was sent and as a consequence did not learn about the address assignment. Windows and Solaris that also join the solicited-node multicast group late (see Sect. 3) send additional NAs during DAD and therefore, were detected by *ndtrack*.

The OpenFlow-based proposed approach would have delivered all NAs to the OpenFlow controller and consequently to the monitoring center and therefore, all address assignments can be detected (see Table 3).

6.3   Network with Stateful DHCPv6

The next experiment tested stateful DHCPv6. We connected computers running Windows 7, 8, 2008 R2, Ubuntu 12.10, and Solaris (one computer for each OS) to a laboratory network depicted in Fig. 7. We verified that *ndtrack* detected all address assignments. Hence, DHCPv6 leases are detected by the proposed approach.

6.4   Comparison to Other Methods

In the last experiment, we compared *ndtrack* with NCP, *addrwatch*, and simple OpenFlow monitoring (all described in Sect. 5) in the network with topology depicted in Fig. 8. Testing was performed with MLD snooping both enabled and disabled. Note, that NCP and Simple OpenFlow yields the same result with or without MLD snooping and consequently, both gathered the same information in each run.

Each run of the experiment followed this scenario:

1. Two Linux hosts were connected to the network.
2. Host A opened a connection to host B and the hosts transferred a file in this connection.
3. Host A initiated an one-way UDP connection outside the network.
4. Host A opened a TCP session to the remote host.
5. Hosts A and B were disconnected.

During the experiment, we monitored NC of the router, and the outputs of the monitoring tools. The results are summarized in Table 4.

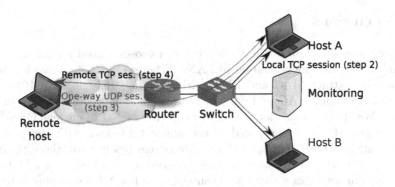

Fig. 8. Network topology used to compare our approach with older methods.

Table 4. Comparison of our approach with older methods ($\checkmark$ = detected).

MLD snooping	NCP	Simple OF	addrwatch		_ndtrack_	
	Does not matter	Inactive	Active	Inactive	Active
A, B connected	-	-	$\checkmark$	-	$\checkmark$	$\checkmark$
Local TCP	-	$\checkmark$	$\checkmark$	-	$\checkmark$	$\checkmark$
One-way UDP	-	$\checkmark$	$\checkmark$	-	$\checkmark$	$\checkmark$
Remote TCP	$\checkmark$	$\checkmark$	$\checkmark$	-	$\checkmark$	$\checkmark$
A, B disconn.	-	-	-	-	$\checkmark$	$\checkmark$

A record for the monitored hosts appeared in the NC of the router only after a packet destined to the host arrived from the Internet. Data transfers inside the LAN and the outgoing UDP session were undetected. In addition, the record stayed in the NC (_stale_ state) after the host was disconnected. Port mirroring and analysis of the traffic traversing the router would detect the outgoing UDP stream. However, local communication would be unnoticed.

While MLD snooping was disabled, _addrwatch_ detected the DAD-NSes issued by the hosts when they connected to the network. Additionally, _addrwatch_ reported NS messages, issued by the hosts or the router, during the data transfers. However, active MLD snooping did not leak any ND message to the monitoring computer and consequently _addrwatch_ did not report any activity in the network. Moreover, _addrwatch_ did not report that the hosts disconnected from the network even without MLD snooping as no ND message was sent to the network.

Both hosts were successfully identified by _ndtrack_ although the tool was behind MLD snooping. In addition, _ndtrack_ was able to detect that the addresses were no longer assigned.

7 Conclusions

The continuing adoption of the IPv6 protocol exposes a need for a redesign of mechanisms for user identification in LANs. Whereas in IPv4, network administrators can extract MAC and IPv4 pairings from DHCP logs, in IPv6, the pairing of IPv6 and MAC addresses is not available on a single device in the network. We studied behaviour of implementation of ND in current OSes [11]. Based on this study, we proposed a mechanism that deals with the problem of the identification of MAC and IPv6 address pairings in networks with MLD snooping both active and inactive. The proposed approach detects all address assignments in networks without MLD snooping. When MLD snooping is active, the proposed approach deals with all addresses in OpenFlow-based networks; in other networks, all addresses are detected except static addresses in FreeBSD and all addresses in OpenBSD.

The proposed approach differs from current methods in several aspects. Firstly, it is completely passive for end devices in the network. In addition, the approach does not need any modification of software or hardware used in the network. Moreover, the proposed approach detects that a new address was generated immediately without polling of active devices in the network. Furthermore, the described approach detects that an address is no longer used. Even more, the approach works for all common methods for IPv6 address distribution, namely SLAAC, stateful DHCPv6, and static assignments.

Acknowledgments. This work is a part of the project VG20102015022 supported by Ministry of the Interior of the Czech Republic. This work was also supported by the research plan MSM0021630528 and BUT project FIT-S-11-1. We would like to thank Marcela Šimková and Jim Wampler for their help during the preparation of this paper.

References

1. Dhamdhere, A., Luckie, M., Huffaker, B., Claffy, K., Elmokashfi, A., Aben, E.: Measuring the deployment of IPv6: topology, routing and performance. In: Proceedings of IMC '12, pp. 537–550. ACM, New York (2012)
2. Hinden, R., Deering, S.: IP Version 6 Addressing Architecture. RFC 4291, February 2006
3. Thomson, S., Narten, T., Jinmei, T.: IPv6 Stateless Address Autoconfiguration. RFC 4862, September 2007
4. Groat, S., Dunlop, M., Marchany, R., Tront, J.: The privacy implications of stateless IPv6 addressing. In: Proceedings of CSIIRW '10, pp. 52:1–52:4. ACM, New York (2010)
5. Narten, T., Draves, R., Krishnan, S.: Privacy Extensions for Stateless Address Autoconfiguration in IPv6. RFC 4941, September 2007
6. Narten, T., Nordmark, E., Simpson, W., Soliman, H.: Neighbor Discovery for IP version 6 (IPv6). RFC 4861, September 2007
7. Vida, R., Costa, L.: Multicast Listener Discovery Version 2 (MLDv2) for IPv6. RFC 3810, June 2004

8. Davies, J.: The Cable Guy: IPv6 Autoconfiguration in Windows Vista. Tech-Net Magazine, August 2007. http://technet.microsoft.com/en-us/magazine/2007.08.cableguy.aspx

9. Dunlop, M., Groat, S., Marchany, R., Tront, J.: The good, the bad, the IPv6. In: CNSR 2011, Ottawa, Canada, May 2011, pp. 77–84 (2011)

10. Droms, R., Bound, J., Volz, B., Lemon, T., Perkins, C., Carney, M.: Dynamic Host Configuration Protocol for IPv6 (DHCPv6). RFC 3315, July 2003

11. Polčák, L., Holkovič, M.: Behaviour of various operating systems during SLAAC, DAD, and ND (2013). http://6lab.cz/?p=1691

12. Polčák, L., Holkovič, M., Matoušek, P.: A new approach for detection of host identity in IPv6 networks. In: Proceedings of the DCNET '13, pp. 57–63. SciTePress - Science and Technology Publications (2013)

13. McKeown, N., Anderson, T., Balakrishnan, H., Parulkar, G., Peterson, L., Rexford, J., Shenker, S., Turner, J.: OpenFlow: enabling innovation in campus networks. SIGCOMM Comput. Commun. Rev. **38**, 69–74 (2008)

14. Grégr, M., Matoušek, P., Podermański, T., Švéda, M.: Practical IPv6 monitoring - challenges and techniques. In: Proceedings of IM 2011, Dublin, Ireland, pp. 660–663. IEEE CS (2011)

15. Groat, S., Dunlop, M., Marchany, R., Tront, J.: What DHCPv6 says about you. In: WorldCIS 2011, London, UK, pp. 146–151 (2011)

16. Kriukas, J.: addrwatch: A tool similar to arpwatch for IPv4/IPv6 and ethernet address pairing monitoring (2012). https://github.com/fln/addrwatch

17. Asati, R., Wing, D.: Tracking of Static/Autoconfigured IPv6 addresses. Internet Draft, version 00 (Work in progress), December 2012

18. Holkovič, M., Polčák, L.: ndtrack (2013). http://www.fit.vutbr.cz/~ipolcak/prods.php?id=308

e-Business

The Use of Twitter by Local Government in Northern Ireland

Tiago Picão[1], Fiona McMahon[2], Valerie Purchase[2],
and Maurice Mulvenna[3(✉)]

[1] Universidade de Aveiro, Aveiro, Portugal
[2] School of Communication, University of Ulster, Belfast, UK
[3] TRAIL Living Lab, School of Computing and Mathematics,
University of Ulster, Belfast, UK
md.mulvenna@ulster.ac.uk

Abstract. This paper presents the results of a survey of Twitter usage in Northern Ireland's twenty-six councils. The data was gathered in Summer 2012. The research questions were developed from a review of the literature on use of social media by government and focused on the role of social media as a communication channel to local government, examining the dialogue between government and citizen and the sentiment of such dialogue. The results show significant heterogeneity in Twitter use amongst the councils; with many not engaging at all, while a small number were highly engaged with their citizens. Regardless of the perspectives of the councils, there was evidence that there was a demand from the citizens for conversations that was not being met by the councils. The paper recommends that councils need to define a social media strategy in order to maximise the use of social media, but reflects that the councils should find it easy to engage with citizens by simply asking them via Twitter. The paper also describes the recent explosion in use of social media by citizens in Northern Ireland to support fractious, polemical argument on identity politics.

Keywords: Social media · Local government · Northern Ireland · Twitter usage

1 Introduction

The social web provides governments with the opportunity to achieve greater citizen engagement and deliberative exchange [22]. Microblogging sites such as Twitter, which allow for the instant sharing of updates, opinions and information, can help governments transform how they relate to citizens [1]. However social media adoption alone does not automatically lead to improved government-citizen relationships [11]. Despite increasing pressure on governments for greater transparency and account-ability, there is limited evidence to suggest that they are capitalising on the interactive properties of social network sites such as Twitter when communicating with citizens [4, 11]. Consequently, recent studies have highlighted the need for research which examines government use of social media and the extent to which it is supporting a collaborative, decentralised approach to governance [10].

© Springer-Verlag Berlin Heidelberg 2014
M.S. Obaidat and J. Filipe (Eds.): ICETE 2013, CCIS 456, pp. 93–106, 2014.
DOI: 10.1007/978-3-662-44788-8_6

2   Literature Review

The transformative potential of social media to help public, private and third sector organisations enhance communication and ultimately democratise relationships with their publics is well documented [5, 16, 22]. Supported by Web 2.0 technologies, which inherently 'facilitate creativity, information sharing, and collaboration amongst users' [20], social media can be defined as a group of Internet applications enabling the creation, sharing and exchange of comments and content in virtual communities or networks [2, 14]. The most popular social media by number of users globally, include the social network sites Facebook, Twitter and Pinterest [24].

Social media's 'interactive and communal' capabilities mean that individuals no longer simply consume content but also produce and share content of their own [14]. From an organisational perspective, social media therefore provides the opportunity to evolve from a 'one to many' broadcast communicative approach to a 'many to many' model of communication, in which collaborative and participatory interactions with stakeholders are proactively encouraged [6, 8, 12]. Social media applications therefore enable organisations to shift their communication style from a 'one-way flow of information' to 'dialogic engagement' whereby views and opinions are openly exchanged and negotiated to achieve mutually beneficial outcomes [19].

'Dialogue' and 'engagement' are core tenets of the UK Government's overall communication policy. The policy aims to encourage more citizen engagement in the democratic process by redefining how Government and constituents interact [23]. Bruning et al. [6] suggest that cities and citizens engaging in dialogic communication have an increased propensity for mutual understanding of each other and the issues at hand. Hand and Ching [11, p. 364] describe social networks as providing an ideal forum for citizen engagement at a local level by supporting interaction between residents and government as well as between resident and resident. Such resident-to-resident inter-actions can lead to personal recommendations or electronic word-of-mouth [13]. They caution however that a council's presence on social networks does not automatically result in increased citizen engagement. Their findings suggest that in order for mean-ingful interaction to occur, careful consideration must be given to the tone and content of posts. Cities that specifically elicited comments by asking questions and posting posi-tive, relevant content in a conversational style tended to have a higher number of comments. Citizens also responded well to timely posts and comments, suggesting the need for city councils to actively monitor and manage their social media presence.

Bonsón et al. [4, p. 123] state that social media are ideally placed to 'enhance interactivity, transparency and openness of public sector entities and to promote new forms of accountability.' They suggest that through social media use the public sector can not only increase access to agendas, policies and news, but also improve both policy making and public services by encouraging the exchange of views and infor-mation. Importantly, the use of social media for interaction and collaboration is more likely to lead to increased trust and empowerment amongst citizens, and social capital within communities [3].

UK Government departments recognise the importance of technology to empower citizens to become more actively involved in local governance issues [26]. Yet there is limited evidence to suggest that technology use by local government extends beyond the automation of administrative processes to facilitate public access to information and services [10]. The extent to which local councils are adopting social media and capitalising on its interactive capabilities remains unclear [3, 10, 11, 25]. The purpose of this study is to investigate the uptake and use of the social network and micro-blogging site Twitter by local councils in Northern Ireland.

Twitter is the one of the fastest growing social network site globally, and is second most popular [24]. It has multiple functionalities providing different levels of interactivity [4, 7]. It allows for instant messages ('tweets') of a maximum of 140 characters, which followers can then read, respond to or share via 'retweets'. Tweets generated can either retweet content from others or can contain and link to original content. The use of hashtags # and mentions @ within tweets makes them more likely to be found by people for whom the content is relevant and interesting. Twitter can also be used to respond to comments and questions publicly through mentions, or engage in private, one to one communication with followers via direct messaging.

This study is designed to ascertain if and how councils in Northern Ireland are using Twitter. It investigates whether councils use Twitter primarily as an additional broadcast channel, or to support a decentralised approach to government by encouraging dialogic, many to many communication with citizens. Finally it will examine whether individuals are exchanging comments and content relevant to local councils outside of official Twitter channels.

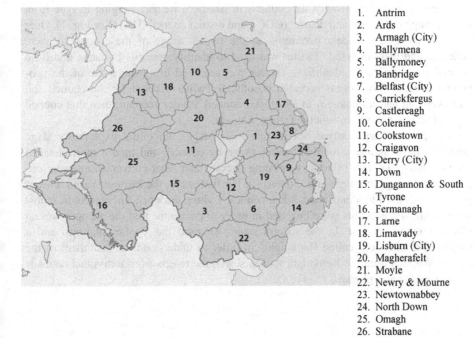

1. Antrim
2. Ards
3. Armagh (City)
4. Ballymena
5. Ballymoney
6. Banbridge
7. Belfast (City)
8. Carrickfergus
9. Castlereagh
10. Coleraine
11. Cookstown
12. Craigavon
13. Derry (City)
14. Down
15. Dungannon & South Tyrone
16. Fermanagh
17. Larne
18. Limavady
19. Lisburn (City)
20. Magherafelt
21. Moyle
22. Newry & Mourne
23. Newtownabbey
24. North Down
25. Omagh
26. Strabane

Fig. 1. Northern Ireland Councils (2012), courtesy Maximilian Dörrbecker.

3   Research Focus and Methodology

Previous studies have tended to discuss use of social media in the public sector in broad terms with little empirical data [9]. As mentioned already, the purpose of this study is to empirically investigate the uptake and use of Twitter by local councils in Northern Ireland. Twitter was identified as the main focus for this study since this social media and micro-blogging platform has been identified as the most commonly used by local governments across Europe [4]. The research focuses on fundamental questions regarding Twitter usage by the councils.

These research questions include:

– Are councils using Twitter? And if so, how?
– Do councils use Twitter primarily as an additional broadcast channel, or to support a decentralised approach to government by encouraging dialogue?
– Do individual citizens exchange comments and content relevant to local councils outside of official Twitter channels?
– What topics are discussed by councils and citizens?
– What kind of sentiment is evident in the dialogue between councils and citizens?

Supported by the conclusions from the literature review, we advanced our first hypothesis: "Councils use Twitter as a broadcast channel of information and events". For our second hypothesis, we assumed that information and events are useful and/or popular subjects, as well as generally neutral and thus that "Citizens follow and comment their Council's tweets with a positive or neutral sentiment".

There are currently twenty-six councils in Northern Ireland, ranging in type from city, borough (BC), city and district (CDC), and district council (DC) (See Fig. 1). Over the Summer of 2012, data pertaining to the twitter usage of these councils were collected and then analysed. Twitter was used to identify councils by name and if no council could be easily identified, Twitter was searched using the name of the geographic area. If this process revealed no official Twitter account for the council and their web site had no linkages to an official council Twitter account, then that council was classed as having no official Twitter account.

The research was carried out in two main stages; an initial exploratory stage gathering basic statistics for the Twitter usage by council, and then a more detailed examination of content of what was being tweeted and what conversations were ongoing between government and citizens. In the first stage, the browser-based Twitter platform was used to identify candidate council Twitter accounts. The tweets from this set of candidate accounts were browsed in order to determine that the account was an official council account. In the second stage, we used the Twitter platform and a sentiment-mining tool called Repknight[1] in order to understand the sentiment of the tweets. We also used the Repknight tool to search the tweets from individual councils for key words and phrases.

---

[1] www.repknight.com

4 Results

The initial approach showed that, among the 26 councils on Northern Ireland, a high number of them (18) have registered a Twitter account, despite the fact that the majority do not advertise it on their webpage (Table 1). However, looking at both the recent and long-term activity of the accounts revealed a large discrepancy on Twitter usage. Five of the existing accounts may be classified as inactive (Antrim BC, Limavady BC, Magherafelt DC, Moyle DC and Strabane DC), since there hasn't been a tweet for more than one year and, while active, they registered a very low number of tweets. Curiously, some of these accounts have a higher number of followers than accounts that are more active. This might indicate that, despite an absence of commitment from these councils, there is demand for such a channel of communication.

Nevertheless, compared to the population of Northern Ireland and their respective councils, the number of followers is very low, less than 1 % in most cases.

The only exceptions are Belfast CC (4.7 %) and Cookstown DC (1.2 %). However, given that Belfast is the capital city of NI, we should not rule out the possibility of outsiders following it. Other cases worth mentioning are the Armagh CDC and Newtownabbey BC, which are followed by more than 0.8 % of the council's population.

The remaining accounts show some activity judging by the month of the last tweet, but with different intensities. Belfast City Council is the champion here with 6,589 tweets and the only one with a history of more than 1,000 tweets. Newtownabbey Borough Council comes close with 726 tweets, but the rest do not even reach 500. Belfast City Council also manages to have both more followers and tweets than the Northern Ireland Assembly's account.

All Twitter accounts are mostly used to broadcast news and publicize events, but some accounts are also used for other purposes. Ards BC and Armagh CDC use twitter for tourism, with information about places to visit and a quiz for visitors. Ballymoney BC, Banbridge CC and Down DC broadcast safety advice. Banbridge CC, Belfast CC and Newtownabbey BC use their accounts for matters concerning governance, like information on public consultation, strategies or plans and calls for grants.

The Northern Ireland Assembly tweets, included here for comparative purposes, announce committee meetings, resolutions and statements. Table 2 shows the relative number of tweets, re-tweets and conversations over a two-month period in the Summer of 2012.

The retweet rate or amplification rate [16] which is the rate at which citizens who follow council's Twitter accounts pass their content on to others, varies from around 6 % for the Northern Ireland Assembly to 10 % for Belfast City Council. The other councils' Twitter volume is too low for the amplification rate to be meaningful statistically.

Another interesting observation is that the majority (10) of the active accounts are following other Twitter users, which could be suggestive of an effort to use Twitter as social network rather than only as a broadcast system. The analysis of 2012's June and July tweets reveals a mixed bag; while it cannot be said that those which follow other users are strongly engaging with them, the bulk of them do re-tweet.

Table 1. General data about Council Twitter Accounts – 08-2012.

Council	No of followers	Percentage of Council/ Assembly Population (2010 Est.)	Total number of Tweets	Month of last tweet	Twitter link on webpage
Northern Ireland Assembly	8,107	0.4505	3,255	08-2012	Y
Antrim Borough Council	25	0,0462	0	N/A	N
Ards Borough Council	199	0,2545	164	08-2012	N
Armagh City and District Council	493	0,8300	234	08-2012	N
Ballymena Borough Council	N/A	N/A	N/A	N/A	N/A
Ballymoney Borough Council	48	0,1569	190	07-2012	N
Banbridge District Council	121	0,2521	140	08-2012	N
Belfast City Council	12,579	4,6814	6,589	08-2012	Y
Carrickfergus Borough Council	91	0,2264	85	08-2012	Y
Castlereagh Borough Council	N/A	N/A	N/A	N/A	N/A
Coleraine Borough Council	73	0,1285	101	08-2012	Y
Cookstown District Council	468	1,2752	386	08-2012	Y
Craigavon Borough Council	238	0,2543	348	08-2012	N
Derry City Council	844	0,7687	141	07-2012	N
Down District Council	98	0,1384	144	07-2012	N
Dungannon & South Tyrone Borough Council	N/A	N/A	N/A	N/A	N/A
Fermanagh District Council	N/A	N/A	N/A	N/A	N/A
Larne Borough Council	N/A	N/A	N/A	N/A	N/A
Limavady Borough Council	254	0,7560	11	11-2010	N
Lisburn City Council	N/A	N/A	N/A	N/A	N/A
Magherafelt District Council	65	0,1454	1	11-2010	N
Moyle District Council	4	0,0235	2	08-2010	N
Newry and Mourne District Council	133	0,1331	73	08-2012	N
Newtownabbey Borough Council	741	0,8864	726	08-2012	Y
North Down Borough Council	N/A	N/A	N/A	N/A	N/A
Omagh District Council	N/A	N/A	N/A	N/A	N/A
Strabane District Council	167	0,4165	6	01-2010	N

Table 2. Data about networking on Council Twitter Accounts – June and July 2012.

Council	Following	No of Tweets	No of re-tweets	No of conversations
Northern Ireland Assembly	802	101	6	4
Antrim Borough Council	0	0	0	0
Ards Borough Council	254	75	16	2
Armagh City and District Council	531	32	5	2
Ballymena Borough Council	N/A	N/A	N/A	N/A
Ballymoney Borough Council	54	63	0	0
Banbridge District Council	0	50	0	0
Belfast City Council	95	400	41	53
Carrickfergus Borough Council	10	36	0	0
Castlereagh Borough Council	N/A	N/A	N/A	N/A
Coleraine Borough Council	0	52	0	0
Cookstown District Council	370	37	12	2
Craigavon Borough Council	0	57	0	0
Derry City Council	5	24	1	2
Down District Council	18	10	0	0
Dungannon and South Tyrone Borough Council	N/A	N/A	N/A	N/A
Fermanagh District Council	N/A	N/A	N/A	N/A
Larne Borough Council	N/A	N/A	N/A	N/A
Limavady Borough Council	14	0	0	0
Lisburn City Council	N/A	N/A	N/A	N/A
Magherafelt District Council	1	0	0	0
Moyle District Council	0	0	0	0
Newry and Mourne District Council	35	51	0	3
Newtownabbey Borough Council	14	90	6	8
North Down Borough Council	N/A	N/A	N/A	N/A
Omagh District Council	N/A	N/A	N/A	N/A
Strabane District Council	16	0	0	0

The exceptions are the Councils of Ballymoney, Carrickfergus, Down and Newry and Mourne. On the other hand, Belfast City Council stands out again, as the one with a stronger engagement with the community, not only by means of re-tweeting, but also through conversation: amid 400 tweets there were 53 conversations.

Newtownabbey Borough Council, while not re-tweeting much, follows Belfast once more, with 8 conversations in the midst of 90 tweets.

The Northern Ireland Assembly only registered 4 conversations amidst 101 tweets. If we examine who initiated these conversations (Table 3), it is easy to conclude that

Table 3. Initiative of conversation – June and July 2012.

Council	Conversations initiated by Council	Conversations initiated by citizens
Northern Ireland Assembly	0	4
Antrim Borough Council	0	0
Ards Borough Council	1	1
Armagh City and District Council	1	1
Ballymena Borough Council	N/A	N/A
Ballymoney Borough Council	0	0
Banbridge District Council	0	0
Belfast City Council	3	50
Carrickfergus Borough Council	0	0
Castlereagh Borough Council	N/A	N/A
Coleraine Borough Council	0	0
Cookstown District Council	1	1
Craigavon Borough Council	0	0
Derry City Council	0	2
Down District Council	0	0
Dungannon and South Tyrone Borough Council	N/A	N/A
Fermanagh District Council	N/A	N/A
Larne Borough Council	N/A	N/A
Limavady Borough Council	0	0
Lisburn City Council	N/A	N/A
Magherafelt District Council	0	0
Moyle District Council	0	0
Newry and Mourne District Council	0	3
Newtownabbey Borough Council	0	8
North Down Borough Council	N/A	N/A
Omagh District Council	N/A	N/A
Strabane District Council	0	0

citizens start the overwhelming majority. Ards, Armagh and Cookstown Councils do show a balance between initiators, but the total number is too low to consider them a real exception.

The initial approach showed quite clearly that most of the existing accounts have very low levels of activity and engagement with followers and/or other twitter users. The major exception is Belfast City Council, while Newtownabbey Borough Council also produces relevant activity, especially if compared with the rest of the councils. The Northern Ireland Assembly's account follows both as the third most active account, which justified, alongside its different power level, its inclusion, together with Belfast and Newtownabbey, in a second, more in-depth, approach.

This second approach introduced new levels of analysis, namely the content of other accounts' tweets which mention the councils' accounts, and the sentiment associated with them. However, the period of time analysed was different from the first approach, encompassing only the month of August 2012. The reason for this was the impact of a single event that occurred in Belfast in the previous month, and originated a large amount of commotion on social networks, thus skewing the results that could have been obtained in a more "neutral" period. Even then, the event, which consisted on the put down of a dog (named Lennox), whose type is forbidden by law, still sent ripples throughout the month, as can be seen in Table 4. Of all the 5 most used keywords, only the word "want" was used on a context not necessarily related to the dog issue.

It is interesting to note the polarisation of sentiment relating to the dog; in particular the significant negative sentiment detected in relation to 'Lennox', effectively flooding the @BelfastCC Twitter account with significantly increased negative sentiment. Despite all the commotion, there were no answers given on the Council twitter account, which triggered some users to "invade" conversations that the Council maintained with other users, on other topics. This "invasion" was also ignored by the Council.

If we filter the content of tweets of other accounts which mention the Belfast City Council account, in such a way that we eliminate tweets related to the dog issue, the remaining most used keywords are all connected to events and/or activities promoted by Belfast City Council (Table 5).

Table 4. Most used keywords for @BelfastCC and their sentiment in August 2012.

Keywords for @BelfastCC				
Keyword	Pos.	Neut.	Neg.	Total
Lennox	2,327	668	1,918	4,913
LennoxArmy	1,321	188	416	1,925
collar	432	141	612	1,185
ashes	232	175	623	1,030
want	748	0	232	980

Table 5. Most used keywords for @BelfastCC, excluding "Lennox", and their sentiment in August 2012.

Keywords for @BelfastCC, excluding "Lennox"				
Keyword	Pos.	Neut.	Neg.	Total
Belfast	199	139	96	434
City	189	41	59	289
today	142	42	30	214
Hall	140	35	28	203
Big	96	24	5	125

The fifth most used keyword, "Big" is actually referring to a panoramic screen on the City Hall Square, where the Olympic Games, Movies and other audio-visual content was displayed. So, other than in the case of the dog issue, followers of the Belfast City Council twitter do not seem to use it as way to communicate with their Council.

The analysis of the content of other account's tweets which mention the New-townabbey Borough Council account also revealed that the five most used keywords are related to events promoted by the council (Table 6). And here it was even more strikingly evident than on the Belfast case, with the first two being the name of the event, or "Shoreline Festival".

Table 6. Most used keywords for @Newtownabbeybc and their sentiment in August 2012.

Keywords for @ Newtownabbeybc				
Keyword	Pos.	Neut.	Neg.	Total
Shoreline	4	2	1	7
Festival	3	2	1	6
Fun	5	0	0	5
Newtownabbey	3	2	0	5
weather	2	0	2	4

5 Discussion

It is clear from the analysed data that councils in Northern Ireland are still in the infancy in their use of Twitter, despite the majority of them (73 %) having set up an account. Some Councils look to have created an account without a strong commitment to it, as can be seen by the low levels of activity and, more strikingly, by the absence of a link for it on their Internet homepage. Furthermore, the generally low number of accounts being followed by a council and equally low amount of re-tweets also point to a lack of understanding of what Twitter, as a social network, is for. Thus, it is not surprising that our first hypothesis was validated, since tweets are mainly broadcasts about local news and events, and, when conversations happen, they are most often than not triggered by citizens.

Another reflex from this lack of understanding, is what we call *displacement*, a phenomenon where the Twitter account was set up to promote specific areas of interest, like Tourism, rather than it being a channel for communication with citizens. On the other extreme, the majority of the accounts are a mixed bag, where everything can go, from announcing events to giving advice on safety issues. At the end of the day, the image given is one of a chaotic use of Twitter by Councils, which does not look to be supported by any well-designed strategy with clear objectives.

On the other side of the fence, as our second hypothesis suggested, citizens look to be ready and available to engage in dialog with their Councils. There is a general trend for accounts to have more followers than total tweets, which is an encouraging signal of some pent-up demand by the citizenry that councils seem to be ignoring. It has already been mentioned earlier that conversations are rare, and that citizen almost always triggers them. However, this does not mean that councils are not responsible for triggering involvement. If we look at the inclusion of a council Twitter account name on tweets from other users, in the cases of Belfast City Council and Newtownabbey Borough Council, we will see that the most used keywords are related to tweets sent by those authorities. Moreover, these keywords were used mostly with a neutral or positive stance, as our hypothesis advanced.

Again, this shows that citizens are paying attention to what the councils are outputting on Twitter, and that it is the task of the councils to put that attention to good use.

The collection of the data for this paper from the Northern Ireland councils took place in June 2012. Since that date, there has been an explosion in the use of social media in Northern Ireland. In December 2012, Belfast City Council democratically ruled that the United Kingdom flag would fly from City Hall on designated days only. There was a vociferous response from the community who sought to keep the flag flying at all times, the so-called Protestant-Unionist-Loyalist (PUL) community.

A full discussion of the issues arising from this event is beyond the scope of this paper. However, it is relevant to note that while the official social media presence in Northern Ireland has been shown to be slow to demonstrate strategic initiative, the same cannot be said for citizens of the communities in Northern Ireland, who use social media to communicate their viewpoint in a lively, forceful and sometimes intimidatory manner. Their use of social media is best exemplified by a group who are parodying some of the spokespersons of the PUL and the equivalent so-called Catholic-Nationalist-Republican (CNR) community, the 'Loyalists Against Democracy' [18, 19].

6 Conclusion and Recommendations

Bonsón et al. [4, p. 123] state that social media including Twitter are ideally placed to 'enhance interactivity, transparency and openness of public sector entities and to promote new forms of accountability.' The analysis presented on this paper began with the observation that the majority of the councils in Northern Ireland have set up a Twitter account. However, there appears to be little clear recognition of the potential benefits for councils in encouraging more citizen engagement in the democratic process, and in building greater understanding and trust [6]. As we dived deeper, we found a reality that was far from such benefits. Many accounts are not active. The use of Twitter by councils is, in most cases, random at best, with tweets covering "what's on" in the moment. On other cases, the account was set up with a specific end, such as tourism or economic development.

However, it is remarkable that, despite the perception of a general lack of objectives, not to mention activity, they are being actively followed by citizens and, in some cases, those numbers of followers significantly exceed the number of tweets output by the councils. The fact that the inclusion of the councils' Twitter account name on other accounts' tweets, happened mostly along words connected to the former's tweets, only strengthens this observation. Thus, it seems to us that the responsibility is on the councils' side to make the best of the attention their citizens are awarding them, and perhaps it justifies something more than a social media policy, but rather a *social media strategy*.

We would recommend that such a strategy starts by identifying clear objectives, in articulation with other strategies and plans in development and/or implementation by the Council. As Hand and Ching [11, p. 364] state for meaningful interaction to occur, careful consideration must be given to content of communication. This could also lead to the definition of specific subjects or content areas (for example, as tourism seems to be prioritised by some councils) which might justify independent Twitter or other social media accounts (or even different social media for different subjects!), thus avoiding the "mixed bag account" that characterises the current reality. This decentralization of social media use by councils could, in effect, trigger a more dialogistic stance, as different teams and/or departments inside the Council took the opportunity to converse with their citizens about choices available to them.

As research has also highlighted, citizens also responded well to timely posts and comments, suggesting the need for city councils to actively monitor and manage their social media presence [11]. Therefore another issue to be addressed by such a strategy would be the "path" or methodology adopted to answer citizen's inquiries, which arguably would not be that much different from what the councils already do in the case of telephone and e-mail contacts. The development of such pathways can support individual staff and the organisation as a whole in avoiding crises and responding in a timely manner to issues as the arise [21]. And last but not least, the strategy should include an evaluation plan, to both evaluate the performance of the council use of social media and allow self-learning about the ways it can be used.

However, as a social media strategy is something that would probably only come into effect in the mid-to-long term, we leave another suggestion for councils, which could be implemented in a very short time: just ask followers on Twitter about what they would like to see the council tweeting about and start from there.

Finally, and in reference to the explosion in use of social media for political point scoring in Northern Ireland in 2013, in his 2012 article on the political blog site Slugger O'Toole, the author points out in his open letter to the (then) US Secretary of State, that "there are two Northern Irelands": "There's a new one that is still trying to give birth to a new way of seeing the wider world, Northern Ireland's place in it and how each citizen might relate positively to one another. And there's the old one, breed by at least one generation of murder, betrayal not to mention remote and dysfunctional government. Every now and then someone presses a tribal button and the door swings open on the abiding suspicion, alienation and loathing between neighbours."

References

1. Aharony, N.: Twitter use by three political leaders: an exploratory analysis. Online Inf. Rev. **36**(4), 587–603 (2012)
2. Ahlqvist, T., Bäck, A., Heinonen, S., Halonen, M.: Road-mapping the societal transformation potential of social media. Foresight **12**, 3–36 (2009)

3. Bertot, J.C., Jaeger, P.T., Grimes, J.M.: Using ICTs to create a culture of transparency: e-government and social media as opened and anti-corruption tools for societies. Govern. Inf. Q. **27**, 264–271 (2010)
4. Bonsón, E., Torres, L., Royo, S., Flores, F.: Local e-government 2.0: social media and corporate transparency in municipalities. Govern. Inf. Q. **29**, 123–132 (2012)
5. Brainard, L.A., McNutt, J.G.: Virtual government-citizen relations. Admin. Soc. **42**(7), 836–858 (2010)
6. Bruning, S.D., Dials, M., Shirka, A.: Using dialogue to build organization-public relationships, engage publics, and positively affect organizational outcomes. Public Rel. Rev. **34**, 25–31 (2007)
7. Burton, S., Soboleva, A.: Interactive or reactive? Marketing with Twitter. J. Consumer Market. **28**(7), 491–499 (2011)
8. Chen, H.: AI, e-government and politics 2.0. IEEE Intell. Syst. **24**, 64–67 (2009)
9. Chun, S., Reyes, L.: Social media in government. Govern. Inf. Q. **29**(4), 441–445 (2012)
10. Dixon, B.E.: Towards eGovernment 2.0: an assessment of where eGovernment 2.0 is and where it is headed. Public Admin. Manag. **15**(2), 418–454 (2010)
11. Hand, L.C., Ching, B.D.: "You have one friend request": an exploration of power and citizen engagement in local governments' use of social media. Admin. Theory Praxis **33**(3), 362–382 (2011)
12. Hearn, G., Foth, M., Gray, H.: Applications and implementations of new media in corporate communications: an action research approach. Corp. Commun. **14**(1), 49–61 (2009)
13. Ho, J.W.C., Dempsey, M.: Viral marketing: motivations to forward online content. J. Bus. Res. **63**(9–10), 1000–1006 (2010)
14. Kaplan, A.M., Haenlein, M.: Users of the world, unite! The challenges and opportunities of Social Media. Bus. Horiz. **53**, 59–68 (2010)
15. Kaushik, A.: Best social media metrics: conversation, amplification, applause, economic value (2011). kaushik.net/avinash/best-social-media-metrics-conversation-amplification-applause-economic-value/. Last accessed 10 Sept 2012
16. Kelleher, T.: Conversational voice, communicated commitment, and public relations outcomes in interactive online communication. J. Commun. **59**, 172–188 (2009)
17. Kent, M.L., Taylor, M., White, W.: The relationship between Web site design and organizational responsiveness to stakeholders. Public Rel. Rev. **29**, 66–77 (2003)
18. LADFLEG.: Loyalists against democracy (2013). https://twitter.com/LADFLEG. Last accessed 21 Oct 2013
19. Mallie, E.: Loyalists against democracy – unveiling and assailing sectarianism (2013). http://eamonnmallie.com/2013/10/loyalists-against-democracy-unveiling-and-assailing-sectarianism/. Last accessed 21 Oct 2013
20. O'Reilly, T.: What is Web 2.0? Design patterns and business models for the next generation of software. http://oreilly.com/web2/archive/what-is-web-20.html?page=5. Last accessed 6 Sept 2012
21. Owyang, J.: Social business readiness: how advanced companies prepare internally. Altimeter, 31 Aug 2011
22. Rishel, N.: Digitizing deliberation: normative concerns for the use of social media in deliberative democracy. Admin. Theory Praxis **33**(3), 411–432 (2011)
23. UK Government.: Review of government direct communication and COI (2011). cabinetoffice.gov.uk/news/review-government-direct-communication-and-coi. Last accessed 26 Sept 2012
24. Viraj.: Top 10 most popular social networking sites in the world 2012 (2012). itechwik.com/2012/07/top-10-most-popular-social-networking-sites-in-the-world-2012/. Last accessed 26 Sept 2012

25. Welch, E., Hinnant, C., Moon, M.: Linking citizen satisfaction with eGovernment and trust in government. J. Public Admin. Res. Theory **15**, 371–391 (2005)
26. Williams, N.: Template Twitter strategy for government departments (2009). slideshare.net/breakingnews/template-twitter-strategy-for-government-departments-1820431. Last accessed 26 Sept 2012

Multi-channel Attribution Modeling
on User Journeys

Florian Nottorf[✉]

Leuphana Universität Lüneburg,
Scharnhorststr. 1, 21335 Lüneburg, Germany
nottorf@uni.leuphana.de
http://www.leuphana.de

Abstract. Consumers are often confronted with multiple types of online advertising before they click on advertisements or make a purchase. The respective attribution of the success of the companies' marketing activities leads to a sophisticated allocation process. We developed a new approach to (1) address consumers' buying decision processes, (2) to account for the effects of multiple online advertising channels, and (3) consequently attribute the success of marketing activities more realistically than current management heuristics do. For example, compared to standardized metrics, we found paid search advertising to be overestimated and retargeting display advertising to be underestimated. We further found that the use of a Bayesian mixture of normals approach is useful for considering heterogeneity in the individual propensity of consumers to purchase; for the majority of consumers (more than 90 %), repeated clicks on advertisements decrease their probability of purchasing. In contrast with this segment, we found a smaller segment of consumers (nearly 10 %) whose clicks on advertisements increase conversion probabilities. Our approaches will help managers to better understand consumer online search and buying behavior over time and to allocate financial spending more efficiently across multiple types of online advertising.

Keywords: Online advertising · User-journey · Consumer behavior · Purchasing probabilities · Clickstream data · Bayesian analysis · Mixture of normals

1 Introduction

In the last decade, the options for online advertising have become increasingly complex. With the increase in options to allocate funds for online advertising, managers have sophisticated decisions to make. Standardized ratios that evaluate the profitability of advertising campaigns are only partly helpful in evaluating the short- and long-term effects of specific advertising channels; such ratios do not address the consumer process that begins with becoming aware of a product or brand through specific channels, such as display or paid-search advertising. This problem may be clearly illustrated with the following example.

© Springer-Verlag Berlin Heidelberg 2014
M.S. Obaidat and J. Filipe (Eds.): ICETE 2013, CCIS 456, pp. 107–125, 2014.
DOI: 10.1007/978-3-662-44788-8_7

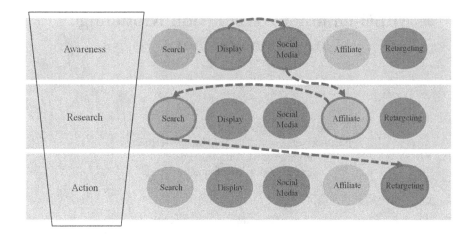

Fig. 1. Illustration of a user-journey across multiple types of advertising.

Suppose we are a company that is engaged in online advertising and we follow a user in his daily routine of Internet surfing; he checks his email, visits his favorite website, reads his blogs, etc. He sees dozens of display advertisements, including video, social media and, retargeted advertisements. Perhaps he clicks one or more advertisements, and maybe he even clicks on one of *our* advertisements; unfortunately, he does not purchase anything. After a few hours have passed, he sees a display advertisement on Facebook and clicks again on one of our advertisements but does not purchase. He might remember our company and our products and search for us using a search engine such as Google or Yahoo; finally, that *specific* user buys something from our company, and our advertising activities have been effective. Such a user-journey across multiple types of online advertising is illustrated in Fig. 1.

However, to measure the overall effectiveness of specific online advertising channels it is important to evaluate which advertisement was crucial for the user to become aware of our company and products. On which type of online advertising should we spend more to increase our chances of acquiring new consumers in future?

Companies often use standalone metrics to evaluate the profitability of specific online advertising campaigns. However, these metrics do not capture consumers' decision-making processes over time and do not account for the interaction effects between multiple advertising activities.[1] Although there have been attempts to attribute online sales success to multiple types of online advertising [26], the effect

---

[1] The profitability and effectiveness of online advertising campaigns may be assessed by using different ratios, such as click-through rate (CTR), which is the ratio of clicks to impressions for a specific type of advertising; conversion rate (CVR), which is defined as the number of purchases in relation to the number of clicks; and cost per click (CPC) and cost per order (CPO) as measures of the efficiency of promotional activities [4,20].

of advertising on the individual behavior of consumers has not yet been comprehensively analyzed.

We build on the specification of Chatterjee et al. [7], who model the probability of a consumer to click on a display advertisement using a binary logit with a normal prior distribution. However, we extend their specification in two principal ways. First, we model the probability of consumers purchasing by including *multiple* advertising channels to address the complex allocating processes used by companies today to manage online advertising campaigns (such as display advertising, social media, and paid search advertising). Second, we employ a Bayesian mixture of normals approach, which offers more flexibility to address consumer heterogeneity than standard normal prior distributions [19, 23]. The proposed model uses anonymized user-level data to help managers understand the effects of specific advertising channels on individual consumer behavior and online purchasing processes.

This paper is structured as follows. First, we will briefly review previous research related to this work. Second, we will examine the general model specification and extend the previous work of Chatterjee et al. [7] to model consumer probabilities of purchasing after clicking on multiple advertising channels. This section is followed by the introduction of our unique dataset that includes detailed user-journeys and consumer interactions with multiple types of online advertising. After outlining our findings and discussing our results, we conclude this work by highlighting its limitations and providing suggestions for future research.

2   Related Work

This work is related to several streams of research because we analyze *multiple* online advertising channels and their influences on consumer online purchasing behavior.

An emerging stream of research is analyzing paid search advertising from the advertiser's perspective and providing important initial insights into consumer clicking and purchasing behavior (see, for instance, Ghose and Yang [11], Rutz et al. [24], or Rutz.2011c). For example, Rutz et al. [25] analyze the long-term effects of consumers' online search activities on subsequent direct-type-in visitors and develop a hierarchical Bayesian elastic net to address the "large p, small n" problem. The authors demonstrate that normal ridge and LASSO regressions push the limits when analyzing the effects of thousands of keywords that are normally used in companies' paid search advertising campaigns.

Focusing on display advertising, Chatterjee et al. [7] and Rutz and Bucklin [23] find significant heterogeneity in the propensity of consumers to click on banner advertisements. In addition, Danaher and Mullarkey [8] introduce user involvement as an important factor that influences the effectiveness of banner advertising; characterizing user intentions as either goal-directed or in surfing mode indicates that there will be significant differences in the effectiveness of banner advertising. Goldfarb and Tucker [12] show that the synergies between different types of banner advertising are negative; targeted and obtrusive banner advertising campaigns independently increase the purchase intent of consumers, whereas combining them is less effective.

Limited research has investigated the online behavior of users while considering multiple advertising channels simultaneously [17,18]. Previous research on media synergy effects has primarily focused on within-media interaction effects of offline advertising efforts, such as television, radio, and print [5,16], or model cross media synergies between offline and online advertising types [3,9,13,15].

Although studies of paid search advertising have increased significantly over the last several years, there have been few attempts to examine an integrated model of online advertising efforts, for example, to explain the effects of the interaction between display and paid search advertising. Although various types of online advertising arrived in the last decade, scientific works on cross channel advertising effects focused on modeling data that is aggregated on a specific time scale (e.g., week or day) on a specific type of advertising channel (e.g., "display" or "search").

Although certain studies have focused on the effects of several types of online advertising, such as display and paid search advertising [10,28], such studies do not investigate the influence of these types of advertising on the online behavior of individual consumers as a result of aggregation biases [1], and they do not consider the interaction effects of different types of online advertising activities on consumers. The possibility of "following" individual users across multiple types of online advertising is relatively new; user-level data is collected through cookie tracking by companies' advertising-servers. Nottorf [19] and Nottorf and Funk [21] employ such data to analyze the effects of repeated paid search advertisements and banner, video and retargeted display advertising on consumer click probabilities; they find both differences in the effects of repeated advertising exposure across multiple types of display advertising and positive interactive effects between display and paid search advertising in influencing consumer click probabilities.

We also use such user-level data to distinguish multiple types of advertising at the level of individual consumers. As opposed to Nottorf [19] and Nottorf and Funk [21], we analyze the effects of multiple advertising-specific clicks on consumers' individual conversion probabilities. Therefore, we contribute to existing research at several junctures because we analyze the effects of *multiple types* of online advertising—such as paid search advertising, display advertising, and newsletter mailings—on consumer *purchasing* behavior at the *individual user-level*.

3 Modeling Individual Conversions Across Multiple Online Advertising Channels

3.1 General Specification

We extend the specification of Chatterjee et al. [7] and follow Nottorf [19] to model the probability of consumer i purchasing at time t in session s, and we consider multiple advertising channels. Therefore, we specify the following:

- advertising-specific *intercepts*, I_{ist},
- variables accounting for *short-term* advertising-specific effects, X_{ist}, and
- variables accounting for *long-term* advertising-specific effects, Y_{is}.

I_{ist}: advertising-specific intercepts

First, we define multiple advertising-specific intercepts that account for the probability of consumers purchasing after clicking on a respective advertisement. We include these advertising-specific intercepts because we expect consumers' likelihood of purchasing to vary strongly with the types of advertising a consumer may click on. For example, while a click on a paid search advertisement is followed by a consumer's active search for specific terms, a click on a display advertisement may occur more or less by accident. Chatterjee et al. [7] denote this intercept as consumers' click-proneness. Because we model consumers purchasing probabilities across multiple advertising channels, we denote these terms as consumers' *advertising-specific conversion proneness*. These intercepts become 1 if a consumer clicks on a respective advertisement and remains at 0 otherwise.

X_{ist}: short-term advertising effects

While a consumer may not purchase after his first click on an advertisement within a current session, that probability may increase with subsequent ones. Furthermore, that probability of purchasing might also vary with the type of advertising the consumer repeatedly clicks on. Therefore, we include the number of consumer clicks on specific advertising channels within a current session. These variables should capture the *short-term effects* (i.e., session-length of one hour) of advertisement-specific clicks on an individual consumer's conversion probabilities. If a consumer does not click on a specific type of advertising in a current session, the respective variable remains at 0.

Y_{is}: long-term advertising effects

The *long-term effects* of advertising clicks on consumer conversion probabilities must also be modeled. We accomplish this because we account for the number of *all* advertising-specific clicks and not just those in a current session. We expect the long-term effects of clicks on conversion probabilities to strongly vary across consumers [8,23]; while we expect the effect of repeated clicks on specific advertisements to be positive for certain consumers (i.e., each click in their respective user-journey increases the awareness that a company might be relevant for their buying process), an increase in clicks on specific advertising channels may decrease the probability of purchasing for other consumers (i.e., no matter how often these consumers click on a specific ad, they cannot be convinced to purchase something). If a consumer does not click at all on a specific type of advertising, the respective variable remains 0.

To model the individual contribution of each advertising effort and its effect on consumer conversion probabilities, we specify a binary logit choice model [7].

The probability that consumer i converts subsequent to a click on an online advertisement at time t in session s is modeled as follows:

$$Con_{ist} = \begin{cases} 1 & \text{if user } i \text{ converts at time } t \text{ in session } s \\ 0 & \text{otherwise,} \end{cases} \tag{1}$$

with the probability

$$Pr(Con_{ist} = 1) = \frac{exp(I_{ist}\alpha_i + X_{ist}\beta_i + Y_{is}\gamma_i + \epsilon_{ist})}{1 + exp(I_{ist}\alpha_i + X_{ist}\beta_i + Y_{is}\gamma_i + \epsilon_{ist})} \tag{2}$$

where I_{ist} are advertisement-specific intercepts modeling the consumers' individual likelihood (proneness) of conversion after clicking on a respective advertisement. X_{ist} are variables varying within (t), across sessions (s), and across consumers (i), whereas Y_{is} are variables varying across sessions (s) and consumers (i), and α_i, β_i, and γ_i are consumer-specific parameters to be estimated.

3.2   Variable Specification

The variable X_{ist} includes the number of consumer advertising-specific clicks within a current session. Furthermore, we follow Chatterjee et al. [7] and define the following additional variables incorporated in X_{ist}: $x^{con}_{is(t-1)}$ is the cumulative number of conversions until $t - 1$ in the current session s for a specific consumer i, and $Con_{is(t-1)}$ is an indicator function that assumes the value 1 if a consumer has already purchased in $t - 1$. We assume both variables to have a negative influence on subsequent consumer conversions; if a consumer has already bought something in $t - 1$ or within his current session s, it might be highly unlikely that he will purchase again in the short-term. Furthermore, we define $TLCon_{ist}$ as the logarithm time since a consumer last made a conversion; if a consumer has never purchased, the variable remains zero.

Modern tracking software also allows companies to capture consumers' on-site clicks and on-site time. The former refers to the number of clicks a user has made on the company's website after he gets redirected by clicking on an advertisement, whereas the latter denotes the time the user browses through the company's website. Therefore, we include the cumulative number of on-site clicks of a user i within session s until time t as $x^{Onsite\text{-}clicks}_{ist}$ and the cumulative logarithm on-site time as $x^{Onsite\text{-}time}_{ist}$. We propose that a user shows a higher involvement in the purchasing process with increasing on-site time and clicks, which may increase the probability of a user to convert.

The same might hold true for the number of brand-related activities. We therefore also include x^{Brand}_{ist}, which refers to the cumulative number of brand-related clicks made by user i within session s until time t, and $Brand_{ist}$, which is an indicator function assuming 1 if a consumer i performs a brand-related activity at time t in session s. We define a brand-related activity as a click on an online advertisement that accompanies prior brand-related knowledge. For example, if a user clicks on a paid search advertisement after searching for brand-related terms (i.e., the keyword includes the name of the company in question, such as "Staples pen" instead of just "pen"), we denote that click as a brand-related click. The same holds true for users' direct visits to the company's website (i.e., the user directly types the name of the company's website into the web-browser or uses bookmarks).

Y_{is} accounts for the long-term effects of advertisement-specific clicks on consumers' individual conversion probabilities, i.e., the cumulative number of clicks on a specific advertisement per consumer i until session s. Furthermore, $y_{i(s-1)}^{con}$ is the cumulative number of conversions in previous sessions. $y_{is}^{Onsite\text{-}clicks}$ and $y_{is}^{Onsite\text{-}time}$ refer to cumulative on-site clicks and time, respectively. The total cumulative number of brand-related clicks is modeled by y_{is}^{Brand}. IST_{is} is the logarithm of the intersession duration between session s and $s-1$; it remains at zero if a consumer is active in only one session. $Session_{is}$ refers to the number of sessions in which a consumer has already clicked on advertisements.

3.3   Data

We use a dataset from a regular online shop that will remain anonymous, at its own request. The dataset consists of information on individual consumers and the point in time at which they clicked on different ads, such as retargeted banner and paid search advertisements. Following consumers across multiple advertising channels and types is performed with cookie-tracking software and respective advertising servers. The data was collected within a one-month period (between 2012 and 2013). To analyze clickstream data, we take into account only those user-journeys that have more than three advertising touch points. The finale dataset still consists several thousand users.[2]

Further, the dataset contains information about the following types of advertising that a user has clicked on:

- *search*: If a user has searched for a keyword, if the company in question advertises on search engines such as Google, and if the user clicked on a respective *paid search advertisement* of that company, then we denote this interaction as a "search" click. Furthermore, the company in question is listed on the results page of a search engine if a user searches specific keywords for which the company has been classified as "relevant" by the search engine. If a user clicks on links of such *organic* results page listings, we also denote this interaction as a "search" click.
- *price*: Companies might pay for becoming linked on *shopping comparison sites* such as Nextag. If a user compares the price of a product and clicks on a link of the company in question, we denote this interaction as a "price" click.
- *retargeting*: Display advertisements, such as banners, may be individualized on a user-specific level. For example, if a user searches for a specific product and gets redirected to the website of a company, the company might individualize the display advertisements in a user's later browsing routines to the extent that it *re-targets* the specific user and displays the specific (or related)

---

[2] The datasets have been sanitized for reasons of confidentiality.

product in the banner advertisement that the user was originally looking for at the company's website. We denote users' clicks on such retargeted display advertisements as "retargeting" clicks.

- *direct*: If a user directly visits the website of the company in question, for example, via bookmarks or *direct-type-ins*, we denote this interaction as a "direct" click.[3]
- *other*: There are other types of advertising contacts, such as *social media* or *newsletter mailings*. Because of their minimal total advertising contacts, we aggregate them and denote a user's click on such types of advertising as an "other" click.

Table 1 lists the number of clicks on each type of online advertising.

Because there is no accessible information available on the number of consumer sessions and their duration, we manually define a session as a sequence of advertising exposures with breaks that do not exceed 60 min. Demographic information is not available. We report the descriptive statistics of our final dataset in Table 2.

Table 1. General information on the dataset.

Clicks in total	100.00 %
On search	51.42 %
On price	16.15 %
On retargeting	11.85 %
On direct	14.95 %
On other	5.63 %
Conversions	2.14 %

Notes: We report the number of advertising-specific clicks, and the number of conversions within our dataset. For privacy reasons, the distribution of the advertising channels have been sanitized.

3.4 Bayesian Mixture of Normals

Although the standard normal model as it has been applied by Chatterjee et al. [7] to model consumers' clickstream is capable of performing analyses with many consumers and properly accounts for heterogeneity [2,14], we use a Bayesian mixture approach to account for consumer heterogeneity and to determine the set of individual parameters. This mixture of normals approach enables us to

---

[3] Although direct visits are not any type of advertising, we will denote and treat it as an advertising channel for the sake of convenience.

find multiple cluster of users whose conversion probability is modeled *significantly* differently from those users of a different cluster (i.e., from a different normal distribution). For example, the conversion probabilities of one cluster of individual consumers may increase with each additional click on a specific type of advertising (wear-in effect), whereas the conversion probabilities of another cluster may decrease (wear-out effect).

For the sake of convenience, we denote the set of consumers' individual parameters to be estimated as:

$$\theta_i = \{\alpha_i, \beta_i, \gamma_i\} \tag{3}$$

Because we assume that the tendency of consumers to purchase will vary significantly (i.e., extensive vs. impulsive buying decision process), a mixture approach offers more flexibility for capturing heterogeneity than the standard normal approach [23]. This assumption is consistent with previous research that classifies the online searches of users according to navigational, transactional, or informational intentions [6] and indicates strong differences in the effectiveness of banner advertising with respect to consumer involvement levels [8,20]. We specify the Bayesian mixture approach, following Rossi et al. [22]:

$$\theta_i \sim N(\mu_{\mathrm{ind}_i}, \Sigma_{\mathrm{ind}_i}), \tag{4}$$

$$\mathrm{ind}_i \sim \mathrm{Multinomial}_K(\mathrm{pvec}), \tag{5}$$

where ind_i is an indicator latent variable from which component observation i is derived. ind takes on values $1, \ldots, K$, and pvec is a vector of mixture probabilities of length K. We use uninformative hyper-priors pvec $\sim Dirichlet(\alpha)$, $\mu_k \sim Gaussian(\mu_0, \Sigma_0)$, and $\Sigma_k \sim Wishart(v, V)$.

We apply a MCMC algorithm including a hybrid Gibbs Sampler with a random walk Metropolis step for the coefficients for each consumer and utilize the R-package bayesm by Rossi et al. [22]. We perform 40,000 iterations and use every twentieth draw of the last 10,000 iterations to compute the conditional distributions.

4   Results

4.1   Benchmarking Alternative Models

We benchmark multiple model specifications by modifying the number of mixture components K. We compute the log likelihood (LL) and the Bayesian information criterion (BIC) to analyze fit performances. The latter criterion penalizes the incorporation of additional parameters—such as an additional number of mixture components—in the model.

As reported in Table 3, the model with two mixture components performs best (BIC = 374.4). There seem to be *two cluster of consumers* who react differently to online advertising as the *two-mixture-components model* exhibits superior performance. The benefit of additional components does not increase the relative fit performance. As expected, the model that is reduced to a prior model with a standard normal distribution performs significantly more poorly than the models with multiple mixture components (BIC = 443.5).

Table 2. Descriptive statistics of the covariates.

Variables	min	max	mean	sd	Variables	min	max	mean	sd
Indicator variables									
I_{ist}^{search}	0	1	0.26	0.44	I_{ist}^{price}	0	1	0.08	0.27
$I_{ist}^{retargeting}$	0	1	0.06	0.24	I_{ist}^{direct}	0	1	0.07	0.26
I_{ist}^{other}	0	1	0.03	0.17					
Intrasession variables									
x_{ist}^{search}	0	16	0.50	1.07	x_{ist}^{price}	0	286	1.23	13.96
$x_{ist}^{retargeting}$	0	13	0.09	0.44	x_{ist}^{direct}	0	46	0.12	1.00
x_{ist}^{other}	0	14	0.06	0.42	$x_{is(t-1)}^{con}$	0	3	0.01	0.11
$Con_{is(t-1)}$	0	1	0.01	0.09	$TLCon_{ist}$	0	7.58	0.15	0.89
$x_{ist}^{Onsite-clicks}$	0	450	2.31	8.95	$x_{ist}^{Onsite-time}$	0	125	1.60	4.47
x_{ist}^{Brand}	0	46	0.15	1.03	$Brand_{ist}$	0	1	0.09	0.29
Intersession variables									
y_{is}^{search}	0	44	0.91	2.61	y_{is}^{price}	0	331	1.71	17.93
$y_{is}^{retargeting}$	0	33	0.31	1.66	y_{is}^{direct}	0	86	0.64	3.80
y_{is}^{other}	0	40	0.19	1.42	$y_{i(s-1)}^{con}$	0	65	0.11	1.92
$y_{is}^{Onsite-clicks}$	0	510	6.28	24.64	$y_{is}^{Onsite-time}$	0	364	4.08	15.24
y_{is}^{Brand}	0	86	0.71	3.85	IST_{is}	0	7.66	1.26	2.02
$Session_{is}$	1	82	2.43	6.38					

Notes: We report both the minimum/maximum and the mean/standard deviation of the covariates used in our study.

4.2   Key Results

The parameter estimates for the two-mixture-component model specification are reported in Table 4. Our findings vary substantially across the two-component groups. The larger group, group 1, has a segment size of 91 % and thus clearly represents the majority of consumers, whereas the second group, group 2, represents a segment size of 9 %, which is a small number of consumers.

We report the results for the intrasession effects, intersession effects, and for the advertising-specific conversion proneness successively for both groups.

Intrasession Effects
Group 1, segment size of 91 %

For the majority of consumers, represented by group 1 (the first component of the mixture model), we find the cumulative number of clicks on all types of advertising within a session to decrease purchasing probability (see x_{ist}^{search} ... x_{ist}^{other}),[4] i.e., the likelihood of consumers purchasing is highest after they have clicked for the first time on a particular advertisement and are redirected

---

[4] The findings are significantly negative for x_{ist}^{direct} and x_{ist}^{other}.

Table 3. Model comparison: benchmarking fit performances.

Model (*Num. of parameters*)	LL	BIC
2 Mixture components (*56*)	−253.9	374.4
3 Mixture components (*84*)	−241.2	421.9
4 Mixture components (*112*)	−241.2	482.2
Standard normal distribution (*28*)	−383.3	443.5

Notes: We report the number of advertising-specific clicks, and the number of conversions within our dataset. For privacy reasons, the distribution of the advertising channels have been sanitized.

to the company's website within a current session. For this segment of consumers, we find further differences in the effects of cumulative clicks during current sessions across different types of advertisements. For example, each additional *direct* visit ($x_{ist}^{\text{direct}} = -4.22$) and click on *other* advertisements such as newsletters or affiliate advertisements ($x_{ist}^{\text{other}} = -4.79$) significantly decreases consumers conversion probability, whereas we find that additional *search, price,* or *retargeting* clicks do not decrease the conversion probability significantly and are not as strong as the other two types. It seems that this group of consumers is either very goal-oriented (i.e., these consumers purchase immediately after they have clicked on an advertisement or directly visited the website of the company in question) or is insecure in their buying process because each additional click decreases their conversion probability.

As expected, the probability of consumers to purchase decreases if they have purchased in the last period ($\text{Con}_{is(t-1)} = -3.70$). The cumulative number of conversions within a current session is not significant and therefore does not affect further purchases (see $x_{is(t-1)}^{\text{con}}$). Contrary to expectations, both on-site time and on-site clicks have no significant influence on the conversion probability of consumers (see $x_{ist}^{\text{Onsite-clicks}}$ and $x_{ist}^{\text{Onsite-time}}$). Notably, information about brand-related activities does not influence consumers' conversion probabilities significantly (see x_{ist}^{Brand} and Brand_{ist}). This result is surprising because we expected an increase in brand-related activities to reflect consumers' intentions to purchase from the company.

Group 2, segment size of 9 %

We now focus on the intrasession effects on consumer probability to purchase in the smaller segment represented by the second mixture component (see the right-hand side of Table 4).

For this small segment of consumers, we do not find the cumulative number of clicks on advertisements within the current session to significantly decrease conversion probabilities; we even find that each additional search with subsequent clicks significantly increases such consumers' probability to purchase ($x_{ist}^{\text{search}} = 3.76$). Therefore, compared to the first segment of consumers, we uncover important differences in the effect of advertisements on consumer's conversion probabilities.

Table 4. Parameter estimates of the two component mixture model.

Variables	Group 1, size: 91 %	Group 2, size: 9 %
	Mean (95 % cov. interval)	Mean (95 % cov. interval)
Indicator variables I_{ist}		
I_{ist}^{search}	$-6.09(-9.17, -3.05)$	$-19.50(-32.75, -6.49)$
I_{ist}^{price}	$-3.98(-6.42, -1.57)$	$-13.30(-26.01, -0.79)$
$I_{ist}^{\text{retargeting}}$	$-4.79(-9.00, -0.57)$	$-12.44(-29.65, 4.67)$
I_{ist}^{direct}	$-3.26(-7.23, 0.68)$	$-15.00(-33.92, 3.67)$
I_{ist}^{other}	$-4.06(-7.40, -0.70)$	$-18.07(-31.28, -5.02)$
Intrasession variables X_{ist}		
x_{ist}^{search}	$-1.27(-4.15, 1.59)$	$\mathbf{3.76(0.54, 6.93)}$
x_{ist}^{price}	$-2.38(-6.02, 1.26)$	$0.44(-20.43, 21.01)$
$x_{ist}^{\text{retargeting}}$	$-1.41(-6.52, 3.69)$	$-6.87(-21.61, 7.47)$
x_{ist}^{direct}	$\mathbf{-4.22(-6.92, -1.52)}$	$3.96(-3.21, 11.06)$
x_{ist}^{other}	$\mathbf{-4.79(-7.57, -2.00)}$	$5.51(-0.57, 11.57)$
$x_{is(t-1)}^{\text{con}}$	$0.38(-2.66, 3.41)$	$\mathbf{-31.76(-49.56, -14.23)}$
$\text{Con}_{is(t-1)}$	$\mathbf{-3.70(-6.38, -1.00)}$	$-12.58(-24.62, -1.07)$
TLCon_{ist} (logarithm hour)	$-0.85(-3.73, 2.13)$	$-10.67(-27.27, 5.24)$
$x_{ist}^{\text{Onsite-clicks}}$	$-1.05(-2.95, 0.83)$	$0.46(-1.61, 2.62)$
$x_{ist}^{\text{Onsite-time}}$ (logarithm hour)	$-1.99(-5.09, 1.02)$	$0.08(-2.95, 3.16)$
x_{ist}^{Brand}	$-1.94(-6.35, 2.40)$	$0.86(-3.31, 5.34)$
Brand_{ist}	$0.45(-2.49, 3.40)$	$1.05(-5.87, 8.05)$
Intersession variables Y_{is}		
y_{is}^{search}	$-2.45(-6.82, 1.91)$	$3.00(-0.60, 6.63)$
y_{is}^{price}	$-3.76(-8.73, 1.20)$	$4.83(-2.19, 11.76)$
$y_{is}^{\text{retargeting}}$	$-1.20(-6.41, 3.99)$	$5.71(-2.24, 13.74)$
y_{is}^{direct}	$0.93(-3.04, 4.93)$	$\mathbf{6.08(2.03, 10.31)}$ '
y_{is}^{other}	$1.83(-1.66, 5.37)$	$-0.25(-4.10, 3.64)$
$y_{i(s-1)}^{\text{con}}$	$2.02(-1.29, 5.33)$	$-19.27(-45.00, 5.99)$
$y_{is}^{\text{Onsite-clicks}}$	$-1.57(-3.74, 0.62)$	$-0.11(-2.13, 1.85)$
$y_{is}^{\text{Onsite-time}}$ (logarithm hour)	$-0.67(-3.39, 2.02)$	$0.42(-2.42, 3.26)$
y_{is}^{Brand}	$-1.45(-4.59, 1.67)$	$-1.40(-8.56, 5.78)$
IST_{is} (logarithm hour)	$-0.99(-3.46, 1.47)$	$0.19(-3.55, 3.99)$
Session_{is}	$-3.97(-8.23, 0.23)$	$-1.58(-6.30, 3.06)$

Notes: We report the mean and the 95 % coverage interval of the parameter estimates of our proposed model using two-mixture-component model. The estimates in boldface are significant as they lie in the 95 % coverage interval.

Furthermore, both variables accounting for past conversions within consumers' current session indicate a very strongly negative influence on future subsequent conversions (see $x^{\text{con}}_{is(t-1)}$ and $\text{Con}_{is(t-1)}$). As for the first segment, neither on-site clicks/time nor brand-related information significantly influences consumers' conversion probabilities.

Intersession Effects
Group 1, segment size of 91 %

We now focus on the long-term effects of clicks on consumers' conversion probabilities. By contrast to prior research that analyzed the long-term effects of repeated display advertisement exposures on consumers and found them to have a significantly positive influence on consumer click probabilities [7], we do not find intersession clicks on any type of advertisement to significantly influence conversion probabilities for the large segment of consumers. There do not appear to be any long-term effects of clicks on conversion probabilities for this group. On the one hand, this is extremely helpful information for the company in question because each consumer nearly has an identical conversion probability when entering a new session. On the other hand, if past clicks on online advertisements do not seem to affect consumer click probabilities, this information may lead managers to question what the long-term success rate of past advertising actually was.

As expected, there is no long-term negative influence of past conversions on future conversions (see $y^{\text{con}}_{i(s-1)}$). Furthermore, as for the short-term, there are no long-term effects of on-site clicks/time and brand-related activities on consumers' conversion probabilities (see $y^{\text{Onsite-clicks}}_{is}$, $y^{\text{Onsite-time}}_{is}$, and y^{Brand}_{is}). Although the parameter estimates are barely not significant, an increase in the number of total sessions reduces consumers conversion probabilities ($\text{Session}_{is} = -3.97$).

Group 2, segment size of 9 %

Compared to the first consumer segment, we again find inherent differences in the effects of clicks on conversion probabilities for the second consumer segment. For example, four out of five click types have a long-term positive influence influences the probability that they will purchase. For this small group of consumers, each *search, price, retargeting,* and *direct* click positively influences the probability that they will purchase.[5] If we compare the influence of each click-type, we find that the cumulative number of *search* clicks does not have that strong of an effect on conversion probabilities as *retargeting* or *direct* clicks, for example (see y^{search}_{is}, $y^{\text{retargeting}}_{is}$, and y^{direct}_{is}). We consider these differences in the next section in formulating managerial implications.

Similar to the intrasession findings, the influence of conversions in prior sessions is negative on futures conversions ($y^{\text{con}}_{i(s-1)} = -19.27$). As with consumers in the first segment, the variables accounting for on-site clicks/time, brand-related

---

[5] Please note that only y^{direct}_{is} is significant, whereas the others are barely not significant.

activities and intersession time may be neglected (see $y_{is}^{\text{Onsite-clicks}}$, $y_{is}^{\text{Onsite-time}}$, y_{is}^{Brand}, and IST_{is}).

Advertising-Specific Conversion Proneness

Group 1, segment size of 91 %

Previous research indicates that the click proneness of consumers in response to display advertisement exposure is minimal [7]), and our findings also confirm this for advertising-specific conversion proneness. For the large segment of consumers, we find that the initial conversion probability is very small across all types of advertisement. Consumer proneness to purchase is smallest after consumers have clicked on companies' links through search engines ($I_{ist}^{\text{search}} = -6.09$). We find the highest probability of purchasing after consumers directly visited the companies website ($I_{ist}^{\text{direct}} = -3.26$) or after they clicked on comparison-shopping sites ($I_{ist}^{\text{price}} = -3.98$). This is not surprising because these two click types typically accompany a high level of intention to purchase (e.g., after comparing prices for a specific product or by directly visiting the company website to purchase).

Group 2, segment size of 9 %

By contrast to the first segment that includes consumers with a low initial conversion probability that decreases with subsequent clicks, we find that the conversion probability of the second and smaller segment of consumers increases with subsequent clicks. By contrast to the first segment, consumers of the second segment show an even smaller initial probability to purchase. All five indicator variables accounting for the type of advertising show a much stronger initial and negative effect (see $I_{ist}^{\text{search}} \ldots I_{ist}^{\text{other}}$). Our prior findings on the intrasession and intersession effects also have shown that this low conversion probability may be increased with subsequent clicks.

5 Implications

5.1 Real-Time Bidding

The knowledge of a consumer's *individual* conversion probability and the respective degree of advertising-specific influence is vital to the relatively new and emerging field of real-time bidding (RTB) settings in which advertising is bought and displayed in real time on an individual consumer level. RTB provides a flexible option of matching individual consumers with suitable advertising content. Within milliseconds, advertisers place bids for individual advertisement impressions in an auction-based process [27].

Assume that the company investigated here is active in a RTB setting and dynamically exposes consumers to display advertising. By accounting for consumers' complete user-journey and applying our parameter estimates, the company may be able to deliver display ads specifically to those consumers who have a higher probability of purchasing compared with consumers with a significantly lower probability of purchasing (i.e., consumers who clicked multiple times but never purchased).

5.2   Alternative Evaluation of Advertising Channels

Table 5. Alternative approach of evaluating profitability of advertising channels.

Channel	Mean estimates			Mean of variables				
	α_i	β_i	γ_i	I_{ist}	X_{ist}	Y_{is}	ASP *(prop.)*	CVR *(prop.)*
Search	-7.30	-0.81	-1.96	0.26	0.50	0.91	1.65 % *(5.43 %)*	1.65 % *(39.70 %)*
Price	-4.82	-2.13	-2.98	0.08	1.23	1.71	0.03 % *(0.03 %)*	0.96 % *(7.25 %)*
Retargeting	-5.48	-1.90	-0.58	0.06	0.09	0.31	33.64 % *(25.46 %)*	1.09 % *(6.04 %)*
Direct	-4.32	-3.48	1.39	0.07	0.12	0.64	54.23 % *(51.80 %)*	4.86 % *(33.99 %)*
Other	-5.32	-3.86	1.64	0.03	0.06	0.19	48.01 % *(17.28 %)*	4.94 % *(13.02 %)*

Notes: We develop an alternative approach to evaluate the profitability of multiple advertising channels on the basis of individual user-level data and compare the average success
probability (ASP) with the conversion rate (CVR). To calculate the proportional ASP
(see the *italicized* number in the brackets), we take into account the total number of
advertisement-specific clicks of the complete campaign/investigation period.

In daily business, there are more- or less-simple heuristics to evaluate the
success of multiple types of online advertising on an individual user-level [26].
In Table 5, we illustrate an alternative approach of evaluating the profitability
of multiple advertising channels and contrast that approach with the conversion
rate (CVR) of each channel type. We will develop that approach simplistically
below because we are not focused on determining an *exact* success rate for each
advertising channel. Instead we want to illustrate how it is generally possible to
account for consumers' individual user-journeys and to evaluate multiple advertising channels in a more realistic way than companies currently are able. By so
doing, we propose an alternative evaluation metric, the average success probability (ASP). The ASP can be interpreted as an advertisement- and campaign-
specific contribution to companies' success probabilities because we account for
both the short- and long-term advertising effects of the complete investigation
period.

We begin the evaluation of each advertising channel by taking into account
the mean (proportional for both mixture segments) of each advertising-specific
parameter. For example, to calculate the mean estimates for the *search* channel,
we take the sum of the mean parameter estimates for the respective parameter
(I_{ist}^{search}, x_{ist}^{search}, and y_{is}^{search}) times the segment size (91 % and 9 %, respectively)
over both segments:

$$\alpha_i = 0.91 * (-6.09) + 0.09 * (-19.50) \qquad = -7.30$$
$$\beta_i = 0.91 * (-1.27) + 0.09 * 3.76 \qquad = -0.81$$
$$\gamma_i = 0.91 * (-2.45) + 0.09 * 3.00 \qquad = -1.96$$

As illustrated in Table 5, a first simplification is that we only take into account
those parameters that measure the advertising-specific influence directly. That is,

we take the advertising-specific intercepts (I_{ist}^{search}, ..., I_{ist}^{other}), the cumulative number of advertising-specific clicks within consumers' current sessions (x_{ist}^{search}, ..., x_{ist}^{other}), and the cumulative number of advertising-specific clicks across all sessions (y_{is}^{search}, ..., y_{is}^{other}).[6]

We take the sum of the mean parameter estimates multiplied by the mean of the applicable variables of the dataset that are reported in Tables 1 and 5, respectively. The logits of each advertisement-specific product are reported as the average success probability (ASP) in Table 5:[7]

$$\text{ASP}^{search} = \frac{exp(-4.09)}{1 + exp(-4.09)}$$

$$\text{ASP}^{search} = 1.65$$

The ASPs differ significantly across multiple channel types. For example, the *price* channel performs very poorly compared to the *retargeting* channel. In analyzing the complete investigation period and evaluating the proportional success of each advertising channel, we take into account the total number of respective clicks (as reported in Table 1) to calculate the proportional ASP (see *italicized* number in brackets).

The standard CVRs and their proportional success rate within the investigation period are reported on the right-hand side of Table 5. The ASPs calculated here offer the first advice on how future advertising spending should be allocated. Compared to the CVRs, we find that the *search* channel is overestimated (5.43 % vs. 39.70 %) and that the *retargeting* channel is underestimated (25.46 % vs. 6.04 %). These differences may be ascribed to the circumstance that consumers seem to be attracted by display advertisements—such as retargeted advertisements—at the early stages of their search-and-decision process before they conduct later searches and click on links of the company. In a test-setting, the company might increase its retargeting advertising spending chargeable to the search channel and then analyze the campaign profitability.

6   Conclusions

We develop a binary logit model with a Bayesian mixture approach to model consumer clickstreams across multiple types of online advertising and analyze the individual conversion probabilities of consumers. The mixture approach we utilize outperforms the standard normal approach and is useful for considering heterogeneity in the individual propensity of consumers to purchase; for the majority of consumers (more than 90 %), repeated clicks on advertisements decrease their probability of purchasing. Thus, for this segment of consumers,

---

[6] Please note that because of simplifications and for convenience, we do not distinguish between significant and non-significant parameter estimates.

[7] Note that we multiply the mean parameter estimates with the mean of the respective variables: $-4.09 = -0.26 * 7.30 - 0.50 * 0.81 - 0.91 * 1.96$.

the probability of purchasing is highest after consumers' first click on an advertisement. In contrast with this segment, we find a smaller segment of consumers (nearly 10 %) whose clicks on advertisements increase conversion probabilities.

We successfully demonstrate how to simultaneously integrate and evaluate multiple types of online advertising to gain knowledge that is indispensable to allocating financial resources. The evaluation of consumers on an individual level along their complete user-journey is essential to optimize the auction-based process, particularly in the emerging new advertising technology of real-time bidding.

Furthermore, we are able to show inherent differences in the effects of consumer clicks on purchasing probabilities across multiple advertising channels. Therefore, on the basis of our parameter estimates, we develop an alternative approach of accounting for the success of advertising channels—the average success probability (ASP)—which may be interpreted as an advertisement-and-campaign-specific contribution to companies' success probabilities as we take into account both short- and long-term advertising effects of the complete investigation period. Compared to standardized advertisement-specific conversion rates, we find the "search" advertising channel to be overestimated and the "retargeting" channel to be underestimated.

In this paper, we analyze a large dataset containing detailed individual consumer-level information. Tracking individual consumers across multiple online advertising types is accomplished by the application of cookies that are stored on the personal computer of each consumer. Thus, we do not have combined information regarding consumer usage of web browsers across multiple devices (i.e., personal computers at work versus at home) and are thus unable to model complete sessions for all consumers. Furthermore, modern web browsers give consumers the opportunity to deny websites access their personal computers to store cookies.

Another limitation of this work is that we do not have any information on consumers' isolated exposures to online advertisements that have not been clicked. The long-term effects of unclicked online advertisements are thought to be positive on conversions [29] but have not been analyzed yet on an individual user-level while analyzing multiple online advertising channels. We leave this question open for future research.

Further, there is room for research analyzing the effects of specific online advertisements on consumer online behavior. For example, the integration of consumer-specific information, such as gender or interests, might uncover further insights into consumers' individual online click and conversion probabilities. We also see the combination of aggregated data (that does not suffer from the cookie-deleting problem) with consumer-level data (as it is analyzed here) as an important and interesting topic for future research.

References

1. Abhishek, V., Hosanagar, K., Fader, P.S.: On aggregation bias in sponsored search data: existence and implications (2011). http://ssrn.com/abstract=1490169
2. Allenby, G.M., Ginter, J.L.: Using extremes to design products and segment markets. J. Mark. Res. **32**(4), 392–403 (1995). http://www.jstor.org/stable/3152175
3. Ansari, A., Mela, C.F., Neslin, S.A.: Customer channel migration. J. Mark. Res. **45**(1), 60–76 (2008)
4. Athey, S., Ellison, G.: Position auctions with consumer search (2009). http://ssrn.com/abstract=1454986
5. Bass, F.M., Bruce, N., Majumdar, S., Murthi, B.P.S.: Wearout effects of different advertising themes: a dynamic bayesian model of the advertising-sales relationship. Mark. Sci. **26**(2), 179–195 (2007)
6. Broder, A.: A taxonomy of web search. SIGIR Forum **36**(2), 3–10 (2002)
7. Chatterjee, P., Hoffman, D.L., Novak, T.P.: Modeling the clickstream: implications for web-based advertising efforts. Mark. Sci. **22**(4), 520–541 (2003)
8. Danaher, P.J., Mullarkey, G.: Factors affecting online advertising recall: a study of students. J. Advert. Res. **43**(3), 252–267 (2003)
9. Deleersnyder, B., Geyskens, I., Gielens, K., Dekimpe, M.G.: How cannibalistic is the internet channel? a study of the newspaper industry in the united kingdom and the Netherlands. Int. J. Res. Mark. **19**(4), 337–348 (2002). http://www.sciencedirect.com/science/article/B6V8R-473FW9H-3/2/6898e255f0f486b1df6be707a03c364a
10. Dinner, I.M., van Heerde, H.J., Neslin, S.A.: Driving online and offline sales: the cross-channel effects of digital versus traditional advertising (2011). http://ssrn.com/abstract=1955653
11. Ghose, A., Yang, S.: An empirical analysis of search engine advertising: sponsored search in electronic markets. Manage. Sci. **55**(10), 1605–1622 (2009)
12. Goldfarb, A., Tucker, C.: Standardization, standards and online advertising (2011). http://ssrn.com/abstract=1745645
13. Ilfeld, J.S., Winer, R.S.: Generating website traffic. J. Advert. Res. **42**(5), 49–61 (2002)
14. Lenk, P.J., DeSarbo, W.S., Green, P.E., Young, M.R.: Hierarchical bayes conjoint analysis: recovery of partworth heterogeneity from reduced experimental designs. Mark. Sci. **15**(2), 173–191 (1996). http://www.jstor.org/stable/184192
15. Naik, P.A., Peters, K.: A hierarchical marketing communications model of online and offline media synergies. J. Interact. Mark. **23**(4), 288–299 (2009)
16. Naik, P.A., Raman, K.: Understanding the impact of synergy in multimedia communications. J. Mark. Res. **40**(4), 375–388 (2003)
17. Neslin, S.A., Grewal, D., Leghorn, R., Shankar, V., Teerling, M.L., Thomas, J.S., Verhoef, P.C.: Challenges and opportunities in multichannel customer management. J. Serv. Res. **9**(2), 95–112 (2006)
18. Neslin, S.A., Shankar, V.: Key issues in multichannel customer management: current knowledge and future directions. J. Interact. Mark. **23**(1), 70–81 (2009)
19. Nottorf, F.: Modeling the clickstream across multiple online advertising channels using a binary logit with Bayesian mixture of normals. Electron. Commer. Res. Appl. **13**(1), 45–55 (2014). http://www.sciencedirect.com/science/article/pii/S1567422313000483
20. Nottorf, F., Funk, B.: A cross-industry analysis of the spillover effect in paid search advertising. Electron. Mark. **23**(3), 205–216 (2013). http://dx.doi.org/10.1007/s12525-012-0117-z

21. Nottorf, F., Funk, B.: The economic value of clickstream data from an advertiser's perspective. In: Proceedings of the 21th European Conference on Information Systems (ECIS), Utrecht, Netherlands 2013 (2013)
22. Rossi, P.E., Allenby, G.M., McCulloch, R.E.: Bayesian Statistics and Marketing. Wiley, Hoboken (2005)
23. Rutz, O.J., Bucklin, R.E.: Does banner advertising affect browsing for brands? clickstream choice model says yes, for some. Quant. Mark. Econ., pp. 1–27 (2011). http://dx.doi.org/10.1007/s11129-011-9114-3
24. Rutz, O.J., Bucklin, R.E., Sonnier, G.P.: A latent instrumental variables approach to modeling keyword conversion in paid search advertising. J. Mark. Res. **49**(3), 306–319 (2012). http://dx.doi.org/10.1509/jmr.10.0354
25. Rutz, O.J., Trusov, M., Bucklin, R.E.: Modeling indirect effects of paid search advertising: which keywords lead to more future visits? Mark. Sci. **30**(4), 646–665 (2011). http://dx.doi.org/10.1287/mksc.1110.0635
26. uniquedigital: Cross-channel management (2012). http://www.uniquedigital.de/downloads/whitepaper-unique-cross-channel-management
27. Way, H.: Real-time bidding: greasing the wheels of digital advertising (2012). http://www.ecommercetimes.com/story/76000.html
28. Wiesel, T., Pauwels, K., Arts, J.: Marketing's profit impact: quantifying online and off-line funnel progression. Mark. Sci. **30**(4), 604–611 (2011). doi:10.1287/mksc.1100.0612
29. Yoon, H.S., Lee, D.H.: The exposure effect of unclicked banner advertisements. Adv. Int. Mark. **7**(18), 211–229 (2007)

When Loyalty Points Become Virtual Currencies: Transforming Business Models for Online Platforms

Uschi Buchinger[(✉)], Heritiana Ranaivoson, and Pieter Ballon

iMinds-SMIT, Vrije Universiteit Brussel, Brussels, Belgium
uschi.buchinger@iminds.be,
{Heritiana.Renaud.Ranaivoson,
Pieter.Ballon}@vub.ac.be

Abstract. Information and Communication Technology is characterized by far-reaching platformisation that affects a wide range of online services. Platforms focalize principally on attracting, and locking-in, various stakeholders groups - and balancing interests of these - rather than on profit maximization in a single market. One option to reach this objective is the implementation of loyalty programs. But rather than a mere adoption of initial mechanisms, digital technology allows platforms to transform loyalty points in order to obtain Virtual Currency (VC), i.e. a tool to support multiple usage options granted to various users and utilizations throughout the value network. This paper enhances knowledge upon tendencies and trends of platform's VC strategies and the corresponding impacts on the business model. It reveals how the implementation of a VC affects a platform's gatekeeper position, the encouragement of loyalty of stakeholder groups and the opening of new income streams for the platform.

Keywords: Loyalty schemes · Virtual currency · Business models · Two-sided markets

1 Introduction

Platformisation is a far-reaching characterization of Information and Communication Technology (ICT) affecting numerous online services [1]. Mostly embedded in larger value networks, platforms build an essential component in mediating and coordinating various stakeholder constituencies, with or without providing own services on top of these activities. Platform's business models focus primarily on attracting, and locking-in of, various stakeholders groups and balancing interests of these groups rather than on profit maximisation in a single market [2].

Platforms' playing field is thus depicted as multi-sided, or, by grouping various stakeholders with similar interests, as at least two-sided markets [3].

An essential characteristic of such markets is the existence of network effects, i.e. utility derived from a good or service correlates to the number of users of this good or service [4]. Hence, platforms (acting as intermediates) need to find a balance supporting the aim to create two mutually equivalent antipoles.

© Springer-Verlag Berlin Heidelberg 2014
M.S. Obaidat and J. Filipe (Eds.): ICETE 2013, CCIS 456, pp. 126–141, 2014.
DOI: 10.1007/978-3-662-44788-8_8

Looking for ways to reinforce this strategic plus, platforms might utilize measures to encourage loyalty on both sides of the market up to lock-in of customers [5, 6]. Especially in the online environment, which is characterized by its low switching costs [7] and the culture of free services [8], such measures are increasingly important. Tailored programs to retain loyalty, now well established by several industries [9, 10], have proven their importance as strategic elements for raising customer retention and influencing the financial performance. One of the most common measures is the rewarding and redeeming of company-related loyalty points [11–14].

But platforms, seeking to implement such loyalty measures, clearly see a need for translation of conventional rewarding points programs to meet the requirements of the respective sectors.

Embedded in digital set-ups where platforms are operating, points loose their status of simple loyalty measures to become Virtual Currency (VC) which have potential to change the platforms' business economics. Contrasting plain loyalty points, VC provides a tool for multiple usage options for all entities in the two-sided market, e.g. by opening it to Third parties (retailers, merchants, commercial sellers) to purchase and reward the platform's VC to their customers.

Hence VC can not only foster loyalty of platform customers but can at the same time encourage Third parties to use the VC when addressing the customer base. Beyond, the currency is a valuable asset itself with potential to open revenue streams for the creator. Hence the option to expand gatekeeper power by purveying VC and deciding upon concessions and usage in the network stands to reason for the platform.

Little research has been conducted on Virtual Currency, in particular on how loyalty measures and strategies, embedded in a digital environment, transform to Virtual currency programs and how they can influence platforms' business models. Within its range of possibilities, VC impacts the edges of the network: the organizational, financial, service and technical design.

Based on four case studies, this paper analyses how online platforms have adopted, altered and/or expanded the initial model of loyalty programs and thus the impact on strengthening their gatekeeper position in the network, encouraging loyal behaviour one or both sides of the market and the opening of new income streams for the platform. Against this backdrop, the paper enhances knowledge about approaching tendencies and trends of platform's VC strategies and the corresponding objectives.

In the remainder of the paper, Sect. 2 describes the applied business model methodology. Section 3 explains loyalty points programs used by organizations have turned into VC used by platforms. Section 4 describes in detail how VC has been implemented in four case studies. Section 5 analyses the impact of a VC implementation by comparing business model parameters. Section 6 concludes and suggests ways for further research.

2 Methodology

The paper uses business modelling to examine variations of VC strategies and their impact on online platforms. More precisely, the platforms' value networks are analysed, i.e. the actors with which they interact, the roles of every actor (including the platforms themselves), and the relationships between them. Actually the platforms are positioned as intermediates between two markets and as purveyors of a dedicated VC. Based on the generic value network, alternative business model scenarios will be depicted and compared.

The paper relies on the business modelling framework developed by Ballon [15] (see also Braet and Ballon [16]) as it provides an holistic approach for the examination of network architectures. While there are several business model frameworks proposed in the literature, notably [17] or [18], these are suited for analysing individual firms rather than value networks.

Braet and Ballon [16] define the business modelling cycle as consisting of four parameters (see Fig. 1): organization, technology, service and finance.

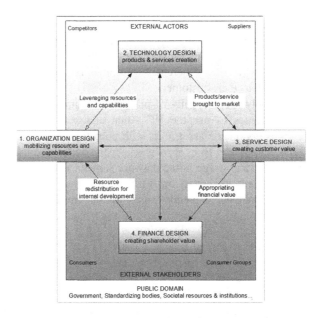

Fig. 1. The business model cycle (Source: [16]).

The organization design corresponds to the value network, i.e. a framework consisting of business actors (physical persons or corporations mobilizing tangible or intangible resources), roles (business processes fulfilled by one or more actors with according capabilities), relationships (the contractual exchanges of products or services for financial payments or other resources). The technology design includes aspects such as modularity, distribution of intelligence and interoperability. The service design refers to the intended customer value. Finally, the finance design includes issues related to costs and revenues.

Virtual Currency has potential to support platforms' objectives of acquiring stakeholders and impact revenue streams concurrently. The organizational and financial parameters are thus going to be extensively examined. This reflects directly in the service offer towards the customer. The technology design is taken as granted and therefore considered with less details in this paper.

3 The Development of VC Schemes on Two-Sided Markets

The section provides an overview of the bases of the succeeding analysis: (i) the particularities and consequences of operations on two-sided market and (ii) the transformation of loyalty concepts to VC fostered by the digital environment.

3.1 Platforms as the Hub of Two-Sided Markets

Information and Communication Technology (ICT) markets are characterized by far-reaching platformisation [1]. A platform can be defined as a product, technology or service that is an essential building block upon which an ecosystem of firms can develop complementary products or services [19]. In ICT markets, crucial gatekeeper roles and functionalities are often conducted by platform leaders. Various business models have emerged that help them to exercise a form of control over the network, and to add and capture value in the processes.

An essential characteristic of platforms is their operation on two-sided markets (or even more than two sides). Two-sided markets can be defined as all markets for which there are inter-group network externalities [20] i.e. the utility of any customer A is correlated to the number of customers B, and conversely. These models were first applied to credit card markets [21]. Actually on such markets, the higher the number of credit card holders, the more interesting it becomes for the shops to be equipped with devices that allow to pay by card. Contrariwise, the higher the number of equipped shops, the more utility one cardholder derives from having such a card [22]. Rochet and Tirole [3] determine various other platforms focusing on two-sides of a market such as software (videogame platforms, operating systems), portals and media platforms or payment systems.

The value network can thus be broken down to three actors building the base of each case study: the platform, the customer and the Third party. The platform mediates interactions between the two sides of the market. Figure 2 illustrates such markets in a simple value network. Relationships are displayed as arrows between the actors.

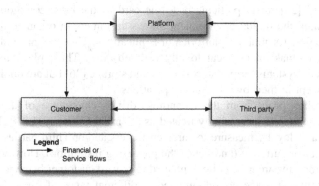

Fig. 2. A stylised representation of two-sided markets.

One of the commonly described obstacles for platforms is incorporating and retaining both sides of the market, not least because of exploiting the gatekeeper position for building financial relations. While one side of the market is often treated as a profit centre, it concurrently needs to cover the loss (or financial neutrality) that is accepted for the other side of the market [3].

It is hence a balancing act of attracting and keeping stakeholders (concretely encourage loyal behaviour or even enforce it by locking stakeholders in) and generating revenue. This is especially relevant for the online environment, which is characterized by its low switching costs [7] and the culture of free services [8]. On the other hand, it is also this environment that facilitates new concepts and concept combination and loyalty schemes are no exception to that.

3.2   Loyalty Points in Transition: Towards Coalition Loyalty and Virtual Currency

The paper follows Sharp and Sharp's [23] definition of loyalty program as "structured marketing efforts which reward, and therefore encourage, loyalty behaviour" [23, p. 474]. Different types of rewards have been developed throughout B2C sectors, notably the implementation of incentives such as points that are redeemable for rebates or prizes within the loyalty scheme [23, 24]. Organizations implement such measures to acquire competitive advantages and loyalty of customers. The latter is often substantiated by the argument of the positive influence on the financial performance and the higher value of customer retention compared to new customer acquisition [11, 13, 14]. Such programs however might become a standard within the industry, diminishing the competitive edge of rewards [10].

One possibility to counteract this tendency is to expand the industries or brands participating in the loyalty program, a method notably exploited by various airlines. The cooperation scheme, defined as coalition loyalty or cross loyalty, describes the facilitation of members' loyalty cards at multiple – sometimes competing – retailers. From a customer perspective, every industry or brand in the network adds incentives – and thus value – for the customer to join [25].

While Baird [25] refers particularly to the card as the most common form of a rewarding design, the digital environment allows customers to organize their loyalty programs on online (or mobile) platforms or applications. They can have all necessary functionalities to make a physical loyalty card obsolete. Thus, platforms not only develop adequate systems for points collection and storage [26] but are on the forefront to use the concept in their own business operations.

Moreover they profit from the technology-driven emergence of digital money where loyalty points are increasingly treated as a Virtual Currency. Like plain loyalty points, it acts as a loyalty measure towards customers and/or Third parties by binding them to a particular currency (and hence the purveying institution). However, whereas pure loyalty programs are mainly implemented to reward customer behaviour [12], VC are tools for multiple usage options granted to different types of users. In the value network representation, these usage options are called roles. This paper identifies eight possible roles bound to the Virtual Currency flows in the value network:

- **Create** (Platform): build up and coordinate the network around a VC
- **Sell** (Platform): Issuing VC in exchange of conventional money
- **Reward** (Platform, Third party): Issuing or awarding VC
- **Redeem** (Platform, Third party): Taking back VC, i.e. accepting it as a payment
- **Buy** (Third party, Customer): Purchase VC for conventional money
- **Store** (Third party, Customer): Accumulating and saving VC in personal or professional accounts or wallets.
- **Spend** (Customer): Using VC as payment instead/alongside conventional money
- **Get rewarded** (Customer): Conduct an activity that is awarded with VC

Some roles can be performed solely by one actor in the network while others can be performed by two or more types of actors. The platform is the creator and purveyor of the VC. It decides upon concession and usage in the network therefore it acts as a gatekeeper. Customers enter into a direct relationship with the platform (mainly by creating an online account or profile). Third parties encompass entities that sell products or services via the platform. They can be included into the VC program being eventually provided with Third party accounts or dashboards to manage the VC.

4 VC Implementation in Platform Schemes – Case Studies

The section provides a detailed study of four cases of platforms that have implemented a VC: Miles & More (Miles), Groupon (Groupon Bucks), Facebook (Facebook Credits), and Mobile Vikings (Vikings Points). They were selected based on their different implementation strategies and thus the multiple options ascribed to VC implementation. The diversity of the platforms that adopted VC and their related business models allow drawing conclusions for trends and tendencies in this area.

Whereas their basic value network is consistent (platforms intermediating two-sided markets), the differentiation is made in the implementation strategy of VC. Platforms follow different strategies with the implementation, such as strengthening their gatekeeper position in the network, encouraging loyal behaviour up to lock-in of one or both sides of the market or opening new income streams.

Actors conduct roles that emerge from daily operations plus additional roles that are related to the VC. They are illustrated as white boxes in the following figures and are reduced to two representative roles for each actor: one for product/services (platform and Third parties provide them, customers receive them) and VC operations (platform creates/manages the VC, Third parties and customers participate).

Relationships and VC flows are displayed as arrows in the value network. Black arrows indicate financial streams; dotted arrows indicate product/service streams (selling and receiving of products or services), grey arrows depict the VC stream. Relations are either bidirectional (exchange between actors) or monodirectional (from one actor to another). The following sections continues with the various use cases.

4.1 Miles

The native intention of the Miles & More program, implemented by the German airline Lufthansa, is to raise customer loyalty towards the airline. The extension of the VC (here: miles) to Third parties increases its value for customers. The platform targets both sides of the market: Miles are rewarded to the customer and sold to Third parties (e.g. banks, retailers, hotels). Miles are valid 36 month of the date of accrual and expire at the end of the respective quarter [27]. In 2011, 20 million members from 234 countries participated in the program, with 250 partners [28].

Figure 3 illustrates the value network with the financial-, product/service- (in the figure, if not specified, abbreviated with <prod./serv.>) and VC flow.

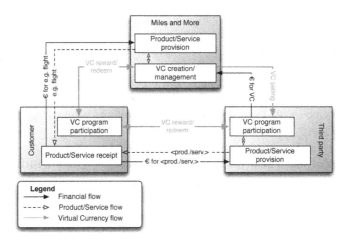

Fig. 3. Miles & More value network.

Miles & More as well as Third parties sell products or services to customers. A purchase initiates the rewarding of VC (e.g. for a flight or a Third party product). The VC stream is bidirectional between platform and customer and customer and Third party (both partners can reward and redeem the VC) and monodirectional between the platform and Third parties. Third parties buy the miles that they reward to the customers. Payment agreements with the platform must apply [29]. Miles can theoretically be purchased from the platform, but these, unlike rewarded ones, can only be used for an immediate redemption (a flight or service provided by the airline (not by a Third party). Hence they diverge from the standard and are thus not considered further).

Contractual agreements regulate the use of VC between the platform and the Third party. The platform cedes control by allowing Third parties to reward and redeem miles. Third parties are largely free in their decisions upon applying terms and conditions (e.g. one mile for every Euro spent). It is possible that the customers gathers and redeems miles only from/for Third party services without any flight purchase.

4.2 Groupon Bucks

Groupon Bucks intend mainly to reinforce customers' loyalty. Groupon is an online group-buying platform that allows Third parties to sell products and services to customers at a discounted price that can be set by the means of economies of scale emerging form group buying. Registered customers are given the possibility to subscribe for offers (called deals) that are validated once enough customers have subscribed. The platform does not provide products or services itself but it relies on Third party services. However, financial movements pass via the platform. The revenue model consists of a fee taken by the platform on every deal sold by a Third party. Customers receive the actual products or services directly from the Third party [30]. Figure 4 displays the flows in the value network.

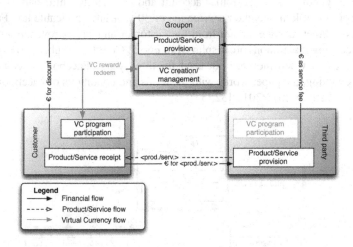

Fig. 4. Groupon value network.

The most common way for the customer to receive Groupon Bucks is conducting a qualifying user activity (e.g. referring someone to Groupon who then conducts a purchase on the platform). The VC is automatically transferred and stored on the customer account and redeemed for any deal purchased at the platform. Bucks can additionally be bought in form of gift cards e.g. to present to other customers. Bucks are restricted to the Groupon platform only, and can be spend on any deal. However, Third parties are not incorporated in the VC. Groupon Bucks do not expire [30].

4.3 Facebook Credits

Facebook Credits act as a loyalty measure towards Third parties; in addition they constitute a source of revenue for the platform as well as for the Third parties. Credits are studied in this paper in the light of game applications.

Launched in 2004, the free platform Facebook has gathered more than 1 billion active users in 2012 [31]. Since 2007, Third party developers can provide apps, including games, via the platform within which they can offer virtual items for sale. Facebook however sets restrictions for the selling activities, making their VC Facebook Credits the obligatory payment mechanism.

While the platform creates and operates the main service and the game embedding, it relies mainly on Third parties for the providing of complementary offering of game apps. Facebook allows its customers to use the Third party services via customer accounts where Credits are stored. Credits can be bought preliminary to -, or whilst playing and are redeemed in games hosted by the platform. If a customer purchases in-game items in a Third party game hosted on the platform, actually he/she buys Facebook Credits that are automatically converted into the requested item. In other words, customers think they buy the virtual item whilst in fact they buy Facebook Credits. Monetary transactions are conducted by the platform who (i) returns each transaction in Credits to the customer account and (ii) credits Third parties with the proceeds from the sale minus their service fee of 30 % + any applicable tax. Facebook thus creates a direct revenue stream from the customer and shares revenue with Third parties. According illustrations are displayed in Fig. 5. Credits are subject to expiration, which takes effect when they are not used for three years. Facebook Credits' use is constantly evolving, the paper works with the terms and conditions of Facebook credits they were in place in 2011/2012 [32, 33].

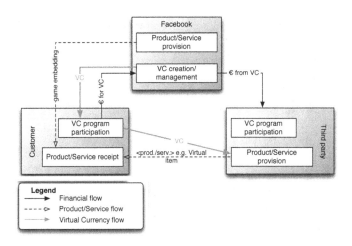

Fig. 5. Facebook value network.

The compulsory VC scheme locks in Third parties (here: game developers) who want to address and sell in-game items to the customer base of Facebook. Customers are locked-in likewise since they can solely play Third party games and buy items via Facebook's platform and VC system.

Apart from purchases, Facebook, in partnership with TrialPay, has implemented a mechanism to reward customers for conducting qualifying user activities (e.g. completing advertiser's offers). This service is meant to attract Third parties that are not game developers but see value in rewarding their customers in Credits [32–34].

4.4 Viking Points

The MVNO (mobile virtual network operator) Mobile Vikings has implemented (Mobile) Viking Points as a rewarding and loyalty measure towards its customers. Additionally they incite Third parties to use this VC thus contributing to customers' loyalty towards both, themselves and the platform. Active in Belgium and the Netherlands, Mobile Vikings sell mobile services such as call minutes, SMS and data packages on Viking SIM cards. Instead of purchasing them for conventional money, Viking Points can be exchanged for these mobile services. For this purpose, Mobile Vikings provides a platform to their customers to organize and manage the VC, create a personal profile or mapping their current location on a virtual map. Since it is however mentioned, that the customer is free to use the VC whenever he wants, it can be assumed, no expiration date is set [35–37]. The flows of product/services, money and VC between the entities are illustrated in Fig. 6.

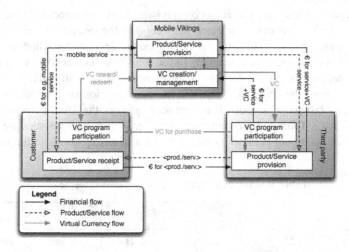

Fig. 6. Mobile Vikings value network.

Comparable to Groupon Bucks and Facebook Credits, Viking Points can be rewarded for certain qualifying user activities (e.g. convincing someone to join Mobile Vikings). Moreover, Viking Points can be bought in form of gift cards mainly as a present for other users. Solely the platform provides the services/products that customers get in exchange for the VC, i.e. its various mobile services, Third parties can not redeem it.

Mobile Vikings incorporate Third parties insofar as they allowing them to register their outlets or shops, thus creating a "spot" on a virtual map provided by the platform for their users. While this service is free, Mobile Vikings offer a product bundle for € 375 (VAT incl.) per year to Third parties, which allows them to add deals connected to the spot. With the bundle, Third parties receive 3000 Viking Points that they must reward their customers with every concluded deal (in Fig. 6 this is illustrated as a VC stream from the VC participation of the Third party to the customer). Third parties can however decide upon the creation and exact configuration of deals that the customers can conduct [35–37].

5 Market Trend Analysis of Virtual Currency Streams

The section compares the cases studied previously to analyse the impact of VC on business models. The cases were chosen for their coverage of a variety of platform solutions, and pursuits of different VC strategies. The paper therefore refrains from drawing general conclusions but identifies trends and tendencies that affect the use of loyalty schemes and VC. Following the business model cycle [15, 16], business models are analysed following four sets of parameters – organization, technology, service and finance. The technological parameters are considered as given and therefore outside the scope of the analysis.

Seven characteristics are subject to comparison. They can directly be linked up to one or more business model parameters: the side(s) of the market on which the VC is oriented; whether the platform itself provides goods or services for which the VC can be redeemed; the strength of enforcement to use the VC in the network; whether Third parties also redeem the VC; if the scheme rewards customer; if the platform generates revenue by selling the VC and if the VC has an expiration date (financial design). For the second last point, a trade-off is necessary between the Third parties (T.P.) and customers (Cust.). Table 1 depicts an overview over which characteristics are ascribed to which business model parameters and their respective executions in the use cases.

Table 1. Characteristics of business model strategies.

		Miles and More		Groupon		Facebook		Mobile Vikings	
Organization design	Orientation of the VC scheme	two sides		one side		two sides		two sides	
Organization and service design	Multifaceted redemption	Y		N		Y		N	
	Enforcement to use VC	Weak		Weak		Strong towards both sides		Strong towards Third Parties	
Service design	Platform provides services/products	Y		N		N		Y	
	Option of rewarding Cust.	Y		Y		Y (with a partner)		Y	
Financial design	Direct Revenue Platform	T.P.	Cust.	T.P.	Cust.	T.P.	Cust.	T.P.	Cust.
		Y	N	N	Y	N	Y	Y	Y
	Expiration	Y		N		Y		N	

Before the analysis of each parameter can be made, this paper already revealed a general increase in the range of roles that accompanies the VC implementation. VC is subject to selling, rewarding, redeeming, creating, buying, spending, getting rewarded and storing by one or more actors in the value network.

The first result is the opening of the loyalty scheme to both sides of the market, as shown in the first line of Table 1 (Orientation of the VC scheme). Here the term "two sides" signifies the issuance of VC (rewarding or selling) to both sides of the market: customers and Third parties. Three of the use cases exert the option to include the second side of the market into the VC program. To establish a balance in the long term, they might primarily try to obtain a critical mass of users on one side of the market. Miles & More and Mobile Vikings concentrate VC measures primarily on the customer-side. A broad user base serves as an argument to get Third parties on board to equally use the VC. Facebook targets principally the Third parties to implement VC standards and concurrently locks customers in. Although platforms control concession and usage and restrict allowances, with the incorporating Third parties, the platform cedes control over the VC program and thus their customer relationship. Only Groupon addresses solely the customer side. It resembles more standard loyalty schemes that are tailored to a single company. The platform profits from boundlessness in decision-making and execution of VC-related measures; they do not require consultation or alignment with other parties and it does not cede power over customer ownership. As a consequence the options for the customers are more limited.

Multifaceted redemption describes the possibility to redeem points at a variety of actors including the platform and the Third parties. Variety can be given throughout industries or within such (e.g. different execution of games for Facebook). Redemption (like rewarding) has an impact on the customer relationship and the intended value. Every additional Third party that redeems the VC enlarges the choices for the customer, and hence the perceived value of the VC. Consequently, platforms need to make a trade-off between single (here: Mobile Vikings and Groupon), or multifaceted redemption (Miles & More, Facebook). Single redemption strategies lower the value for the customer but guarantee for the platform a greater control over customer loyalty. In contrast, multifaceted redemption requires that the platform cede more control to Third parties, which however increases the value for the customer in return.

The second aspect of the organization and service design is the enforcement to use the VC in the network. It is weak when no or only loose obligations are set for the usage and participation is optional (Miles & More and Groupon). In case of obligations, they can affect both sides (Facebook) or one side (Mobile Vikings) of the market. Facebook developers need to use the payment schemes if they want to sell virtual items while customers must use the VC for purchases. Mobile Vikings' Third parties are obliged to reward the VC to every customer.

A fourth characteristic of platforms is whether platforms provide their own products/services on top of their platform activity. Those who do (here: flights in the Miles & More program, and mobile services from Mobile Vikings) are less dependent on the Third parties' performance. Their VC is valuable for the customer even without the other side of the market. Additionally customers may be more aware of products/services they can receive in exchange for VC, the redemption mechanisms and the distribution channels. For platforms that do not provide own products/services (Groupon and Facebook), the VC has only as much value as the Third parties create. The platform is more dependent on the Third parties' capacity and willingness to fulfil their engagements. Platforms face increased risks due to the unpredictability of the Third parties' products and services to cover the demands of the market in the long term. If the Third parties fail, the VC loses its value.

The fifth characteristic is the option of rewarding customers for desired user actions. It is based on the report that attaining benefits from rewards is the principal motivating factor for customers subscribing to – initially - loyalty programs [38]. It remains a consistency throughout all cases. This aspect shows the connection to the initial loyalty schemes that fosters customer involvement.

Influencing the financial parameter, VC can constitute a direct source of revenue for some platforms on top of their principal revenue models, albeit, the principal intention of most platforms remains the rewarding of VC for qualifying user activities (which should reflect indirectly in increased revenue). However, selling VC to the customers in form of gift cards applies also as a possibility. In most cases, the platforms choose either side of the market for deriving revenues with the VC. Miles & More generate revenue from Third parties that pay for the VC, which is then used to reward their customers. In this case, Third parties need to compensate the expenses, e.g. by increased price or additional sales. Facebook sell the VC to customers, by making it the obligatory payment method for buying in-game items. Revenue that emerges from selling VC is shared between the Third party and the platform. Miles & More and Mobile Vikings allow the former to decide on conversion rates, terms and conditions for VC, nonetheless, Third parties cannot sell VC (and generate revenue).

The final parameter, which belongs to the financial design, is the expiration date. Unused VC that expires does not require an exchange in products/services from the platform or Third party and thus represents income for the respective business Miles & More and Facebook implemented expiration dates, both setting a valid period of three years before the implemented terms and conditions take effect.

The counterpart of using VC as a source of revenue is nevertheless that it can slow its adoption process by Third parties or customers. The higher the fee (e.g. per transaction using VC), the less interesting for the customer to use the VC. The platform is thus required to invest in- and provide adequate, competitive applications that are able to support the conduction of all roles allowed to the other entities in the market.

6   Conclusion

Based on the business model approach developed by Ballon [15], (see also Braet and Ballon [16]) the paper has analysed the implementation of Virtual Currency schemes by online platforms. Value networks were represented, which illustrated the interplays between three types of actors: platforms, customers and Third parties (i.e. partners that sell products or services via the platform). The platform mediates the two sides of the market in terms of service and financial flows but also by the implementation of a Virtual Currency. Four cases were analysed in detail: Miles & More (Miles), Groupon (Groupon Bucks), Facebook (Facebook Credits), and Mobile Vikings (Vikings Points). The case studies were compared upon seven characteristics that are directly linked to organisation, service and financial design of the business models. Each case followed a different strategy, which prevents the drawing of general conclusions. Nonetheless, some findings derive from the comparison.

Loyalty schemes, embedded in a digital environment, have transformed into VC schemes allowing the two sides of the market – mediated by a platform – a broader range of options for using VC. While VC answers in its basic functionalities the same purposes as loyalty points, namely rewarding desirable (loyal) customer behaviour, it expands its roles towards multiple usage options granted to different types of users.

Second, loyalty schemes can be opened to both sides of the market, rather than limited to the customers. The realization ranges from weak measures, where VC is handled as benefit or bonus program, to strong measures where loyalty is enforced by usage obligations in the network. The VC can in some cases be redeemed at the Third parties and at the platform, rather than only at the platform, which has an impact on the perceived value for the customer. Platforms must have own products/services in return for VC and are therefore less dependent on the Third parties' performance.

Third the analysis revealed that all platforms use the VC as a source of revenue, albeit to a different extent. Purchasing VC can either be an additional option granted to customers or obligatory for customers or Third parties. In line with the two-sided market theory, in the examples where both sides are included, revenue can be generated on one side of the market while the other one is included for free (with the option to buy VC made available as incentive).

In spite of this trend towards a greater diversification of the usage options related to VC, the paper has finally shown that – based on the selected set of examples - the implementation of the VC requires some consistency in the roles. Thus, the platform creates, coordinates and decides upon a VC program and owns a customer base. The latter is in direct interaction with the platform because of the platform's own - and/or the Third parties' products/services that are accessible via the platform.

In summary, being purveyor and owner of the VC, the platforms can decide upon how they make use of their bottleneck position, notably by defining which roles are allowed in the VC program and under which conditions. It can be concluded that VC has the necessary attributes to support platforms strategies in their service and financial design by encouraging loyal behaviour and opening a source of revenue.

The authors acknowledge that industries are still in an early phase of experimenting with new business models concerning VC strategies, in particular with mobile devices opening up new possibilities. Further research is thus required reflecting the market development and new entities in this field, also from a technical point of view.

Acknowledgements. CoMobile is a R&D project cofounded by IWT (Agentschap voor Innovatie door Wetenschap en Technologie), the government agency for innovation by science and technology founded by the Flemish Government. Companies and organizations involved in the project are C2P–ClearPark, Alcatel-Lucent, Netlog, CityLive–Mobile Vikings, Colibri, BDMA, K.U.Leuven/COSIC, K.U.Leuven/CUO, K.U.Leuven/ICRI, UGent/MICT, iMinds/iLab.o.

References

1. Ballon, P.: The platformisation of the european mobile industry. Commun. Strat. **75**, 15–33 (2009)
2. Cortade, T.: A strategic guide on two-sided markets applied to the ISP market. Commun. Strat. **61**(1), 17–35 (2006)
3. Rochet, J.C., Tirole, J.: Platform competition in two-sided markets. J. Eur. Econ. Assoc. **1**(4), 990–1029 (2002)
4. Varian, H.R.: Introduction à la microéconomie, 4th edn. De Boeck Université, Bruxelles (2000)
5. Balabanis, G., Reynolds, N., Simintiras, A.: Bases of e-store loyalty: perceived switching barriers and satisfaction. J. Bus. Res. **59**(2), 214–224 (2006)
6. Ranaweera, C., Prabhu, J.: On the relative importance of customer satisfaction and trust as determinants of customer retention and positive word of mouth. J. Target. Meas. Anal. Mark. **12**(1), 82–90 (2003)
7. Shimizu, K.: The Cores of Strategic Management. Routledge, New York (2012)
8. Anderson, C.: Free: The Future of a Radical Price. Random House, London (2009)
9. O'Malley, L.: Can loyalty schemes really build loyalty? Mark. Intell. Plan. **16**(1), 47–55 (1998)
10. Palmer, A., Mcmahon-Beattie, U., Beggs, R.: Influences on loyalty programme effectiveness: a conceptual framework and case study investigation. J. Strat. Mark. **8**(1), 47–66 (2000)
11. Christopher, M., Payne, A., Ballantyne, D.: Relationship Marketing. CRC Press, Oxford (2008)
12. Kumar, V., Shah, D.: Building and sustaining profitable customer loyalty for the 21st century. J. Retail. **80**(4), 317–330 (2004)
13. Reichheld, F.F., Sasser, E.W.: Zero defections: quality comes to services. Harward Bus. Rev. **14**(3), 497–507 (1990)
14. Webster, F.E.: The changing role of marketing in the corporation. J. Mark. **56**(4), 1–17 (1992)
15. Ballon, P.: Business modelling revisited: the configuration of control and value. Info **9**(5), 6–19 (2007)
16. Braet, O., Ballon, P.: Business Model Scenarios for remote management. J. Theor. Appl. Electron. Commer. Res. **2**(3), 62–79 (2007)
17. Chesbrough, H.W.: Open Business Models: How to Thrive In The New Innovation Landscape. Harvard Business Press, Boston (2006)
18. Osterwalder, A.: The Business Model Ontology: A Proposition in a Design Science Approach. HEC, Lausanne (2004)
19. Gawer, A., Cusumano, M.A.: Platform Leadership: How Intel, Microsoft, and Cisco Drive Industry Innovation, 1st edn. Harvard Business Review Press, Boston (2002)
20. Armstrong, M.: Competition in two-sided markets. RAND J. Econ. **37**(3), 668–691 (2006)
21. Rochet, J.C., Tirole, J.: Cooperation among competitors: some economics of payment card associations. The RAND J. Econ. **33**(4), 549–570 (2002)
22. European Central Bank: Virtual Currency Schemes. Frankfurt am Main (2012)
23. Sharp, B., Sharp, A.: Loyalty programs and their impact on repeat-purchase loyalty patterns. Int. J. Res. Mark. **14**(5), 473–486 (1997)
24. Dowling, G.R., Uncles, M.: Do customer loyalty programs really work? Sloan Manage. Rev. **38**, 71–82 (1997)
25. Baird, N.: Coalition loyalty programs: the next big thing? Chain Store Age **83**(7), 14 (2007)

26. Perez, S.: PassRocket Lets Any Business Create Loyalty Cards For Apple's New Passbook App for Free, TechCrunch (2012). http://techcrunch.com/2012/09/19/passrocket-lets-any-business-create-loyalty-cards-for-apples-new-passbook-app-for-free/. Accessed 02 Oct 2012
27. Miles & More. http://www.miles-and-more.com/online/portal/mam_com/de/homepage. Accessed 06 Feb 2013
28. Lufthansa, Lufthansa Press Releases, Miles & More: 20 million members (2011). http://presse.lufthansa.com/en/news-releases/singleview/archive/2011/february/11/article/1875.html. Accessed 03 Jul 2012
29. Mason, G., Barker, N.: Buy now fly later: an investigation of airline frequent flyer programmes. Tour. Manag. **17**(3), 219–223 (1996)
30. Groupon (2012). http://www.groupon.com. Accessed 26 Jul 2012
31. The Associated Press: Hits and misses in Facebook history over the years, The Big Story (2013). http://bigstory.ap.org/article/hits-and-misses-facebook-history-over-years. Accessed 03 Feb 2013
32. Facebook Sign Up (2013). https://www.facebook.com/. Accessed 06 Feb 2013
33. Facebook Developers (2013). http://developers.facebook.com/. Accessed 06 Feb 2013
34. Kincaid, J.: Facebook To Make 'Facebook Credits' Mandatory For Game Developers (Confirmed), TechCrunch (2011). http://techcrunch.com/2011/01/24/facebook-to-make-facebook-credits-mandatory-for-game-developers/. Accessed 31 Oct 2012
35. CityLive NV, VikingSpots (2012). https://vikingspots.com/en/. Accessed 06 Feb 2013
36. Mobile Vikings Home (2013). https://mobilevikings.com/bel/en/. Accessed 06 Feb 2013
37. Mobile Vikings: What are Viking Points? (2013). https://mobilevikings.com/bel/en/vikingpoints/. Accessed 06 Feb 2013
38. Kumar, V., Reinartz, W.: Customer Relationship Management: Concept, Strategy, and Tools, 2nd edn. Springer, Heidelberg (2012)

Digital Cities Web Marketing Strategies in Italy: The Path Towards Citizen Empowerment

Elena Bellio[(⊠)] and Luca Buccoliero

CERMES, Department of Marketing, Bocconi University,
Via Roentgen 1, 20136 Milan, Italy
{elena.bellio,luca.buccoliero}@unibocconi.it

Abstract. The concept of 'digital city' has been introduced as a strategic way of designing a city by highlighting, in particular, the importance of Information and Communication Technologies. Nowadays the performance of our cities depends only in small part on its infrastructure, as an increasing importance is given to the availability, quality and delivery of public services. In this context, citizens have new expectations based on involvement, collaboration and participation. The aim in managing a city becomes making citizens actors in the decision making process creating engagement and involvement, providing ways of direct relationships with politicians and civil servants.

This paper attempts on the one hand to assess the web strategies of Italian municipalities to see their level of "citizen empowerment" by adopting a revised version of the Citizens Web Empowerment Index (CWEI) designed to benchmark administrations' official web portals – and on the other hand, to present some best practices: initiatives which, according to the CWEI, allow the creation of empowerment by answering at citizens' needs.

The analysis was made on the web portals of the 104 Italian cities with over 60,000 inhabitants in 2012 and 2013. Results show a low level of the indicator which testifies that the path towards citizen empowerment is still long. Despite this, the good examples spread around the country allow to believe in a close future where marketing strategies will be more and more oriented towards empowerment creation.

Keywords: Citizens · CWEI · Empowerment · Italy · Participation · Public administrations · Smartcities · Web 2.0 · Web portals

1 Introduction

A frequently adopted definition states that a digital city may be called 'smart' "when investments in human and social capital and traditional (transport) and modern (ICT) communication infrastructure fuel sustainable economic growth and a high quality of life, with a wise management of natural resources, through participatory government" [1]. According with Schaeffers et al. [2], this holistic definition balances different economic and social demands as well as the needs implied in urban development and this characterization implicitly builds upon the role of the Internet and Web 2.0 as

© Springer-Verlag Berlin Heidelberg 2014
M.S. Obaidat and J. Filipe (Eds.): ICETE 2013, CCIS 456, pp. 142–159, 2014.
DOI: 10.1007/978-3-662-44788-8_9

potential enablers of urban welfare creation through social participation, for addressing hot societal challenges.

Moving from this perspective, how to assess and benchmark the web strategies of digital cities in term of their "citizen empowerment" effectiveness? How to measure the "smartness" of the "empowerment effectiveness" in Italian Municipalities? Are Italian Municipalities ready to face the smartcity challenge?

Citizen empowerment represents one of the major challenges that public systems face today and citizens are the bearers of new demands, which include:

- access to official, customized and "on demand" information and services;
- new opportunities for direct and informal relationships with politicians and civil servants;
- willingness to be "active players" within the network, also by sharing their own problems and complaints with others and seeking information on experiences of others with the same problems; Web 2.0 logic [3] has considerably amplified this latter development [4].

As web sites and portals are the strategic tool needed to meet this growing empowerment demand, their design has moved from a technology-centric vision to a content-centric one and, more recently, to a citizen-centric approach [5].

The impact of ICT on urban environments governance and planning is typically linked with challenging problems. A successful city must balance social, economic and environmental needs but it should also put the needs of its citizens at the forefront of all its planning activities. A "smartcity" makes conscious efforts to adopt innovative ICT-based solutions to improve conditions of living and working and to support a more inclusive, and sustainable urban environment. The strategy is built on the principles to use technologies to improve the City and to empower its citizens by making them active players in the decision making process. In the Web 2.0 age, Internet represents the key tool of this strategy [4].

This paper describes a methodological framework for the assessment of citizen empowerment provided by municipalities' web sites and analyses the trend of citizen web empowerment in a sample of Italian municipalities in the years 2012 and 2013. In Sect. 2, a review of relevant literature is shown. In Sect. 3, the research framework and results are presented. In Sect. 4, some managerial implications of the study and future research developments are discussed.

2 Background and Related Works

According with Richards [6], Web communication platforms, such as blogs, wikis, and social networks have allowed average users to change from passive receivers of information to active producers of information [7]. These tools and the ways that they have empowered individuals to take control of their Internet experiences have been categorized as Web 2.0 technology [8].

Tim O'Reilly has first attempted to provide a clear definition of web 2.0: *"Web 2.0 is the business revolution in the computer industry caused by the move to the Internet as a platform, and an attempt to understand the rules for success on that new platform.*

Chief among those rules is this: "Build applications that harness network affects to get better the more people use them" [9]".
The identified key points are:

1. User participation: the web should be the medium that enables its users to participate and share information. The services offered are developed under the open-source paradigm, where users' interaction is a source of development and growth for the site.
2. Transformation of data ('remixability'): 'Remixability' stems from the desire of users and developers to be able to use and share information and then process and change it by developing new concepts and ideas.
3. Design centered on the user's needs.

It is increasingly important to understand not only how Web 2.0 tools work, but also how the sharing and distribution of information through these tools can promote civic engagement [7].

It has been a long time since public administrations have begun to investigate the potential of Web 2.0 to improve service delivery, democratic responsiveness and citizen participation [10]. According with European Commission [11]: *"public sector institutions are beginning to recognise the need to shift to services that are closer to people's everyday lives, to use innovative tools to reach citizens and to better engage employees and to share information and knowledge within and between organisations [12]. Also, public institutions are increasingly making use of collective intelligence and user-generated content to encourage real-time interaction and facilitate participation [13] Social Computing-enabled governance mechanisms could enhance collaboration within government agencies and interaction with stakeholders, transforming processes into more user-centric, cost-effective solutions and bringing public value to end-users [14, 15]".*

A recent study [16] emphasizes that the current objective is to provide online services customized to match users' profiles and requirements, and to personalize the relationships users have with public institutions. The emergence of Web 2.0 and rise of social networks have revealed new perspectives that challenge public institutions. These institutions are particularly attentive to the possibilities of taking advantage of these tools in the context of e-government.

Given these trends, business models and governance modes must necessarily adapt and sometimes be rethought. Public organizations are not immune to these developments, and the e-government 2.0 concept refers to specific applications of social media in the sphere of public services [17].

The annual meeting of the Gov2.0 Summit has brought together figures from the U.S. administration and some researchers to discuss experiments, problems and questions concerning e-government 2.0 implementation since 2009. Few recent academic publications tackle explicitly e-government 2.0 and the problems it raises: in Niehaves' paper [18], specific applications of the concept in the process management field; in Nam's study [19], the adoption of e-government 2.0 by citizens; or in Scholl's paper [20] factors that promote openness, collaboration and citizen participation.

Several papers have been published on web site quality evaluation methodology [21–26]. Many of these publications offer frameworks containing groups of quality dimensions that are similar to the SERVQUAL (Service Quality) model proposed by Parasuraman [27]. Also some publications have proposes evaluation methodologies for specific web sites such as e-government web sites [28, 29] hotel web sites [30], online library web sites [31, 32], and health care web sites [21, 33, 34]. Recently, Kuo [35] has presented a new point of view by integrating quality function deployment aspects into web site quality assessment methodology.

In a number of publications, quantitative methods for Web site quality evaluation are used. Statistical methods are the most widely used assessment tool [24, 26, 36, 37].

3 The Research

3.1 Citizen Web Empowerment Index

In this study, we combine both service and web site quality assessment methodologies by adopting an index named "Citizen Web Empowerment Index" (CWEI) [4, 38, 39], whose components are listed in Table 1.

Table 1. CWEI components (adapted by [38, 39]).

	Sub-indicator	Assesses variables
CWEI	E-information	Government structure
		Segmentation or life event
		Contact details
		Policies, procedures
		Budget
		Council minutes
		Newsletter and/or web magazine
	Web tools & strategies	Blog and Forum
		Chat
		Social networks
		Mobile services
		Web TV
		Open data strategy
		Web strategy evaluation EGRI (UN, 2008)
	E-consultation	On-line polls, surveys
		On-line complaints
		Reputation systems
		Mayor's direct on-line relation with citizens
	E-decision making process	Evidence that the opinion of citizens is considered
		Evidence of other complaints

Our study attempts to extend previous empirical research to understand and to measure the degree of citizen web empowerment in local Italian governments' portals by developing and index for benchmarking citizens' empowerment through web portals (CWEI).

The baseline research hypothesis is that the information and services provided by local governments via the web are capable of enhancing citizen empowerment regarding two key dimensions: information held by citizens and control of the information with respect to his/her needs.

The various typologies of web information which allow evaluation of the level of e-participation were used to develop an indicator by means of which ratings could be given for the websites of all the cities considered. This indicator, CWEI, is given by the aggregation of four components, each of which is calculated on the basis of the presence of certain elements characterizing the structure of the website considered (during the stage of quantitative determination, the value 1 was ascribed to the presence of the service or of the information considered, value 0 to absence). The maximum theoretical value is 100 while each sub-indicator has a different theoretical value:

CWEI =e-information + web tools & strategies + e-consultation + e-decision making process

During spring 2012 and spring 2013, the indicator was used to assess the websites of local Italian governments with populations over 60,000 inhabitants (104 cities assessed even if from 2012 to 2013 the number decreased to 102); the aim was to arrive at certain assessments of the current state of maturity of their web strategy in relation to their potential to increase citizens' empowerment.

Analysis and rating of sites was based on two fundamental criteria:

- the immediacy with which information or services can be obtained while navigating the site, without impediments and time-consuming procedures coming into play when attempting to access information or services;
- systematic (as opposed to sporadic) presence of the information or services required from the site.

CWEI, as pointed out in Table 1, is a multidimensional indicator because it is composed of a series of sub-indicators the objective of which is the measurement of various aspects of citizen participation via the web.

*The first sub-indicator has been termed **E-information**. It relates to the presence on the website of some general information regarding the city and its policies.*

Assessment was conducted on a number of these characteristics: the presence of a city politician list, considering if there are only name and surnames or a wider range of details in order to contact the municipality officials. Clear presentation of the city government organizational structure was also assessed since it is considered as an important way of orientation among the total number of services provided. The on-line availability of policies, procedures and legislation also helps. The last element considered in this sub indicator is the on-line presence of the budget and the way it is addressed.

The second component of the indicator consists of **Web tools & strategies**. It refers to the existence of social networking applications made for a high level of citizen participation - empowerment. However not only was the presence of the main instruments assessed (e.g. forums, blogs, newsletters, Facebook, Twitter, Flickr, YouTube), also specific services provided through mobile were included. The presence of "open data" and "GIS" strategy was also considered as an interesting element that makes a difference to citizens.

To construct sub-indicator **E-consultation**, various elements relative to the way of exchanging information with citizens were considered as reputation systems, online polls or e-surveys, and on-line complaints. Also the direct relation between citizens and the mayor was evaluated by searching for the presence of direct on-line involvement of citizens.

The fourth component of the indicator is termed **E-decision making process**. This sub-indicator assesses evidence that the municipality considers the opinion of citizens in decision making processes and provides evidence as to what decisions have been taken starting from the consultation process (e.g. publication of on-line pools, e-surveys results and subsequent actions taken) [4].

3.2   Cwei Assessment 2012–2013

The evaluation task was randomly assigned to two coders (the authors). The intercoder reliability of each CWEI sub-indicator was tested on a 20-site subset using Krippendorff's alpha coefficient [40].

Overall, use of the CWEI rating system was found to be highly reliable in the two annual evaluations (Table 2).

Table 2. Intercoder reliability (Krippendorf's alpha values for the sub-indicators, yearly subset n = 20).

CWEI Sub-indicator	α 2012	α 2013
CWEI E-information	0.9714	0.9797
CWEI WEB Tools and strategies	0.9552	0.9765
CWEI E-consultation	0.9509	0.9412
CWEI E-decision making process	0.9009	0.9319

When looking at the CWEI values, we observe that none of the surveyed websites has reached a score close to the maximum theoretical value of 100; in fact the average CWEI value was 37.30 in 2012 and 40.24 in 2013. A moderate increase was registered during the last year but the value is still low, this testifies that it is hard to find local governments which have developed web-based strategies oriented toward information and user participation.

Considering the average CWEI values per sub-indicators (Table 3), a little increase among the two years of analysis can be noticed, but the score order remains unvaried. The higher value is E-information; this does not surprise since it is the only component of the index which stands in the middle between a traditional website structure and a participatory one. On the contrary, the lowest level is registered by E-decision making process sub-indicator. This demonstrates that the awareness of local governments on the potentials of the web is only partial; in fact the tools for citizen participation in many cases exist (for example forms that allow problems to be reported very easily on-line, polls to evaluate initiatives, etc.), but what is missing is something that makes citizens aware that they have been taken into account, something that gives evidence on how a citizen's opinion was used in the decision making process, something that develops e-participation to empower citizens.

Table 3. Average CWEI values by sub-indicators.

Average CWEI sub-indicator values	2012	2013
CWEI E-information	64.42/100	68.21/100
CWEI WEB Tools and strategies	29.29/100	32.53/100
CWEI E-consultation	22.12/100	23.08/100
CWEI E-decision making process	7.21/100	8.89/100

Figure 1 shows the map of Italy and contains the average CWEI values per geographic area (Nielsen Areas).

The highest value has been registered in the North-East of the Country (Area 2: 46.61/100 in 2012 and 50.00/100 in 2013), North-West and the Centre have a similar value both in 2012 and 2013 (Area 1: 37.25/100 in 2012 and 40.99/100 in 2013, Area 3: 36.32/100 in 2012 and 39.20/100 in 2013), while a lower value is obtained by the South of Italy (Area 4: 32.84/100 in 2012 and 35.17/100 in 2013). For all the four geographical areas an increase is shown between the two years of analysis.

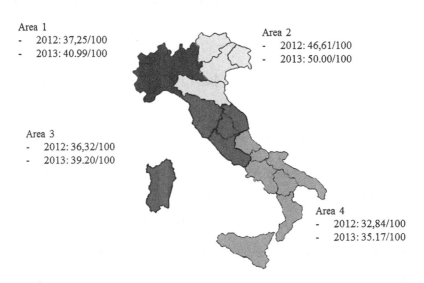

Fig. 1. Average CWEI values per geographic area (Nielsen areas).

Table 4. Number of cities that have obtained the maximum value per sub-indicator.

	Cities with maximum value			
	N 2012	% 2012	N 2013	% 2013
E-information	8/104	7.69 %	10/104	9.62%
WEB tools and strategies	0/104	0	0/104	0
E-consultation	1/104	0.96 %	1/104	0.96 %
E-decision making process	3/104	2.88 %	3/104	2.88 %

When looking at the "top scores" per sub-indicator, we find a number of interesting and significant "best practices" even if just in very few cases the maximum value per sub-indicator is obtained as shown in Table 4. By comparing numbers in 2012 and 2013 it can be seen that the number of cities increased only for sub-indicator E-information.

The fact that only this sub-indicator was fully accomplished by new cities shows, once again, that the web strategies perceived by administrations are still oriented at providing the most traditional form of information to citizens, those which guarantee little interaction and participation.

With regard to **E-information** the component site structure was examined. Ratings show that sites enabling the life events model for navigation (i.e. navigation starting out from events which may characterize the life of citizens, such as "studying", "giving birth" "using public transport" or "life as a senior citizen"), or which provide clear segmentation of citizens by cluster (the elderly, women, children, foreigners, etc.) have increased between 2012 and 2013 probably because it has been understood that menus constructed according to these approaches aid consultation by citizens who can now receive immediate answers targeted for their specific needs.

The research reveals that in 2013 about the 35 % of the sample had information provision based on visitor-type clusters and 41 % had chosen the life event logic. Both approaches were adopted only in 22 cases over the 104 cities of the sample.

A good example is given by Venice where already on the website homepage both approaches are used. As can be seen in Figs. 2 and 3, citizens can choose to find the information they need though a cluster partition (the elderly, women, children, for-eigners etc.) or navigating starting out from events which may characterize the life, in health terms, such as "giving birth", "growing" or "life as a senior citizen".

The highest score in **WEB Tools and Strategies** sub-indicator was obtained both in 2012 and 2013 by the city of Turin where there is a wide offer of mobile services as can be seen in Fig. 4.

The use of blogs and forums, social networks, videos and Web TV channels was also registered. The city of Milan for example has developed an intense use of Face-book and Twitter by opening many different "city pages" or accounts according to different service (Fig. 5).

In the last few years public GIS applications have been introduced not only to allow interactive consultation of different cartographies but also to help to personalize and share maps of the city. Open data strategies have been adopted in most of big cities (Fig. 6) as Rome, Florence and Bologna, but the best solutions are found where there is an integration between GIS and open data strategies as in Venice (Fig. 7).

Fig. 2. Venice: information provision based on visitor-type clusters (www.comune.venezia.it).

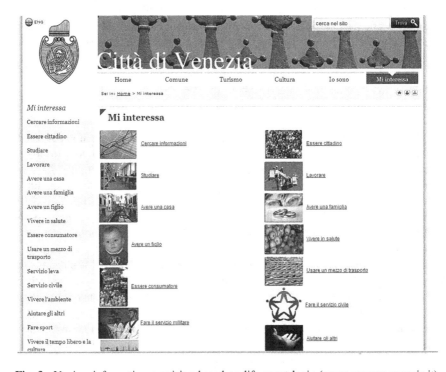

Fig. 3. Venice: information provision based on life event logic (www.comune.venezia.it).

Fig. 4. Turin: services provided through mobile (www.comune.torino.it).

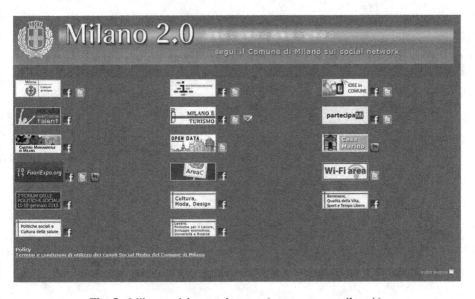

Fig. 5. Milan: social network pages (www.comune.milano.it).

Fig. 6. Rome: open data strategy (www.comune.roma.it).

Fig. 7. Venice: open data and GIS strategy (www.comune.venezia.it).

The research also shows that there is an increase in the presence of some specific information as for example the list of politicians and their personal pages or on-line details about the budget. This trend is due to the Italian legislation's recent requirements.

Analysis of Web tools and strategies reveal that the use of social networks by local governments has increased between 2012 and 2013 (29.81 % in 2012 and 41.35 % in 2013 among the sample). The most used social networks are Facebook, YouTube and Twitter as shown in Table 5, but also my Space, Flickr, G+ and Skype were considered.

Table 5. Number of cities using each social network (SN) and percentage among the sample.

	Cities using each SN			
	N 2012	% 2012	N 2013	% 2013
Facebook	26/104	25.00	38/104	36.54
You Tube	21/104	20.19	29/104	27.88
Twitter	16/104	15.38	29/104	27.88
G+	5/104	4.81	7/104	6.73
Flickr	5/104	4.81	5/104	4.81
My Space	4/104	3.85	4/104	3.85
Skype	1/104	0.96	1/104	0.96

In 2013 only 11 local governments out of 104 offer mobile services. As in 2012, the most significant examples are given by services for tourists which are often combined with QR codes which allow cultural and historical information to be read.

The use of open data was also explored, numbers confirm that only a few cities are considering this strategy but findings show that there was a significant increase in 2013 compared to the previous year: a set of 10 cities has now introduced open data as for example Florence, Palermo, Rome, Venice, while others are starting to consider it.

Turning to **E-consultation**, the involvement of the mayor in on-line relations with citizens was assessed but it was hard to find tools for a true interaction.

Only in few cases special forms are used or the mayor's presence on Facebook or Twitter is shown.

A wider presence of internet polls, surveys, complaint platforms and reputation systems is registered, even if in many cases they are still just electronic forms to fill in which do not allow a complete participatory behaviour.

The only city which has obtained the maximum score in this sub-indicator was in 2012 and still was in 2013 Rimini. Its website offers reputation systems not only to evaluate the general agreement on the website but also on specific areas, as for example police services. In addition there are direct online ways to put citizens in contact with the administration and also ways to report the needs of a specific area, such as maintenance, repairs and removal of litter in certain districts and public parks (Fig. 8).

The theme of reporting problems in a collaborative and interactive way is addressed by some specific project in Udine or Venice (Fig. 9) where open source softwares have been developed to allow citizens to directly report problems related to the city using a digital map, providing a new method of networking and sharing knowledge and orienting the user to become a generator of web contents.

Fig. 8. Rimini: reporting system and citizens in contact with the administration (www.comune.rimini.it).

Fig. 9. Udine: complaint platform (www.comune.udine.it).

In terms of **E-decision making process** there is still much work to do across the country.

It's possible to see that except for a few cases there is no evidence on how decisions are taken. Often there are tools which allow a participatory atmosphere but rarely results are shown. On the whole sample only in 3 cases both evidence that citizens' opinion has been considered and evidences about other's compliant are shown. When considering some best practices, we can think at Venice or Udine, two cities which websites offers a range of services built to allow citizens to "speak" by reporting something, interacting with others and seeing what the administration does or says.

Figure 10 shows a full area of Udine's website where it is asked citizens to express an opinion and to vote. In the same page it is also possible for citizens to see the results of their participation.

Fig. 10. Udine: participation results (www.comune.udine.it).

In the case of reporting systems normally platforms are designed not only to allow to indicate a problem but also to follow on the screen if and when they are taken into account. Figure 11 represent how this has been implemented in Udine where two different columns show the "beginning" and the "end" of works to repair the reported damages. Colours are also used: yellow for the approval phase and green when a procedure is over.

With this regard it can be said that not much has changed between year 2012 and year 2013 in the Italian context.

In addition, correlation analyses (Pearson correlation coefficient) between elements were evaluated using the statistical package SPSS to determine if there is a link between the city population and the scores of each sub-indicator (Table 6). Results show that in 2012 there was not significant correlation between the number of inhabitants and the level of the CWEI nor between the number of inhabitants and the sub-indicators. Instead in 2013 some significant correlations (two tailed) are found between the population and the CWEI score and also between the number of inhab-itants and CWEI 2 - Web Tools and Strategies and CWEI 3 - E-Consultation.

Fig. 11. Udine: complaint status (www.comune.udine.it).

These results show that in 2012 on-line investments in citizen empowerment didn't depend on the dimension of the city while in 2013 the opposite trend was found. Probably the 2013 result could be explained by some elements of CWEI 2 and CWEI 3 which were observed in an increased number of cities and which require some big

Table 6. Correlation between population and CWEI.

		Population	
		2012	2013
CWEI_TOT	Pearson's correlation	.086	.212[*]
	Sig. (2-code)	.388	.031
	N	104	104
CWEI_1	Pearson's correlation	−,016	.093
	Sig. (2-code)	.873	.350
	N	104	104
CWEI_2	Pearson's correlation	.100	.217[*]
	Sig. (2-code)	.310	.027
	N	104	104
CWEI_3	Pearson's correlation	.162	.223[*]
	Sig. (2-code)	.100	.023
	N	104	104
CWEI_4	Pearson's correlation	−,009	.013
	Sig. (2-code)	.931	.899
	N	104	104

financial and organizational investment. For example the development and adoption of online complaint platforms or the adoption of open data strategies which have increased during 2013.

4 Conclusions

A number of conclusions may be reached on the basis of the analysis of the CWEI.

The very low CWEI scores obtained by the Cities of the sample (average CWEI value is 37.30 over 100 in 2012, 40.24 over 100 in 2013) testifies there is still a substantial immaturity of web strategies, which appear modulated on structures and organizational responsibilities rather than on the needs and on the demand of citizens' empowerment; no substantial improvement has been detected in the two-years period considered.

There is still a low but increasing penetration of Web 2.0 tools and strategies (average sub-indicator "Web tools and strategies" value is 29.29 over 100 in 2012, 32.53 over 100 in 2013). This moves an emphasis from the individual for whom information equates to power to a more collaborative, collective "group cooperation culture" that is hard to be understood and accepted by most public employees.

Surprisingly, also a limited diffusion of mobile applications was registered. This finding moves in the same direction of Web 2.0 tools adoption since also mobiles, especially smartphones, if properly used, can turn citizens into active players in the relationship with the Administration, involving them in service co-creation, evaluation and use.

Although there is theoretical and practical recognition that citizens must be more involved in public decisions, many administrators are, at best, ambivalent about public involvement or, at worst, they find it problematic. Administrators need help in addressing problems but find that the help they seek from citizens often creates new sets of problems. As a result, although many public administrators view close relationships with citizens as both necessary and desirable, most of them do not actively seek public involvement. If they do seek it, they do not use public input in making administrative decisions. Future research hints include a focus on this specific topic, in order to fully understand the different behaviours of public organization and the relationship with variables such as the political parties ruling the municipality and the degree of political continuity. It could be interesting to observe if there is a link between the CWEI values and the political orientation of the city or between the results and the phase of the mayor's mandate.

Overcoming the highly significant limits shown above may turn out to be a prerequisite for concrete development of the provision of services for empowered citizens.

The CWEI index (if further evaluated) could be used also at international level to benchmark and monitor the web strategies of smartcities across countries. Furthermore the CWEI index could support a citizen-centered web design of information and services. This could help a faster development of official web solutions aimed to citizen empowerment, developing trust and partnership relationships, which are essential to deliver quality and value for money.

References

1. Caragliu, A., Del Bo, C., Nijkamp, P.: Smart cities in Europe, in series research memoranda 0048. VU University Amsterdam, Faculty of Economics, Business Administration and Econometrics, Amsterdam (2009)
2. Schaffers, H., Komninos, N., Pallot, M., Trousse, B., Nilsson, M., Oliveira, A.: Smart cities and the future internet: towards cooperation frameworks for open innovation. In: Domingue, J., et al. (eds.) Future Internet Assembly. LNCS, vol. 6656, pp. 431–446. Springer, Heidelberg (2011)
3. O'Reilly, T.: O'Reilly Network: What Is Web 2.0 (2005)
4. Bellio, E., Buccoliero, L.: Citizen Web Empowerment across Italian Cities: a benchmarking approach. In: Nunes Silva C. (ed.) Citizen E-Participation in Urban Governance Crowdsourcing and Collaborative Creativity. IGI Global, (2013)
5. King, S., Cotterill, S.: Transformational government? The role of information technology in delivering citizen-centric local public services. Local Gov. Stud. 33(3), 21 (2007)
6. Richards, R.: Digital citizenship and web 2.0 tools. MERLOT J. Online Learn. Teach. 6(2), 7 (2010)
7. Budin, H.: Democratic education and self-publishing. In: Crocco, M. (ed.) Social Studies and the Press: Keeping the Beast at Bay?. Information Age Publishing, Greenwich (2005)
8. Pachler, N., Daly, C.: Narrative and learning with Web 2.0 technologies: Towards a research agenda. J. Comput. Assist. Learn. 25(1), 12 (2009)
9. O'Reilly, T.: What is web 2.0: design patterns and business models for the next generation of software. Int. J. Digit. Econ. 65(1), 20 (2007)
10. Fountain, J.E. (ed.): Building the Virtual State: Information Technology and Institutional Change. Brookings Institution Press, Washington, DC (2001)
11. Ala-Mutka, K., et al.: The impact of social computing on the EU information society and economy. European Commission Joint Research Centre Institute for Prospective Technological Studies, Seville (Spain) (2009)
12. Berce, J., et al.: Towards the eGovernment Vision for the EU in 2010: Research Policy Challenges. European Commission Joint Research Centre Institute for Prospective Technological Studies, Seville (Spain) (2006)
13. Dutton, W., Peltu, M.: Reconfiguring Government-Public Engagements: Enhancing the Communicative Power of Citizens. Oxford Internet Institute, Oxford (2007)
14. Di Maio, A., et al.: Government in 2020: Taking the Long View. Gartner Inc, Stamford (2005)
15. Osimo, D.: Web2.0 in Government: Why and How? European Commission Joint Research Centre Institute for Prospective Technological Studies, Seville (2008)
16. Assar, S., Boughzala, I.: E-Government evolution priorities from a Web 2.0 perspective: an exploratory field study. In: 46th Hawaii International Conference on System Sciences (HICSS), Maui (2013)
17. Baumgarten, J., Chui, M.: E-government 2.0. McKinsey Quarterly 4 (2009)
18. Niehaves, B.: Open Innovation and Public Sector Business Process Management - A Multi-Method Study. In: Americas Conference on IS (AMCIS) (2009)
19. Nam, T.: New ends, new means, but old attitudes: citizens' views on open government and government 2.0. In: 44th HICSS Conference 2011 (2011)
20. Scholl, H.J., Luna-Reyes, L.F.: Uncovering Dynamics of open government, transparency, participation, and collaboration. In: 44th HICSS Conference (2011)
21. Bilsel, R.U., Büyüközkan, G., Ruan, D.: A fuzzy preference-ranking model for a quality evaluation of hospital web sites. Int. J. Intell. Syst. 21, 1181–1197 (2006)

22. Aladwani, A., Palvia, P.: Developing and validating an instrument for measuring userperceived Web quality. Inf. Manag. **39**, 467–476 (2002)
23. Van Iwaarden, J., et al.: Perceptions about the quality of Web sites:Asurvey amongst students at Northeastern University and Erasmus University. Inf. Manag. **41**, 947–959 (2004)
24. Cox, J., Dale, B.: Key quality factors in Web site design and use: An examination. Int. J. Q. Reliab. Manag. **19**, 862–888 (2002)
25. Van Iwaarden, J., Van derWiele, T.: A study on the applicability of SERVQUAL dimensions for Web sites (2002)
26. Kim, S.-E., Shaw, T., Schneider, H.: Web site design benchmarking within industry groups. Internet Res. **13**, 17–26 (2003)
27. Parasuraman, A., Zeithaml, V., Berry, L.: SERVQUAL: A multi-item scale for measuring consumer perceptions of service quality. J. Retail. **64**, 2–40 (1988)
28. Kaylor, C., Deshazo, R., Eck, D.: Gauging e-government: a report on implementing services among American cities. Gov. Inf. Q. **18**, 293–307 (2001)
29. Smith, A.: Applying evaluation criteria to New Zealand government websites. Int. J. Inf. Manag. **21**, 137–149 (2001)
30. Chung, T., Law, R.: Developing a performance indicator for hotel websites. Int. J. Hosp. Manag. **22**, 119–125 (2003)
31. Chao, H.: Assessing the quality of academic libraries on the Web: the development and testing of criteria. Lib. Inf. Sci. Res. **24**, 169–194 (2002)
32. Novljan, S., Maja, Z.: Web pages of Slovenian public libraries: Evaluation and guidelines. J. Doc. **60**, 62–76 (2004)
33. Buccoliero, L., Bellio, E., Prenestini, A.: Patient web empowerment index (PWEI): a tool for the assessment of healthcare providers'web strategies. A first benchmark of Italian NHS Hospitals. In: Safran, C., Reti, S., Marin, H. (eds.) MEDINFO 2010 Proceedings of the 13th World Congress on Medical Informatics, pp. 38–42. IOS PRESS, Amsterdam (2010)
34. Bedell, S., Agrawal, A., Petersen, L.: A systematic critique of diabetes on the World Wide Web for patients and their physicians. Int. J. Med. Informatics **73**, 687–694 (2004)
35. Kuo, Y.-F.: Integrating Kano's model intoWeb-community service quality. Total Q. Manag. **15**, 925–939 (2004)
36. Jeong, M., Oh, H., Gregoire, M.: Conceptualizing Web site quality and its consequences in the lodging industry. Int. J. Hosp. Manag. **22**, 161–175 (2003)
37. Kim, S., Stoel, L.: Dimensional hierarchy of retail Website quality. Inf. Manag. **41**, 619–633 (2004)
38. Buccoliero, L., Bellio, E.: Citizens web empowerment in european municipalities. J. E-Governance **33**(4), 11 (2010)
39. Bellio, E., Buccoliero, L.: Emerging trends in local governments web strategies, citizen web empowerment assessment in italy. In: ICE-B 10th International Conference on E-Business, SCITEPRESS – Science and Technology Publications, Reykjavik (2013)
40. Hayes, A.F., Krippendorff, K.: Answering the call for a standard reliability measure for coding data. Commun. Methods Measures **1**, 77–89 (2007)

Estimating the Effort in the Development of Distance Learning Paths

Milena Casagranda[1], Luigi Colazzo[2], and Andrea Molinari[1(✉)]

[1] Department of Economics and Management, University of Trento,
Via Inama, 5, 38122 Trento, Italy
{milena.casagranda,andrea.molinari}@unitn.it
[2] Department of Industrial Engineering, University of Trento,
Via Sommarive 2, 38122 Trento, Italy
luigi.colazzo@unitn.it

Abstract. In this paper we present a model for better understanding the ratio between costs, production of didactic material and activity of monitoring and facilitating e-learning tasks. The quantification of the effort required to produce e-learning material has been always subject to the proposal of some "magic numbers" not always supported by a method or analytical data. In this paper we propose a method for calculating the effort required to design and develop e-learning paths. Our model is based on a systematic gathering of data regarding the effort of the different actors involved (teachers, tutors, instructional designers etc.) from a series of e-learning projects carried out at the Laboratory of Maieutics over the last five years. In the first two years we collected ex-post data on design and development times, being careful to include a variety of different teaching methodologies. In the following years we identified critical variables which allowed us to abstract and generalize a possible costing model. The model proposed could be used as a reference point for professionals working on the development of content in their estimation of costs linked to the design and development of learning materials, providing a calculation basis which takes a number of methodological approaches and educational objectives into account.

Keywords: E-Learning cost modeling

1 Introduction

This paper presents an analysis of the problem never completely solved of the costs of e-learning. It tackles it through a pragmatic approach based on the experience of our group gained in designing and implementing a training process in blended mode. The attention focuses in particular on the aspects linked to e-learning costs and the various modalities that ICT offer to people who design training, especially concerning the evaluation of online activities that can support "face-to-face" situations in a blended way.

Organizations have always calculated a series of factors such as costs, duration, quality of learning, customer satisfaction, in order to choose the most suitable training approach to be employed. None of these variables is easily defined and measured but the

© Springer-Verlag Berlin Heidelberg 2014
M.S. Obaidat and J. Filipe (Eds.): ICETE 2013, CCIS 456, pp. 160–179, 2014.
DOI: 10.1007/978-3-662-44788-8_10

cost analysis, in particular, seems to be the most complex. One of the elements frequently emerging from existing studies is that e-learning is less expensive compared to the residential editions of the same course at the increase of numbers of participants [1].

Over the years the fortunes of Distance Learning (DL) have see-sawed, for reasons both cultural and technological: among them, a reluctance to replace face-to-face interaction with instructors; inadequate communication lines for the transmission of complex learning objects (LOs); insufficient bandwidth for the reliable streaming of multimedia material and also a lack of standards for tracking and certification of on-line courses. Most of these problems have now been overcome: it therefore seems that the hesitant progress of e-learning – always on the point of spreading extensively and then for some reason never really succeeding - should not have to continue any longer, given the disappearance of most of the technological barriers.

In fact, we believe, there is another - considerably more insidious, not being linked to the inevitable progress of technology - obstacle which threatens to further slow the spread of DL. This obstacle is the economic advantage of instructors in the production of LOs in relation to the traditional method of being paid an hourly or daily rate, linked to their verifiable, physical presence in a classroom. This point seems rather crass and mercenary, but we have observed early signs of such resistance, especially as it is now clear, at the industrial level above all, that e-learning will become indispensable.

To associate a cost model that is limited to the traditional retribution of a teacher/tutor calculated per hour, is to run the risk of overestimating the low cost of e-learning initiatives with respect to traditional training and, on the other hand, of demotivating all the people involved in an e-learning process, given the constant contribution they are called upon to give. We are convinced that the use of Web 2.0 tools can intensify the learning process, especially when conceived as relation created or facilitated by the teacher. On one side, integrating traditional educational tasks with web 2.0 tools (like forums, wikis, FAQs etc.) can help to avoid that the participant should perceive the value of e-learning as simply downloading didactic material and filling in final progress tests. On the other hand, this is undoubtedly an extra effort for trainers, therefore amplifying the problem, as normally these web 2.0 activities require a lot of time and resources.

In this paper we will present a model for better understanding the real costs and efforts to produce didactic material for e-learning paths. In our opinion, when a blended or a full on-line course is being designed, it is necessary to be prepared to understand the various factors involved in the development and delivery of the training process, by building up a list of cost factors applicable to the needs of the organization and the context.

2 The Origin of the Problem

e-Learning has always been considered mainly as a way of saving money over training budgets. Others are the benefits of e-learning, as widely demonstrated, but for this paper we refer to those cases where e-learning has unquestionable advantages independently from budget considerations, for example: a) large numbers of people to be trained in a short time; b) people widely dispersed or hard to access physically; c) training regarding software or ICTs usage.

All the above cases include factors which could be considered to "justify" fair pay for the creators of LOs (instructors, instructional designers, tutors, etc.). A comparison of the production costs of the LOs with how much it would have cost to run a face-to-face course normally justify the choice for an e-learning initiative. On the other side, however, we find the perspective of the creator of the LOs, who should be highly paid due to the number of users involved and due to the strategic value of the training itself. We are thus witnessing an extension of the online course offer, which is going to involve an increasing range of subjects, ever more closely linked to those areas (like soft skills) traditionally not "favorable" to e-learning. Nevertheless, this potential burst of growth in LOs production presents a number of criticalities:

- a more detailed planning is required in order to create interactive, reflective, self-rating situations for the learning of soft skills;
- LOs are delivered by instructors who are often unfamiliar with ICTs;
- LOs represent an area of the market which is still very profitable for traditional classroom based education.

Regarding the last item, resistance on the part of instructors, who have always been the authors of the destiny of e-learning initiatives, is presumable – and, as far as we are concerned, already verifiable. By instructors we mean everybody involved in the development of courses and related educational objects. The argument is very simple: considering for example the business of professional training, teaching a given subject requiring 20 classroom hours to 100 people allows an instructor to suppose N repetitions of the course, each multiplied by 20 h, multiplied by their hourly pay. The economic final reward (FR) for the instructor, by which to calculate the threshold of convenience in creating the LOs, is function (at least) of the following parameters:

$$FR = f(r, h, hr, d, ph, hpc)$$

where

r = No. of course repetitions;
h = No. of hours of each edition;
hr = hourly rate of the teacher for that course
d = rate for design activities
ph = preparation hours needed for LOs creation
hpc = hourly preparation costs

Other elements should be considered, like the location of the course, travel expenses, credibility of the organization etc. Sometimes, moreover, a flat rate is paid for design, or it is not always recompensed, since instructors receive a good hourly rate for classroom hours (particularly as they become more senior).

In the simplest situations, the function can be easily calculated as follows:

$$FR = r * h * hr + d - ph * hpc$$

There's no doubt that unless a pay scheme for e-learning courses at least as attractive to instructors as that for traditional courses is provided, there will be a further brake on the spread of e-learning. A number of studies have focused on the determining of parameters, and many authors have already pointed out the complexity resulting from methodologically and educationally based choices in the construction of e-learning courses. [2–4].

To a great degree, over-simplifying the idea risks, we believe, the reoccurrence of the initial problem, the "inexpedience" for experts of transferring their knowledge through DL. We have already drawn attention [5] to criteria for calculating the production costs of LOs, but extensive subsequent trials have revealed the need to refine and integrate the model, especially in the LOs design stage. In this paper we will propose these extensions and refinements to our e-learning costs model. We have added more importance to the design stage, in order to allow the a priori estimation of the work done by the different experts involved in project development.

3 The Design of Educational Projects

The detailed preparation of an e-learning course or environment needs to be done in advance. The instructional designer should identify the subject matter, define it operatively, decide how to evaluate students' knowledge and skills and introduce occasions for feedback in order to support learning. Therefore, we begin by identifying the different phases of planning stages and then suggest how times and costs might be calculated.

All e-learning projects include at least four basic stages which lead to the delivery of a course. We believe that in the evaluation of the effort involved, we should quantify, optimize and recognize:

- the design of the educational project;
- the design of LOs through an analysis of subject matter, which we introduce as modeling in this article;
- the development of educational material, the utilization of which has already been described by other researchers [6];
- the management of interactions with students in order to further learning, mostly following web 2.0 approaches and tools (forums, blogs, wikis, social network interactions etc.), as already mentioned in previous articles [5]

When discussing the design phase, we include a number of dimensions, already mentioned elsewhere [7]:

- demand assessment: information about clients' expectations is collected, clarified and selected, through hypotheses which designers develop considering technological issues about the creation of LOs;
- the proposal of hypotheses: the variables and points of view involved are multiple and it is hoped that decisions / solutions can lead to the presentation to clients of a number of possibilities;
- fine tuning of the project: when a possibility has been chosen the – almost inevitable – next step is the development of the project, a recursive research process in which the direction of the project is defined.

We started from the presumption that the infinite variants of training initiatives make it difficult to immediately comprehend the main characteristics of each. We believe that the concept of model could help us to organize and coordinate the various phases of a process required, offered, chosen and the operative design of a training activity. For this reason, as a starting point we have used and adapted two models:

- model CLEAAB 16 [2, 3, 8], to describe the process of phases and activities that characterize the design of a blended training path. Five macro activities of design have been chosen, later distinguished for further relative under-activities: planning, preparation of material resources, human resources training, implementation and evaluation;
- the study of G. Battaglia [9], suggesting the identification of the various models through a three dimensional matrix and a check list descriptive of the main characteristics of the components of the training product, has been used for the selection of the four didactic models of reference. The three dimensional matrix representative of the models is then developed considering three dimensions:
  1. type of the main didactic objectives: knowledge, knowing how to do, knowing how to decide/act;
  2. importance of the vertical interactions according to the principle of authority of the teacher, distinguishing the role of the moderator, facilitator and main figure of reference for the path; we have integrated the model by inserting also the figure of tutor who generates a further vertical interaction. Thus we can note how the role of teacher and tutor are strictly correlated and interdependent: when the teacher is the main person of reference for the course the tutor supports him mostly as observer. On the contrary, when the role of the teacher is that of moderator, generally the tutor acquires major relevance in the training context, especially in the possible distance versions of the didactic process;
  3. relevance of the horizontal interaction according to the principle of collaboration and confrontation on a large scale that goes from collective learning to individual learning.

The combination of the three dimensions generates a "training space" in which it is possible to identify twelve training models. Among these, four can represent relatively "pure" models and, therefore, usable for general reference:

- the didactic model aimed at knowledge: characterised by strong vertical interaction between trainer-trainee, by a weak horizontal interaction among trainees and a training objective identified in "knowledge";
- the didactic model aimed at method: characterized by a s strong vertical interaction, by a weak horizontal interaction identified as "knowing how to do";
- the didactic model aimed at ability: characterized by a strong vertical interaction, by a strong horizontal interaction and the training objective of "knowing how to do";
- the didactic model aimed at competence: characterized by a weak vertical interaction, by a strong horizontal interaction and the training objective of "knowing how to act/decide".

The collocation of a specific training course within a training model supports and "justifies" the identification of the roles of teacher and tutor, as well as the choice of instruments coherent with the didactic objectives and the vertical interaction, from the design phase to the phase of realization and it offers a departure point for the estimate of costs.

If we take as reference the courses, object of the experiment, and try to collocate them within the model, we see that, for example, an Excel™ course focused on training people in the usage of the software uses a format aimed at method. The training objective is indeed that of "knowing how to do", while the vertical interaction is strong since the teacher represents the main point of reference while the horizontal one is weak since learning in this case is mainly individual.

Conversely, a course aimed at training people on "Safety on the building site" is collocated in a format aimed at ability where the teacher is the main point of reference, but the horizontal interaction is strong. Here the objective is to know how to do, meaning knowing how to apply the norms learnt during the training course, and the objective is reached both through individual study and collaborative work.

Through a consideration of these three critical variables we can create a 3-dimensional matrix representing the educational models:

- the principal teaching objectives;
- the importance of vertical interaction according to the principle of instructors' authority;
- the importance of horizontal interaction according to the principle of collaboration and dialogue.

As said, the combination of educational objectives has been graded in three segments: knowledge, technological skills, the development of cognitive skills.

The second dimension focuses on the importance of instructors as a source of knowledge and as an expert in the field. The two ends of the continuum are the "Central figure" or "reference point" at one extreme, on whom the learning process depends, and the "Neutral moderator" of students' study, at the other (Fig. 2).

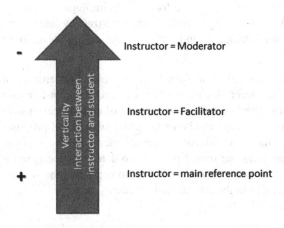

Fig. 1. The vertical interaction dimension of an educational model.

Fig. 2. The horizontal interaction dimension of an educational model.

In our terminology, "Verticality" represents the degree of interaction between instructor and student, while "Horizontality" refers to the degree of interaction between students. Note that the two dimensions are independent, allowing four different combinations: the weak vertical - weak horizontal combination represents independent learning, while the strong-strong combination represents the development of elaborate educational projects, in which the instructor assumes the role of project manager and strong group leader. The combination of the three dimensions generates an cubic "educational space" in which twelve educational models can be identified. Some of these models are relatively "pure" and can therefore be used as general points of reference.

We can place the tutor in this educational space, alongside the instructor. This allows us to see how closely correlated and dependent on each other these roles are: when an instructor is the central role for a course, the tutor – to a large extent an observer – supports him; conversely, when the instructor's role is that of moderator, the teaching role of the tutor is potentially greater, particularly for any Distant Learning versions of a course. In our studies, four educational models have been identified:

1. models aimed at the acquisition of knowledge: characterized by strong vertical interaction between instructor and student, weak horizontal interaction between students;
2. models focusing on method: characterized by strong vertical interaction, weak horizontal interaction and a focus on technological skills;
3. models aimed at increasing ability: characterized by strong vertical interaction, strong horizontal interaction and a focus on technological skills;
4. models aimed at increasing expertise: characterized by weak vertical interaction, strong horizontal interaction and with a focus on the development of cognitive skills.

Note that the variable of technology is not one of the dimensions of the model: the characteristics of the technological tools used to deliver on-line courses cannot be considered primary criteria for the classification of educational models (Fig. 3).

We could have different models for the same educational proposal, depending on the methodology that is considered more effective for the learning process. The detection of the predominant model is useful to determine the educational objectives, while it is relevant for our cost model in order to determine the type and the extension of the support activities in the educational processes, as presented in Tables 1 and 2 at the end of this paper.

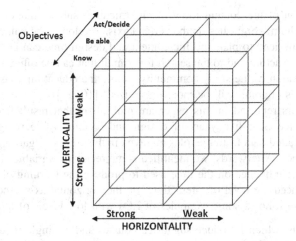

Fig. 3. The "educational space" through the identification of educational formats.

The central role at this stage and across the other proposals is the e-learning project managers, who support and coordinate those involved in the development of the educational project. The overall organization and implementation of the e-learning system is their responsibility.

They supervise the planning, development and administration of the project and are responsible for its educational content. The project manager undertakes to:

- schedule and coordinate the e-learning program
- identify users' profiles of the e-learning system
- analyze the educational requirements / demand of users
- define the objectives of the e-learning system
- define the type of service to set up
- define the criteria and indicators for the monitoring and evaluation of the service

We examine the roles of the collaborators later on, in particular those of the content manager and instructional designer.

4 Learning Objects Design Through Content Analysis

When LOs are being planned, after the appropriate educational model has been identified, we can start to apply our costing model. The most significant variables, which we introduce for the first time in this model, are [7]:

- content "definability": can the content be processed in a standard way, or does it require discussion and comparison and need to be created for a specific group of participants?
- content "interactivity": can the content be conveyed through text, images and graphics, or does it require interactivity? Simulations, for example?

The definition of the content (how much structured subject matter there is, on a scale: low – medium – high) lies on the vertical axis. The lower the value, the less time the instructor will need to plan specific content and design time can be devoted to the methodological structure and to the search for stimuli that can be offered along a study path (e.g. facilitation of the study community, where the educational task and support while the work is ongoing will be more recognized) [10, 11].

The indicators reported in this paper are multipliers that result from an ex-post analysis conducted over five years of design and creation of learning objects. We collected the detailed data from the roles involved in the process regarding design times and creation times. Afterwards, we identified some recurring variables in the process, and their average influence on the time used to produce the learning objects (Fig. 4).

We have placed the level of interactivity on the horizontal axis. According to our formulation, here follows some examples of LOs with low levels of interactivity:

- narrative LOs, which introduce suggested courses and/or single modules;
- expository LOs, which refer to text based information and concepts, images.

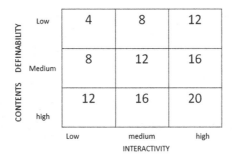

Fig. 4. Model for the calculation of multipliers in the planning of material.

The following are examples of medium levels of interactivity:

- Demonstrations: animations which illustrate a series of operations
- Interactive LOs: participants are required to interact with the material – providing answers, commands, links, etc.
- Tests: drag and drop, classification tests that start with given possibilities, problem solving tests, etc.
- Guided exercises: step by step instructions on what to do
- Case studies

The following involve high levels of interaction:

- Simulations: presentations of simulated situations in which the student must achieve an objective (e.g. using particular software)
- Role based LOs: contexts in which participants are asked to take decisions, etc.

Each cell in this model is assigned a different value which is multiplied by the expected length of the material being developed. We have excluded "serious games" from the calculation / estimate that can be made at this stage of our experiments / trials. The serious games category is a broad one, nevertheless it always entails, at all stages of development, a quantity of work which definitely cannot be reduced to the elements represented in our model. Currently, there are experiments / trials on-going in this field, but they are still at too early a stage to provide accurate data.

At least two figures are involved at this stage of design, their contributions can be identified using the same parameters (from the point of view of co-planning), using the matrix above:

- the instructor, who:
  - participates in the definition of course structure
  - identifies the possible testing and evaluation methods to be included in the program
  - supports and collaborates with the instructional designer in the creation of LOs

- the instructional designer, who:
  - gives advice on educational methods and strategies for the delivery of content and resources for e-learning
  - decides which software to use for the generation of content
  - manages the multimedia resources
  - identifies the strategies and tools for evaluation and practice most appropriate to the purposes of the course.

5 The Development of Educational Material

Regarding another component in our model for determining the cost of production, i.e., the development of educational material, in other studies [5] we suggested a method for estimating the amount of time spent by instructors on the creation of LOs. We will shortly present this part, considering the following questions: (a) will all the material be new, or is there any material available for reuse? (b) to what extent might the material be reusable in the future?

The possibility of reusing existent material for the development of LOs has a great impact in the perception that end users have about the originality of the creator's work, and sometimes is even subject to negotiation between the educational institution and the instructor. In our model, this aspect lies on the vertical axis, on a scale: absent – low – medium – high. The higher the value, the less time the instructor needs for the preparation of the LO.

The replicability of material – how possible it is to reuse the same LOs for other courses or users [11] – lies on the horizontal axis. The scale we use is the same as the last one: the higher the replicability the bigger the multiplier, as the same material can be used for many versions and subjects and costs can thus be recouped. In contrast, if there is little or no possibility of replicating the material and an LO is useful only in one, or a limited number of, context/s, instructors will be paid proportionately less since they will soon have either to generate new material or update old.

We hypothesize that the values of the variables of the multiplier on this axis will be lower than those on the vertical. All the cells in the model are assigned a different value which serves as a multiplier for the expected useful life of the material being developed. Moreover, the concept of "reuse" can be based on an estimate of the number of versions expected and on the number of possible users, or even on estimates of re-combinability in other contexts.

The following factors are to be considered when determining the "reuse of material" variable:

- Absent: it is the first time that instructors have developed a course like this, so they have neither classroom nor online material available with which to begin the preparation and must start from zero, or near zero;
- Medium: instructors can adapt material which they have previously used in the classroom for use online, or have a limited amount of relatively unstructured online material available;
- High: instructors have some structured material available, suitable for their chosen type of distance education, and only small changes or updates are required.

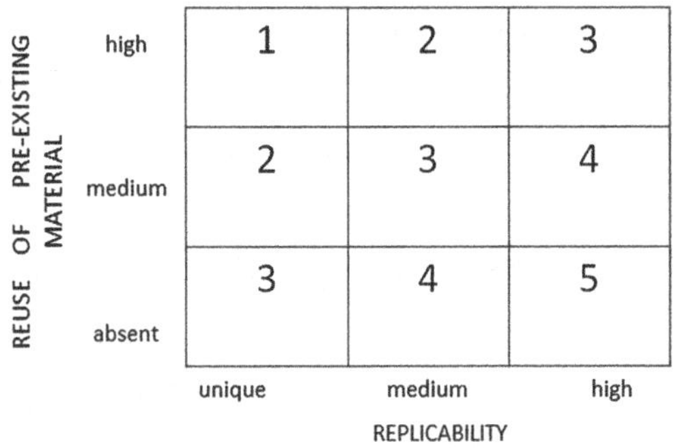

Fig. 5. Model for calculation of multipliers in the creation of material.

The variable regarding the replicability has been constructed referring to the average participation to courses held for University and public administrations in our territory. It is complicated to "universalize" this parameter of replicability, that in our case sets a "high replicability" when courses involve up to 100 participants.

This parameter could hence be a limit in different contexts respect to those used in our analysis, and should be recalculated and adapted. At the same time, having collected data from several courses editions, in environments very close to what the market nowadays provides, we are confident to have a good basis for future analysis.

Instead, on the horizontal axe we put the repeatability, meaning the possibility to be able to reuse the same LO for other training courses or further users. The scale here is developed on three parameters (univocal – medium – high), converse proportion to the previous one: the higher this value, the larger will the multiplier be since it will be possible to reuse the same material for more editions and participants, and, therefore costs will be amortized. In order to identify the degree of repeatability in this training context, in our context we base ourselves on a future estimate of the number of predictable editions and the number of possible users.

Finally, we have substantiated our hypothesis through the analysis of a large number of historical courses held by our partners, verifying the distribution of frequency of participants in similar areas of training courses. The hypothesis emerging from the analysis made during the last training years is the following division:

- univocal, as inferior to 40 participants
- medium, from 40 to 100 participants
- high, more than100 participants.

The calculation becomes crucial in complex and articulated situations such as the one of our context, in which courses are offered with extremely varying number of participants. At the moment, an experimentation and an application on various training types is being carried out in order to be able to evaluate the validity of the first hypotheses and to identify possible updating of the parameters so far identified.

At this stage we are also faced with the following questions:

- What are the best technologies for the running of the course? For content management? (We are here referring to LMS and LCMS.)
- What technical support is needed for the production of the material?

Sometimes the instructor him/herself will be able to produce the educational material, sometimes a specific person will carry out this function. The person producing material will have the time recognized using the model in Fig. 5. It is important to add, however, that it would be helpful to add an extra multiplier to our model, both to quantify the work involved in reviewing the content / work, in checking that the material meets established LO standards, and for the professional editing of the material itself, as set out below.

At this stage we add another value, when two roles dominate the work: the content manager and the LO editor / LO production expert, who guarantee the quality of the LO at all stages of its production, and especially:

- when the stages of production and their durations are being decided;
- for the writing of LO storyboards;
- for managing professional standards in the multimedia content (videos, narrators, graphics, etc.)
- for editing of the LO

From our evidences, we derived these multiplying factors, that must be confirmed in further analysis:

Content manager	Responsible for there view of video content: video time multiplied by 3
LO editor	Responsible for editing: video time multiplied by 33

Fig. 6. Model for calculating the multiplier for creating material.

The incidence of this element on the production time of LOs is clearly relevant, and in our experience this is particularly true for those institutions that do not have a LO editor at their disposal, thus forcing them to turn to external expertise (Fig. 6).

Accessibility of learning objects is a serious issue, and the attention devoted to people with disabilities is never too much. Thus, we observed in our tests to which extend the impact of enriching / modifying material to be usable by this category of users was. When accessible materials are being created, we have identified a further increase in time to be recognized for this activity (Fig. 7):

Accessible materials generated by the LO editor
- Addition of Text: Creation of material + Video time
- Addition of Subtitles: Creation of material + Video time multiplied by 1.5

Fig. 7. Model for calculating multipliers in the case of accessible material.

6   Supporting the Learning Process

Finally, as already discussed in other papers, [5], we consider the choice of teaching model to be very important for the estimation of the maximum number of hours that tutors and instructors will spend on the delivery of a course. The estimate of this effort for the people involved in e-learning is one of the main obstacles in estimating the e-learning costs: well known are the studies on the frontal hours / didactic material preparation ratio (even if such a ratio is quite questionable, subjective and depending on context), and there are some hints at an estimate of the overall engagement of the people involved in e-learning paths.

We believe that such information is not sufficient to guarantee an equal compensation to who creates work on the implementation side. Furthermore, as already mentioned, teachers, tutors, instructional engineers, multi media designers, etc., need updated models able to suitably calculate the respective efforts and the right retribution for such efforts. To associate a simplified cost model to these activities, that limits itself to the traditional hourly retribution of the teacher and/or tutor, could contribute to nourish two important risks for e-learning:

- on the one hand, there is the risk of over-estimation of the costs of the e-learning initiatives compared to traditional training. Often e-learning appears enormously more advantageous in the economy scale compared to the same editions of frontal paths and relative retribution to who is in the classroom. But, if we want to compensate all the activities that a complete, interactive, collaborative e-learning environment creates, the centre of attention should be moved from the costs (still present but not so high) to the quality of the training service offered.
- on the other hand, it could mean an economic disincentive towards people who are involved in an e-learning experience, if the activity carried out by the teacher and tutor is not suitably recognised. Qualified teachers and tutors could be little stimulated to participate in e-learning initiatives, given the amount of hours to be

dedicated to the various activities, the loss of income on the repetition of the e-learning editions, the complication linked to the use of less known instruments and technologies.

These risks emerge above all when the e-learning initiatives are carried out on large scale, as in our case, where we are facing a Public Administration that has a very ample training catalogue. Therefore, the necessity arises for adopting an adequate model of costs that should guarantee to teacher and tutor an appropriate economic compensation in the administration of the didactic phase in order to thus favour a legitimization of the competences and contribute to the motivation towards e-learning.

On the basis of these presuppositions our group's aim is to define for each type of didactic model, on the basis of experimentation and taking into consideration various combinations of classroom and e-learning that we have activated, maximum percentages of recognition of the hours worked in e-learning on various services and instruments, both for teacher and tutor (Fig. 1).

For the final calculation of the cost estimate for the production of didactic material we have hypothetically introduced another fundamental parameter, meaning the total number of participants in that specific course and, consequently, multiplied the hours resulting from this percentage by the number of participants.

The calculation of these hours is based on the application of a percentage on the total number of course hours for face-to-face and DL, shown below:

Table 1. Adjusting factor for distance learning courses based on teaching model for teaching.

% in class room	% in Distance Learning	Expertise	Ability	Method	Knowledge
100	0	///	///	///	///
70	30	5%	4%	3%	2%
50	50	6%	5%	4%	3%
30	70	7%	6%	5%	4%
0	100	8%	7%	6%	5%

This table presents the Percentage of the maximum number of instructor's hours recognized based on combinations of classroom and/or DL hours (supporting students' learning and communication during the course). The following figure, instead, represents the percentage of the maximum number of tutor's hours recognized based on combinations of classroom and/or DL hours (supporting students' learning and communication during the course).

The percentage is doubled if it is expected that an instructor's presence in the medium term will be required, either to allow students more time to complete certain activities (e.g. in blended courses: within 3 months of the last classroom based lesson), or to guarantee that the course web pages are updated (e.g. the instructor agrees to update FAQs, regulations, etc.).

Table 2. Adjusting factor for distance learning courses based on teaching model for tutoring.

% in class room	% in Distance Learning	Expertise	Ability	Method	Knowledge
100	0	///	///	///	///
70	30	4%	3%	3%	2%
50	50	5%	4%	4%	3%
30	70	6%	5%	5%	4%
0	100	7%	6%	6%	5%

7   Application of the Model

In this article we describe the application of the model to a self-study course run in 2011 and 2012. Our results were extremely encouraging: a deviation of about 10 % between the "ex-ante" calculation, based on the a priori application of the suggested parameters, and the "ex-post" statement of accounts (allowing an a posteriori evaluation of the hypothesis).

See below a short summary of the course characteristics:

• Course title: "Digital signatures and Certified electronic mail";
• Participants: almost 22,000 private businesses;
• Course objectives: divided into two areas;
• Information component: a presentation of the main characteristics of digital signatures and certified electronic mail, the related legal aspects, the main uses of these tools, the necessity of adopting them, limits to their use, opportunities for their use;
• Application component: showing how digital signatures and certified electronic mail work and making available practical demonstrations of their use.
• Effective duration of the educational material–information component: 6 h, application component: 2 h (Figs. 8, 9).

Choice of Educational Model
-     Information component: model directed towards knowledge
-     Application component: model directed towards method

Fig. 8. Educational model.

In summary, the original course has been planned as a 6 h + 2 h course. With the application of our model to this specific instance, the global effort has been calculated as follows:

– Planning Time: 72 h + 72 h + 40 h + 40 h = 224 h
– production Time: 30 h + 18 h + 198 h + 9 h + 10 h + 6 h + 66 h +3 h = 340 h
– Support time: n/a

Total Effort: 564 h respect to an effective duration of the educational material of 8 h (Figs. 10, 11).

Calculation of planning time

- Information component: narrative and expository LOs
  - o Instructor/expert: 6 hours (effective duration) * 12 (multiplier: high definability of the content/ low levels of interaction) = 72 hours
  - o instructional designer: 6 hours (effective duration) * 12 (multiplier: high definability of the content / low levels of interaction) = 72 hours

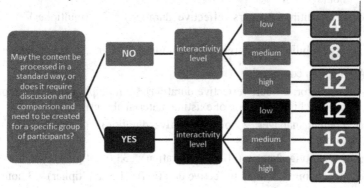

- Application component: simulations
  - o instructor/expert: 2 hours (effective duration) * 20 (multiplier: high definability of the content/ high interactivity) = 40 hours
  - o instructional designer: 2 hours (effective duration) * 20 (multiplier: high definability of the content/ high interactivity) = 40 hours
  - o total planning hours: 224

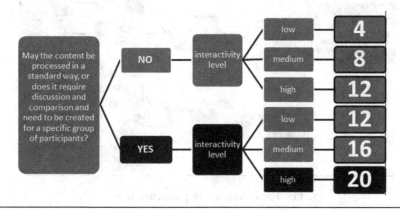

Fig. 9. Calculation of planning time.

Calculation of production time

- Information component
   - o instructor: 6 hours (effective duration) * 5 multiplier (material replicability high and reuse of existing material absent) = 30 hours
   - o content manager: 6 hours (effective duration) * 3 (multiplier) = 18 hours
   - o LO editing: 6 hours (effective duration) * 33 (multiplier) = 198 hours;
   - o accessibility 6 hours (effective duration) * 1.5 (multiplier) = 9 hours
- Application component
   - o instructor: 2 hours (effective duration) * 5 multiplier (material replicability high and reuse of existing material absent) = 10 hours
   - o content manager: 2 hours (effective duration) * 3 (multiplier) = 6 hours
   - o LO editing: 2 hours (effective duration) * 33 (multiplier) = 66 hours;
   - o accessibility 2 hours (effective duration) * 1.5 (multiplier) = 3 hours
   - o Total LO production hours: 100

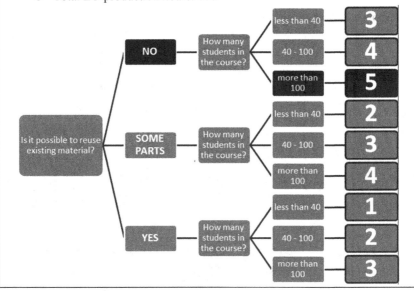

Fig. 10. Calculation of production time.

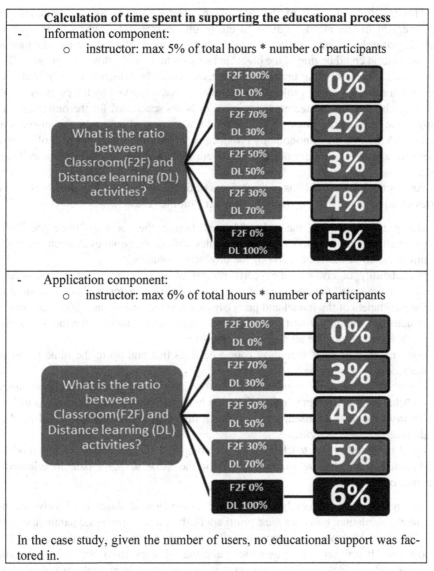

Fig. 11. Calculation time spent supporting the educational process.

8   Conclusions

This article describes a model for the estimation of the time spent by the various people involved in the planning and production of distance learning material. We attempt to address the problem of calculating total numbers of hours worked by all the actors, providing a general framework for this complex calculation (in the sense of quantity of variables and situations to be considered).

This is largely a result of the lack of an adequate model for standardizing the measurement of the effort required to create online material, leading to instructors receiving completely inadequate recompense for their work. We believe that the lack of this calculation could be one of the possible factors which could slow the spread of DL. Our model calculates, using multipliers and reference tables which have been trialed in the field in some revealing projects, the number of hours worked by the creators of DL courses to be recognized against the number of hours scheduled for the online course. Most of the trials / experiments with this model were carried out under the auspices of the DL program of the Autonomous Province of Trento and the University of Trento, where we applied the model on a set of 37 editions of different courses run in 2011/ 2012.

As mentioned, the model is in the process of being refined, but has already shown a series of advantages that encourage us to carry on the research:

- clarity in calculating the acknowledged hours: the teacher "undergoes" the parametrization of the model, yet contributes with his/her own evaluation and has a direct match at the conclusion of the production phase
- predictability of costs in the yearly budget phase: the organization can indeed classify "ex-ante" the courses that it intends to offer, categorize them according to the parameters of the model and precisely estimate the cost of the various e-learning initiatives without having to resort to less "stimulating" models for the actors and while having a precise idea of the expenditure
- comparability of costs regarding course editions that end up in the same boxes of the model
- clarity in the temporal engagements taken on and the modality of implementation on behalf of the actors: the roles of teacher /tutor can be precisely defined, as well as the instruments to be used, and how much time (approximately) they will need to dedicate to these activities
- more profitability for teacher and tutor compared to traditional costing models: doubtlessly an element of motivation for the same to participate in e-learning initiatives

Our results were extremely encouraging: a deviation of about 10 % between the "ex-ante" calculation, based on the a priori application of the suggested parameters, and the "ex-post" statement of accounts (allowing an a posteriori evaluation of the hypothesis), based on the systematic gathering of data from the roles involved (teachers, tutors, instructional designers, etc.). Further experiments are needed to confirm or adjust the multipliers stated in the model, especially regarding new media and new educational models and approaches. The evaluation of the multiplier for multimedia learning objects is a crucial component: we are already working on a method that progressively decreases progressively the effort respect to the length of multimedia learning objects to be produced.

References

1. Rumble, G.: The costs and costing of networked learning. JALN **5**(2), 72–76 (2001)
2. Bacsich, P., Ash, C.: The Costs of Networked Learning. Sheffield Hallam University, Sheffield (1999)
3. Bacsich, P., Ash, C.: The Costs Of Networked Learning Phase Two. Sheffield Hallam University, Sheffield (2001)
4. Levin, H.M.: Cost-effectiveness analysis. In: Carnoy, M. (ed.) International Encyclopedia of Economics of Education, 2nd edn, pp. 381–386. Pergamon, Oxford (1995)
5. Casagranda, M., Colazzo, L., Molinari, A., Tomasini, S.: E-learning as an opportunity for the public administration: results and evolution of a learning model. Int. J. Teach. Case Stud., **2**(3/4), ISSN (Online): 1749-916X - ISSN (Print): 1749-9151, InterScience (2010)
6. Bartley, S.J.E., Golek, J.H.: Evaluating the cost effectiveness of online and face-to-face instruction. Educ. Technol. Soc. **7**(4), 167–175 (2004)
7. Ranieri, M.: E-learning: modelli e strategie didattiche, Trento, Erikson (2005)
8. Boccolini, M., Perich, C.: I costi dell'e-learning. Metodi e applicazioni per l'analisi costo-efficacia, Erickson, Trento (2004)
9. Battaglia, G., Serpelloni, G., Simeoni, E.: Apprendere e lavorare nell'era digitale – Online collaborative e-learning per le organizzazioni sanitarie, Verona (2008)
10. Cohen, A., Nachmias R.: A case study of implementing a cost effectiveness analyzer for web-supported academic instruction: an example from life science. Paper for the EDEN 2008 Annual Conference –New Learning Cultures, How do we learn? Where do we Learn? Portugal (2008)
11. Huddlestone, J., Pike, J.: Learning object reuse – a four tier model. In: IEEE and MOD HFI DTC Symposium on People and Systems - Who are We Designed for (2005)

Optical Communication Systems

Modal and Chromatic Dispersion Analysis Within a Measured 1,4 km MIMO Multimode Channel

Andreas Ahrens[✉], Steffen Schröder, and Steffen Lochmann

Department of Electrical Engineering and Computer Science,
Communications Signal Processing Group, Hochschule Wismar,
University of Technology, Business and Design,
Philipp-Müller-Straße 14, 23966 Wismar, Germany
{andreas.ahrens,steffen.lochmann}@hs-wismar.de, sschroeder81@web.de
http://www.hs-wismar.de

Abstract. In the recent past the concept of MIMO (multiple input multiple output) transmission over multimode fibers has attracted increasing interest in the optical fiber transmission community, targeting at increased fiber throughput or improved bit-error rate performance. Mostly, the possible performance improvements are calculated by computer simulations, which require some knowledge about the underlying system. Here, measurements results can be helpful to improve the quality of the estimated performance improvements. That's why in this contribution a signal theoretic multiple-input multiple-output (MIMO) system model for estimating modal and chromatic dispersion is developed. Based on channel measurements within a 1,4 km MIMO multimode channel parameters for modal and chromatic dispersion are estimated. Furthermore, taking given parameters of the dispersion into account, the introduced signal theoretic MIMO system model enables a reconstruction of the MIMO specific impulse responses.

Keywords: Multiple-input multiple-output (MIMO) system · Optical fibre transmission · Multimode fiber (MMF) · Modal dispersion · Chromatic dispersion

1 Introduction

The increasing desire for communication and information interchange has attracted a lot of research since Shannon's pioneering work in 1948. A possible solution was presented by Teletar and Foschini in the mid 90's, which revived the MIMO (multiple-input multiple-output) transmission philosophy introduced by van Etten in the mid 70's [5,13–15].

Since the capacity of wireless multiple-input multiple-output (MIMO) systems increases linearly with the minimum number of antennas at both, the transmitter as well as the receiver side, MIMO schemes have attracted substantial

© Springer-Verlag Berlin Heidelberg 2014
M.S. Obaidat and J. Filipe (Eds.): ICETE 2013, CCIS 456, pp. 183–196, 2014.
DOI: 10.1007/978-3-662-44788-8_11

attention [7,17] and can be considered as an essential part of increasing both the achievable capacity and integrity of future generations of wireless systems [6,16].

Optimizing the transmission on high-data rate links is in particular of great practical interest for delivering voice or video services in mobile IP (Internet Protocol) based networks in the access domain. That's why the MIMO transmission has influenced nearly any standard of wireless communication. However, the MIMO principle is not limited to wireless communication channel and a lot of scenarios can be described by the MIMO technology [3,6,12].

In comparison to the wireless MIMO channel, the optical fibre is an important type of a fixed-line medium, which is used in several sections of telecommunication networks, where single- and multi-mode fibres are distinguished. Unfortunately, the inherent modal dispersion limits the maximum data speed within the multimode fiber (MMF). In order to overcome this limitation, the well-known single-input single-output systems, also called SISO systems, should be transferred into systems with multiple-inputs and multiple-outputs, also called MIMO systems.

Within the last years, the concept of MIMO (multiple-input multiple-output) transmission over multimode and multicore fibers has attracted increasing interest in the optical fiber transmission community, e.g. [2,3,12], targeting at increased fiber throughput or improved bit-error rate performance.

Unfortunately, the multimode fibre capacity is limited by the dispersion. In multimode fibres the modal dispersion dominates the chromatic dispersion by orders. Only systems with Restricted Mode Launching (RML), e.g. the 10 Gbit Ethernet system standard 10GBASE-SR, focus on the description of both dispersion effects [4,10].

Since the modal and the chromatic dispersion are considered to be independent, the system impulse response is given by the convolution of these individual impulse responses.

Mostly, the possible performance improvements are calculated by computer simulations, which require some knowledge about the underlying system. Here, measurements results can be helpful to improve the quality of the estimated performance improvements. Against this background, the novel contribution of this paper is that based on channel measurement with a 1,4 km multimode fibre, a signal theoretic MIMO system model for estimating modal and chromatic dispersion is developed. By taking given parameters of the dispersion into account, the introduced system model enables a reconstruction of the MIMO specific impulse responses. Thus, a fundamental algorithm for further studies on the impact of dispersion and for a comparison of different MIMO systems utilizing different wavelengths is presented.

The remaining part of this contribution is organized as follows: Sect. 2 introduces our system model. The measurement setup for estimating the channel impulse responses is presented in Sect. 3. In Sect. 4 our signal theoretic system model is introduced and discussed. The associated performance results are presented and interpreted in Sect. 5. Finally, Sect. 6 provides our concluding remarks.

2   Multimode MIMO Channel

In order to form the optical MIMO channel, different sources of light have to be launched into the multimode fibre. In this work a (2×2) optical multimode MIMO channel is studied. The corresponding electrical MIMO system model is highlighted in Fig. 1.

In Fig. 2 the optical MIMO setup is shown schematically. On the left side the transmitter side is represented for launching different sources of light into the fibre. By coupling light in the center of the multimode core, described by TX_1, low-order mode groups are activated (e.g. fundamental mode). For activating high order mode groups, described by TX_2, light has to be launched into the fibre with an given eccentricity.

At the receiver side, different spatial filters are used to separate the different mode groups. For low-order mode groups the spot filter (described by RX_1) and for higher order mode groups the ring filter is used (described by RX_2). Together

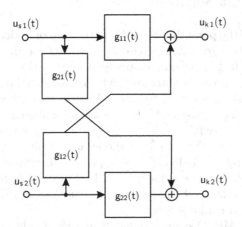

Fig. 1. Electrical MIMO system model (example: $n = 2$).

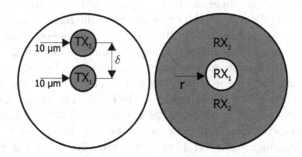

Fig. 2. Forming the optical MIMO channel (left: light launch positions at the transmitter side with a given eccentricity δ, right: spatial configuration at the receiver side as a function of the mask diameter r).

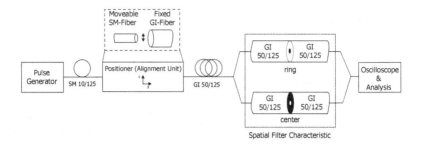

Fig. 3. Measurement setup for measuring the MIMO specific impulse responses.

with the mode group coupling along the 1,4 km long fibre, the MIMO system model according to Fig. 1 can be formed [8].

3   Measurement Setup

In order to evaluate the potential of MIMO in the field of optical multimode communication channels, a good knowledge of the MIMO specific impulse responses and their corresponding dispersion parameter is needed. For analyzing the MIMO specific impulse responses, the measurement setup depicted in Fig. 3 is used. For measuring the impulse responses, the input impulse was generated by using the Picosecond Diode Laser System (PiLas). For the measurement campaign two different laser diodes are used: The spectral properties of each laser diode are determined by measurement. The first laser diode has a center wave length (CWL) of 1326 nm and a spectral half width of approximately 8 nm. The second laser diode has a CWL of 1576 nm and a spectral half width of approximately 10 nm. Figure 4 shows exemplarily the measured spectrum of the 1576 nm Fabry-Perot laser with the typical modal structure.

For generating a MIMO system, different sources of light have to be launched into the multimode fibre. For the measurement campaign the laser light will be launched through a single mode waveguide into the core of a multimode waveguide. For the (2 × 2) MIMO System two different sources of light are needed. This part is realized by the first coupler component using a splicer. In a splicer the end of the transmitter waveguide and the beginning of the transmission path are clamped together where they are aligned exactly to each other (Fig. 5). By using the center launch condition only the fundamental mode is stimulated, represented by the signal $u_{s\,1}(t)$ in Fig. 1. The signal $u_{s\,2}(t)$ in Fig. 1 represents the offset launch condition for activating higher order mode groups. For the measurements an eccentricity of 10 μm was chosen. As a transmission channel a graded-index fibre of 1,4 km length was chosen. At the receiver side, for separating the different optical channels, different spatial filters (i.e, the spot filter with a diameter of $r = 15$ μm for low order mode groups and the corresponding ring filter for higher order mode groups) are used (Fig. 6). These spatial filters have been produced by depositing a metal layer at fibre end-faces

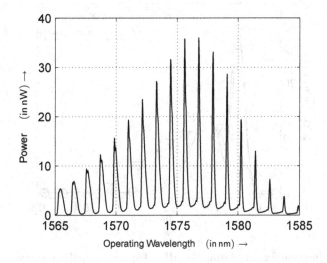

Fig. 4. Spectrum of used Fabry-Perot Laser (resolution bandwidth (RBW) of optical spectrum analyzer 0,07 nm).

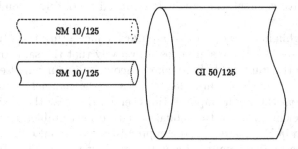

Fig. 5. Transmitter side configuration with center and offset light launch condition.

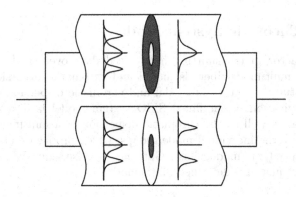

Fig. 6. Receiver side filter configuration for separating the different channels.

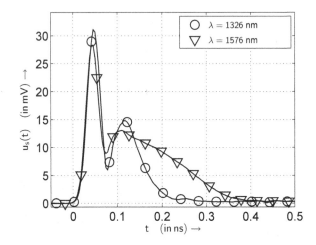

Fig. 7. Input impulse for calculating the MIMO-specific impulse responses at different operating wavelength.

and subsequent ion milling [1,8]. To determine the appropriate impulse response for the respective channel, the particular transmitter/receiver combination has to be chosen.

Figure 7 highlights the electrical impulse for measuring the MIMO-specific impulse responses. The pulses are chosen in a way that the same optical power is coupled into the multimode fibre core. Theoretically, an impulse like a dirac delta pulse has to be chosen in order to measure the channel impulse response unaffectedly from the input impulse. However, in this case the optical power is no longer sufficient to make the modal structure measurable. Thus, the input impulses shown in Fig. 7 are a good compromise to an impulse like a dirac delta impulse at a reasonable amount of coupled transmit power. The MIMO-specific impulse responses are obtained after deconvolution with the measured impulse responses.

4   Signal Theoretic System Model

The limiting factor in transmitting high speed data over single input single output (SISO) multimode fibers is modal and chromatic dispersion. In order to be able to study the effect of modal and chromatic dispersion especially in MIMO communication, a simplified SISO system model is developed, which takes the modal as well as the chromatic dispersion of a multimode fibre into account. Thereby the individual mode groups, which propagate along the fibre with different speed, are modeled as a Gaussian impulse sequence as highlighted in Fig. 8. This sequence is described mathematically as

$$g(t) = \sum_{\ell=0}^{q-1} a_\ell \, \delta(t - \tau_\ell) \tag{1}$$

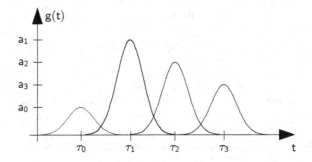

Fig. 8. Approximated impulse responses.

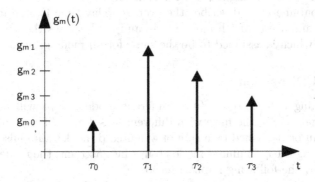

Fig. 9. Weighted Dirac delta impulse pulse response for the description of the SISO specific mode dispersion.

by taking q dominant mode groups into account which propagate along the fibre. The delay time of each mode group is described τ_ℓ and the mode group dependent weighting factor by a_ℓ.

Since the modal as well as the chromatic dispersion are independent from each other, the gaussian impulse sequence can be decomposed into two parts: a weighted dirac delta impulse response $g_m(t)$ for the description of the modal dispersion (Fig. 9) and a common gaussian part $g_c(t)$ for the description of the chromatic dispersion (Fig. 10). The resulting SISO specific impulse response can be obtained by convolution of $g_m(t)$ and $g_c(t)$ and results in:

$$g(t) = g_m(t) * g_c(t). \tag{2}$$

Figure 8 shows an exemplarily impulse response decomposed into individual gaussian impulses. In this work it is assumed that all mode groups are described by Gaussian impulses with individual delay and spread parameters. This sequence of weighted Gaussian pulses can now be decomposed into a sequence weighted dirac impulses (Fig. 9), for the description of the modal dispersion, and into a Gaussian pulse (Fig. 10), for the description of the chromatic dispersion.

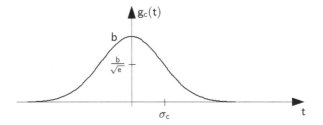

Fig. 10. Gaussian pulse to describe chromatic dispersion.

Figures 9 and 10 also highlight the parameters of the presented SISO system model. The parameter τ_ℓ describes the average delay time for the mode group ℓ, $g_{m\,\ell}$ is the amplitude of ℓth mode group and σ_c describes the spread of each mode group, which is assumed to be the same for all mode groups.

4.1 Modal Dispersion

When launching light into the fibre, different mode groups will be activated which propagate along the fibre with different speed and different attenuation. This effect can be described by a sum of weighted dirac delta impulses as shown in Fig. 9. Taking the q dominant mode groups into account, the mode dispersion is described by the following impulse response

$$g_m(t) = \sum_{\ell=0}^{q-1} g_{m\,\ell}\,\delta(t - \tau_\ell) \tag{3}$$

with the parameter τ_ℓ as the delay time and the parameter $g_{m\,\ell}$ as the weighting coefficient of the ℓ-th mode group.

The amount of modal dispersion included in the measured impulse response can now be described according to wireless transmission channels by a delay spread parameter σ_m [9]. The parameter σ_m describes the spread of the whole impulse response and can be used as a reference value for the modal dispersion. The delay spread is given by:

$$\sigma_m = \sqrt{\frac{1}{A}\sum_{\ell=0}^{q-1}\left(\tau_\ell\,g_{m\,\ell}\right)^2 - \left(\bar{t}_m\right)^2}. \tag{4}$$

Therein, the average delay of all modal groups (i.e. $\bar{t}_m$) results in

$$\bar{t}_m = \frac{1}{A}\sum_{\ell=0}^{q-1}\tau_\ell\left(g_{m\,\ell}\right)^2 \tag{5}$$

with normalization parameter $A = \sum_{\ell=0}^{q-1}\left(g_{m\,\ell}\right)^2$. With this normalization parameter, the mode-group dependent weighting coefficients fulfil the boundary condition

$$\frac{1}{A} \sum_{\ell=0}^{q-1} (g_{m\,\ell})^2 = 1. \tag{6}$$

4.2   Chromatic Dispersion

Theoretically, in the absent of chromatic dispersion, each mode group can be described by a single dirac delta impulse with a mode dependent delay and weighting factor. However, as the operating wavelength increased, the modes within a mode group travel with different speed and therefore the delay time between the different modes within a mode group become visible. This results in a broadening of the beforehand analyzed individual mode group dirac delta impulses. The parameter for this widening is the spread parameter σ_c. However, through the widening of the mode group dependent dirac delta impulses, the amplitude of impulse response is also weighted, i.e., the amplitude of impulse response a_ℓ and the modal dependent weighting factors $g_{m\,\ell}$ depend on the parameter σ_c.

The chromatic dispersion of each mode group is described by a normalized Gaussian impulse (Fig. 10) and is given as

$$g_c(t) = \frac{1}{\sigma_c \sqrt{2\pi}}\, e^{-\frac{t^2}{2\sigma_c^2}} \tag{7}$$

The parameter b in Fig. 10 represents the normalization factor of the Gaussian impulse and results in

$$b = \frac{1}{\sigma_c \sqrt{2\pi}}. \tag{8}$$

4.3   Spread Parameters

For the SISO system model, modal and chromatic dispersion are described by their corresponding spread parameters. Assuming that the individual mode groups are described as Gaussian pulses

$$g(t) = \sum_{\ell=0}^{q-1} a_\ell\, \delta(t - \tau_\ell), \tag{9}$$

the parameter a_ℓ is obtained by combining (3) and (7) and results in

$$a_\ell = g_{m\,\ell}\, \frac{1}{\sigma_c \sqrt{2\pi}}. \tag{10}$$

Taking this equation into account, the mode group dependent weighting factor $g_{m\,\ell}$ can be obtained as

$$g_{m\,\ell} = a_\ell\, \sigma_c\, \sqrt{2\pi} \tag{11}$$

by taking into account that the measured amplitude a_ℓ contains the information about the width of the gaussian pulse (i.e. chromatic dispersion) as well as the mode-dependent weighting factor. Therefore, the weighting factor $g_{\mathrm{m}\,\ell}$ can be determined with the predetermined spread parameter σ_{c} and the measured amplitude a_{ℓ}, i.e.

$$g_{\mathrm{m}\,\ell} = a_{\ell}\,\sigma_{\mathrm{c}}\,\sqrt{2\,\pi}. \tag{12}$$

Since the weighting of each mode group is described by the modal dispersion completely, the chromatic dispersion corresponding spread parameter σ_{c} can be calculated by taking the measured amplitudes a_{ℓ} into account.

4.4   MIMO System Model

In this work a (2×2) MIMO system model is investigated and the beforehand introduced signal theoretic SISO system model has now to be extended to the MIMO system model. The corresponding electrical MIMO system model is highlighted in Fig. 1 with the four existing transmission paths $g_{\nu\,\mu}(t)$ (with $\nu = 1, 2, \ldots, n_{\mathrm{R}}$ and $\mu = 1, 2, \ldots, n_{\mathrm{T}}$), which will be measured and analyzed separately. The number of transmitters is given by the n_{T} and the number of receivers by n_{R}, respectively. Therefore, the impulse response is given by

$$g_{\nu\,\mu}(t) = g_{\mathrm{m}}^{(\nu\,\mu)}(t) * g_{\mathrm{c}}^{(\nu\,\mu)}(t). \tag{13}$$

According to Eq. (14) the modal dispersion can be described by

$$g_{\mathrm{m}}^{(\nu\,\mu)}(t) = \sum_{\ell=0}^{q-1} g_{\mathrm{m}\,\ell}^{(\nu\,\mu)}\,\delta(t - \tau_{\ell}^{(\nu\,\mu)}) \tag{14}$$

with the delay of ℓth mode group $\tau_{\ell}^{(\nu\,\mu)}$ and the corresponding weighting factors $g_{\mathrm{m}\,\ell}^{(\nu\,\mu)}$. The average delay of the mode groups can be calculated by

$$\bar{t}_{\mathrm{m}}^{(\nu\,\mu)} = \frac{1}{A^{(\nu\,\mu)}} \sum_{\ell=0}^{q-1} \tau_{\ell}^{(\nu\,\mu)} \left(g_{\mathrm{m}\,\ell}^{(\nu\,\mu)}\right)^2 \tag{15}$$

with the normalization factor $A = \sum_{\ell=0}^{q-1} \left(g_{\mathrm{m}\,\ell}^{(\nu\,\mu)}\right)^2$ [9]. Finally, the modal dispersion results in:

$$\sigma_{\mathrm{m}}^{(\nu\,\mu)} = \sqrt{\frac{1}{A^{(\nu\,\mu)}} \sum_{\ell=0}^{q-1} \left(\tau_{\ell}^{(\nu\,\mu)} \cdot g_{\mathrm{m}\,\ell}^{(\nu\,\mu)}\right)^2 - \left(\bar{t}_{\mathrm{m}}^{(\nu\,\mu)}\right)^2}. \tag{16}$$

Assuming that the same laser is used for measuring all four impulse responses, the chromatic dispersion can be considered to be same within all four transmission path. Taking (7) into account, the following equation holds

$$g_{\mathrm{c}}^{(\nu\,\mu)}(t) = g_{\mathrm{c}}(t). \tag{17}$$

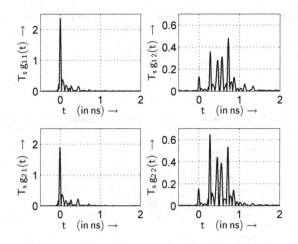

Fig. 11. Measured electrical MIMO impulse responses with respect to the pulse frequency $f_T = 1/T_s = 5{,}00\,\text{GHz}$ at 1326 nm operating wavelength.

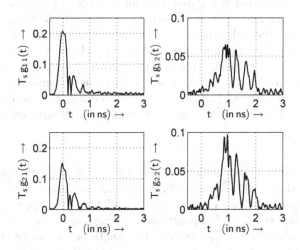

Fig. 12. Measured electrical MIMO impulse responses with respect to the pulse frequency $f_T = 1/T_s = 5{,}00\,\text{GHz}$ at 1576 nm operating wavelength.

5   Results

Within this paper, channel measurements within a 1,4 km (2×2) MIMO system are carried out. For the investigated optical MIMO channel an eccentricity δ of 10 μm and a mask diameter r of 15 μm were chosen (Fig. 2). Figure 11 shows the four impulse responses for an operating wavelength of 1326 nm according to Fig. 1. Compared to 1576 nm depicted in Fig. 12 the influence of the chromatic dispersion is highly visible.

Table 1. Parameters of the calculated chromatic dispersion.

λ (in nm)	σ_c in (ps)
1326	15
1576	129

Table 2. Parameters of the calculated modal dispersion.

λ (in nm)	σ_c (in ps)			
-	$g_{11}(t)$	$g_{12}(t)$	$g_{21}(t)$	$g_{22}(t)$
1326	38	215	62	199
1576	159	424	185	353

The impulse responses are obtained after deconvolution with the input impulse depicted in Fig. 7. Furthermore it is assumed that each optical input within the multimode fiber will be fed by a system with identical mean properties with respect to transmit filtering and pulse frequency $f_T = 1/T_s$. For numerical assessment within this paper, the pulse frequency is chosen to be $f_T = 5{,}00\,\text{GHz}$. Taking the measured impulse responses, depicted in Figs. 11 and 12, into account, the obtained parameters for the chromatic dispersion are presented in Table 1. For the same operating wavelength, the chromatic dispersion is assumed to be the same for all propagation paths and all individual mode groups. For comparison reason, the chromatic dispersion can be approximated by the following equation

$$\tau_c = D_c\,\delta_\lambda\,\ell. \tag{18}$$

The impulse spread τ_c can be described as the width of each impulse or mode group, measured at a 50 % decay of the maximum amplitude and to be assumed to be approximately twice as large as the calculated spread parameter σ_c. The dispersion parameter D_c at the operating wavelength of 1576 nm can be assumed to be 20 ps/(nm km) [11]. Together with the length of the measured multimode fibre of $\ell = 1{,}4\,\text{km}$ and the spectral width δ_λ (FWHW, Full Width Half Maximum) of the laser diode of 10 nm, an impulse spread τ_c of approximately 280 ps is obtained. With $\tau_c \approx 2\,\sigma_c$ the measured values of σ_c can be justified. At a operating wavelength of 1326 nm the chromatic dispersion tends to be zero. At this particular operating wavelength no chromatic dispersion appears. Therefore, at the operating wavelength of 1326 nm, the chromatic dispersion is not exactly zero, but much lower compared with an operating wavelength of 1576 nm.

The estimated parameters of the modal dispersion are highlighted in Table 2.

Next to analyzed parameters of modal and chromatic dispersion, the introduced system model enables a reconstruction of the MIMO specific impulses responses by taking the estimated dispersion parameters into account. In Figs. 13 and 14 the approximated impulse response $g_{22}(t)$ is shown exemplarily at different operating wavelength by using the beforehand introduced system model and the estimated parameters of modal and chromatic dispersion. As shown by

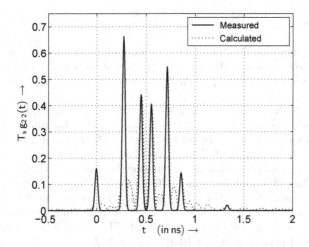

Fig. 13. Calculated and measured impulse response $g_{22}(t)$ at 1326 nm operating wavelength.

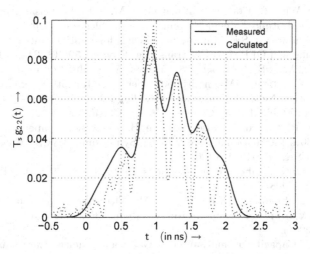

Fig. 14. Calculated and measured impulse response $g_{22}(t)$ at 1576 nm operating wavelength.

Figs. 13 and 14 the approximated impulse responses show a good correlation with the measured impulse responses.

6   Conclusions

Based on channel measurements, in this work a signal theoretic MIMO system model for estimating modal and chromatic dispersion is introduced and parameters for modal and chromatic dispersion for an 1,4 km multimode MIMO channel are estimated.

References

1. Aust, S., Ahrens, A., Lochmann, S.: Channel-encoded and SVD-assisted MIMO multimode transmission schemes with iterative detection. In: International Conference on Optical Communication Systems (OPTICS), Rom, Italy, pp. 353–360 (2012)
2. Bülow, H., Al-Hashimi, H., Schmauss, B.: Stable coherent MIMO transport over few mode fiber enabled by an adiabatic mode splitter. In: European Conference and Exhibition on Optical Communication (ECOC), Torino, Italy, p. P4.04 (2010)
3. Bülow, H., Al-Hashimi, H., Schmauss, B.: Coherent multimode-fiber MIMO transmission with spatial constellation modulation. In: European Conference and Exhibition on Optical Communication (ECOC), Geneva, Switzerland (2011)
4. Castro, J., Pimpinella, R., Kose, B., Lane, B.: The interaction of modal and chromatic dispersion in VCSEL based multimode fiber channel links and its effect on mode partition noise. In: 61th International Wire & Cable Symposium (IWCS), pp. 724–730. Providence, Rhode Island, USA (2012)
5. Foschini, G.J.: Layered space-time architecture for wireless communication in a fading environment when using multiple antennas. Bell Labs Tech. J. $1(2)$, 41–59 (1996)
6. Kühn, V.: Wireless Communications Over MIMO Channels - Applications to CDMA and Multiple Antenna Systems. Wiley, Chichester (2006)
7. Mueller-Weinfurtner, S.H.: Coding approaches for multiple antenna transmission in fast fading and OFDM. IEEE Trans. Sig. Process. $50(10)$, 2442–2450 (2002)
8. Pankow, J., Aust, S., Lochmann, S., Ahrens, A.: Modulation-mode assignment in SVD-assisted optical MIMO multimode fiber links. In: 15th International Conference on Optical Network Design and Modeling (ONDM), Bologna, Italy (2011)
9. Pätzold, M.: Mobile Fading Channels. Wiley, Chichester (2002)
10. Pimpinella, R., Castro, J., Kose, B., Lane, B.: Dispersion compensated multimode fiber. In: 60th International Wire & Cable Symposium (IWCS), Charlotte, North Carolina, USA, pp. 410–418 (2011)
11. Senior, J.: Optical Fiber Communications: Principles and Practice. Prentice Hall, New Jersey (2008)
12. Singer, A.C., Shanbhag, N.R., Bae, H.-M.: Electronic dispersion compensation-an overview of optical communications systems. IEEE Sig. Process. Mag. $25(6)$, 110–130 (2008)
13. Telatar, E.: Capacity of multi-antenna Gaussian channels. Eur. Trans. Telecommun. $10(6)$, 585–595 (1999)
14. van Etten, W.: An optimum linear receiver for multiple channel digital transmission systems. IEEE Trans. Commun. $23(8)$, 828–834 (1975)
15. van Etten, W.: Maximum likelihood receiver for multiple channel transmission systems. IEEE Trans. Commun. $24(2)$, 276–283 (1976)
16. Zheng, L., Tse, D.N.T.: Diversity and multiplexing: a fundamental tradeoff in multiple-antenna channels. IEEE Trans. Inf. Theor. $49(5)$, 1073–1096 (2003)
17. Zhou, Z., Vucetic, B., Dohler, M., Li, Y.: MIMO systems with adaptive modulation. IEEE Trans. Veh. Tech. $54(5)$, 1073–1096 (2005)

Long-Reach PONs Employing Directly Modulated Lasers for Provisioning of OFDM-UWB Radio Signals in Sparse Geographical Areas

Tiago M.F. Alves and Adolfo V.T. Cartaxo[⊠]

Instituto de Telecomunicações, Department of Electrical and Computer Engineering,
Instituto Superior Técnico, Universidade de Lisboa, 1049-001 Lisboa, Portugal
{tiago.alves,adolfo.cartaxo}@lx.it.pt

Abstract. Directly modulated long-reach (LR) passive optical networks
(PONs) are experimentally assessed for the distribution of orthogonal
frequency division multiplexing (OFDM) ultra wideband (UWB) bands
along sparse geographical areas. Particularly, we propose and demonstrate useful system design guidelines enabling the distribution of UWB
signals along directly modulated LR-PONs with maximum reach exceeding 100 km. Adequate selection of the UWB signal applied to the directly
modulated laser (DML) and fixed in-line optical dispersion compensation are shown as effective solutions to reach between 75 km and 130 km
of standard single-mode fibre. The analysis performed for a wavelength
division multiplexing system comprising three optical channels showed
also that, for optical channel spacing as narrow as 0.2 nm, the proposed system suffers from negligible linear inter-channel crosstalk. These
results demonstrate that directly modulated LR-PONs can be employed
as a reliable solution for provisioning of UWB signals to users' premises
located in sparse take-up geographies.

Keywords: Long-reach passive optical networks · Orthogonal frequency
division multiplexing · Ultra wideband · Directly modulated lasers ·
Optical dispersion compensation

1 Introduction

Ultra wideband (UWB) radio communication systems have been receiving a
special attention over the last years. Such systems can benefit from several
UWB advantages as high data rate broadcasting (480 Mbits/s [1,2]), tolerance to
multi-path fading, possibility of co-existence with other already employed technologies (IEEE 802.11 and IEEE 802.16), position monitoring and low power
consumption allowing small size/low cost integration [3]. UWB is an unlicensed
technology that uses radio modulation techniques with a minimum bandwidth
of 500 MHz or at least 20 % greater than the centre frequency of operation.

M.S. Obaidat and J. Filipe (Eds.): ICETE 2013, CCIS 456, pp. 197–206, 2014.
DOI: 10.1007/978-3-662-44788-8_12

UWB channels must be allocated in the band between 3.1 and 10.6 GHz with a maximum equivalent isotropic radiated power (EIRP) of -41.3 dBm/MHz [4,5]. The UWB radio signals broadcasting is indicated for small environments like homes and offices premises. Impulse-radio (IR) and orthogonal frequency division multiplexing (OFDM) were proposed as UWB signal modulation formats [3]. The OFDM-UWB solution has shown enhanced features such as higher flexibility to provide multiple access inherent to multi-band techniques, tolerance to multipath fading and intersymbol interference (ISI), and reduced band limitations in the UWB transceiver due to the 528-MHz-wide channelization of OFDM-UWB signals rather than 7.5 GHz of bandwidth for IR-UWB signals. Furthermore, devices for OFDM modulation and demodulation are already available due to the use of OFDM in other wireless applications like IEEE 802.11 and IEEE 802.16. Hence, this work is focused only on OFDM-UWB radio signals.

Significant efforts from microelectronic companies developing UWB terminals and devices at low cost have been accomplished in order to reach a large scale penetration of the UWB technology in the access telecommunication networks [6]. The Wimedia Alliance, a non-profit organization that defines, certifies and supports enabling wireless technology for multimedia applications, defined data rates up to 1 Gbit/s and the creation of a global UWB radio standard with guaranteed inter-operability as main targets for the UWB radio specifications. Hence, UWB technology presents the advantage of broadcasting higher data rate between electronic devices than traditional communications and it is indicated to be used by high quality multimedia equipment as personal digital video recorders (DVR), high definition television (HDTV), laptops and cable/satellite set-top boxes [2,7].

The transmission of UWB radio signals along optical fibre in short-range environments was already investigated [8]. The application target of such investigation is to cover buildings/offices with an integrated optical fibre distribution/wireless broadcasting solution that allows the end-users to benefit from the high mobility and high bit-rate over short ranges capabilities provided by the UWB-based wireless networks. The transmission of these UWB radio signals over fibre-to-the-home (FTTH) infrastructures is a powerful solution to address the distribution of UWB signals along longer distances. Moreover, avoiding transmodulation or frequency conversion of the UWB radio signals at the end-users' premises, the subscribers can benefit from low cost transponders and a deep penetration can be expected worldwide. The considered FTTH paths correspond to standard lengths used in passive optical networks (PONs) to connect distribution hubs (DH) to UWB end users (up to 60 km).

Recently, the increase of the reach of the FTTH paths has been a hot research topic supported by the operators' point of view [9]. The main target of this topic is to reach 100 km between the central office and the users' premises, and it is indicated for the metro and access networks integration envisaged by long-reach (LR) PONs [9]. In LR-PONs, the optical line termination (OLT) at the central office (CO) is connected to an active remote node (RN) via a fibre span denominated feeder or trunk line [9]. The target reach of this span is around

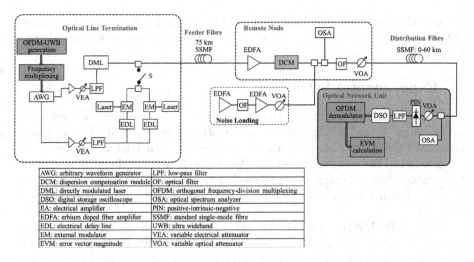

AWG: arbitrary waveform generator	LPF: low-pass filter
DCM: dispersion compensation module	OF: optical filter
DML: directly modulated laser	OFDM: orthogonal frequency-division multiplexing
DSO: digital storage oscilloscope	OSA: optical spectrum analyzer
EA: electrical amplifier	PIN: positive-intrinsic-negative
EDFA: erbium doped fiber amplifier	SSMF: standard single-mode fibre
EDL: electrical delay line	UWB: ultra wideband
EM: external modulator	VEA: variable electrical attenuator
EVM: error vector magnitude	VOA: variable optical attenuator

Fig. 1. Schematic diagram of the experimental setup implemented in the laboratory to emulate the distribution of the UWB signals along a directly modulated LR-PON.

80 km and optical amplification is performed at the RN in order to compensate for the losses introduced along the optical link. The different optical network units (ONUs) are then connected to the RN via a completely PON with reach around 20–30 km. From the operators' viewpoint, some of the benefits of the LR-PONs are [9]: (i) decrease the number of OLTs deployed and provide a full integration between the metro and access networks with the corresponding system cost savings, (ii) sharing the OLT and the feeder fibre by several users in a sparse take-up geography and (iii) decrease the configuration and management issues of the network.

External and direct modulation have been recently proposed and demonstrated as effective solutions to be employed in LR-PONs supporting radio-over-fibre signals [10]. External modulated LR-PONs have shown better performance, whereas directly modulated LR-PONs are viewed as a cost-effective and alternative solution. However, the maximum reach of directly modulated LR-PONs is commonly assumed shorter than when external modulation is employed due to the combined effect of the chirp introduced by the directly modulated laser (DML) and the fibre dispersion.

The study of the directly modulated LR-PON work proposed in [10] for the provisioning of different wired and wireless OFDM-based services to the end users showed that the performance of the bundle of OFDM signals is impaired mainly by the UWB signals. This is due to the higher bandwidth of UWB signals and also due to their higher central frequencies [10].

In this work, we focus our attention only in the transmission of the UWB signals along directly modulated LR-PONs. Particularly, we propose and demonstrate experimentally useful system design guidelines enabling the distribution of UWB signals along directly modulated LR-PONs with maximum reach exceeding

100 km. This directly modulated extended LR-PON is a powerful solution to distribute the UWB signals to users' premises located at sparse geographical areas in a cost-effective manner.

2   Experimental Setup

Figure 1 depicts the diagram of the experimental setup employed to assess the performance of the OFDM-UWB signals distribution along the directly modulated LR-PON. Figure 1 depicts a multi-wavelength setup comprising three optical channels. However, in this section, we focus the system description only on the single-channel operation, i.e., the switch S presented in Fig. 1 is in the open position. Further information about the multi-wavelength setup is provided in Sect. 3.2.

The OFDM-UWB bands #1, #2 and #3 are generated and frequency multiplexed through digital signal processing (DSP) in Matlab. The raw data rate of each UWB band is 320 Mbaud and the UWB bands #1, #2 and #3 are centred at the frequencies of 3.4 GHz, 3.9 GHz and 4.4 GHz, respectively, and each UWB band occupies a bandwidth of 528 MHz. Hence, after multiplexing, the spectral occupancy of the three UWB bands is between 3.1 GHz and 4.7 GHz. Quadrature phase-shift keying (QPSK) mapping and similar power levels between the three OFDM-UWB bands are considered. Only these three bands are considered in these experiments because most of the UWB devices commercially available nowadays operate only in these UWB bands and also due to the limited bandwidth of the DML available in the laboratory. The electrical signal is generated by an arbitrary waveform generator operating at 20 Gsamples/s. A radio frequency (RF) amplifier and a variable electrical attenuator are used to set the modulation index of the signal applied to the DML. After amplification, the electrical noise power is reduced by using a low-pass filter (LPF) with -3 dB bandwidth of 7.6 GHz. The DML is a low-cost multi-quantum well DFB laser characterized by a threshold current of $I_{th} = 8.1$ mA, a bias current of $I_b = 30$ mA, a chirp parameter of 2.6, nominal wavelength of 1552.85 nm and an intensity response bandwidth of about 4 GHz [11]. The OFDM-UWB signal is launched into a 75 km-long feeder standard single-mode fibre (SSMF), with dispersion parameter of 17 ps/nm/km, with an average optical power of 0 dBm.

At the remote node (RN), an optical amplifier compensates for the fibre loss and a dispersion compensating module (DCM) is used to reduce the degradation induced by the combined effect of the DML's chirp and the fibre dispersion. A noise loading circuit is used to set the optical signal-to-noise ratio, in a 0.1 nm bandwidth, to 30 dB. The amplified spontaneous emission noise power is reduced by using an optical filter with -3 dB bandwidth of 16 GHz. The average optical power at the input of the distribution fibre is also 0 dBm.

Different distribution fibre reaches are considered along the study in order to measure the performance of the OFDM-UWB signals distribution for different LR-PON distances. Particularly, distribution fibres with reach between 0 km and 60 km are analysed. These distribution fibre reaches correspond to LR-PON with reaches between 75 km and 135 km.

At the ONU, the average optical power at the photodetector input is set to -12.5 dBm. The signal is photodetected by a 10 GHz PIN including a transimpedance amplifier stage. After photodetection, the UWB signal is filtered by a LPF with -3 dB bandwidth of 10 GHz and sampled by a real-time oscilloscope operating at 20 Gsamples/s. DSP algorithms are then applied to the sampled signal waveform in order to demodulate each OFDM-UWB band. These algorithms comprise RF carrier recovery, time synchronization, down-conversion, ideal filtering, FFT window synchronization, common phase error compensation and equalization. After DSP, the EVM of each received OFDM-UWB band is evaluated and compared with the EVM limit (-14.5 dB for QPSK) of UWB standard [12]. The EVM limit of UWB standard is defined at the output of the wireless transmitter, i.e., before wireless radiation. Therefore, it can be used as performance threshold of the UWB signals at the output of optical fibre link.

3 Experimental Results and Discussion

3.1 Single-Wavelength Operation

In this section, the EVM of each of the three OFDM-UWB bands simultaneously distributed along the LR-PON infrastructure described in Sect. 2 is evaluated experimentally and discussed.

Initially, the optimization of the modulation index of the OFDM-UWB signal applied to the DML (in order to optimize the level of nonlinear distortion induced by the combined effect of the DML and the PIN) and of the optical dispersion compensation level of the DCM (to minimize the degradation due to the joint effect of DML's chirp and fibre dispersion) located at the RN is performed. The optimization outcomes depend on the reach of the LR-PON considered due to the interaction between the accumulated dispersion of the link and the chirp introduced by the DML. Thus, we decided to perform the optimization for a RN-ONU distance of 25 km (total LR-PON reach of 100 km). The system optimization is accomplished for this reach as it represents a compromise between two LR-PON reaches. First, we want to ensure the distribution of UWB signals along a minimum LR-PON reach (the feeder fibre length, 75 km) with acceptable performance. Second, we want to extend the maximum LR-PON reach for a distance longer than 100 km while keeping the reception of UWB signals with acceptable conditions.

The modulation index is defined as $m = I_{RMS}/(I_b - I_{th})$, where I_{RMS} is the root mean square (RMS) current of the OFDM-UWB signal applied to the DML. Figure 2(a), (b) and (c) depict the PSD of the optical signal at the RN for different modulation indexes levels. Figure 2(a), (b) and (c) show that the modulation index increase leads not only to the power increase of the UWB bands but also to the power increase of the distortion components generated due to the nonlinear characteristic of the DML.

Figure 2(d), (e) and (f) show the EVM of each OFDM-UWB band as a function of the residual dispersion (defined as the difference between the accumulated dispersion of the feeder and distribution fibres, and the dispersion compensated

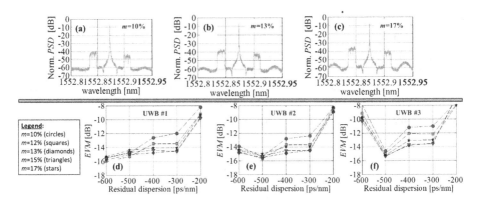

Fig. 2. (a), (b) and (c) PSD of the signal after the DCM inserted at the RN for different modulation indexes. (d), (e) and (f) EVM of UWB band #1, #2 and #3 as a function of the residual dispersion of the link and for different modulation indexes. In (d), (e) and (f), the LR-PON reach is 100 km and $m = 10\%$ (circles), $m = 12\%$ (squares), $m = 13\%$ (diamonds), $m = 15\%$ (triangles), $m = 17\%$ (stars).

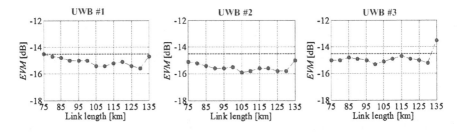

Fig. 3. EVM of UWB band #1, #2 and #3 as a function of the LR-PON reach. The DCM is compensating for 2200 ps/nm and the modulation index is 13%.

by the DCM) of the link. The EVM results are presented for different modulation indexes. Figure 2(d), (e) and (f) show that the behavior of the EVM when the residual dispersion varies depends on the UWB band under analysis. Particularly, the inspection of Fig. 2(d), (e) and (f) show that the tolerance of the EVM to negative residual dispersion levels decreases when the number of the UWB band increases, i.e., when the central frequency of the UWB band increases. This effect occurs because the intensity response of the link is remarkably affected by the residual dispersion. Further investigation showed that, if the residual dispersion of the link changes from -300 ps/nm (DCM adjusted to compensate for 2000 ps/nm of dispersion) to -600 ps/nm (DCM adjusted to compensate 2300 ps/nm), an amplitude gain close to 9 dB occurs at the frequency of 3.4 GHz (central frequency of UWB band #1). However, this gain is reduced to 5 dB at the frequency of 4.4 GHz (central frequency of UWB band #3).

On the other hand, Fig. 2(d), (e) and (f) show also that the performance of the UWB bands is remarkably dependent on the modulation index. For low

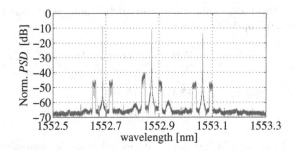

Fig. 4. PSD of the WDM signal after the DCM inserted at the RN.

modulation indexes, the EVM improves when the modulation index increases due to the improvement of the signal-to-noise ratio. However, for high modulation indexes, this EVM improvement is counterbalanced by the degradation induced by the nonlinear distortion caused by the DML nonlinear characteristic and the PIN square law detection.

In the following, the analysis of the EVM of the three UWB bands when the LR-PON reach varies between 75 km and 135 km is performed. This study is accomplished with a fixed dispersion compensation level in the DCM. From the results of Fig. 2(d), (e) and (f), the DCM is adjusted to compensate 2200 ps/nm of dispersion. In a 100 km-long LR-PON, this compensation level leads to a residual dispersion of −500 ps/nm. The modulation index of the multiplexed UWB signal applied to the DML is 13 %. The fixed dispersion compensation level of the DCM and the modulation index value chosen correspond to the optimum system operating point shown in Fig. 2(d), (e) and (f).

Figure 3 shows the EVM of UWB band #1, #2 and #3 as a function of the LR-PON reach. LR-PON reaches between 75 km and 135 km are considered, which correspond to distribution fibre distances between 0 km and 60 km. Figure 3 shows that the EVM of the three UWB bands meets the EVM requirements of UWB standard (−14.5 dB) for LR-PON reaches between 75 km and 130 km. Moreover, Fig. 3 shows also that, for almost all the LR-PON reaches analysed, UWB band #3 is the UWB band with worst performance. This is attributed to the limited frequency response of the electrical devices used in the experiments and also due to the reduced gain of the intensity response of the optical link observed for higher frequencies.

3.2 Multi-wavelength Operation

Our investigation of the single-channel LR-PON was also extended to a wavelength division multiplexing (WDM) LR-PON. This extension allows assessing the impact of the inter-channel crosstalk induced by adjacent optical channels on a WDM LR-PON. To perform this activity, two optical channels adjacent to the one used in the single-channel system were introduced into the system, as shown in Fig. 1. However, these two additional optical channels were deployed using

Table 1. EVM of the UWB signals transmitted by the central channel of a WDM signal comprising three optical channels.

EVM [dB]	UWB #1	UWB #2	UWB #3
75 km	−14.8	−15.0	−15.1
100 km	−15.1	−15.4	−15.3
130 km	−15.6	−15.6	−15.1

Table 2. EVM of the UWB signals transmitted in single-channel operation.

EVM [dB]	UWB #1	UWB #2	UWB #3
75 km	−14.5	−15.1	−15.0
100 km	−15.0	−15.5	−15.3
130 km	−15.6	−15.8	−15.2

external modulation instead of direct modulation due to the lack of DMLs in our laboratory with adequate features to generate a dense WDM signal. Figure 4 shows the PSD of the WDM signal after the DCM inserted at the RN. Figure 4 shows that the spectra of the optical signal generated by the directly or externally modulated solutions are similar and, consequently, crosstalk features similar to the ones obtained if only directly modulated channels were employed are expected.

The two adjacent channels are generated through a distributed feedback laser (DFB) and an external cavity laser (ECL), and using 10 GHz Mach Zehnder modulators. The nominal wavelengths of the adjacent optical channels are set to 1552.65 nm and 1553.05 nm and, therefore, the channel spacing is 0.2 nm. The average optical power of the WDM signal launched into the feeder and distribution fibres is kept below 0 dBm to avoid degradation due to the nonlinear fibre transmission effects. The impact of the inter-channel linear crosstalk was performed for LR-PONs with reach of 75 km, 100 km and 130 km. As our focus is in directly modulated LR-PONs, we only evaluated the performance of the UWB bands transmitted in central optical channel.

Table 1 presents the EVM results of the central channel of the WDM signal. Table 2 presents the EVM results of the UWB bands in single-channel operation, corresponding to the results of Fig. 3(d), (e) and (f), as a reference. The comparison between the EVM results of Tables 1 and 2 shows an EVM variation lower than 0.3 dB between single and WDM operation. This variation is mainly due to the fluctuation of the EVM measurements resulting from e.g. the noise introduced along the system. Those reduced EVM variations indicate that, for the channel spacing and the optical power levels considered in this work, the inter-channel linear and nonlinear crosstalks are not a relevant concern.

4 Conclusions

The distribution of OFDM-UWB radio signals along LR-PONs employing directly modulated lasers has been demonstrated experimentally as an effective solution to serve users' premises located at 130 km away from the central office. Directly modulated LR-PONs has been also demonstrated as an effective solution to be deployed in sparse geographical areas, as EVM levels compliant with UWB standard are achieved for LR-PONs with reach between 75 km and 130 km, i.e., for a maximum distribution fibre reach of 55 km. In addition, the performance of the directly-modulated optical channel has shown an EVM variation lower than 0.3 dB when two adjacent channels (with a spacing of 0.2 nm) were introduced to assess the impact of the WDM operation.

This successful demonstration has been achieved by using fixed optical inline dispersion compensation at the RN and through adequate selection of the level of the UWB signal applied to the DML.

Acknowledgments. This work was supported by Fundação para a Ciência e a Tecnologia from Portugal under the TURBO-PTDC/EEA-TEL/104358/2008 project.

References

1. Staccato Communications, Intel and Philips: Demonstration to show future of high-speed wireless USB. MBOA UWB Techzone at CES, CES Las Vegas (2005)
2. Pulse LINK demonstrates UWB wireless, cable and power line communications. In: Global Conference on Ultra Wideband: Demonstrations of new high bandwidth technology showcase opportunities for connected home, Boston, MA (2004)
3. Siriwongpairat, W., Liu, K.: Ultra Wideband Communications Systems - Multiband OFDM Approach. Wiley, New Jersey (2008)
4. European Union: Commission decision of 21 February 2007 on allowing the use of the radio spectrum for equipment using ultra-wideband technology in a harmonised manner in the Community. Official Journal of the European Union (2007)
5. FCC: Revision of part 15 of the Commission's rules regarding ultra-wideband transmission systems: first report and order. Technical Report (2002)
6. European Project Ultra-wide band radio over fiber technology, FP6-2005-IST-2005-033615 (2005)
7. Wimedia. http://www.wimedia.org/en/index.asp
8. Guo, Y., Pham, V., Yee, M., Ong, L., Luo, B.: Performance study of MB-OFDM ultra-wideband signals over multimode fiber. In: Proceedings of the Optical Fibre Communication Conference, California, pp. 429–431 (2007)
9. Davey, R., Grossman, D., Wiech, M., Payne, D., Nesset, D., Kelly, A., Rafael, A., Appathurai, S., Yang, S.: Long-reach passive optical networks. J. Lightwave Technol. **27**, 273–291 (2009)
10. Alves, T., Morant, M., Cartaxo, A., Llorente, R.: Wired-wireless services provision in FSAN NG-PON2 compliant long-reach PONs: performance analysis, In: Proceedings of the Optical Fibre Communication Conference, OM3D3, California (2013)

11. Morgado, J., Fonseca, D., Cartaxo, A.: Experimental study of coexistence of multi-band OFDM-UWB and OFDM-baseband signals in long-reach PONs using directly modulated lasers. Opt. Express **19**, 23601–23612 (2011)
12. ECMA Int.: High Rate UltraWideband PHY and MAC Standard, 2nd edn. Geneve, Switzerland (2007)

Security and Cryptography

InCC: Evading Interception and Inspection by Mimicking Traffic in Network Flows

Luis Campo Giralte, Isaac Martin de Diego, Cristina Conde,
and Enrique Cabello$^{(\boxtimes)}$

Universidad Rey Juan Carlos, Madrid, Spain
{luis.campo.giralte,isaac.martin,cristina.conde,enrique.cabello}@urjc.es

Abstract. This article proposes and implements a network covert channel called InCC capable of hiding information on the Internet, which is designed to produce a undetectable communication channel between systems. This network channel is fully transparent to any network analysis and for hence to any interception and inspection on a network. InCC is capable to send messages on the same production network without compromising the existence of source and destination. By using techniques like encryption, address spoofing, signature poisoning and traffic analysis, the channel is able to hide the flows on the network without implicating the source and destination.

Keywords: Storage covert channel · Network flow · p2p applications · rc4

1 Introduction

Traditionally, network covert channels were classified into storage and timing channels despite the fact that there is no fundamental distinction between them [1]. The storage channels involve the direct/indirect writing of object values by the sender and the direct/indirect reading of the object values by the receiver. Otherwise, timing channels involve the sender signaling information by modulating the use of resources over time so that the receiver can observe and decode the information properly.

One of the main problems of existing network covert channels is that they only send small amounts of information, since otherwise the connection could be detected. When using timing channels, the amount of packets needed to send information is quite high. It is well known that timing channels use variable time in order to encode the binary information. Nevertheless, network storage channels are capable of sending more information in comparison with timing channels, but by using DPI (Deep packet inspection) technique renders most of them detectable.

In this article we propose and implement a storage network covert channel called InCC (Invisible Covert Channel) which is capable of hiding the communication between two peers without compromising their existence. One of the

© Springer-Verlag Berlin Heidelberg 2014
M.S. Obaidat and J. Filipe (Eds.): ICETE 2013, CCIS 456, pp. 209–225, 2014.
DOI: 10.1007/978-3-662-44788-8_13

main differences of the proposed system as compared with the existing ones is that InCC learns from the network and generates traffic that mimics the existing one on the network. This feature makes InCC a perfect network covert channel, capable of going undetected by any DPI technique.

The proposed system has been tested using some open-source traffic engines and to test the effectiveness of the covert channel, we have implemented a prototype on Python that enables secure communication between transparent network systems over UDP. The main idea of the proposal is to camouflage the flows on the network traffic in order to remain unnoticed for any type of network analysis. So even if the flows are detected by a network analysis, the traffic generated by the channel cannot be identified. InCC learns the traffic most commonly used by the network, being capable of hiding the new flows generated in this traffic in order to communicate systems.

The organization of this paper is as follows. The related work is discussed in Sect. 2. The discussion of the methods proposed, together with the description, is presented in Sect. 3. The implementation details are presented in Sect. 4. The experiments carried out can be found in Sect. 5 and, finally, a conclusion is reached in Sect. 6.

2   Related Work

The most common techniques for hiding information on network flows are network covert channels [2–6], which focus on hiding data in various network protocols like IPv4, TCP, DNS, HTTPS, etc. Applications like Skype use covert channels [7] on HTTP traffic in order to hide their communications, and many others use these techniques in order to comply with ISP network restrictions. The most relevant works are shown next, with the most interesting techniques by the different authors classified in Table 1.

Dittmann *et al.* [8] examine the existing VoIP applications with respect to their extensibility to steganographic algorithms. They have also paid attention to the part of steganalysis in PCM audio data that allows us to detect hidden communications while running VoIP communication with the usage of the PCM codec. They show the results for their PCM steganalyzer framework that is able to detect this kind of hidden communication by using a set of 13 first and second order statistics.

Liu *et al.* [9] use covert timing channels by encoding the modulated message in the inter-packet delay of the underlying overt communication channel such that the statistical properties of regular traffic can be closely approximated. The system was designed for UDP traffic by hiding the covert traffic on networks with on-line gaming traffic.

Most timing channels are based on the use of a time variable in order to encode the information. This increases the number of packets sent on the network -an evidence of the channel's existence, which is the largest disadvantage of timing channels [10]. In addition, jitter and delays are of no avail on these channels.

Storage channels are becoming of increasing interest for the research community. This is due to the arrival of new techniques that allow the hiding of information, such as stenography. The most interesting research will now be evaluated and later classified.

Zander et al. [11] compare the different encoding techniques and also propose two new improved encoding schemes based on the IP TTL field. They group the existing techniques for encoding covert information into the TTL field into three classes: (a) Direct encoding encodes covert bits directly into bits of the TTL field, (b) Mapped encoding encodes covert bits by mapping bit values to specific TTL values and (c) Differential encoding encodes covert bits as change between subsequent TTL values. The weakness of this model is the high amount of packets that have to be sent to the destination, since the limitation of the TTL field is 8 bits.

Nussbaum et al. [5] propose a system called TUNS which is an IP over DNS tunnel. Their system only uses the CNAME record of the DNS header. It encodes the IP packets using a Base32 encoding without splitting the IP packets into several smaller DNS packets. The main problem of this model resides in the fact that, by using a good DNS analyzer most of the bogus packets could be detected due to modify the use of the DNS CNAME record.

Luo et al. [12] propose a system called CLACK, which encodes covert messages into the TCP acknowledgements (ACKs). Their system is based on a persistent flow of TCP data. They find two objectives: to provide a reliable covert channel, similar to the reliable data service provided by TCP, and increase the cost of detecting the covert channels. Their weakest point is that they assume that all transmissions are perfect, i.e. lossless, packet order preserved and no duplicate packets, and this is not very common on the Internet network.

Wendzel et al. [13] shows a method for detect switching covert channels (PSSCCs). PPCSSs transfer hidden information by sending networks packets with different selected network protocols such as HTTP, POP3, etc. Protocols are therefore linked to secret values, e.g., a HTTP packet could represent the value '1' and a SMTP packet could represent the value '0'. The weakness of this model relay on the high amount of packets that the sender needs to sent in order to encode the information.

Mazurczyk et al. [14] present steganographic methods that utilize mechanisms for handling over-sized IP packets: IP fragmentation, PMTUD (Path MTU Discovery) and PLPMTUD (Packetization Layer Path MTU Discovery). They modify the offset value of the fragmented packets to add the information payload and also modify certain IP flags. However, the detection of these methods are trivial due to the short number of IP fragmented packets on the networks.

Lucena et al. [15] describe an approach to application-layer protocol steganography, showing how they can embed messages into commonly used TCP/IP protocols such as SSH and HTTP. They also introduce the notion of semantics preservation, which ensures that messages still conform to the host protocol, even after embedding. Strong semantics preservation ensures that the meaning of the message is unchanged, while weak semantics preservation only guarantees the less stringent condition that the message be semantically valid. Their main shortcoming is that their model only works in specific protocols such as HTTP.

Fu *et al.* [16] present a flow-based architecture for network traffic camouflaging. They hide both the message traffic pattern and the fact that camouflaging itself is taking place, while at the same time guaranteeing the QoS requirement of the message flow. The idea is to embed the packets of the message flow into the packets of another flow, denoted as carrier flow, which in turn may be generated by a well-known network service. The system's main drawback is that it replaces the carrier payload, making changes in the payload vulnerable to detection simply by checking the same packet in different paths.

Burnett *et al.* [17] present a system called Collage, which allows users to exchange messages through hidden channels in sites that host user-generated content, such as photo-sharing sites. To send a message, the user embeds it into covert traffic and posts the content onto some site, where receivers retrieve the content using a sequence of tasks. Their evaluation shows that performance overhead is acceptable when sending small messages such as web articles, emails and so on. The system's weakest point is that the communication cannot be interactive due to its architecture.

Rios *et al.* [6] examine the Dynamic Host Configuration Protocol (DHCP) for search new forms of covert communications. They shows that is possible to create covert channels on specific fields (xid, Sname, File and Option) of the DHCP messages. The problem of the solution proposed lies in the DHCP scope and also the fields are easily detectable using a dedicated analyzer.

Below, Table 1 offers a classification of the reviewed papers under the following labels: Cryptography, if the system uses some type of cryptography functions for hiding the information; Modify L7, if the system modifies application layers such as HTTP, DNS, etc.; Modify IP, if the technique involves the modification of some IP fields for hiding information; Modify TCP/UDP, if it includes the modification of TCP/UDP fields for enclosing the covert message; Timing, if it uses timing techniques to hide messages on the flow; and finally, Network, if the system reacts in a different way to network traffic.

Notice that most covert channel classifications are based on storage or timing channels, as shown in Table 1. Most of the studies are actually related to storage channels, since the amount of information in storage channels is larger than in timing channels. One of the weaknesses of timing channels is that they need a high amount of packets to send information to the destination. According to the Table, InCC could be classified as a storage channel, dynamically adapted to network traffic.

3   INvisible Covert Channel

The purpose of this section is to introduce the network channel, first by describing the system (detailed further below in Subsect. 3.1), then by reviewing the different parts and techniques involved (Subsects. 3.2–3.5).

Table 1. Network covert channels techniques.

Author	Cryptography	Modify L7	Modify IP	Modify TCP/UDP	Timing	Network
Zander [11]			*		*	
Luo [12]			*		*	
Wendzel [13]		*			*	
Lucena [15]		*				*
Burnett [17]	*	*				
Fu [16]		*	*	*		
Rios [6]		*				
Dittmann [8]		*			*	
Mazurczyk [14]			*			
Nussbaum [5]	*	*				
Liu [9]					*	
InCC	*	*		*		*

InCC offers a solution for communicating two systems by using storage covert channels. This is achieved by combining several hiding techniques which allow the systems to share information without compromising source and destination.

3.1 System Description

InCC supports the following specifications in order to avoid being detected: (a) The channel uses a port-walking technique (inspired by the port-knocking [18–20] technique), which consists in emulating P2P traffic management of ports in order to disturb any traffic analysis. P2P applications generate a huge amount of disturbing traffic to random ports previously negotiated by the applications. (b) Encryption of the main payload packet by using RC4 [21], with the introduction of some variations such as key rotation. RC4 is chosen due to the simplicity of the code and the negligible CPU overload. (c) The channel uses IP spoofed addresses for both source and destination. Consequently, only source and destination will know the spoofed IP addresses. And finally, (d) it uses signatures from other systems, such as Snort [22] or OpenDPI [23]. The channel is capable of inserting the signatures on the generated flows in order to camouflage the flows with those existing on the network.

Figure 1 illustrates how the channel operates. Notice that the sender and the receiver may belong to either the same or to different networks, being A and B users who are sharing files via P2P, as detailed in Fig. 7. Both sender and receiver are authenticated by RSA [24] or port-knocking [18–20] mechanisms at the initialization state. In our design, InCC uses standard RSA authentication, but notice that the authentication phase is out of scope of the paper. As seen in Fig. 1, once the authentication state has passed the sender and the receiver could

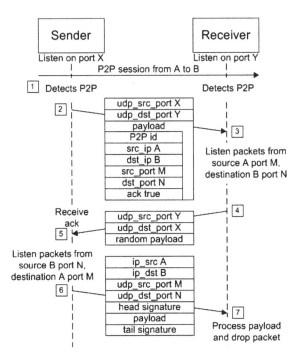

Fig. 1. InCC description.

receive messages on ports X and Y. Elements A and B are P2P users sharing a file. The different states in the channel may be summarized as:

1. The source detects a P2P session between A and B, the detection being made by signatures.
2. The sender sends out a message to the receiver including the following information: a P2P identifier which identifies the signature detected at the P2P session; A's IP address (src_ip) and source port (src_port); B's IP address (dst_ip) and destination port (dst_port); and optionally, an acknowledgement flag. All the messages have been previously encrypted by RC4.
3. Once the message has been decoded and the fields processed by the receiver, the receiver's behavior changes.
4. The receiver sends out an acknowledgement message to the sender because the ACK flag had been previously activated. The payload of the message is made up of random bytes whose only purpose is to disturb the flow's analysis.
5. The sender gets the acknowledgement and understands that new messages should use A and B's IP addresses and ports, as well as the signature detected in the previous message.
6. The sender sends out a datagram with the P2P signature detected and all the payload encrypted by RC4. Notice that the IP addresses and the ports used are A and B's.

7. The receiver intercepts the message, decodes it and processes its fields, then sends it one layer up enclosing an incident report. Note that the receiver drops the packet in order to avoid ICMP unreachable port packets that could be suspicious.

After describing the network channel, we proceed to the different techniques involved in the system. This has the following options: 'Port walking', so the flow can change from different ports; 'Payload noise', which adds trash noise to the payload; 'IP randomness', which enables the use of spoofed addresses in order to communicate source with destination; and finally, 'Signature poisoning', which inserts known traffic signatures into the generated payload. These options will be discussed next.

3.2 Port Walking

Port knocking [18–20] is a technique whereby authentication information is transmitted across closed network ports. A machine using port knocking closes all network ports to all hosts but logs incoming packets. A program watches the firewall logs for certain sequences of packets, which encode authentication information and make a request for opening or closing ports. Based on this information, the port knocking system can choose to open network ports to the originating host. In essence, port knocking enables or disables services which are invisible most of the time, and which appear on the network by a combination of special IP packets. So secure systems could enable or disable their reporting mechanism by using this type of technique.

By using the same principle as port knocking, we have created port walking (refer to Fig. 2). This is a technique which consists in generating several flows between the source and the destination machines, much in the same way as P2P applications. P2P applications generate a lot of flows in order to send and receive

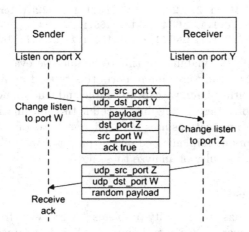

Fig. 2. InCC port walking.

information over the distributed network. By using this idea, the InCC behaves like P2P applications, which use random ports in order to avoid filtering and shaping. Thus, for every object sent to the destination a new port parameter is added to the payload. If the object size is too large, then InCC splits it into several packets (only when this option is enabled at the initialization state or when AB identifies P2P traffic). This feature is recommended when BitTorrent [25], Gnutella, Skype, or similar applications which use random ports for signaling, file-transfer, etc. are detected.

As shown in Fig. 2, to synchronize the destination and the source ports of both sender and receiver, InCC sends out the following ports (src_port for the sender and dst_port for the receiver), either randomly or by using the distribution ports previously detected in a P2P session.

The tcpdump output below shows a port Walking technique without acknowledgement, where 192.168.1.1 represents the sender, 192.168.1.2 the receiver, and 2000 the initialization port.

```
IP 192.168.1.1. 47578 > 192.168.1.2. 2000: len 123
IP 192.168.1.1. 35690 > 192.168.1.2. 7030: len 157
```

By contrast, a tcpdump output of a port Walking technique with acknowledgement is shown next. Notice that the acknowledgement uses the same port. Ports 2000 and 7949 in the output are used to verify the acknowledgement.

```
IP 192.168.1.1. 47578 > 192.168.1.2. 2000: len 123
IP 192.168.1.2. 2000 > 192.168.1.1. 33225: len 53
IP 192.168.1.1. 36347 > 192.168.1.2. 7949: len 163
IP 192.168.1.2. 7949 > 192.168.1.1. 36347: len 23
```

It is possible to use full random ports to make the flow analysis more difficult, allowing the receiver to send the acknowledgements from different ports as shown in the output below.

```
IP 192.168.1.1. 47578 > 192.168.1.2. 2000: len 123
IP 192.168.1.2. 1280 > 192.168.1.1. 33225: len 53
IP 192.168.1.1. 36347 > 192.168.1.2. 7949: len 163
IP 192.168.1.2. 98634 > 192.168.1.1. 36347: len 23
```

In order to check the viability of this technique, we evaluate the most use BitTorrent clients for study how many ports this type of applications uses. As shown on Table 2, during 4 min we capture traffic and study how many ports and flows this applications uses. Taking into account this information we can argue that on average this applications uses 2628 different ports on a single session. So by having this technique implemented on our proposal we will disturb network analysis due to the difficulty of analyze these flows.

3.3   Payload Noise

The algorithm RC4 has vulnerability problems [26–28], with frequency analysis-based attacks. However, by using techniques such as key rotation these vulnerabilities could be partially solved. The behavior of the mentioned techniques

Table 2. BitTorrent port usage.

Application	Flows	Ports
BitComet	10890	8617
BitLord	890	587
Vuze	1704	1528
Azuerus	2512	2257
uTorrent	1865	1668
BitTorrent	1819	1112

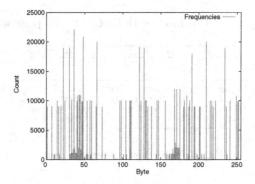

Fig. 3. 10.000 objects with RC4.

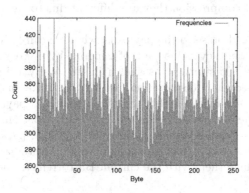

Fig. 4. 10.000 objects with RC4 and random key.

can be observed in Figs. 3, 4 and 5. These figures represent the dispersion of the packet payload frequency generated by InCC without any signature. The byte is represented on the x-axis, whereas on the y-axis we find the number of occurrences of the x byte. As shown in Fig. 3, when we encrypt 10.000 objects by using the same key, the byte frequency distribution of RC4 is poor and a frequency attack could be launched. However, when the channel uses a random key, as shown in Fig. 4, the resiliency is better than in the previous case.

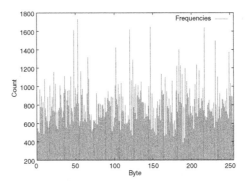

Fig. 5. 10.000 objects with RC4 and noise payload.

Fig. 6. Noise payload serialization.

Notice that the dispersion of the frequency data in Figs. 4 and 5 are similar, whereas in terms of compression they are different due to the trash noise added to the payload.

We propose to add noise to the payloads, what we call 'payload noise'. This consists in adding the key value pair of random bytes to some parts of the object, in our case a dictionary, as shown in Fig. 6. By using this technique we get the same frequency distribution (see Fig. 5) as the one in Fig. 4, which uses random key. Nevertheless, this technique fixes the payload to a specific size in order to generate payload sizes which already exist on the network. For example, if the AB process detects BitTorrent with size packets of 300 bytes, then the packet generated with this technique will generate packets of 300 bytes in order to camouflage them with the current BitTorrent traffic detected by the AB process.

The process of adding noise to the payload is achieved by using dictionaries and JSON (JavaScript Object Notation), as shown in Fig. 6. The addition of random key value pairs in this figure gives us a fuzzy frequency value and increases the object size. However, this technique only gives us extra bytes to cope with specific payload sizes, and does not give us an encryption method like RC4.

3.4   IP Randomness

One of the interesting things about InCC is that the IP addresses of the generated data-grams do not belong to any of the systems trying to communicate with each other (see Fig. 7). This is achieved by learning the most used IP addresses on the network, or by configuring the IP address with spoofed addresses from the source and destination networks.

This technique consists of the following points:

- When Sender and Receiver are in the process of learning from the networks, all the IP addresses identified by the signatures are stored on a temporary memory (called temporary IP address). These IP addresses are temporary because they depend on the flow duration and on the type of user. For example, if a user spends 20 min downloading a large file from a torrent client, the temporary IP of this user will have a duration of 20 min due to the flows generated by the torrent application.
- If node Sender wants to send messages to node Receiver the channel has two options: first, using the temporary addresses, or second, using random addresses. Random addresses are IP addresses generated by changing the last digit of the source network's IP address.

Thus, if an advance administrator manages a transit network, our flows will be completely hidden to any analysis the attacker could conduct because the IP addresses are spoofed or even used by other systems such as web-servers, email-servers, etc.

The use of temporary IP addresses by the channel has the advantage of learning from active IP addresses, for instance the address of a P2P user from another network. For our purposes, we use C class addressing, so for a 192.168.0.0 network the random address would range from 192.168.0.1 to 192.168.0.254.

In Fig. 7, the Sender node represent the system which wants to share information, the R routers are transient routers, and A and B are two users sharing a file with a P2P application. When the Sender and Receiver detects P2P activity they stores the source and destination addresses (A,B), as seen in point t1 of the figure. Then, when the Sender needs to transfer information to the Receiver, it sends IP traffic with B's destination address and A's source address, as observed in point t2. Notice that the Receiver will never forward the traffic to B, since this flow is generated in a non-natural way and will always be destroyed after being processed by destination (see point 7 in Subsect. 3.1).

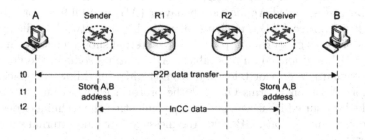

Fig. 7. IP usage mechanism.

One of the strengths of the temporary addresses is that the datagrams generated by InCC can be camouflaged with the source traffic detected by A and B. This gives more robustness to the channel with respect to the random addresses, which do not depend on the network IP addresses. On the contrary, random addresses using spoofed addresses could be more suspicious because the IP addresses generated would be unique in the network and an advance attacker could notice the lack of response of the IP address, for example by using port scanning techniques. One of the main drawbacks of this technique is that Sender and Receiver should be on the same network path than A and B, in order to spoof properly the IP addresses. However, this could be solved having installing BitTorrent clients on the network path.

3.5   Signature Poisoning

NIDS and tools like tcpdump [29] can be used by network administrators in order to inspect the traffic. Normally commercial systems and open source solutions use network signatures in order to identify the network flows. So by using signatures from different tools [22,23,30], the channel hides the flows with the network's current traffic. The channel is only implemented on UDP for the proof of concept, so our flows are capable of hiding with DNS, BitTorrent, Gnutella, Skype or any other application that uses UDP and may have a signature for identifying the flow.

The following tcpdump output shows an InCC message. This packet contains the initial payload bytes $0 \times 474e$ and 0×4403, which correspond to a signature for the Gnutella protocol. The rest of the packet is encrypted by RC4.

```
IP 192.168.1.1.55728 > 192.168.1.2.4399: UDP
0x0000: 4500 00ce 2e5b 4000 4011 8870 c0a8 0101
0x0010: c0a8 0102 d9b0 112f 00ba 2044 474e 4403
0x0020: 578e df02 9088 bd1b e3db d268 5bf4 4ffc
0x0030: d626 4e10 9440 c93e c1a1 6249 ce2d 92df
```

4   Prototype Implementation

The channel consists of a light-weight multi-platform library with two differentiated processes, called Application behavior (AB) and Obfuscator (OB). As shown in Fig. 8, process AB is in charge of analyzing the network traffic by using signatures. These signatures are provided by external subsystems like Snort, or even OpenDPI, and loaded on a database. AB identifies some of the flows with the traffic signatures provided, learning from the identified flows the packet size distribution. AB then informs OB that the protocol identified at the previous stage is the best suited for usage, and, by implementing the techniques described in the previous subsections, OB sends the message from the external subsystem to the destination.

Taking into account these options, the flows generated will be camouflaged on the network. This allows the external systems to share information without

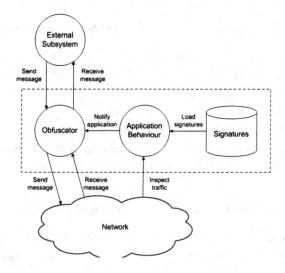

Fig. 8. InCC process.

compromising their existence on the network. Our method does not modify the packets, as happens with Xinwen *et al.* [16], and does not depend on specific protocols as Lucena *et al.* explain in their model [15]. On the contrary, our channel depends on traffic signatures, where the amount of available signatures from different open-source projects [22, 23, 30] is high.

5   Experiments

The tests were carried out by two PC Linux with kernels 2.6.38, one of them having a CPU Intel core duo 3.16 GHz, and the other with a CPU Intel core duo 2 GHz. First we generated Gnutella traffic with an application on one of the PCs. We chose the signatures from Gnutella because generating real traffic is achieved just by downloading the application and capturing the traffic on a pcap file. Secondly, we generated one flow between the two PCs (with the characteristics described in previous sections) by using InCC and by setting up the behavior to Gnutella. Then the traffic generated was captured on a pcap file.

All capabilities were implemented in our configuration, developing a complete test of all the modules presented. This is because the costs of having a real environment are much higher due to the expenditure in routers, web-servers, links, etc. But as shown in Fig. 7, which is just a small part of the previous figure, we can emulate this environment with only a single network LAN and two PCs as a proof of concept.

Thirdly, we merge the traffic generated by Gnutella with the one generated by the channel. By using tools like Snort [22] and OpenDPI [23], we analyze network traffic and we inject the merged traces, resulting in the fake flows being completely hidden from the rest of the traffic. Also, the flows will be identified with the provided signature as shown in the following tables.

Table 3. Gnutella traffic.

Protocol	Packets	Bytes	Flows
Unknown	61215	19031577	17
Dns	10	960	3
Http	115	44107	11
Netbios	53	7679	3
Gnutella	102656	30658221	270
Icmp	563	52454	21

Table 4. Gnutella traffic and InCC.

Protocol	Packets	Bytes	Flows
Unknown	61215	19031577	17
Dns	10	960	3
Http	115	44107	11
Netbios	53	7679	3
Gnutella	**102707**	**30672048**	**271**
Icmp	563	52454	21

Table 5. BitTorrent traffic.

Protocol	Packets	Bytes	Flows
Unknown	7600	1644465	1412
Dns	296	29542	84
Http	701	278328	55
Igmp	3	166	3
BitTorrent	116	25633	15
Icmp	242	22738	126

Table 6. BitTorrent traffic and InCC.

Protocol	Packets	Bytes	Flows
Unknown	**7603**	**1644804**	**1413**
Dns	296	29542	84
Http	701	278328	55
Igmp	3	166	3
BitTorrent	116	25633	15
Icmp	242	22738	126

Table 7. BitTorrent traffic.

Protocol	Packets	Bytes	Flows
Unknown	12011	3976878	746
Dns	104	10082	28
BitTorrent	70	21786	9
Icmp	3	8630	54
Igmp	3	166	3

Table 8. BitTorrent and InCC with Battlefield.

Protocol	Packets	Bytes	Flows
Unknown	12011	3976878	746
Dns	104	10082	28
BitTorrent	70	21786	9
Battlefield	**4**	**385**	**1**
Icmp	3	8630	54
Igmp	3	166	3

Tables 3 and 4 represent the detection rates obtained by OpenDPI in order to check InCC's viability. Table 2 shows OpenDPI detecting a Gnutella session, including byte distribution, and number of flows and packets. On the other hand, Table 3 shows how the new flow generated by InCC is detected by OpenDPI as Gnutella. Notice that the flow generated by InCC contains 51 packets, 13.827 bytes and a packet average size of 271 bytes, an amount which is large enough for reporting network incidents.

On the other hand, Tables 5 and 6 represent the detection rates but in this case the tool was unable to detect properly as bittorrent and couldnt identify properly the InCC flow as shown bellow. This is due to the lack of having implemented the signature on the OpenDPI source code.

The following Tables 7 and 8 shows the detection rates obtained by OpenDPI by generating a different traffic profile on the network. In this case, the traffic generated was Battlefield [31], Battlefield is a first person shooter game world wide spread. On this experiment InCC was capable of generate different traffic than detected, this gives more flexibility to the system in order to avoid the traffic analisys by other systems.

To test the performance of the channel, particularly the library's CPU overload, 10.000 objects were generated using the different options described in Subsects. 3.2–3.5. The results shed light on the consumption, negligible for all the options supported by InCC that was approximately 76 microseconds with all the options enabled.

6 Conclusions

This article presents a light-weight library for network covert channels, capable of communicating with other systems from different networks. By using the options described in the previous sections the channel is capable of sending information to other systems without compromising their existence. The channel is modular and any of the options can be configured independently. The source code is under the terms of the GPL and is available on https://github.com/camp0/incc.

We propose a new technique which evades detection by camouflaging the flows with the existing ones on the network. InCC was designed for UDP traffic in order to check the viability of its implementation and test its functionality. However, it would be possible to extend it to TCP flows in order to camouflage the generated flows with the ones detected on the network. The proposed technique is independent of the existing traffic of the network, also the system is capable to adapt the behaviour depending of the different type of traffic, such as p2p, voip, gaming, and so on.

The majority of P2P applications send packets garbage in order to disrupt the traffic analysis of the ISP networks. One possible extension to InCC is the production of fake datagrams to disturb all sorts of analysis during the transmission of InCC flows. When there is not enough traffic for InCC to identify, the administrators could install P2P applications in order to help camouflage the InCC flows, thus making the channel more resilient and robust.

Acknowledgements. This work has been partially funded by Vulcano project (ref 442808215-8215-4-9) funded by Spanish ministry of Science and Innovation.

References

1. 5200.28-STD, D.: Trusted Computer System Evaluation Criteria. Dod Computer Security Center (1985)
2. Llamas, D., Miller, A., Allison, C.: An evaluation framework for the analysis of covert channels in the tcp/ip protocol suite. In: ECIW, pp. 205–214. Academic Conferences Limited, Reading (2005)

3. Zander, S., Armitage, G.J., Branch, P.: A survey of covert channels and counter-measures in computer network protocols. IEEE Commun. Surv. Tutorials **9**, 44–57 (2007)

4. Sellke, S.H., Wang, C.C., Bagchi, S., Shroff, N.B.: Tcp/ip timing channels: theory to implementation. In: INFOCOM, pp. 2204–2212. IEEE (2009)

5. Nussbaum, L., Neyron, P., Richard, O.: On robust covert channels inside DNS. In: Gritzalis, D., Lopez, J. (eds.) SEC 2009. IFIP AICT, vol. 297, pp. 51–62. Springer, Heidelberg (2009)

6. Rios, R., Onieva, J.A., Lopez, J.: HIDE_DHCP: covert communications through network configuration messages. In: Gritzalis, D., Furnell, S., Theoharidou, M. (eds.) SEC 2012. IFIP AICT, vol. 376, pp. 162–173. Springer, Heidelberg (2012)

7. Freire, E.P., Ziviani, A., Salles, R.M.: On metrics to distinguish skype flows from http traffic. J. Netw. Syst. Manage. **17**, 53–72 (2009)

8. Dittmann, J., Hesse, D., Hillert, R.: Steganography and steganalysis in voice-over ip scenarios: operational aspects and first experiences with a new steganalysis tool set. In: Delp, E.J., Wong, P.W. (eds.) Security, Steganography, and Watermarking of Multimedia Contents. Proceedings of SPIE, vol. 5681, pp. 607–618. SPIE (2005)

9. Liu, Y., Ghosal, D., Armknecht, F., Sadeghi, A.-R., Schulz, S., Katzenbeisser, S.: Hide and seek in time — robust covert timing channels. In: Backes, M., Ning, P. (eds.) ESORICS 2009. LNCS, vol. 5789, pp. 120–135. Springer, Heidelberg (2009)

10. Zhang, D., Askarov, A., Myers, A.C.: Predictive mitigation of timing channels in interactive systems. In: Proceedings of the 18th ACM Conference on Computer and Communications Security, CCS '11, pp. 563–574. ACM, New York (2011)

11. Zander, S., Armitage, G.J., Branch, P.: An empirical evaluation of ip time to live covert channels. In: ICON, pp. 42–47. IEEE (2007)

12. Luo, X., Chan, E.W.W., Chang, R.K.C.: Clack: a network covert channel based on partial acknowledgment encoding. In: ICC, pp. 1–5. IEEE (2009)

13. Wendzel, S., Zander, S.: Detecting protocol switching covert channels. In: 37th Annual IEEE Conference on Local Computer Networks, pp. 280–283 (2012)

14. Mazurczyk, W., Szczypiorski, K.: Steganography in handling oversized ip packets. CoRR abs/0907.0313 (2009)

15. Lucena, N.B., Pease, J., Yadollahpour, P., Chapin, S.J.: Syntax and semantics-preserving application-layer protocol steganography. In: Fridrich, J. (ed.) IH 2004. LNCS, vol. 3200, pp. 164–179. Springer, Heidelberg (2004)

16. Fu, X., Guan, Y., Graham, B., Bettati, R., Zhao, W.: Using parasite flows to camouflage flow traffic. In: Proceedings of the 2002 IEEE Workshop on Information Assurance (2002)

17. Burnett, S., Feamster, N., Vempala, S.: Chipping away at censorship firewalls with user-generated content. In: Proceedings of the 19th USENIX Conference on Security, USENIX Security'10, pp. 29–29. USENIX Association, Berkeley (2010)

18. Miklosovic, S.: Pa018 - term project - port knocking enhancements (2011). http://www.portknocking.org/view/resources

19. Degraaf, R., Aycock, J., Jacobson, M.: Improved port knocking with strong authentication. In: Proceedings of the 21st Annual Computer Security Applications Conference (ACSAC 2005), pp. 409–418. Springer (2005)

20. Tariq, M., Baig, M.S., Saeed, M.T.: Associating the authentication and connection-establishment phases in passive authorization techniques (2008)

21. Rcf4557: The rc4-hmac kerberos encryption types used by microsoft windows (2006). http://www.ietf.org/rfc/rfc4757.txt

22. Snort: Snort (2013). http://www.snort.org/

23. OpenDPI: Opendpi (2013). http://www.opendpi.org/opendpi.org/index.html
24. Rfc2246: The tls protocol (1999). http://www.ietf.org/rfc/rfc2246.txt
25. BitTorrent: The bittorrent protocol specification, version 11031 (2013). http://bittorrent.org/beps/bep_0003.html
26. Klein, A.: Attacks on the rc4 stream cipher. Des. Codes Crypt. **48**, 269–286 (2008)
27. Mantin, I.: Predicting and distinguishing attacks on RC4 keystream generator. In: Cramer, R. (ed.) EUROCRYPT 2005. LNCS, vol. 3494, pp. 491–506. Springer, Heidelberg (2005)
28. Paul, S., Preneel, B.: A new weakness in the rc4 keystream generator and an approach to improve the security of the cipher, pp. 245–259 (2004)
29. Tcpdump: Tcpdump (2013). http://www.tcpdump.org/
30. Hippie: Hi-performance protocol identification engine (2013). http://sourceforge.net/projects/hippie/
31. Battlefield: Battlefield (2013). http://www.battlefield.com/

A Trust Management Framework for Secure Cloud Data Storage Using Cryptographic Role-Based Access Control

Lan Zhou, Vijay Varadharajan$^{(\boxtimes)}$, and Michael Hitchens

Advanced Cyber Security Research Centre, Department of Computing,
Macquarie University, North Ryde, Sydney, NSW, Australia
{lan.zhou,vijay.varadharajan,michael.hitchens}@mq.edu.au

Abstract. In recent times, there has been an increasing development of storing data securely in the cloud. The Role-based access control (RBAC) model, a widely used access control model, can provide a flexible way for data owners to manage and share their data in the cloud environment. To enforce the access control policies in the cloud, several cryptographic RBAC schemes have been proposed recently, which integrate cryptographic techniques with RBAC models to secure data storage in an outsourced environment such as a cloud. However, these schemes do not address the issue of trust in such a data storage system. In this paper, we introduce a trust management framework which can enhance the security of data in cloud storage systems using cryptographic RBAC schemes. The trust management framework provides an approach for each party in such a cloud storage system to determine the trustworthiness of other parties. The framework consists of a series of trust models, which (i) enable the users and the data owners to decide whether to interact with a particular role for accessing and sharing data in the system and (ii) allow the role managers to evaluate the trustworthiness of users and data owners. These trust models take into account role inheritance and hierarchy in the evaluation of trustworthiness of the roles. In addition, we present a design of a trust-based cloud storage system which shows how the trust models for users and roles can be integrated into a system that uses cryptographic RBAC schemes.

Keywords: Role-based access control · Trust model · Cryptographic RBAC

1 Introduction

Controlling the access to data is an important issue in data storage systems. A proper access control mechanism is needed depending on the context and the requirement of the system. Many access control models have been proposed over the years in the literature. Role-based access control (RBAC) is a well-known access control model which can help to simplify security management especially

© Springer-Verlag Berlin Heidelberg 2014
M.S. Obaidat and J. Filipe (Eds.): ICETE 2013, CCIS 456, pp. 226–251, 2014.
DOI: 10.1007/978-3-662-44788-8_14

in large-scale systems. In RBAC, roles are used to associate users with permissions on resources. Users are assigned roles and permissions are allocated to roles instead of individual users; only users who have been granted membership to roles can access the permissions associated with the roles and hence can access the resources. Since being first formalised in the 1990's [5], RBAC has been widely used in many systems to provide users with flexible controls over the access to their data. The RBAC model was extended and updated in 1996 [11], and a NIST RBAC standard was proposed in 2000 [12].

In traditional systems, access control policies are usually specified and enforced by a central authority who has administrative control over all the resources in the system. With the rapid increase in the amount of digital information that needs to be stored, cloud storage has attracted much attention in recent years because of its ability to deliver storage resources to users on demand in a cost effective manner. In such an environment, there may not exist a central authority as the data may be stored in distributed data centres which cannot be under the control of a single authority. One approach to control the access to data in an untrusted environment is to encrypt the data and give the key to users who require access to the data.

Several cryptographic schemes have been developed to allow data encryption in the context of the RBAC model. A hierarchical cryptographic access control scheme [1] was proposed in 1983. Because of the similarity in structures between hierarchical access control and RBAC, a hierarchical cryptographic access control scheme can be easily transformed into a cryptographic RBAC scheme. The problem of access control for securely outsourcing data using cryptographic techniques was first considered in [7]. Some other schemes were proposed afterwards, such as in [3,10,16]. Recently, a new role-based encryption (RBE) scheme has been proposed in [15]. In this scheme, the user memberships are managed by individual roles as opposed to a central administrator as in other cryptographic RBAC schemes. These schemes combine cryptographic techniques and access control to protect the privacy of the data in an outsourced environment where data can be encrypted in such a way that only the users who are allowed by the access policies can decrypt and view the data.

In some cases though the access control policies may be specified by the cloud provider authority itself in a centralised way, there could be multiple authorities to enforce these access policies distributed throughout the cloud system. Therefore there would be a need to trust these authorities to correctly specify the access control policies and enforce them properly. In some cryptographic RBAC schemes, roles and their users are managed by administrators who hold the master secrets of the systems. All the administration tasks in these schemes are centralised. Therefore, if one wants to know if a RBAC system is secure, it is primarily dependent on the trustworthiness of the administrator of the system.

However, in large-scale RBAC systems, it is impractical to centralise the task of managing these users and permissions, and their relationships with the roles in a small team of security administrators. Reference [15] proposes a new cryptographic RBAC scheme called Role-based Encryption (RBE) in which the user management can be decentralised to individual roles; that is, the administrators only manage the roles and the relationship among them while the role managers have the flexibility in specifying the user memberships themselves. In this paper, we consider trust models for cloud storage systems that are using cryptographic RBAC schemes like RBE, where each individual role manager can manage their user memberships without the need of involving the administrators. We believe this case is more general and can be used in large-scale RBAC systems. In such systems, the trust on the individual roles needs to be considered instead of the trust on the administrators.

There have been several trust models [2,14] for RBAC proposed in the literature. These trust models considered the trust on users to assist the decision making about whether or not to grant permissions to the users. In a cloud storage system using cryptographic RBAC schemes, it would be helpful if a user could determine whether or not a role in the system is trusted before joining it. This would be useful especially in systems where there is a cost for users to join a role, for example, users need to pay the subscription fee for joining roles. When a user evaluates the trust value of a role, she or he will only proceed with joining the role if the trust value of the role is above a certain trust threshold (this threshold being set by the users, and being different for different applications and context dependent). In a system where owners are allowed to choose the roles to which to assign their data, from the users' perspective, malicious owners can also cause negative behaviours of roles by assigning bad resources (e.g. virus, malware) to roles. Therefore, roles will also need to consider the trust of the data owners so that only data from well-behaved owners will be accepted.

In this paper, we introduce a trust management framework for securing data storage in cloud storage systems that are using cryptographic RBAC schemes. Though much work exists on trust models in RBAC, none of this work considers the trust on the RBAC system itself. The proposed trust management framework addresses this missing aspect of trust in cryptographic RBAC schemes to improve the decision making for entities in the cloud system. This framework consists of trust models which can assist (i) the users to evaluate the trust in the roles in a RBAC system and use this trust evaluation to decide whether to join a particular role or not, (ii) the role managers to evaluate the trust in the owners in the RBAC system and use this trust in the decision to accept data from an owner, (iii) the data owners to evaluate the trust in the roles in a RBAC system and use this trust evaluation to decide whether to store their encrypted data in the cloud for a particular role, and (iv) the role managers to evaluate the trust in the users in the RBAC system and use this trust in the decision to grant the membership to a user. Theses trust models take into account the effect of role inheritance in RBAC systems on trust evaluation. If a role A inherits all the permissions that a role B has, then we say role A is a ancestor role of role B, and role B is a descendent role of role A.

We give the formal definition of the first two trust models, users' trust in role managers and role managers' trust in data owners. These two trust models form a natural pair as they consider trust from a user's perspective.

We refer to these trust models as User-Role RBAC and Role-Owner RBAC trust models respectively. These two trust models can not only prevent users from joining roles which have bad historical behaviour in terms of sharing poor quality resources or misleading users on the content of resources, but also assist the role managers to identify the malicious owners who have caused a negative impact on the roles' trustworthiness. We also present the architecture of a trust-based cloud storage system which integrates the these two trust models in a cryptographic RBAC system. Then we describe the other two trust models, data owners' trust in role managers and role managers' trust in users. Furthermore, we describe the relevance of all the trust models in the framework by considering practical application scenarios and then illustrate how the trust evaluations can be used to enhance the quality of secure decision making by different entities of cloud storage service.

The paper is organised as follows. Section 2 reviews relevant preliminary knowledge that is needed for the design of our trust models. Section 3 describes the trust issues in a cryptographic RBAC system and discusses the trust requirements for each type of entities. We give the formal User-Role and Role-Owner RBAC trust models in Sect. 4. The architecture of our secure cloud storage system is presented in Sect. 5. We describe the owners' trust models in Sect. 6. In Sect. 7, we illustrate how the trust models in the framework can be used in a cloud service application to enhance the quality of security decision making. Section 8 discusses relevant related works and compares them with our proposed trust management framework. Section 9 concludes the paper.

2   Preliminaries

2.1   Experience-Based Trust

Trust has played a foundational role in security for a long period of time. It is clear that two entities may not trust each other on the basis of identity alone. There are a range of other attributes and credentials such as different types of privileges, the state of the platform being used as well as reputations, recommendations and histories that come into play in decision making. An experience-based trust model is a trust management system which enables the trust decisions to be made based on the historical behaviour of an entity. Such a system allows an entity to rate the transactions with other entities, and the trustworthiness of an entity is determined using the collection of ratings of the transactions that other entities have had with this entity. In most experience-based trust systems, one entity derives the trustworthiness of another entity from both experience of the former with the latter and the feedback on transactions provided by other entities which have had interactions with target entity in the past. An entity is able to evaluate its trust in another entity and the former can make a decision as to whether to not to continue its transaction with the latter, based on whether the trust value exceeds a certain threshold; this threshold is dependent on the context of the application at hand.

2.2   Bayesian Trust Model

Many approaches have been proposed that use probabilistic models to evaluate trust based on evidence which contains the number of "positive" and "negative" transactions in which a given entity have been involved. Perhaps the most common probabilistic model is the one based on Bayesian trust [6,8,9] using the beta probability distribution function. The beta family of distributions is a collection of continuous probability density functions defined over the interval $[0, 1]$. Suppose a beta distribution used for a parameter θ is defined as

$$P(\theta) = \frac{\Gamma(\alpha + \beta)}{\Gamma(\alpha)\Gamma(\beta)}\theta^{\alpha-1}(1 - \theta)^{\beta-1}$$

where α and β are two parameters controlling the distribution of the parameter θ, and $0 \le \theta \le 1$, $\alpha > 0$, $\beta > 0$. Assume $X = \{x_1, \ldots, x_n\}$ is the collection of the feedbacks from the past n transactions, and X has r "positive" feedbacks and s "negative" feedbacks. Then the likelihood function can be defined as

$$P(X|\theta) = \prod_{i=1}^{n} P(x_i|\theta) = \theta^r(1 - \theta)^s$$

The posterior distribution $P(\theta|X)$ is proportional to the multiplication of the prior $P(\theta)$ and the likelihood function $P(X|\theta)$, and we then have

$$P(\theta|X) = \frac{P(X|\theta)P(\theta)}{P(X)}$$
$$= \frac{\Gamma(r + \alpha + s + \beta)}{\Gamma(r + \alpha)\Gamma(s + \beta)}\theta^{r+\alpha-1}(1 - \theta)^{s+\beta-1}$$

Now let x_{i+1} be the possible feedback of the next transaction. The probability that x_{i+1} is a "positive" feedback given the transaction history X can be represented as

$$P(x_{i+1}|X) = \int_0^1 d\theta\ P(x_{i+1}|\theta)P(\theta|X)$$
$$= \int_0^1 d\theta\ \theta P(\theta|X)$$
$$= E(\theta|X)$$

Then we write the probability that the next transaction will be a "good" one as follows:

$$\mathcal{E}(r, s) = P(x_{i+1}|X) = \frac{r + \alpha}{r + \alpha + s + \beta} \tag{1}$$

Using Eq. 1, one entity can derive the probability that the next transaction with another entity will be positive from the transaction history of the other entity. Most Bayesian trust systems assume that the parameters $\alpha = \beta = 1$, such as in [6]. Some other approaches allow the parameters α and β to be chosen depending on the system context.

3   Trust Issues in Using Cryptographic RBAC Schemes in Secure Cloud Storage

Cryptographic RBAC schemes integrate cryptographic techniques with RBAC models to secure the data storage. They inherit the features and concepts from RBAC models, and also have additional components that are specific to data storage systems. In the standard RBAC model, permissions are assigned to roles by the administrator of the system. However, in a system using cryptographic RBAC schemes, "permissions" are the data encrypted to roles, and the security policies are specified to control the users' access to data. Because data are usually not owned by a single party, cryptographic RBAC systems assume that data can be encrypted to a role by whoever owns the data as opposed to the administrator in the standard RBAC system. In this paper, we address trust issues for cryptographic RBAC systems. Therefore we adopt the above described concepts for cryptographic RBAC systems in our trust models.

Using cryptographic RBAC schemes in cloud storage systems, a data owner can encrypt the data to a role, and only the users who have been granted membership of that role or an ancestor role of that role can decrypt the data. In this paper, we assume that the data owners and users reside outside this role system infrastructure (where the roles are being administered). Hence the entities in a cloud storage system need to consider the following issues. Users consider their trust in roles (role managers) in order to ensure that joining roles guarantee access to data assigned to these roles, and data owners consider the trust of role managers in order to ensure that their data is secure after being assigned to the roles. The role managers need to consider trust on both data owners and users; role managers consider their trust in data owners to ensure that data owners who have assigned malicious data to the roles will not be allowed to assign data to the roles any more, and they consider the trust of users so that users with negative behaviours are excluded from the roles, which in turn makes owners trust these roles. In this section, we discuss the trust issues that need to be considered by different entities of a cryptographic RBAC system.

3.1   Data Users' Trust in Role Managers

In some RBAC systems, user-role assignment is managed by administrators of the systems where the administrators check the qualification of users and grant role membership to them. In these systems, users trust all the roles at the same level as they are all managed by the same administrators. The roles are trusted as long as the administrators are trusted.

In RBAC systems that use cryptographic RBAC schemes, users-role assignment can be decentralised to individual role managers to allow more flexibility in user management, especially in large-scale systems. Assume for example in these systems users join a role based on subscription for accessing the data assigned to that role. It is clear that users need to choose a trusted role when subscribing.

If the data that a user wants to access is encrypted to one role only, the user considers the trustworthiness of that role in deciding whether or not to join that role. When the same data is encrypted to multiple roles, users will need to evaluate the trustworthiness of these roles to choose the most reliable role to join. From the user's perspective, a trusted role should meet the following requirements:

- *Requirement 1: The role manager should grant membership to the users who are qualified for that role.*
  In order to access data, a user needs to join a role to which the data is encrypted. When the user requests to join the role, the role manager should give access (grant the membership) to the user if the user qualifies for that role, e.g. the user has paid the subscription fee. Refusing to give access will be considered as bad behaviour of the role manager.
- *Requirement 2: The data that a role claims to have should have been encrypted properly to that role.*
  When users want to access data, they need to know what data has been encrypted to which role so that they can choose a particular role to join. The list of the data is provided by roles. However, a user may find that she or he cannot locate or decrypt the data even after she or he has joined that specific role. This may happen if the data was not encrypted properly to that role by the owner, or the role claims to possess data that has not been encrypted to the role. Each role should take the responsibility of providing a valid and up-to-date list of the data that is in its possession.
- *Requirement 3: The data that the descendant roles of the role claim to have should have been encrypted properly to the descendant roles.*
  Since a role can inherit permissions from its descendant roles, a user who has joined a role should be able to access the data that is encrypted to any of its descendant roles. Each role is liable for the validity of the data that its descendant roles claim to have, as it is considered to be part of the data that this role has.

3.2   Role Managers' Trust in Data Owners

In cryptographic RBAC systems, owners can encrypt their data to any role. Obviously, role managers do not want owners to encrypt malicious data (e.g. virus, malware) to their roles. Therefore, role managers need to decide whether or not to accept data that owners want to assign to them. Having malicious data assigned to a role may result in a low trust value of the role because users who have joined the role will place negative trust records against the role if they detect that the data they get from the role is malicious. In the case where roles are profiting from users' subscriptions, low trust values in roles imply the risk of losing business.

To help role managers detect malicious owners, and hence avoid accepting data from them, another trust model is required to assist role managers in evaluating the trustworthiness of owners. Each time an owner wants to assign data to a role, the role manager will use the trust model to determine whether the data is coming from a trusted owner or not. From a role manager's perspective, a trusted owner should meet the following requirements:

– *Requirement 1: The data from the owner should be the same as its description.*
When owners encrypt and assign data to a role, the role manager may not be
able to verify each individual record from the owners. When a user who has
joined a role finds that the data she or he has accessed is not the data it claims
to be or contains malicious records, the user will inform the role manager about
the malicious data, and the role manager should place a negative trust record
against the owner who owns that data. Then next time this owner wishes to
assign data to the role, this trust record will be used by the role manager in
making the decision whether or not to accept the data.

– *Requirement 2: The owner should not be considered as untrusted by role managers of any role to which the owner has assigned data before.*
An owner may have had interactions with more than one role in the system.
A trusted owner is supposed to act consistently in the interaction with different roles. An owner may still be considered untrusted even though she or
he has good interaction histories with a small portion of roles in the system.
Therefore a trusted owner should try to maintain good interaction histories
with all the roles in the system. When a role manager is interacting with an
owner with which it has not interacted before, the trust opinions from the
role managers of other roles can assist this role manager to determine the
trustworthiness of the owner.

3.3 Data Owners' Trust in Role Managers

In a cloud storage system, owners are the parties who want to share the data.
When they encrypt their data to the roles (in an RBAC system), they need
to determine the trustworthiness of the role managers to reduce the risks of
unauthorised parties accessing their data. For instance, a data owner may choose
not to encrypt the data to a specific role if the role manager is found to have
"bad" behaviour histories. Let us now consider some of the key requirements
that the owner must consider in determining whether a role manager should
be trusted or not. From the owner's perspective, a trusted role manager should
meet the following requirements.

– *Requirement 1: The role manager should grant membership to users who are qualified for that role.*
When a data owner encrypts her or his data to a role, the intention of the
owner is to allow the data to be decrypted by the users who are qualified to be
in that role. Therefore, it is a basic requirement that the qualified users should
have the access to the data. The violation of this requirement is detected by
checking whether or not the qualified users can decrypt the data. Not granting
the membership to a qualified user is therefore considered as a bad behaviour
of a role.

– *Requirement 2: The role manager should not grant membership to users who are not qualified to that role.*
Another requirement that is expected by a data owner is to prevent users who
are not qualified from accessing the permissions to decrypt the data stored

in the cloud. A trusted role manager should only grant membership to a user when the qualifications of the user are verified. Granting membership to an unqualified user is therefore considered as a bad behaviour.

– *Requirement 3: The qualified users in a role should not leak the data to unqualified users.*

Even if a role manager grants membership only to the qualified users, it is possible that a qualified user may leak the data to unqualified users. For example, consider the situation whereby a user, who is allowed to access the private information that an owner has stored in the cloud, leaks it to another user to whom the owner does not want to reveal the information. The violation of this requirement is detected if it is found that an unqualified user has knowledge of the data. It may or may not be possible to discover this situation. In general, we assume that it is not possible to track down the user who leaks the data; this implies that all the users in that role will need to be under suspicion when such a data leak is detected.

In a hierarchical RBAC system, a role can inherit permissions from other roles. The users of a role have access to the data encrypted to any of its descendant roles. When a leakage is detected in the data encrypted to one of the descendant roles of a role, the users of this role are also under suspicion as they have the potential ability to cause the leakage. Therefore, when an owner wants to determine the trustworthiness of a role manager, the behaviour histories of role managers of descendant roles of this role need to be taken into account in the evaluation, as the users in this role could be the cause of the leakage of its descendant roles' data which are not reflected in the behaviour history of the role manager of this role.

– *Requirement 4: The role managers of ancestor roles of the role under consideration should be trusted.*

Since a role's permissions are inherited by all its ancestor roles, when an owner encrypts data to a role, all its ancestor roles also have access to the data. So the data owners need to consider the trustworthiness of not only the role to which they want to encrypt the data, but also of all the ancestor roles of this role, as encrypting data to this role is equivalent to encrypting data to any of the ancestor roles of this role.

3.4 Role Managers' Trust in Data Users

Since roles have the role managers to manage their user memberships, it is role managers' responsibility to build up their own reputation. Therefore it is important for each role manager to be able to evaluate the trustworthiness of users. Role managers can exclude malicious users from the roles; so these users would not affect the trustworthiness of the roles. The ability to evaluate the trust of users is also useful when a user wants to join the role. The role manager can determine the trustworthiness of the new user and decide whether or not to grant the membership to that user. The proper management of users can result in a good behaviour history for a role manager, which in turn affects the owners' decisions on the role manager. From the role managers' perspective, a trusted user should meet the following requirements.

- *Requirement 1: The user should not be involved in the event of leaking resources of the role.*
  When a leak of data is detected, we assume that the role manager can track which users have accessed the data but the role manager does not know who leaked the data. Here we say that a user is involved in leaking data if the data was found to be leaked, and this user has accessed the data before the leakage is detected. A user who has been involved in a leaking event m times will be considered as less trusted than the user who has been involved in a leaking event n times if $m > n$.
- *Requirement 2: The user should not be considered as untrusted by role managers of any role of which the user is or was a member.*
  A user may belong to different roles in a RBAC system. Therefore, the role managers of some other roles to which the user belongs may also hold trust opinions on the user. A trusted user is supposed to act consistently in different roles. Though a user may behave well in one role, she or he will still be considered as untrusted if she or he has bad behaviours in the other roles. The trust opinions of the role managers of other roles on a user can support the evaluation of the user's trustworthiness. A role manager who does not have any trust records in regards to a user (e.g. when a new user requests to join the role) will still be able to determine the trust of the user.

4   User's Trust Models for Cryptographic RBAC

In this section, we consider the user's trust models for a cryptographic RBAC system. There are three types of entities in our trust models, *Owner*, *User* and *Role*. Our trust models can assist a *User* to decide whether a *Role* to interact with is trusted, and assist a *Role* in determining the trustworthiness of an *Owner*. We first review these three entities. *Owner* is the entity who owns the data and stores it in an encrypted form for particular roles in the cloud. *User* is the entity who wishes to access the data stored in the cloud. *Role* is the entity that associates users with the access to owners' data, and each role manages the user membership of itself. Here when we say that users are managed by a role, we refer to the managers of the role who determine the user set of that role.

In our trust models, we assume that all the feedback and recommendations provided are honest. In other words, we assume that the trust system has the ability to verify the submitted feedback and recommendations, and only the valid ones will be considered in the trust evaluations.

4.1   User-Role RBAC Trust Model

In this subsection, we consider the trust model for user's trust in roles in a RBAC system.

Definition 1 (Interaction). From a user's perspective, an interaction is a transaction in which a user accesses data that is encrypted to a role to which the user belongs.

A successful interaction is an interaction where a user has successfully accessed the data. An unsuccessful interaction is an interaction where a user failed in accessing the data to which she or he should have legitimate access. Next we define two types of unsuccessful interactions.

User Management Failure: User management failure is an unsuccessful interaction caused by incorrect user membership management of a role; that is, the role did not grant the membership to the user even when the user qualifies for the role.

Permission Management Failure: Permission management failure is an unsuccessful interaction where the data encrypted to a role is invalid, or the data is not encrypted to the role. In other words, the owner of the data did not encrypt the data to the role in question or encrypted an invalid data to the role.

Definition 2 (Trust Vector). We define a trust vector to represent the behaviour history of a role as follows:

$$v = (r, s_U, s_P)$$

In the trust vector, r is the value related to successful interactions that users have had with a given role, s_U is the value related to *User Management Failure* of the role, and s_P is the value related to the *Permission Management Failure*.

Using the function $\mathcal{E}$ in Eq. 1, we define the trust function $T(v)$ that represents the trust value derived from the trust vector v as

$$T(v) = \mathcal{E}(r, s_U + s_P)$$

Definition 3 (Interaction History). We assume that there exists a central repository in the system that collects and stores the ratings from users on the interactions between users and roles. We define the trust record history derived from the ratings of the role R from n users as

$$Hist_\mathcal{U}(R) = \{H_1^R, H_2^R, \cdots, H_n^R\}$$

Each entry H_i^R in $Hist(R)$ is defined as a pair of parameters, $H_i^R = \langle U_i, v_{i,R} \rangle$, where $v_{i,R} = (r, s_U, s_P)$ is a trust vector that represents the trust record of interactions that the user U_i has had with the role R. r is the number of U_i's positive feedbacks on the interactions with R, s_U is the number of negative feedbacks on the interactions with R due to *User Management Failure*, and s_P is the number of negative feedbacks on the interactions with R due to *Permission Management Failure*.

In a cryptographic RBAC system, a user who belongs to a role not only has access to the data of the role, but also has access to the data of descendent roles. Therefore, an invalid resource from a descendent role may also cause an unsuccessful interaction. Since a role knows whether a resource comes from its descendent roles, we assume that users give feedback to the roles to whom the resources are directly assigned; that is, if a user detects an invalid resource from a descendent role, she or he will update the feedback for the descendent role directly instead of the role she or he belongs to.

As discussed in Sect. 3.1, from the users' perspective, the trustworthiness of a role is affected by the interaction history of the role and its descendant roles. Therefore users need to consider the following types of trust classes when evaluating the trustworthiness of roles.

Individual Trust. Individual trust is a belief that is derived directly from the interaction history of the role R.

When a user U_k wishes to evaluate the trust value of a role R, the user first obtains the interaction history $Hist_\mathcal{U}(R)$ of the role from the central repository. Assume that w_u is the weight that the user U_k assigns to the feedbacks from other users. Then the individual trust value of the role R can be computed as follows,

$$T_\mathcal{U}(R)^D = \mathcal{T}(v_{k,R}^D),$$

$$\text{where} \quad v_{k,R}^D = v_{k,R} + w_u \cdot \sum_{i=1, i \neq k}^{n} v_{i,R}$$

where the trust vector $v_{k,R}^D$ is a combination of all trust vectors in $Hist_\mathcal{U}(R)$ considering the weighting for the trust vectors from other users.

Inheritance Trust. Inheritance trust is a belief that is derived from the interaction history of the descendant roles of a given role.

Assume a role R has m immediate descendant roles $\{R_1, \cdots, R_m\}$, and a weight vector w_{R_i} is defined as $(w_{R_i}^R, 0, w_{R_i}^R)$ where $w_{R_i}^R \in [0, 1]$ is the weight assigned to the inheritance relationship between R and R_i. The second element is set to zero because *User Management Failure* is not considered in inheritance trust as user management of descendant roles will not cause any unsuccessful interaction for this role. The inheritance trust of roles in a hierarchy is computed as follows:

$$T_\mathcal{U}(R)^I = \mathcal{T}(v_{k,R}^I),$$

$$\text{where} \quad v_{k,R}^I = \sum_{i=1}^{m} [(v_{k,R_i}^D + v_{k,R_i}^I), w_{R_i}]$$

In the above equation, $[v, w] := v^T w$ is the usual dot product on $\mathbb{Z}_q^3$.

Combination Trust. To compute the trust value of a role, we define a combination trust function for a role R as $T_\mathcal{U}(R)$ to combine the above described two types of trust together. Assume that $w \in [0, 1]$ is the weight of the inheritance trust. The trust value is computed as

$$T_\mathcal{U}(R) = (1 - w) \cdot T_\mathcal{U}(R)^D + w \cdot T_\mathcal{U}(R)^I$$

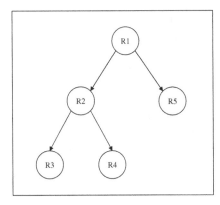

Fig. 1. Hierarchical RBAC example.

4.2   Example of User-Role RBAC Trust Model

Now we use an example to show how the users' trust in a role is affected by feedback for different roles in a RBAC system. In this example, we consider all the bad feedback as *Permission Management Failure*, as our intention is to show how the role hierarchy affects the trust value of roles. Consider the role hierarchy example shown in Fig. 1.

In Fig. 1, the role R_1 inherits from role R_2 and role R_5, and the role R_2 inherits from R_3 and R_4. We set the weight between every two roles and the weight of other owners' feedback to 1; that is, the weight vector for each role R_k where $k \in [1, 5]$ is defined as $\boldsymbol{w}_{R_i} = (1, 0, 1), \forall\, i \in [1, 5], i \neq k$, and $w_u = (1, 1, 1)$. When a user wants to access a resource that has been assigned to the role R_2, she or he will need to evaluate the trust value of R_2 to decide whether R_2 is reliable to join. In Fig. 2, we show the trust values of R_2 when only different individual roles in the RBAC system have feedback. For example, the curve for $R_1, GFP = 75\,\%$ shows the trust values of R_2 when only R_1 in the RBAC system has feedback, and $75\,\%$ of the feedback is positive.

When the good feedback percentage is $75\,\%$, the trust value for R_2 goes up with the increasing number of feedbacks that R_2 and R_3 have. This trend implies that the more resources a role has, the more impact the good feedback percentage has on the trust value of the role. Note that the feedback for R_1 does not affect the trust value of R_2. This is because an untrusted R_1 will not cause an unsuccessful interaction of R_2. When the feedback is only given for R_2, the increase in the trust value is the fastest. This is because the individual trust of the role has more weight than the inheritance trust by our assumption. It is clear that the increase in the trust value of R_2 is slower when the feedback is for R_3 only, because inheritance trust has less weight in this example.

When the good feedback percentage is $25\,\%$, the trust value for R_2 goes down with the increasing number of feedbacks that R_2 and R_3 have. Similarly, this trend implies that the more resources a role has, the more impact the good feedback percentage has on the trust value of the role. The feedback for R_1 does

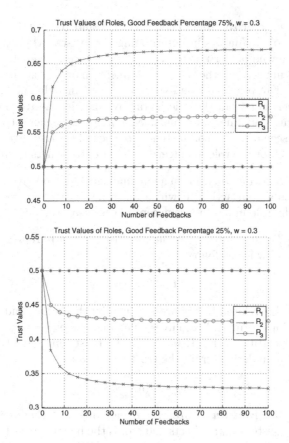

Fig. 2. Trust values on R_2 for users from feedback on different roles.

not affect the trust value of R_2 either. When feedback is only given for R_2, the decrease in the trust value is the fastest. This is because the individual trust of the role has more weight than the inheritance trust by our assumption. Therefore the decrease in the trust value of R_2 is slower when the feedback is for R_3 only.

From Fig. 2, we see that the feedbacks for different roles in the system have different impacts on the trust value of R_2. Firstly, the feedback for ancestor roles does not affect the trust of the role. Secondly, the more resources that have been assigned to a role, the more impact the feedback for the role will have on its ancestor roles as well as itself. These results show that our users' trust model is useful in assisting users to determine properly the trust of roles in RBAC systems.

4.3   Role-Owner RBAC Trust Model

In the case when any owner can choose roles to encrypt their resources to, assigning malicious resources or invalid resources to a role may cause the *Permission*

Management Failure of the role. Therefore, it would be useful to have a trust model to assist role managers in determining the trustworthiness of an owner, and hence decide whether or not to accept the resources from the owner.

As discussed in Sect. 3.2, the trust requirement on owners is simpler compared to the users' trust in roles, and we see some important differences. The trust in owners is independent from the role hierarchy; that is, the role hierarchy does not affect the trustworthiness of owners. We note that a general trust model can be used in this scenario. For completeness purposes, we also give the definition of the trust model for the role managers' trust in data owners in this subsection.

Definition 4 *(Interaction).* From a role manager's perspective, an interaction with an owner is a transaction in which an owner assigned a resource to that role, and that the role manager has accepted the resource.

Definition 5 *(Trust Vector).* We define a trust vector to represent the behaviour history of an owner as follows:

$$v = (h, s)$$

where h is the value related to resources owned by the owner, and s is the value related to malicious or invalid resources owned by the owner.

Using the function $\mathcal{E}$ in Eq. 1, we define the trust function $T(v)$ that represents the trust value derived from the trust vector v as

$$T(v) = \mathcal{E}(h - s, s)$$

Definition 6 *(Interaction History).* We assume that there exists a central repository in the system that collects and stores the behaviour histories provided by role managers to which the owner has assigned the resources. We define the trust record history provided by a set $\mathcal{R}$ of n roles as

$$Hist_{\mathcal{R}}(O) = \{H_1^O, H_2^O, \cdots, H_n^O\}$$

Each entry H_i^O in $Hist(O)$ is defined as a pair of parameters, $H_i^O = \langle R_i, v_{i,O} \rangle$ where $v_{i,O} = (h, s)$ is a trust vector that represents the trust record of the owner O on the resources that she or he has assigned to the role R_i. h is the total number of O's resources that has been assigned to R_i, and s is the number of bad resources assigned by O.

We assume that an owner O has a resource and wants to assign it to a role R_k. When this resource is assigned to the role R_k, R_k updates the trust record of the owner by increasing the value h in the trust vector H_k^O of O by 1. Now assume that a user has found the resource to be invalid, and then she or he reports to the role of this resource. If the role has confirmed that the user's complaint is true after verifying the resource, R_k will find out that it is O who uploaded this resource, and R_k will increase the value s in trust vectors H_k^O for this owner by 1.

A user that belongs to a role has the permission to access resources of the descendant roles of the role. When the user reports a bad resource from its descendant role, this role may not be able to identify the owner of the resource as the resource is not assigned to this role directly. Hence the role cannot update the trust records of the owner. In this case, the role can notify all its descendant roles about this bad resource, and the role to which the resource is assigned to will update the trust record of the owner who owns the resource.

Assume that w is the weight that the role R_k assigns to the feedback from other roles. Taking as input the interaction history of an owner, the trust value of the owner can be computed as follows:

$$T_{\mathcal{R}}(O) = T(v_{k,O}^T), \quad v_{k,O}^T = v_{k,O} + w \cdot \sum_{i=1, i \neq k}^{n} v_{i,O}$$

This trust value is evaluated based on a combination of all trust records in $Hist_{\mathcal{R}}(O)$ considering the weighting for the trust records from other roles.

5 Architecture for User's Trust Models

In this section, we present the design of a secure cloud storage system by combining the user's trust models for RBAC proposed in Sect. 4 with a cryptographic RBAC system. This architecture provides a practical solution for building a reliable and trusted RBAC system while retaining the use of cryptographic techniques. We have implemented a prototype of this architecture and have been conducting a range of experiments.

5.1 System Overview

Consider the system architecture shown in Fig. 3. Each solid line in the figure shows the communication channel set by the system between two components

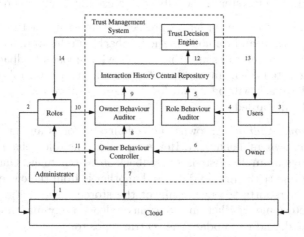

Fig. 3. Architecture for using user's RBAC trust models in a cryptographic RBAC system.

joined together by the line, and the arrows indicate the direction in which the information flows. Since our trust models are based on cryptographic RBAC schemes, our system contains all the entities that a cryptographic RBAC scheme has, including an administrator, roles, users, and owners. The administrator is the certificate authority of the RBAC system, and it generates the system parameters and issues all the necessary credentials. In addition, the administrator manages the role hierarchy of the system. To put a role into the role hierarchy, the administrator needs to compute the parameters for that role. These parameters represent the position of the role in the role hierarchy. They are stored in the cloud, and are available publicly. Roles are the entities that associate users and owners together. Each role has its own role parameters which define the user membership. These role parameters are stored in the cloud, and a role needs to update them in the cloud when updating the user membership of the role. Owners are the parties who possess the data and want to store the encrypted data in the cloud for other users to access, and they specify the roles who can access the data. In the RBAC model, they are the parties who manage the relationship between permissions and roles. Users are the parties who wish to acquire certain data from the cloud. When a user wishes to access stored data in the cloud, she or he first sends the request to the cloud, and decrypts the data upon receiving the response from the cloud.

In addition to these four entities in a basic cryptographic RBAC scheme, our trust models enhanced the cryptographic RBAC system by integrating an extra trust management system, which consists of five components.

Central Repository. In our trust models, all the interaction histories and trust records related to roles and users are stored in a central repository. The central repository is used to keep the records of all these interaction histories and trust records which are used by the Trust Decision Engine (described below) in evaluating the trust value of roles and owners. Any entity that is residing outside the trust management system is not able to access the central repository.

Role Behaviour Auditor. In order to protect the integrity of the feedback on roles, a role behaviour auditor collects the feedback on roles from users. The role behaviour auditor needs to ensure that a user who uploads feedback against a role has been granted the membership of the role or an ancestor role of that role. All the valid feedback will be forwarded to the central repository, and invalid feedback will be discarded.

Owner Behaviour Auditor. An owner behaviour auditor is an entity to collect the feedback on owners' behaviour. However, unlike the role behaviour auditor, the owner behaviour auditor listens for feedback on two channels. One is from the roles who may report the invalid data, and another is from the owner behaviour controller which reports the ownership of the stored data in the cloud. This auditor will determine whether an owner has uploaded any malicious or invalid data to the cloud, and can update the central repository.

Owner Behaviour Controller. Owner behaviour controller acts as a proxy server between owners and the cloud. It controls and forwards the owners' encrypted data to the cloud. The controller can decide whether to store data in the cloud based on the decision from the role to which the data is assigned. The controller will inform the owner behaviour auditor about which owner the uploaded data belongs to.

Trust Decision Engine. The trust decision engine is the entity which evaluates the trust of the roles for users and the trust of the owners for roles. The trust decision engine takes as input the interaction histories or trust records stored in the central repository, and outputs the trust value of a particular role or owner.

5.2   System Workflow

All the entities in the system are connected through different communication channels which are labelled with numbers in Fig. 3. We explain how the system works by describing the information flow through these channels.

First, the administrator initialises the system and specifies the role hierarchy of the system. The generated system parameters are uploaded to the cloud via (1). Roles grant the membership to users, and upload role parameters to the cloud via (2). Users download and decrypt data from the cloud via (3). When an owner wants to encrypt and store data in the cloud to a particular role, she or he first encrypts the data and sends a request to the owner behaviour controller via (6). Then the owner behaviour controller notifies the role via (11) and forwards the request to the cloud through (7) if the role agrees to accept the data from this owner. The cloud then communicates with the owner as in a normal cryptographic RBAC scheme. The controller also sends the owner behaviour auditor the information about the owner's identity and the resource's identity via (8).

When a user wants to access a resource in the RBAC system, the system first returns a list of roles who claim to have this resource. Then the user requests the trust evaluation on these roles from the trust management system. The trust value of the roles will be returned to the user through the (13). The user may choose a role who has the highest trust value to send the join request. When a user has found that the data she or he has accessed from the role is malicious or invalid, she or he then provides feedback on the role to whom the resource is encrypted to the role behaviour auditor through (4). Once the role behaviour auditor verifies that the feedback is from an authorised user, it will forward the feedback to the central repository.

When a negative feedback of a role has been raised by a user because of an invalid resource, the role will send the identity of the resource to the owner behaviour auditor via (10) if it believes that the resource was invalid when the owner uploaded the resource. The auditor then updates the trust records of the owner of this resource to the central repository via (9). When an owner wants to assign a resource to a role, the role can ask the trust management system about the trust evaluation for an owner, and the trust value will be returned by the trust decision engine through (14). Upon receiving the trust values for the owner from the trust decision engine, the role can inform the owner behaviour controller via (11) whether to accept the data. Moreover, this trust evaluation process can be made automatically by connecting the owner behaviour controller to the trust decision engine directly. Roles can pre-determine a trust threshold for accepting data from owners. Every time an owner wants to upload a resource, the owner behaviour controller can check the trust value of the owner from the trust decision engine directly, and decide whether to accept the resource by comparing the trust value with the role's threshold.

6   Owner's Trust Models for Cryptographic RBAC

In this section, we consider the remaining two trust relationships in crypto-graphic RBAC systems, data owners' trust in role managers and role man-agers' trust in users. We refer to these trust models as Owner-Role RBAC and Role-User RBAC trust models respectively. The Owner-Role RBAC trust model assists the data owners to evaluate the trust in role managers in a RBAC system and use this trust evaluation to decide whether to store their encrypted data in the cloud for particular roles. The Role-User RBAC trust model helps the role managers to evaluate the trust in users in the RBAC system and use this trust in deciding whether to grant membership to the users. These trust models can not only prevent the owners from interacting with role managers which have a poor track record in terms of carrying out their functions properly, but also assist the role managers to identify the malicious users who caused the negative impacts on the role managers' trustworthiness. This can in turn be used to reduce the risks associated with interacting with the RBAC system for the data owners and help role managers to keep the RBAC system authentic. The Owner-Role RBAC and Role-User RBAC trust models are independent of each other and serve different purposes.

6.1   Owner-Role RBAC Trust Model

An important feature of the proposed trust models is that they take role inheri-tance into account. Since our trust models are for cloud storage systems dealing with hierarchical RBAC schemes, the trustworthiness of a role manager is also affected by the historical behaviour of the role managers of its ancestor roles and/or descendent roles. Hence in our trust evaluation, we take into account the impact of role hierarchy and inheritance on the trustworthiness of the role managers and users.

In Sect. 3.3, we discussed the trust requirements that an owner should con-sider when deciding whether or not to trust a role. From that discussion, we see that the factors which can affect the owners' decision come from the interaction history of the role with whom owners have interacted as well as its ancestor roles and descendant roles. When an owner evaluates the trust of a role R, the owner needs to consider the interaction history of other roles that have inheritance relationships with the role R.

First we consider the inheritance trust where only the interaction history of the descendant roles is included. When an owner detects that a user of a descen-dant role R_d of a role R leaked data to unqualified users, the feedback that the owner provided should not only be applied to that descendant role R_d, but should also affect the trust of R as users belonging to the role R also have the access to owner's data assigned to R_d and hence are under suspicion of causing an unsuccessful interaction. Therefore, while evaluating the trust of the role R, the interaction history from all its descendant roles including R_d needs to be considered.

Then we look at the interaction history of ancestor roles' impacts on the trust of the role. Consider the scenario where the trust score of a role is higher than the trust score of one of its ancestor roles. Then the owners will trust this role at the same level as its ancestor role which has a lower trust score, as the users of its ancestor role have the same level of access as the users in this role. So the trust score of the role will be the minimum value of the trust of this role and the trust of all its ancestor roles.

6.2   Role-User RBAC Trust Model

Since the trustworthiness of a role is primarily determined by the behaviour of users of the role, it is important for the role to ensure that only users with good behaviour are granted membership. If roles do not have a way to evaluate the trust of their users, it would be difficult for them to distinguish the malicious users from those with good behaviours.

When a role wishes to evaluate the trust value of a user, the role first considers the user's trust record rated by the role itself. Then the role needs to consider the trust records of the user from other roles in the system. Therefore, the trust score of the user is evaluated based on all the trust records of this user including the trust records from other roles.

This trust model can either work independently or work together with the Owner-Role RBAC trust model. Roles can use this model to periodically check the trust value of the existing users in the roles, and revoke the memberships from users whose trust values are below the preset threshold. This trust model can also be used by roles to determine the trust value of a new user requesting to join; the request from the users whose trust values are below the threshold will be rejected.

7   Application Scenario

In this section, we use application examples to illustrate how the trust models in the framework can be used in a cloud service application to enhance the quality of security decision making.

7.1   Application for User's RBAC Trust Models

In this subsection, we describe a digital library system which uses our proposed user's trust models to illustrate how the trust models can assist security decision making in this system. The digital library system uses an external public cloud

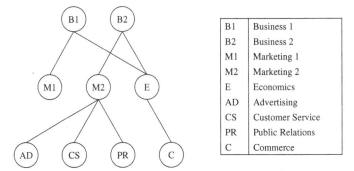

Fig. 4. Digital library system example for user's RBAC trust models.

to store all the digital format resources such as books, papers, theses, and other types of publications. There are many distributors who use the platform provided by the digital library system to share digital resources. Each distributor can get the authorisations for sharing the digital resources from the publishers directly. A party who subscribes to a distributor can access all the resources of the distributor. Assume that the distributors have two types of subscription licenses; personal licenses that allow only the subscribed user to access the resources, and business licenses that allow another distributor to resell the resources to other users or distributors.

Now let us consider the example of a distributors' network for this digital library system. The hierarchical relationship of the distributors is shown in Fig. 4. In this system, distributors choose the resources to share by their categories. The distributors AD, CS, PR, C, and M_1 get the authorisations for selling digital resources in the categories *Advertising*, *Customer Service*, *Public Relations*, *Commerce* and *Marketing* respectively from the publishers. Distributors M_2 and E sell a wider ranger of resources which cover all the categories in *Marketing* and *Economics* respectively, and these two distributors get authorisations from the distributors of sub-categories instead of the publishers directly. Note that the categories of resources sold by M_1 and M_2 are overlapped. The difference is the channels they get the resources from: M_1 from publishers, and M_2 from sub-distributors. Similarly, distributors B_1 and B_2 get authorisations from M_1, E, and M_2, E respectively, and their resources both cover the categories *Business*.

To use cryptographic RBAC schemes to protect the resources so that only the authorised users can access them, the administrator of the digital library system first sets up the system parameters based on the relationships of the distributors. Then the publishers can encrypt their resources to the distributors whom they authorised to sell the resources. Here we consider the distributors as roles in the RBAC, and publishers as owners of the resources. When a user subscribes to a distributor, the distributor simply adds the user to the role. Then the user can use the key given by the system administrator to decrypt the resources of the role. Because the cryptographic RBAC schemes support role hierarchy, in this example, users who subscribed to the role M_2 can also access the resources of the role AD, CS and PR, and users subscribed to B_1 can access the resources of all the roles M_1, E, and C.

First let us consider how the trust model can assist the users. Assume that the distributor M_2 also gets some resources, which the distributors AD, CS, and PR do not have directly from the publishers. To save the cost of storing resources in the cloud, M_2 chooses to reprint some resources in a lower quality to reduce the file size. Users subscribed to M_2 may give negative feedbacks on M_2 because they have difficulties in reading some of the resources. Later on, when a user want to access marketing resources, she or he evaluates the trust of M_1 and M_2, and the trust model will output a higher trust value for M_1 than for M_2 because of the negative feedbacks of M_2. Then the user will know the quality of resources from M_1 is better than those from M_2. However, the distributors AD, CS, and PR will not be affected because the poor quality resources are not coming from them. When a user wants to subscribe to a distributor for *Business*, B_2 will have lower trust value than B_1 as resource the user would get from B_1 may come from M_2.

Now let us look at the trust model for roles' trust in owners. Assume that publishers want to promote their digital resources, and they actively assign their resources to distributors. The resources that have come from some publishers may be of poor quality or alternatively some resources are not what the publishers claim them to be. The distributors may not be able to verify each individual resource due to the lack of expertise in certain areas. When users complain about a bad resource, the role can give a negative feedback on the publisher who owns the resource, after confirming that the users' complaints is valid. The feedback of the publisher can be accessed by all the distributors so they can avoid using this publisher in the future.

7.2 Application for Owner's RBAC Trust Models

Finally, we consider another application scenario based on a digital library system. Similarly, assume that the digital library system uses an external cloud storage platform to store all the resources. A party can subscribe to the publisher for particular resources in order to access the resources stored in the cloud, and the subscription to a publisher needs to be authorised by the publisher. The publisher may reject the subscription request for reasons such as the party is not reliable in paying the subscription or the party has the potential to leak the resources to unauthorised parties.

Now assume that there is an organisation with several branches in different geographical locations and that each branch consists of several departments. When employees of the organisation need to access the digital resources stored in the cloud, the relevant department or the branch (where the employee works) can subscribe to the publisher. Let us assume that the organisation uses a RBAC system to control the access to resources, and the role hierarchy is shown in Fig. 5.

In this example, the organisation consists of two branches B_1 and B_2, and each branch has two departments MD_1 and PD_1, MD_2 and PD_2 respectively.

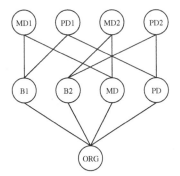

ORG	Organisation
B1	Branch 1
B2	Branch 2
MD	Marketing Department
PD	Production Department
MD1	Marketing Department 1
PD1	Production Department 1
MD2	Marketing Department 2
PD2	Production Department 2

Fig. 5. Digital library system example for owner's RBAC trust models.

Assume that the head office has two head departments MD and PD which manage the relevant departments in both branches. Recall that a role can inherit from other roles in the RBAC system. For example, when PD has subscribed to a resource from a publisher, both PD_1 and PD_2 will have access to the resource. Similarly, a resource subscribed by the role ORG can be accessed by all the roles in the system.

By using a cryptographic RBAC scheme in this system, a publisher is able to encrypt the resource to the branch or department (who subscribes to the resource) and store it in the cloud so that the employees who work in the branch or department can access it. There is an assumption that these employees are trusted and will not redistribute resources of the publisher to employees who are not in that branch or department. However, it is possible that an employee leaks the content of a resource to others. Therefore, the publishers will need a trust system to assist them in identifying the roles who have malicious users, and hence avoid accepting the subscriptions from them.

Let us now consider how our trust model can be used in this system to assist the publishers (owners). Assume that no publisher has ever interacted with the role PD_1, PD_2, and now a publisher wishes to evaluate the trust of these two roles. We also assume that B_1, MD_1 and PD_1 are the same as B_2, MD_2 and PD_2 in terms of the number of employees and percentage of good feedbacks for B_1 is higher than that for B_2. Since the trust of the role is affected by descendant roles in our model, the publisher will get the result where the role PD_1 is more trusted than PD_2. This result aligns to the fact that if the branch B_1 is more trusted than the branch B_2, then the department PD_1 of the branch B_1 will also be considered more trusted than the department PD_2 of the branch B_2.

Now assume that the role ORG only has good feedbacks; that is, the resources the role ORG has subscribed have never been leaked. Since the trust value of a role is taken from the minimum value of the trust value for all its ancestor roles, when a publisher evaluates the trust of the role ORG, its trust value may be low if the good feedback percentage for B_2 is low. This is because employees in the role B_2 inherit permissions from the role ORG, and employees in this branch could potentially leak the resources.

When the role B_2 realises that its trust value is low, it may decide to warn or even exclude some potential malicious users. Then our Role-User RBAC trust model can be useful to assist roles in identifying the potential malicious users. Our trust model allows the trust for employees in B_2 to be evaluated based on the feedbacks from all the roles in the organisation. That is, if an employee was working in the branch B_1 and relocated to B_2 recently, the feedbacks on the user from B_1 when the user was working in B_1 is also taken into account when B_2 determines the trustworthiness of the user.

From this digital library system example, we see that our owner's trust model can be used in the cloud storage system using cryptographic RBAC schemes where role managers themselves have the flexibility in managing the user membership.

8 Related Works

There have been some related works which have addressed only trust on users in RBAC systems. Reference [2] proposed a trust model for RBAC system which considers users' trust by assigning trust levels to users. These trust levels are based on a number of factors such as user credentials, user behaviour history and recommendations from other users. Trust levels are then mapped to roles. Another trust model for RBAC was proposed in [13] to assist roles with the decision of user-role assignment based on a wide range of criteria of users, including behaviour history and reputation. In [4], a trust model for RBAC was introduced which evaluates the trust in the users based on user behaviours and context, in a context-aware access control model. Another trust model was discussed in [14] which also uses trust level to determine the access privileges of users. All these trust models only consider the trust on users in a RBAC system. None of these works address the other trust relationships in the RBAC system. The trust for role managers is critical in cloud storage systems which has been addressed in this paper. Our trust models have also addressed the roles's trust on data owners and users. Another difference between our model and the previously proposed ones is that our trust models work in RBAC systems which use cryptographic RBAC schemes. That is, our models take into account cryptographic operations and the access privileges to decrypt the data stored in the cloud, which none of the previous works address.

9 Conclusions and Future Work

In this paper, we have addressed trust issues in cryptographic role-based access control systems for securing data storage in a cloud environment. We have proposed trust models for different entities in RBAC systems which are using cryptographic RBAC schemes to secure stored data. These trust models assist the users and role managers to determine the trustworthiness of individual role managers and data owners, and data owners and role managers to evaluate the trustworthiness of individual role managers and users, in the RBAC system respectively. They allow the users and the data owners to perform the trust evaluation to decide whether or not to access/share a resource from/to a particular role. Our trust model takes into account role inheritance and hierarchy in the evaluation of trustworthiness of roles. The models also enable the roles to use the trust evaluation in their decision to accept the resources from a particular owner and grant the role membership to a user. We have given the design of an architecture of a trust-based cloud storage system which has integrated the user's trust models with the cryptographic RBAC schemes. We have also described the application of the proposed trust models by considering a practical scenario and illustrating how the trust evaluations can be used to reduce the risks and enhance the quality of security decision making by different entities of the cloud storage service.

The proposed trust models used a centralised trust management system to assist entities with their trust evaluations. Though these entities in the system still need to trust the centralised trust management components, we believe that this approach has much improved the cases where entities need to trust every other individual entity in the system. We note that the auditing components in our designed architecture need to collect all the provided feedback. In large-scale systems, the load of these auditing components could be high. One solution to this issue is using decentralised auditing components which will be considered in our future work. In addition, we only considered two types of feedbacks in our trust models, positive and negative. However, a user who has unsatisfactory experiences with roles may want to provide varying levels of negative feedback. For example, the user may have retrieved a malware instead of valid data from a role and a poor quality data instead of a good quality one from the same role. It is clear that some cases are more harmful than others, and the user may want to rate the role less untrusted when it is more harmful. We will also consider this issue in our future work.

References

1. Akl, S.G., Taylor, P.D.: Cryptographic solution to a problem of access control in a hierarchy. ACM Trans. Comput. Syst. 1(3), 239–248 (1983)
2. Chakraborty, S., Ray, I.: TrustBAC - integrating trust relationships into the RBAC model for access control in open systems. In: 11th ACM Symposium on Access Control Models and Technologies, SACMAT 2006, pp. 49–58. ACM, 7–9 June 2006
3. De Capitani di Vimercati, S., Foresti, S., Jajodia, S., Paraboschi, S., Samarati, P.: Encryption policies for regulating access to outsourced data. ACM Trans. Database Syst. 35(2), 12:1–12:46 (2010)
4. Feng, F., Lin, C., Peng, D., Li, J.: A trust and context based access control model for distributed systems. In: 10th IEEE International Conference on High Performance Computing and Communications, HPCC 2008, pp. 629–634. IEEE, 25–27 September 2008

5. Ferraiolo, D.F., Kuhn, D.R.: Role-based access controls. In: Proceedings of the 15th NIST-NCSC National Computer Security Conference, pp. 554–563. National Institute of Standards and Technology, National Computer Security Center, 10–13 October 1992

6. Jøsang, A., Ismail, R.: The beta reputation system. In: Proceedings of the 15th Bled Conference on Electronic Commerce (2002)

7. Miklau, G., Suciu, D.: Controlling access to published data using cryptography. In: Proceedings of 29th International Conference on Very Large Data Bases, VLDB 2003, pp. 898–909, 9–12 September 2003

8. Mui, L., Mohtashemi, M., Ang, C., Szolovits, P., Halberstadt, A.: Ratings in distributed systems: a bayesian approach. In: Workshop on Information Technologies and Systems (2001)

9. Mui, L., Mohtashemi, M., Halberstadt, A.: A computational model of trust and reputation for e-businesses. In: HICSS, p. 188 (2002)

10. Samarati, P., De Capitani di Vimercati, S.: Data protection in outsourcing scenarios: issues and directions. In: Proceedings of the 5th ACM Symposium on Information, Computer and Communications Security, ASIACCS 2010, pp. 1–14. ACM, 13–16 April 2010

11. Sandhu, R.S., Coyne, E.J., Feinstein, H.L., Youman, C.E.: Role-based access control models. IEEE Comput. 29(2), 38–47 (1996)

12. Sandhu, R.S., Ferraiolo, D.F., Kuhn, D.R.: The NIST model for role-based access control: towards a unified standard. In: ACM Workshop on Role-Based Access Control, RBAC00, pp. 47–63 (2000)

13. Takabi, H., Amini, M., Jalili, R.: Trust-based user-role assignment in role-based access control. In: AICCSA, pp. 807–814. IEEE, 13–16 May 2007

14. Toahchoodee, M., Abdunabi, R., Ray, I., Ray, I.: A trust-based access control model for pervasive computing applications. In: Gudes, E., Vaidya, J. (eds.) Data and Applications Security XXIII. LNCS, vol. 5645, pp. 307–314. Springer, Heidelberg (2009)

15. Zhou, L., Varadharajan, V., Hitchens, M.: Enforcing role-based access control for secure data storage in the cloud. Comput. J. 54(13), 1675–1687 (2011)

16. Zhu, Y., Hu, H., Ahn, G.-J., Wang, H., Wang, S.-B.: Provably secure role-based encryption with revocation mechanism. J. Comput. Sci. Technol. 26(4), 697–710 (2011)

IPv6 Network Attack Detection
with HoneydV6

Sven Schindler[1(✉)], Bettina Schnor[1], Simon Kiertscher[1], Thomas Scheffler[2],
and Eldad Zack[3]

[1] Department of Computer Science, University of Potsdam, Potsdam, Germany
{sschindl,schnor,kiertscher}@cs.uni-potsdam.de
[2] Department of Electrical Engineering, Beuth Hochschule, Berlin, Germany
scheffler@beuth-hochschule.de
[3] EANTC AG, Berlin, Germany
zack@eantc.de

Abstract. During 2012, we conducted a long term IPv6-darknet experiment. We observed a relatively high number of interesting events and therefore needed additional network security tools to capture and analyse potentially harmful IPv6 traffic. This paper presents *HoneydV6*, a low-interaction IPv6 honeypot that can simulate entire IPv6 networks and which may be utilized to detect and analyze IPv6 network attacks. Our implementation is based on the well-known low-interaction honeypot *Honeyd*. To the best of our knowledge, this is the first low-interaction honeypot which is able to simulate entire IPv6 networks on a single host. Enticing attackers to exploit an IPv6 honeypot requires new approaches and concepts because of the huge IPv6 address space. We solved this problem through a dynamic instantiation mechanism that increases the likelihood for an attacker to find a target host in our IPv6 honeynet.

Keywords: IPv6 · Honeypot · Darknet · IPv6 traffic analysis

1 Introduction

In June 2012, the Internet Society arranged the World IPv6 Launch Day, an event where well-known service providers and web companies like Google or Yahoo! started to enable IPv6 support for their customers.

With the increasing number of service providers offering IPv6, the number of attackers aiming for these networks may increase. In order to get an idea of the current threat level in IPv6 networks, we started an IPv6-darknet experiment in March 2012 using a /48 network. A darknet is an address space that is advertised and routed but does not provide any services [1]. All traffic entering a darknet can be considered malicious. This eases classification and subsequent analysis, because we do not have to separate production traffic from attack traffic.

Due to the huge IPv6 address space, brute-force network scanning of IPv6 addresses is not attractive for an attacker and hence the probability to catch

© Springer-Verlag Berlin Heidelberg 2014
M.S. Obaidat and J. Filipe (Eds.): ICETE 2013, CCIS 456, pp. 252–269, 2014.
DOI: 10.1007/978-3-662-44788-8_15

attackers in a darknet is low. Nevertheless, the results of our darknet experiment show that malicious IPv6 traffic is existent and increasing.

There may also arise new threats that are aimed at specific weaknesses in the IPv6 design. A well-known example for this trend is the published THC-IPv6 Attack Toolkit [2] which exploits several protocol-specific features, such as the IPv6 Stateless Address Autoconfiguration [3].

In order to analyse IPv6-related attacks, IPv6-enabled security tools like Intrusion Detection Systems or virtual honeypots have to be deployed that allow a deeper analysis of attack patterns.

Virtual honeypots provide an excellent mechanism to collect information about network attacks and vulnerabilities, because they provide a level of interactivity that cannot be achieved by darknets. A virtual honeypot is a security device that has no production value [4]. This can be something like a computer or even a mobile phone which only purpose is to attract attackers, so that their attacks can be analysed. Low-interaction honeypots like *Honeyd* [5] may even be used to simulate large networks with thousands of routers and hosts.

We chose to extend the low-interaction IPv4 honeypot *Honeyd* to *HoneydV6*, since it is able to simulate entire IPv4 networks on a single computer and provides a lot of components that could be reused in our IPv6 implementation. Further, *Honeyd* is the fundamental part of a number of honeypot solutions like *Tiny Honeypot* or the *SCADA HoneyNet Project* and can be used to improve the capabilities of honeypots like Nephentes [6]. Therefore, by implementing IPv6 functionality into *Honeyd*, the aforementioned honeypots may be adapted so that they are able to handle IPv6 connections as well.

Honeyd implements a customized network stack to handle t multiple simulated hosts on a single machine. The large number of available addresses in a single IPv6 network requires a new honeynet design approach. The static placement of virtual components does not work, because an attacker is unlikely to find a deployed honeypot within the large IPv6 address space by chance. We therefore developed the concept of *random IPv6 request processing* to allow attackers to dynamically find and exploit our simulated hosts.

The next section presents the results from our darknet experiment. Section 3 summarizes related work. In Sects. 4 and 5, we present the IPv6 extension of *Honeyd*. Section 6 shows the results of performance measurements of *HoneydV6* and Sect. 7 concludes our work.

2   Examining the Threat Level in IPv6 Networks

A couple of years ago, it was hard to find any malicious or even unintentional traffic in IPv6 networks. In 2006, Matthew Ford et al. published a traffic statistic of their IPv6 darknet with a /48 prefix, which may have been the world's first IPv6 darknet [1]. Within approximately 16 months, they captured about 12 ICMPv6 packets which were most probably caused by misconfiguration and typographical errors resulting from the long and unwieldy IPv6 addresses. In comparison, Pang et al. observed in 2004 about 30,000 packets of background radiation per second in a class A IPv4 network [7].

In 2010, Geoff Huston presented the results of his darknet experiment where he examined the background radiation in a 2400::/12 network provided by APNIC for 9 days [8].

The darknet received about 21,000 packets. However, the used /12 address block was not vacant and about 1.6 % of the network addresses had already been allocated. Therefore, it is hard to compare the results of this experiment to earlier darknet results even though traffic which was directed to allocated addresses was filtered before further analysis. It is assumed that the received traffic is caused by misconfiguration and probably a small number of guess probes. Scans that are definitely produced by bots or viruses could not be detected.

We set up a new /48 IPv6 darknet and monitored the incoming traffic for 9 months including the time around the World IPv6 Launch to confirm this assumption. The address space was provided by the tunnel broker "Hurricane Electric" and the incoming traffic was tunnelled to our machine using a SIT tunnel.

While the probability that an attacker choses an IPv6 address from our darknet is about 2^{-48}, we observed a total number of 1172 packets. The whole traffic consists of TCP packets, much to our surprise, we didn't receive a single UDP or ICMPv6 packet. Figure 1 shows the temporal distribution of the received packets, As predicted, we received most of the traffic around the World IPv6 Launch day.

Even though the number of received packets has decreased since the World IPv6 Launch, we are still constantly receiving packets.

2.1 Backscatter

Most of the TCP traffic (1157 packets) seems to be backscatter. This kind of traffic can be caused by misconfiguration or by attackers who intentionally use spoofed source addresses when sending packets to a destination. The destination

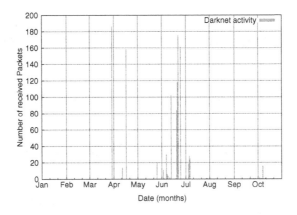

Fig. 1. Number of received packets per day, increased number of packets around the World IPv6 Launch day.

Table 1. Source ports of the received backscatter packets.

Number of packets	Source port	Description
486	113	auth
327	22	ssh
186	6667	ircd
158	80	http

under attack creates a respond packet to the spoofed source address. So in our case, attackers spoofed addresses that belong to our darknet address space.

In case of TCP it is rather simple to spot backscatter traffic. A TCP handshake is essential to enable the connection setup. Normally, this handshake cannot be completed if the initiating client uses a spoofed source address. If a target receives the initial TCP handshake packet, where the SYN flag is set in the TCP header, it tries to complete the handshake by answering with a TCP packet where SYN and ACK flags are set. Hence, the reception of TCP darknet traffic, where SYN and ACK flags are set, is a good indication of backscatter. Of course, it is possible to generate TCP packets with SYN and ACK flags set and send it directly to a destination. However, we concluded that the intentional forwarding of such packets to our darknet is very unlikely, since they would serve no known purpose.

We continued our attack evaluation with an analysis of the attacked ports. Table 1 provides a source port statistic for the received backscatter traffic.

Port 113 belongs to the most occurring source ports in our backscatter traffic. It is actually used by the Ident protocol [9] which is able to identify an owner of a TCP connection on a remote multi-user system. The protocol is still used, for example by IRC servers which connect back via Ident to a requesting source in order to ensure a user's identity [10].

The 486 received packets with source port 113 came from 8 different source IPs. They are aimed for 457 different destination IPs. This indicates that 457 different clients tried to connect to 8 different servers. A peculiar aspect of all packets received on port 113 is an unaltered acknowledgment number for most of the sources with different destination addresses. Hence, the TCP handshake must have always been initiated with the same initial sequence number with different source addresses. In some cases, even the sequence number as well as acknowledgment number stay unaltered.

As you can see in Table 1, we received 327 packets from source port 22 (ssh). The packets came from 8 different sources and were targeted at 295 different destinations. Two of the source addresses are also contained in the set of packets coming from port 113. Similar to the packets coming from port 113, most packets from the same source share the same acknowledgment number even though the targets are different.

Furthermore, we received 186 packets targeted at port 6667, commonly used by IRC [10]. All packets came from the same source but had a different destination addresses. The acknowledgment number of all packets is equal. We received further 158 packets coming from one source IP using source port 80. Like the packets coming from port 6667, the acknowledgment number and the target port always stays the same, with one exception. The last packet received contains a different destination port and a different acknowledgment number.

Geoff Huston also reported a huge amount of TCP backscatter traffic where ACK and SYN flags are set. He assumes misconfiguration as one possible explanation for receiving these packets in his darknet. In our case, almost all packets coming from the same source, even packets with different target addresses, share the same target port and acknowledgment number. This indicates a deliberate use of spoofed source addresses when connecting to the server. It is possible that these packets belong to a denial of service attack. Because we might have seen only a subset of all packets belonging to an attack, we are not able to provide a clearer statement about the attack's purpose.

2.2 Ack Scans

We also received 15 packets where only the ACK flag of the TCP header is set without any sign of a prior TCP handshake. All 15 packets are coming from the same /64 subnet, which belongs to the address space of the tunnel broker "Hurricane Electric".

The missing handshake suggests that these packets are part of an ACK scan, which is usually used to evaluate filter rules of firewalls. The source port of these packets, however, is Microsoft's file sharing port 445, which belongs to the most attacked ports in the IPv4 darknet experiment presented in [7]. Geoff Huston also received 141 TCP packets without an initial handshake and he also concludes that these packets belong to a network probe and rules out that these packets may belong to backscatter traffic.

2.3 Summary

Even though our /48 IPv6 darknet recorded only light traffic, we can say that the IPv6 network is not free of threats anymore. Almost all received packets were caused by spoofed source addresses and may belong to denial of service attacks and we even received packets that may be network probes.

From this evidence we draw the conclusion that, in contrast to earlier darknet reports, the IPv6 internet has become more interesting for attackers.

Since an darknet is not well suited to analyse network-level attacks in greater detail, the next section looks at IPv6 honeypots.

3   IPv6 Honeypots and Related Work

The only IPv6-capable general purpose low-interaction honeypot is Dionaea [11], a honeypot which emulates well-known services like SMB or SIP. It is able to detect remote shellcode attacks using the emulation library *libemu* [12]. In contrast to *Honeyd*, Dionaea does not implement a customized network stack and a single instance of Dionaea is not able to simulate entire IPv6 networks. Although it is possible to create honeynets by setting up multiple instances of Dionaea, it is more challenging to maintain multiple machines and expenses increase as additional performance is needed. This approach is not usefully applicable for IPv6 networks if a huge number of honeypots needs to be deployed.

There already exist different approaches to set up *honeyfarms* consisting of thousands of honeypots: In [13], the authors presented *Potemkin*, an architecture to create a honeyfarm with thousands of virtual machine based honeypots. A gateway dynamically creates virtual machines for incoming requests and forwards the traffic to the machines. It is not clear whether the gateway is able to process IPv6 traffic. The approach needs to filter network scans because otherwise, a new machine would have to be created for each scanned IP address which would lead to performance problems. Of course, Potemkin faces the same performance issues as most high-interaction honeypots do. While Potemkin needs a handful of servers to simulate 64,000 machines, low-interaction honeypots like *Honeyd* are able to simulate the same number of hosts on a single end user machine.

Recently, *HoneyCloud* was proposed [14], a cloud based honeypot that aims to be able to handle thousands of attackers and to utilize various log mechanisms and IDS'. HoneyCloud creates new virtual machine based high-interaction honeypots for each attacker and is deployed in an elastic compute cloud (EC2) using Eucalyptus.

The system utilizes different log mechanisms and is even able to capture keystrokes. While the Potemkin honeyfarm may assign multiple attackers to the same target machine, HoneyCloud assigns each attacker to a separate high-interaction honeypot which writes events into own log files in order to avoid log file mixtures. HoneyCloud accepts SSH connections only and is currently not able to handle other services or even network scans. That is a drawback when trying to gather valuable information about bots and viruses in IPv6 networks because it is necessary to monitor the whole range of ports and services. Furthermore, the need for a cloud infrastructure makes it hard for smaller businesses or even private researchers to deploy the honeypot without falling back on commercial solutions.

4   Extending Honeyd to Honeyd V6

Honeyd is a low-interaction honeypot which has been developed by Niels Provos in the C programming language and is currently available in version 1.5c on the project website[1]. We chose *Honeyd* as base for our IPv6 honeypot since it is able to simulate entire IPv4 networks on a single host. It provides a framework that enables users to write various service scripts for the simulated machines, e.g. a script that simulates a telnet service and captures all log-in attempts of

---

[1] http://www.honeyd.org/

an attacker. These service scripts can be bound to addresses which are managed by *Honeyd*.

The simulation of entire networks in *Honeyd* is accomplished by a customized network stack implementation using the network capture library *libpcap*[2] to bypass the host's network stack. Even though this approach is very flexible, it impedes the IPv6 extension because the existing IPv6 functionality of the host's operating system cannot be reused. The packet processing has to be modified and essential parts of entirely new protocols such as ICMPv6 or the Neighbor Discovery Protocol (NDP) have to be implemented.

In this section, we will describe the major IPv6 specific implementations. A number modifications require a deeper understanding of *Honeyd's* architecture. We will therefore provide a deeper insight into the technical background when required.

4.1 Adapting the Configuration of Virtual Hosts

Honeyd can be configured by defining all hosts to be simulated in a configuration file. The behaviour of a simulated host can be specified via so-called system templates. A template specifies system properties such as open ports and their assigned scripts. Listing 1.1 shows a configuration file for an IPv4 network containing two system templates called *windows* and *linux*.

```
create windows
set windows default tcp action reset
add windows tcp port 21 "scripts/ftp.sh"

create linux
set linux default tcp action reset
add linux tcp port 80 "scripts/web.sh"

set windows ethernet "aa:00:04:78:98:76"
set linux ethernet "aa:00:04:78:95:82"

bind 192.168.1.6 windows
bind 192.168.1.7 linux
```

Listing 1.1. Honeyd example configuration.

A template is created using the *create* statement followed by the template name. In this example, the FTP port 21 of the *windows* template is opened and attached to a script called *ftp.sh*. The *ftp.sh* script contains just enough functionality to capture all log-in attempts, an actual log-in is not possible. The **set** statement assigns a MAC address to the template. By using the **bind** statement, the *windows* template is bound to the address *192.168.1.6* whereas the *linux* template is bound to the address *192.168.1.7*.

Internally, *Honeyd* creates a new template for each IP address binding which are basically copies of the original defined template. The names of the copied templates are changed from *windows* or *linux* to their defined IP addresses so

---

[2] http://www.tcpdump.org/

that a template belonging to an incoming connection can easily be found by its name.

The different templates are maintained in a splay tree ordered by their names. A splay tree is a self balancing binary tree where recently accessed elements are located close to the root [15]. This allows an efficient search for a connection belonging to an incoming packet.

In *HoneydV6*, the syntax to define templates and to assign scripts to configured ports in the configuration file is left unchanged. Our modified configuration parser allows users to bind templates to an IPv6 address in the same way as an IPv4 address. A **bind** statement with a given IPv6 address followed by the template name is sufficient to bind a template to an IPv6 address.

The fact that the honeypot maintains templates in a splay tree ordered by their names in a string representation allows us to store IPv6 and IPv4 templates in the same tree. It might be possible to improve the performance by storing IPv4 and IPv6 templates in two separate trees. However, our performance tests show that the current performance is sufficient for most scenarios (see Sect. 7).

4.2   Modifying Packet Processing

As soon as *Honeyd* receives an IPv4 packet, it searches for the corresponding template based on the target address. If it cannot find a template, the packet will silently be discarded. If a packet is received for which *Honeyd* is responsible, the packet will be forwarded to a dispatcher. The dispatcher moves the packet further to a TCP, UDP or ICMP processor, depending on the IP payload. If the packet is a fragment, then *Honeyd* will wait for all fragments to arrive and will assemble the fragment before forwarding it to the dispatcher.

The service scripts, such as the *ftp.sh* script of the previous example, are connected to the matching connection via socket pairs. *Honeyd* forwards incoming traffic to the standard input of the assigned script while the standard output of a script is sent back to the attacker. In addition, scripts are able to print logging information using their standard error output.

Similar to the IPv4 approach, *HoneydV6* assembles and forwards incoming IPv6 packets to a new IPv6 packet dispatcher. We had to modify the original TCP and UDP processor, so that they are able to process both kinds of connections, IPv4 as well as IPv6. The IPv6 dispatcher forwards received packets to the new ICMPv6 or to the extended TCP and UDP processor based on the payload type.

Fragmented IPv6 packets get reassembled before they are forwarded to the IPv6 packet dispatcher. This function required the implementation of an IPv6 packet assembler which evaluates the fragment extension header, if available, of each incoming packet. The offset and length of each incoming fragment is logged so that attacks which are based on packet fragmentation can easily be analysed.

Honeyd provides a number of further settings and mechanisms such as proxy connections to high-interaction honeypots, conditional templates and fingerprinting. However, these features are out of the scope of this document.

4.3   TCP and UDP

Honeyd's packet dispatcher passes incoming TCP and UDP packets to the corresponding callbacks. These callback functions are named tcp_recv_cb and udp_recv_cb respectively. After our modifications, these functions wrap around tcp_recv_cb46 and udp_recv_cb46 which are able to handle IPv4 as well as IPv6 packets.

Fortunately, these callbacks needed only minor modifications. Depending on the address family, an incoming packet is now mapped to the corresponding structure as shown in the following code snippet of the UDP callback:

```
if (addr_family == AF_INET) {
ip = (struct ip_hdr *)pkt;
udp = (struct udp_hdr *)(pkt + (ip->ip_hl << 2));

}else if (addr_family == AF_INET6) {
ip6 = (struct ip6_hdr *)pkt;
get_ip6_next_hdr((u_char **)&udp,ip6,IP_PROTO_UDP);
}
```

Listing 1.2. Protocol switches to handle IPv4 and IPv6.

The use of the two different structures in the same functions had quite an impact on multiple code segments. However, this way a lot of code fragmentation could be avoided and the packet processing is easier to understand.

In quite a few sections of the TCP and UDP code, the IPv4 functionality could not be reused and a protocol switch had to be implemented. One example is the checksum and data length calculation, which had to be updated in both callbacks.

The IPv6 packet processing needs to be aware of possible extension headers. As shown in the previous example, the actual payload cannot be retrieved directly, we first have to parse the chain of possible extension headers. The function get_ip6_next_hdr provides a pointer to a certain extension header or the actual payload.

The structures to maintain UDP and TCP connections (udp_con and tcp_con) include a pointer to a tuple structure which holds address details of a connection. Honeyd uses the variables ip_src and ip_dst of type ip_addr_t to store IPv4 addresses of a connection. This type is too small to store IPv6 addresses, so we had to add the fields src_addr and dst_addr to store IPv6 addresses.

4.4   Fragmentation

IPv6 fragmentation handling differs from IPv4 insofar, as only source nodes may fragment packets. We implemented the functions ip6_send_fragments and ip6_fragment that handle fragmentation of outgoing IPv6 packets that are larger than the maximum transmission unit (MTU) and reassemble fragmented incoming packets. All fragments are maintained in a splay tree using a special fragment6 structure.

Besides address, length and ID, the structure contains a queue which stores received fragments belonging to a packet. When a packet arrives, the function ip6_fragment_find is used to search for already received fragments in the splay tree. If the received packet is the first received fragment then ip6_fragment_new is used to insert a new entry into the splay tree. If other fragments have already been received, then ip6_insert_fragment is used to add the packet to the fragment queue.

Outgoing packets bigger than the Honeyd MTU are fragmented using the function ip6_send_fragments. Path MTU discovery has not yet been implemented and a fixed defined size HONEYD_MTU is used instead. ip6_send_fragments computes the number of fragments needed and prepares the fragments by inserting a fragmentation extension header before using honey_deliver_ethernet6 to send each single fragment.

4.5 Implementation of the Neighbor Discovery Protocol

While IPv4 uses ARP for address resolution, IPv6 is based on the new so-called Neighbor Discovery Protocol (NDP). Therefore, *HoneydV6* has to implement the essential parts of NDP.

For every IPv4 template that is created, *Honeyd* creates an ARP entry which contains the Ethernet address in a splay tree that can be used later to handle ARP requests. For IPv6 templates, *HoneydV6* creates a further splay tree representing a neighbor cache. It contains the Ethernet addresses of all IPv6 templates needed by the NDP.

We implemented the essential parts of NDP that are required to properly advertise the simulated machines in the network:

- Send and Process Neighbor Solicitations - If a machine needs the Ethernet address of a node in the local network, it sends a neighbor solicitation message to that node. A host receiving a neighbor solicitation answers with a neighbor advertisement containing the corresponding Ethernet address.
- Send Router Solicitations and Process Router advertisements - It is very probable that in practice *HoneydV6* will run behind a router. In order to find all routers and their Ethernet addresses, *HoneydV6* sends a router solicitation to the all routers multicast address and afterwards collects incoming router advertisements.

Because NDP goes hand in hand with ICMPv6, the core functionality to handle NDP packets is contained in *icmp6.c*. Honeyd's dispatcher was modified to forward ICMPv6 packets to the ICMPv6 dispatcher function icmp6_recv_cb. The function passes the incoming packet to the corresponding handler depending on the ICMPv6/NDP type.

4.6 Support for the Monitoring of Network Scans

One of *Honeyd's* advantages is its ability to simulate entire network topologies containing virtual routers and virtual low-interaction hosts. This mechanism

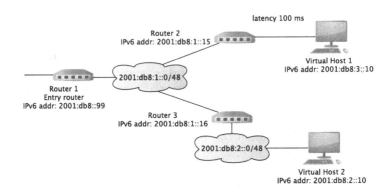

Fig. 2. An example IPv6 network that can be simulated using *HoneydV6* and the configuration presented in Listing 1.3.

allows researchers to analyse the way network scans are performed and how bots try to find new hosts to infect.

RFC 5157 [16] suggests a number of possible ways to reveal IPv6 hosts more efficiently than brute-force network scanning. Network scanning tools like *scan6* of the *SI6 Networks' IPv6 Toolkit* [17] already started to implement these scanning techniques.

In order to allow researchers to observe new kinds of scanning methods in IPv6 networks, we adapted the internal routing mechanisms of *Honeyd* to support IPv6 packet routing.

Listing 1.3 shows an example configuration for the network topology presented in Fig. 2. In order to simplify the configuration, the configuration syntax corresponds with the syntax used to define IPv4 network topologies. Our example contains three virtual routers and two virtual low-interaction hosts. Incoming network packets need to traverse an entry router, which in this example has the IPv6 address 2001:db8::99. An entry router can be defined using the `route entry` statement followed by the router address and the reachable network which in this case is 2001:db8::0/32.

By using the `add net` and the `link` statement, the entry router is directly connected to *Router 2* and *Router 3* with the addresses 2001:db8:1::15 and 2001:db8:1::16 respectively. *Router 2* covers the network 2001:db8:3::/48 and has the virtual low-interaction *Host 1* with address 2001:db8:3::10 attached.

Because of the first `add net` statement, *HoneydV6* knows that packets targeting the network 2001:d8:3::/48 need to be forwarded to *Router 2*. A `link` statement defines what addresses are directly reachable through a router. In case of *Router 2*, all addresses within the network 2001:db8:3::/48 are directly reachable which includes *Host 1*.

In order to simulate a realistic network packet routing, the following ICMPv6 types had to be implemented:

– Time Exceeded - Each time an IPv6 packet traverses a router, its hop limit
  gets decreased. As soon as the hop limit reaches zero, *HoneydV6* sends an
  ICMPv6 *Time Exceeded* message back to the source.
– Destination Unreachable - If a packet is sent to an address within *Honeyd's*
  address space to an undefined virtual host or to a closed UDP port then the
  honeypot replies with an ICMPv6 *Destination Unreachable* message.,

Both packet types are essential in order to make network scanning tools like
traceroute6 work and to allow attackers exploring the virtual network.

The simulation of physical network properties, as provided by the *Honeyd*
IPv4 version, was adapted to also work with IPv6 packets. This includes the
computation of the hop limit of a packet and functions that find and compare
IPv6 networks. It is possible to define factors like packet loss or network latency
as shown in Listing 1.3. In this example, a packet transfer from *Router 1* to
Virtual Host 1 is configured to take approximately 100 ms. If no latency is set,
then a packet is passed to the next hop without any extra delay except the time
needed for computation.

Of course, the simulated network configuration requires that the covered
prefixes are advertised throughout the global IPv6 Internet and attacking traffic
is forwarded to the machine *HoneydV6* is running on.

```
route entry 2001:db8::99 network 2001:db8::0/32

bind 2001:db8::99     router1
bind 2001:db8:1::15 router2
bind 2001:db8:1::16 router3
bind 2001:db8:3::10 host1
bind 2001:db8:2::10 host2

route 2001:db8::99
    add net 2001:db8:3::0/48 2001:db8:1::15 latency 100 ms

route 2001:db8::99
    add net 2001:db8:2::0/48 2001:db8:1::16

route 2001:db8::99 link 2001:db8:1::0/48
route 2001:db8:1::15 link 2001:db8:3::0/48
route 2001:db8:1::16 link 2001:db8:2::0/48
```

Listing 1.3. Extract of HoneydV6 configuration to simulate the network shown in
Fig. 2.

5   Pitfalls

We faced two major issues when we extended *Honeyd* to *HoneydV6*. One problem
was that scope IDs, which were embedded in link-local addresses, complicated
address comparisons needed to route packets. Besides that, we had to deal with
memory access violations caused by dynamic arrays. The following two subsections explain both issues in more detail.

5.1   Scope IDs Stored in Link-local Addresses

The link-local interface addresses that we retrieved using the *libdnet* network library function intf_get contained scope IDs directly embedded in the address. In order to convert these addresses into valid link-local addresses, the scope IDs had to be removed. We wrote a simple function called addr_remove_scope_id to remove the scope ID from link-local addresses.

```
static void addr_remove_scope_id(struct addr* ip6) {
  if (ip6->addr_data8[0]==0xfe && ip6->addr_data8[1]==0x80) {
    /* delete scope id */
    ip6->addr_data8[2]=0;
    ip6->addr_data8[3]=0;
  }
}
```

Listing 1.4. Function to remove scope IDs.

HoneydV6 retrieves the interface of an incoming packet by using *libpcap*. Therefore there is no need to store a removed scope ID. When *HoneydV6* initializes and inspects an interface, it removes scope IDs of all it's IPv6 address aliases directly after acquiring the interface information with intf_get.

5.2   Use of Dynamic Arrays

The original *Honeyd* version maintains information about an interface in a custom interface structure. This structure has a field of type intf_entry followed by other fields.

The intf_entry structure contains a dynamic array which may overwrite the following fields.

The function intf_get, which is used in *interface.c* to retrieve interface information, fills the dynamic array with address aliases depending on the amount of reserved memory. If no further memory is available then no alias will be returned. This was not a problem in the IPv4 version because no address aliases needed to be requested. In the IPv6 version, we need to find out the address aliases to get information about assigned IPv6 addresses too. Therefore, we extended the memory allocation for the interface and moved the intf_entry structure to the end of the interface structure.

6   Covering Huge Address Spaces using Random IPv6 Request Processing

The huge address space of an IPv6 subnet makes it hard, if not almost impossible, for an attacker to find a single host on the network by pure chance. While this fact is very welcome in common networks, it impedes the behavioral analysis of an actual attacker who may or may not be able to find a machine.

We want to observe IPv6 network scan techniques and analyse the attacker's actions when he actually finds a running host. In order to accomplish this, we extended *HoneydV6* with a mechanism that dynamically creates simulated hosts on-demand and randomly accepts IPv6 connections. Hence, after a certain number of connection attempts, an attacker will definitely find a machine to exploit.

Furthermore, all connection attempts are logged, even to IPv6 addresses that are not defined in the configuration file. It allows us to analyze IPv6 network scans and to find new scan patterns.

When a packet arrives, *HoneydV6* tries to find the matching virtual low-interaction host. If no host can be found, then a new template will be dynamically created with a specified *acceptance probability*.

A user can enable the so-called *IPv6 random mode* by using the `randomipv6` statement followed by the acceptance probability. In order to define what template to use for dynamically created machines, the name of a default template has to be specified right after the acceptance probability.

Consider the example configuration in Listing 1.5 where we define the template *randomdefault* to be the default template. The default template has the web server and the FTP port open and assigned to the corresponding scripts. Besides the configured open ports and the matching script assignments, the template has a defined Ethernet address. *HoneydV6* replaces the last three bytes of this Ethernet address with randomly generated bytes for each newly created template. This corresponds to *Honeyd's* default behavior in the IPv4 version. Currently, we are supporting only one default template.

```
create randomdefault
set randomdefault default tcp action reset
add randomdefault tcp port 80 "scripts/web.sh"
set randomdefault ethernet "aa:00:04:78:98:78"

randomipv6 0.5 randomdefault 256

randomexclude 2001:db8::1
randomexclude 2001:db8::2
```

Listing 1.5. Honeyd configuration to randomly accept IPv6 connections.

If the honeypot randomly decides to reject a request and not to create a machine for it, then the target address will be blacklisted. Future requests to a blacklisted address will always be ignored to keep the system state consistent and to avoid revealing the honeypot.

In some cases it may be useful to exclude certain addresses from the automatic template creation, e.g. if other nodes are in the same network. This can be done by using the `randomexclude` statement. An excluded address is automatically blacklisted and *HoneydV6* will ignore requests to this address.

It is possible to define an upper bound for the number of dynamically created templates by the honeypot. This number can be set after the default template name. In the example above, the maximum number of allowed templates is 256. It is important to restrict the number of dynamically created virtual low-interaction hosts in order to avoid memory-exhaustion attacks. Each created machine and each blacklisted address causes memory consumption until the maximum number of allowed machines is reached.

We recommend to restrict the number of dynamically created machines as well as the acceptance probability to an appropriate low value depending on the use case. A large number of uniformly distributed host may easily reveal the honeypot.

7   Performance Tests

Our modified version of *Honeyd* still fully contains the original IPv4 implementation. Thus it is able to handle IPv4 and IPv6 packets at the same time. When we implemented the IPv6 functionality, we tried to modify the IPv4 code as little as possible in order to avoid new programming errors and negative impact on the IPv4 performance. Nevertheless, in some cases minor modifications to the IPv4 work flow had to be done. We conducted some measurements to quantify the performance of the new IPv4 and IPv6 code in *HoneydV6*.

7.1   Comparison: IPv4 and IPv6 Throughput

In order to evaluate the performance impact of our IPv6 modification, we compared the average application layer throughput of the original IPv4 *Honeyd* 1.5c with *HoneydV6*. We developed a simple *Honeyd* benchmark service script and a corresponding client which allow us to measure the time needed to transfer larger files over the network to the honeypot. The original honeypot as well as the IPv6 modification were installed on a Fujitsu PRIMERGY TX200 S5 Server with an Intel Xeon processor 5500 series and 4096 MB of RAM running Ubuntu 12.04. The benchmark client was installed on a Lenovo ThinkPad L520 with an Intel i5-2450M CPU and 4096 MB of RAM. Both computers were connected via a Brocade FWS648G FastIron switch using Gigabit Ethernet.

Table 2 shows the results for transferring 50 MB and 100 MB from the client via IPv4 and IPv6 to the honeypot benchmark service.

For each experiment, Table 2 shows the median from 5 runs. It takes about 16 s to transfer 50 MB to the honeypots and about twice as much time to transfer 100 MB. In case of transferring 50 MB over IPv4, the original 1.5c version of *Honeyd* is approximately 0.2 s faster than *HoneydV6*. For sending 100 MB, the original Version was about 0.09 s faster than our modified version. This indicates that the overhead is in the magnitude of the measurement error and neglectable. The overhead is most probably caused by a number of newly added IPv4/IPv6 switches in the source code. Furthermore, the IPv6 transfer is insignificantly

Table 2. Comparison of transmission time in seconds between the original Honeyd version 1.5c and HoneydV6.

Filesize	1.5c (IPv4)	V6 (IPv4)	V6 (IPv6)
50 MB	15.98 s	16.19 s	16.33 s
100 MB	31.85 s	31.94 s	32.36 s

slower than the IPv4 transfer of both versions. *HoneydV6* needed approximately 0.35 s longer than the original 1.5c version to transfer 50 MB and about 0.51 s to transfer 100 MB over IPv6.

7.2 Scalability of HoneydV6

While throughput measurements can help to get an impression of the performance impact caused by the IPv6 modifications, throughput is not a very useful criteria to evaluate a honeypot for its suitability in a network. A honeypot like *Honeyd* rather needs to be able to handle a large number of connections than transferring huge files.

Provos and Holz measured for example the number of TCP requests per second that *Honeyd* is able to process [18]. Since we are particularly interested in the performance impact on the application layer, we used the web server benchmark *servload* [19][3] to measure the number of HTTP GET requests that *HoneydV6* is able to process per second. Servload is capable of replaying a previously captured traffic log file based on the timestamps of the contained packets. We generated a log file containing 20,000 HTTP GET requests from different source addresses with 600 requests per second. *HoneydV6* was configured to simulate a single machine which was bound to an IPv4 and an IPv6 address and which delivers the *web.sh* script that is shipped with the original Honeyd version 1.5c when getting requests on port 80. The *web.sh* script simulates a Microsoft IIS 5.0 and delivers either a directory listing of the server or a 404 NOT FOUND page. Our generated requests demanded a non-existing *index.html* page so that the *web.sh* script responses with an HTTP 404 NOT FOUND error code and a short explanation.

We repeated the test run for the original Honeyd 1.5c and compared the results with the IPv6 and IPv4 requests of HoneydV6. Table 3 shows that the original Honeyd version and HoneydV6 were able to process about 212 IPv4 requests per second. HoneydV6 managed to handle about 205 IPv6 request/s without any packet loss, which is currently more than sufficient in an IPv6 network and only slightly less than its IPv4 counterpart is able to process.

We configured HoneydV6 to simulate just a single target for our test runs. Since Honeyd maintains one connection entry for each connection in a splay tree, regardless of existing connections with the same target address, the performance difference between benchmarking a single target compared to benchmarking multiple targets is insignificant.

Table 3. Comparison of the number of HTTP GET requests per second that Honeyd 1.5c and HoneydV6 is able to handle without any packet loss.

1.5c (IPv4)	V6 (IPv4)	V6 (IPv6)
212.57	214.00	205.75

---

[3] Download available from http://www.salbnet.org/

8   Conclusions and Future Work

While the general threat level in IPv6 networks is still low compared to IPv4 networks, the results of our IPv6-darknet experiment show the raising interest of attackers in IPv6.

The honeypot *HoneydV6* presented in this paper provides an excellent foundation for future IPv6 network security research. It can be used to observe attacks in IPv6 networks and to reveal new network scan approaches. *HoneydV6* is based on the well-known honeypot *Honeyd* which is the fundamental part of a number of honeypot solutions like *Tiny Honeypot* or the *SCADA HoneyNet Project*. These projects can easily be extended to IPv6 networks using *HoneydV6*.

HoneydV6 is the first low-interaction honeypot which is able to simulate entire IPv6 networks. Besides IPv6 packet processing, *HoneydV6* implements necessary parts of the ICMPv6 and the Neighbor Discovery Protocol. In order to observe new kinds of scanning methods in IPv6 networks, we adapted the internal routing mechanisms of *Honeyd* to support IPv6 packet routing. In our performance tests *HoneydV6* performed comparable to *Honeyd* for both, IPv4 and IPv6 networks. Further, we developed a mechanism that randomly and dynamically generates low-interaction IPv6 hosts, based on the requests of an attacker, in order to increase the chances that an attacker will encounter the honeypot within the huge IPv6 address space.

Honeyd still contains some features that are supported in IPv4 networks only. One example is the operating system fingerprinting mechanism, which allows *Honeyd* to emulate system-specific behavior. We currently investigate how the new nmap IPv6 fingerprint format [20] can be reused to simulate the network stack parameters of different operating systems.

Further, we are working on a connection between our IPv6 honeypot and the shellcode detection library *libemu* [12] with the aim of simplifying remote exploit detection.

In order to promote further IPv6 research, the sources of our *HoneydV6* implementation are publicly available at http://www.idsv6.de.

References

1. Ford, M., Stevens, J., Ronan, J.: Initial results from an IPv6 darknet. In: ICISP '06: Proceedings of the International Conference on Internet Surveillance and Protection, Washington, DC, USA, p. 13. IEEE Computer Society (2006)
2. Heuse, M.: THC IPv6 attack tool kit. http://www.thc.org/thc-ipv6/
3. Thomson, S., Narten, T., Jinmei, T.: IPv6 Stateless Address Autoconfiguration. RFC 4862, September 2007
4. Seifert, C., Welch, I., Komisarczuk, P.: Taxonomy of honeypots. Technical report, Victoria University of Wellington, Wellington (2006)
5. Provos, N.: Honeyd: A virtual honeypot daemon. Technical report, Center for Information Technology Integration, University of Michigan, February 2003
6. ENISA Honeypot Study - Proactive Detection of Security Incidents (2012).   http://www.enisa.europa.eu/activities/cert/support/proactive-detection/proactive-detection-of-security-incidents-II-honeypots

7. Pang, R., Yegneswaran, V., Barford, P., Paxson, V., Peterson, L.: Characteristics of internet background radiation. In: Proceedings of the 4th ACM SIGCOMM Conference on Internet Measurement, IMC '04, pp. 27–40. ACM, New York (2004)
8. Huston, G.: Background Radiation in IPv6, October 2010. https://labs.ripe.net/ Members/mirjam/background-radiation-in-ipv6
9. Johns, M.S.: Identification Protocol. RFC 1413 (Proposed Standard) February 1993
10. Kalt, C.: Internet Relay Chat: Architecture. RFC 2810 (Informational) April 2000
11. Dionaea: dionaea catches bugs. http://dionaea.carnivore.it/
12. Baecher, P., Koetter, M.: libemu - x86 Shellcode Emulation. http://libemu. carnivore.it/
13. Vrable, M., Ma, J., Chen, J., Moore, D., Vandekieft, E., Snoeren, A.C., Voelker, G.M., Savage, S.: Scalability, fidelity, and containment in the potemkin virtual honeyfarm. In: Proceedings of the Twentieth ACM Symposium on Operating Systems Principles, SOSP '05, pp. 148–162. ACM, New York (2005)
14. Clemente, P., Lalande, J.F., Rouzaud-Cornabas, J.: HoneyCloud: elastic honeypots - on-attack provisioning of high-interaction honeypots. In: International Conference on Security and Cryptography, Rome, Italy, July 2012, pp. 434–439 (2012)
15. Sleator, D.D., Tarjan, R.E.: Self-adjusting binary search trees. J. ACM **32**(3), 652–686 (1985)
16. Chown, T.: IPv6 Implications for Network Scanning. RFC 5157 (Informational) March 2008
17. SI6 Networks: SI6 Networks' IPv6 Toolkit - A security assessment and troubleshooting tool for the IPv6 protocols (2012). http://www.si6networks.com/tools/ ipv6toolkit
18. Provos, N., Holz, T.: Virtual Honeypots - From Botnet Tracking to Intrusion Detection. Addison-Wesley, Boston (2008)
19. Zinke, J., Habenschuß, J., Schnor, B.: Servload: generating representative workloads for web server benchmarking. In: International Symposium on Performance Evaluation of Computer and Telecommunication Systems (SPECT), Genoa (2012)
20. Nmap: Nmap Network Scanning - IPv6 fingerprinting. http://nmap.org/book/ osdetect-ipv6-methods.html

Youtube User and Usage Profiling: Stories of Political Horror and Security Success

Miltiadis Kandias[(⊠)], Lilian Mitrou, Vasilis Stavrou,
and Dimitris Gritzalis

Information Security and Critical Infrastructure Protection Laboratory,
Department of Informatics, Athens University of Economics and Business,
76 Patission Ave., GR10434 Athens, Greece
{kandiasm,l.mitrou,stavrouv,dgrit}@aueb.gr

Abstract. Social media and Web 2.0 have enabled internet users to contribute online content, which may be crawled and utilized for a variety of reasons, from personalized advertising to behaviour prediction/profiling. In this paper, our goal is to present a horror and a success story from the digital world of Social Media, in order to: (a). present a political affiliation profiling method, the Panopticon method, in order to reveal this threat and contribute in raising the social awareness over it. (b). describe an insider threat prediction method by evaluating the predisposition towards law enforcement and authorities, a personal psychosocial trait closely connected to the manifestation of malevolent insiders. The experimental test case of both methodologies is an extensive Greek community of YouTube users. In order to demonstrate our cases, we performed graph theoretic and content analysis of the collected dataset and showed how and what kind of personal data can be derived via data mining on publicly available YouTube data. As both methodologies set user's privacy and dignity at stake, we provide the reader with an analysis of the legal means for each case, so as to effectively be prevented from a privacy violation threat and also present the exceptional cases, such as the selection of security officers of critical infrastructures, where such methodologies could be used.

Keywords: Awareness · Behavior prediction · Insider threat · Panopticon · Privacy · Social media · Surveillance · User profiling · Youtube

1 Introduction

The exponential growth of Information and Communication Technologies (ICT) and the rapid explosion of social media have contributed to substantive changes in the social dimensions of information sharing and (mis)use. However, several inherent features of Internet (and especially Web 2.0) supported technologies and platforms (e.g., digitization, availability, recordability and persistency of information, public or semi-public nature of profiles and messages, etc.) encourage not only new forms of interaction but also surveillance behaviors and tendencies [1]. ICT have often been accused for facilitating surveillance via CCTV, or the Internet [2].

The common conception of surveillance is this of a hierarchical system of power between the observer and the observed, represented in metaphors, such as the

© Springer-Verlag Berlin Heidelberg 2014
M.S. Obaidat and J. Filipe (Eds.): ICETE 2013, CCIS 456, pp. 270–289, 2014.
DOI: 10.1007/978-3-662-44788-8_16

"Panopticon" of J. Bentham, i.e. a theoretical prison structure, an "ideal" prison building designed in a way that allows observing of the prisoners from a central location at all times. The observed subject is never sure of whether or not she is under surveillance. Foucault, who elaborated extensively on the modern implications of the Panopticon, emphasized that the conscious and permanent visibility assures the automatic functioning of power [3]. The Panopticon creates "a consciousness of permanent visibility as a form of power, where no bars, chains and heavy locks are necessary for domination, anymore" [4].

May Web 2.0 become an Omniopticon, in which "the many watch the many"? [5]. Is the "social" and "participatory network" [6] the ideal "topos" for "social surveillance" [1] and "participatory panopticism" [7]? By being subject of communication and engaging in social networking activities the users are becoming objects of a lateral surveillance [8]. In social media users monitor each other. Moreover, such sites and interaction platforms are, by design, destined for users to continually digital traces left by their "friends" or persons they interact with – often by simply consuming or commenting user-generated content.

Social media activities produce user generated information flows. These flows may be – in fact have been – utilized for purposes ranging from profiling for targeted advertising (on the basis of analyzing online features and behavior of the users), to personality profiling and behavior prediction. Along with consumer and configuration based offerings, exploitation/use of user generated data has contributed to the shaping of the "Open Source Intelligence" [9]. This data may be used for both, the social good/in the interest of the society (e.g. Forensics), or in a way that infringes fundamental rights and liberties or private interests (e.g. social engineering, discriminations, cyber bullying, etc.) [10–14]. Another aspect of user generated content is insider threat detection and prediction within Critical Infrastructures. Shaw's et al. [15] research examined the trait of social and personal frustrations. The most important observation is the "revenge syndrome" they develop and the anger they feel towards authority figures. Thus, an employee negatively predisposed towards law enforcement and authorities, is considered to be more possible to manifest delinquent behavior against the organization.

However, such information aggregation and profiling of political beliefs/affiliations and psychosocial traits may result to a "nightmare" for a democratic State, especially in the case that such practices concern a large thus disproportional number of citizens/netizens. Users' political profiling implicates the right to decisional and informational privacy and may have a chilling effect on the exercise of freedom of expression.

In order to prove our horror story hypothesis we have developed a proof-of-concept Panopticon and applied it on real-life data. We crawled the YouTube social medium and created a dataset that consists solely of Greek users, hence a Greek YouTube community. We examined the data (comments, uploads, playlists, favorites, and subscriptions) using text classification techniques via comments classification. The Panopticon can predict the political affiliation of a video and then predict the political affiliation expressed in a list of videos. The method applies the above on users' comments, uploaded videos, favorite videos and playlists, so as to aggregate the results and extract a conclusion over the users' political affiliation (Radical, Neutral, and Conservative).

On the other hand, the success story relies on the same dataset; however it utilizes a differentiated methodology and purpose. Our goal is to extract conclusions and statistics over the users, regarding the personality trait of predisposition against law enforcement and authorities. Our methodology has been found to be able to extract a user's attitude towards that trait. We further utilized the aforementioned Greek community of YouTube users and classified them via comment classification. Users are divided in two categories, i.e., those who are predisposed negatively towards law enforcement and authorities (Category P), and those who are not (Category N). The user attitude is extracted by aggregating the individual results from the attitude expressed in comments, uploads, favorites and playlists.

2 Related Work

The rise of social media usage has challenged and directed researchers towards opinion mining and sentiment analysis [16]. Opinion mining and sentiment analysis constitute computational techniques in social computing. Social computing is a computing paradigm that involves multi-disciplinary approach in analyzing and modeling social behavior on different media and platforms to produce intelligence and interactive platform results. One may collect and process the available data, so as to draw conclusions about a user mood [17]. Choudhury and Counts present and explore ways that expressions of human moods can be measured, inferred and expressed from social media activity. As a result, user and usage profiling and conclusion extraction from content processing are, today, more feasible and valuable than ever.

Several methods have been utilized in order to process online data and materialize the above mentioned threat. These methods include user behavior characterization in online social networks [18], as well as analysis of the relationship between users' gratifications and offline political/civic participation [19]. Park et al. examine the aforementioned relationship through Facebook Groups and their research indicated the four needs for using Facebook groups. The analysis of the relationship between users' needs and civic and political participation indicated that informational uses were more correlated to civic and political action than to recreational uses.

Users often appear not to be aware of the fact that their data are being processed for various reasons, such as consumer behavior analysis, personalized advertisement, opinion mining, user and usage profiling, etc. Automated user profiling [20] and opinion mining may be used for malevolent purposes, in order to extract conclusions over a crowd of users. Balduzzi et al. utilized the ability of querying a social network for registered e-mail addresses in order to highlight it as a threat rather than a feature. Furthermore, they identified more than 1.2 million user profiles associated with the collected addresses in eight social networks, such as Facebook, MySpace and Twitter. Alternative approaches have, also, been proposed to this extend [21, 22].

Magklaras et al. [23] introduced a threat evaluation system based on certain profiles of user behavior. Kandias et al. [24] proposed a combination of technical and psychological approaches to deal with insider threats. Personal factors that may increase the likelihood someone to develop malevolent behavior are presented by the FBI, too [25]. Personal traits such as anger, revenge or greed along with certain circumstances present in an organization could lead to the manifestation of an insider. An approach of studying personality traits, described by Shaw, has been introduced by studying the trait of narcissism using Graph Theoretic Analysis [26].

3 Methodology and Data Crawling

In our research, we focus on a Greek community of YouTube and on information gathered from our previous work [27]. In comparison with our previous work, this paper builds upon our previous research and poses a significant extension mainly in terms of further analysis and comparison of our methods.

3.1 Methodology and Testing Environment

We utilized the dataset we crawled during our previous work. Dataset collection was performed using YouTube's REST-based API (https://developers.google.com/youtube/v3/), which simplifies and accelerates the procedure and does not cause any harm to YouTube's infrastructure. With respect to user privacy, we added an anonymization layer to the collected data, thus usernames have been replaced with MD5 hashes, so as to eliminate possible connections between collected data and real life users. However, it is in principle possible, to reverse this process by using indirect means. The dataset includes: (a) 12.964 users, (b) 207.377 videos, and (c) 2.043.362 comments. The time span of the collected data covers a period of 7 years (Nov. 2005 Oct. 2012). In addition, data was divided into three categories: (a) user-related information (profile, uploaded videos, subscriptions and favorites), (b) video-related information (license, number of likes and dislikes, category and tags) and (c) comment-related information (comment content and number of likes/dislikes).

3.2 Graph-Theoretic Approach

The main conclusions from the graph-theoretic and content analysis, as initially presented in [27], based on the forms of interactions in YouTube, are:

(a). The *small world* phenomenon does apply to the collected Greek community, as every user of the community is 6 hops away from everyone else. (b). A *small group of users have the most subscribers,* while the rest of the users have considerably fewer subscribers. Also, user content is generated mostly by a small fraction of users, while the rest is significantly lower than the one from the above mentioned small fraction. (c). *Users join YouTube to participate.* We detected one large and strongly connected component consisting of 175.000 users, 2 small connected components with approximately 20 users, and 3.795 consisting of 1 user. As a result, most nodes in the graph have an outgoing tie to another node. Only a considerably small number of nodes had no outgoing ties (were inactive). (d). *Users of interest may be easily spotted within the limits of the medium.* Tag cloud and manual content analysis of our dataset concluded to a core axis of the medium's users' frames of interest. Most videos are related to *music* and *entertainment.* Several of them refer to *comedy, sports,* and *political issues.*

3.3 Youtube Social Medium Selection

We carried out the experimentation on a real environment i.e. YouTube, in order to prove that such an approach is feasible and a social medium could be used to tackle the insider threat issue. Also, we offer a real-life proof-of-concept application of the proposed methodology. Observations indicate that users tend to participate in the medium and generate personalized content. YouTube videos and comments contain political characteristics and the appropriate phraseology of interest (anti-authority and negatively predisposed towards law enforcement). Thus, we formed the hypothesis that attitude towards law enforcement may be extracted via content analysis. Based on these observations, we consider that: (a) YouTube often contains content expressing negative attitude towards law enforcement and the authorities, (b) users often feel free to express their opinions, especially when it comes to law enforcement and even work place superiors (because of the anonymity they assume and the emotional content of the medium), (c) most users join YouTube to participate, so one can reasonably expect that they will reveal, among others, their personal data.

3.4 Drawing Conclusions

We demonstrate that one can identify (a) the political affiliation of a user via the political beliefs and (b) the predisposition towards law enforcement, expressed within the comments of her videos. The reason why videos are examined is because video is YouTube's basic module. Since we cannot process the video itself, we draw a conclusion for the video through its comments.

We detect the political affiliation expressed in a comment by performing text classification into three main categories: (a) category R, which contains expressions related to radical affiliation, (b) category C, which contains expressions related to conservative affiliation and (c) category N, which contains all the comments that hold a neutral political stance or have no political content.

The classification categories used to detect the attitude towards law enforcement are the following two: (a) category P, which contains expressions holding negative attitude towards law enforcement, and (b) category N, which contains all the comments that hold a neutral attitude towards law enforcement and authority, or have no such content. Category N may also contain expressions holding positive attitude towards law enforcement. However, in this paper we are interested only in the prevalence or absence of negative attitude towards law enforcement.

Text classification uses machine learning techniques to classify a comment in the appropriate category. Regarding the political profiling case, assigning a comment into one of the categories is equivalent to the fact that the comment contains the respective political affiliation its category depicts. In the case of insider threat prediction, the assignment of a comment into one of the two categories is equivalent to the fact that the comment contains the respective attitude towards law enforcement its category depicts. An alternative approach for both cases would be to create a vocabulary including words of each category and scan each comment to detect specific words. Machine learning leads to a more reliable result than a simple word existence check. Also, text classification performs better than scanning lists of words in a vocabulary.

Comment classification enables us to extract conclusions over a video's content regarding either the political affiliation or the predisposition towards law enforcement expressed its comments. The conclusion drawn helps us to classify any video into one of the defined categories of each case. So, by assigning a comment into a category implies that the conclusion drawn for the comment is the political affiliation or the attitude towards law enforcement, respectively, expressed in the category. The same applies to a list of videos, such as favorite videos and playlists. Having the category in which a video falls into, a conclusion can be drawn for the list. Being able to classify user's content, we may extract conclusions for user's comments, uploaded videos, favorite videos and playlists. This way we can draw a final conclusion about user's political affiliation or attitude law enforcement regarding for each case.

As it gets obvious, we can apply the same core methodology to achieve a dual goal. On the one hand we use the core methodology to highlight the social threat of political profiling, while on the other hand we describe how the same methodology can be extended and used to predict potential insiders in critical infrastructures. First we describe the Panopticon methodology regarding the political affiliation detection and afterwards the insider threat prediction approach via predisposition towards law enforcement detection.

4 Panopticon – The Horror Story

We store the crawled data in a relational database for further analysis. The first step of the process is to train a classifier that will be used to classify comments into one of the three categories of political affiliation (radical, neutral, conservative). Comment classification is performed as text classification [28], which uses machine learning techniques to train the system and decide in which category a text falls into. The machine is trained by having as input text examples and the category the examples belong to. Label assignment requires the assistance of an expert, who can distinguish and justify the categories each text belongs to.

We formed a training set so as to perform comment classification. By studying the collected comments, we noticed that a significant percentage of the comments are written in the Greek language. Another characteristic of the Greek YouTube community is that users write Greek words using Latin alphabet in their communication ("greeklish"). This is the dominant way of writing in Greek YouTube (the 51 % of our dataset's comments are written in greeklish). Most users prefer to use greeklish, instead of Greek, because they do not care about correct spelling of their writings.

The appearance of those two different types of writing in comments has led us to pick two different approaches in comment classification, i.e., analyze them as two different languages. Another issue is due to the use of both greeklish and Greek. In order to mitigate this problem we have chosen to merge these training sets into one and train only one classifier. Forming Greek and greeklish training sets requires the selection of comments from the database and proper label assignment for each one of them, based on the category it belongs to. We consulted a domain expert (i.e., Sociologist), who could assign and justify the chosen labels on the training sets. Thus we created a reliable classification mechanism. We chose 300 comments from each category (R,C,N) of the training set for each language. The expert contributed by assigning a category label to each comment.

Apart from the training set, we also created a testing set, which is required to evaluate the efficiency of the resulting classifier. The testing set contains pre-labeled data that are fed to the machine to check if the initial assigned label of each comment is equal to the one predicted by the machine. The testing set labels were also assigned by the domain expert.

We performed comment classification using: (a) Naïve Bayes Mutlinomial [29] (NBM), (b) Support Vector Machines [30] (SVM), and (c) Multinomial Logistic Regression [31] (MLR), so as to compare the results and pick the most efficient classifier. We compared each classifier's efficiency based on the metrics of precision, recall, f-measure and accuracy [32].

Accuracy measures the number of correct classifications performed by the classifier. Precision measures the classifier's exactness. Higher and lower precision means less and more false positive classifications (the comment is said to be related to the category incorrectly) respectively. Recall measures the classifier's completeness. Higher and lower recall means less and more false negative classifications (the comment is not assigned as related to a category, but it should be) respectively. Precision and recall are increased at the expense of each other. That's the reason why they are combined to produce f-score metric which is the weighted harmonic mean of both metrics.

Table 1 presents each classifier's efficiency, based on accuracy, precision, recall, and f-score metrics. Multinomial Logistic Regression and Support Vector Machines achieve the highest accuracy. The accuracy metric is high due to the dominant number of politically neutral comments. Precision and recall are proper metrics to evaluate each classifier [32].

Table 1. Metrics comparison of classification algorithms.

Metrics									
Classifier	NBM			SVM			MLR		
Classes	R	N	C	R	N	C	R	N	C
Precision	65	93	55	75	91	74	83	91	77
Recall	83	56	85	80	89	73	77	93	78
F-Score	73	70	60	76	89	73	80	92	77
Accuracy	68			84			87		

Multinomial Logistic Regression achieves better precision value and SVM better recall value. Multinomial Logistic Regression achieves a slightly better f-score assessment. Support Vector Machines and Multinomial Logistic Regression achieve similar results regarding both recall and precision metrics. As a result, we chose Multinomial Logistic Regression because of the better f-score value achieved for each one of the categories.

4.1   Video Classification

Regarding the extraction of the political affiliation expressed in a video, we studied each video, based on its comments, classified to one of the three categories. Also, we know the number of likes/dislikes each comment has received. Likes and dislikes represent the acceptability a comment has from the audience, so it may be an indication of the comment's importance to the overall video's result. Thus, a comment that receives a significant number of likes should be treated differently than a comment with no likes, as the first one is acknowledged as important by more users. This assumption has been confirmed by the data mining process. Subsequently, in order to extract a conclusion for the video, we take into consideration only comments that belong either to category R or C. Neutral comments are ignored.

Each comment's importance is measured via its number of likes and dislikes. In order to come to a video overall result we utilize two sums, one for category R and one for C. For every comment that belongs to categories R or C we add the following quantity to the respective aggregation:

$$1 + \{(likes/total\_likes) - (dislikes/total\_dislikes)\}$$

The quantity added to each sum shows that a comment that has received more likes than dislikes should affect the overall score more than a comment with more dislikes than likes. Finally, the category with the larger sum is the category that represents video's political affiliation. Table 2 illustrates the procedure described above.

Sum R equals to: $(1 + 90/150 - 10/40) + (1 + 30/150 - 5/40) + (1 + 10/150 - 3/40) = 4.1$, whereas Sum C equals to $(1 + 15/150 - 20/40) = 0.6$. Sum $R \geq C$, so video "Example" is classified into category R and expresses radical political affiliation.

Table 2.   Example of video classification decision.

Video "Example"			
Comment	Political affiliation	Likes	Dislikes
#1	R	90	10
#2	C	15	20
#3	R	30	5
#4	N	5	2
#5	R	10	3
Total		150	40

4.2   List Classification

The procedure followed to extract a conclusion about a list of videos is similar to the above mentioned video method. The only difference is that we utilize videos instead of comments. The two sums are also applied, one for category R and one for C. In this case, instead of likes and dislikes we used the video ones. In the end, the category with the greater sum indicates the list's political affiliation. This procedure is applied to the "favorite videos" list, as well as to the other playlists that the user may have created.

4.3   User Classification

User political affiliation can be identified based on the category she is assigned to. The procedure, as shown in Fig. 1, takes into account a user's comments, uploaded videos, favorite videos, and playlists. A user is able to: (a) write a comment to express her feelings or her opinion, (b) upload a video (the content may have a distinctive meaning for her), (c) add a video to her favorites list (it may have an emotional or intellectual meaning for her), and (d) create a playlist and add videos to it.

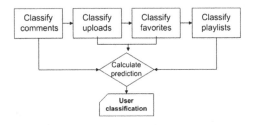

Fig. 1.   User classification process.

Based on these observations one may look for indications of political beliefs within the user generated content. For the needs of our experimentation, we have defined ad-hoc weights for each of the cases we examine (Table 3). Each phase of the process generates a result on the category each user belongs to. In comment classification, the result is based on the number of political comments that exhibit the highest aggregation. If the number of comments classified in category R is more than those classified in C, then the result is that user tends to be Radical. The results on uploaded videos, favorite videos and playlists are extracted as described in the list result extraction process. User comments are the most important factor to decide of a user's political affiliation.

Table 3.   Ad-hoc weights of each element.

	Comment	Upload	Favorite	Playlist
Weight	3	2	2	1

Regarding the aggregation of the results, we utilize two sums, one for category R and the other for C. Comments, videos, and lists classified as neutral do not contribute to the aggregation. The sub-results are appropriately weighted and added to the final sums, in order to extract the final result. An example of this procedure appears in Table 4. Sum R equals to 3 + 2 = 5, while Sum C equals to 1. Sum R ≥ Sum C, which implies that the user belongs to category R. A user is classified to categories R, or C, if there is at least one political comment or political video detected to her content. A user may not express a political stance via her comments or uploaded videos; however, she may have added a video with political content to her playlists.

Table 4. User classification example.

	User "Example"	
	Political beliefs	Weight
Comments	R	3
Uploaded videos	N	2
Favorite videos	R	2
Playlists	C	1

The result for the user will be that she belongs either to category R or C, depending on the political thesis expressed in the video. The weights are defined on an ad-hoc basis. Further meta-training is required for better determination of the weights.

4.4 Statistical Analysis

Based on the analysis, the 2 % of the collected comments exhibit a clear political affiliation (0.7 % was classified as R, while 1.3 % was classified as C). On the contrary, 7 % of the videos were classified to one of these categories, 2 % as R and 5 % as C. On the other hand, 50 % of the users have been found to clearly express, at least once, their political affiliation. Out of them, the 12 % of the dataset has been found to express Radical affiliation and 40 % Conservative.

Regarding users classified as radicals, we found that - on average - the 20 % of their comments has a political position expressed. Also, they tend to prefer the Greek alphabet (i.e., 54 % of their comments are written in Greek, 33 % in greeklish, and 13 % use both Greek and Latin alphabet).

On the other hand, users classified as conservatives tend to prefer the greeklish way of expression, namely 55 % of the comments are in greeklish, 35 % written using the Greek alphabet and 10 % use both Greek and Latin alphabet. In Table 5 the average number of characters that a comment consists of is depicted.

Table 5. Average number of characters in a comment.

Alphabet	Average no. of characters (R)	Average no. of characters (C)
Greek	294	179
Greeklish	245	344
Both	329	227

Comments written in greeklish tend to be shorter and more aggressive. On the contrary, comments written in Greek tend to be larger, more explanatory, and polite. Another finding is that the more aggressive a comment, the more misspelled it is.

Regarding the license assigned to each video (Typical YouTube or Creative Commons), the 7 % of the videos are published under the Creative Commons license. A 55 % of these videos were uploaded by users classified as Radicals, 10 % by Conservatives and 35 % by Neutrals.

Radicals tend to massively comment on the same videos. We found that these videos have unequivocal political content, namely political events, music, incidents of police brutality, etc. Moreover, the videos that radicals tend to add to their favorites are mainly documentaries and political music clips. Conservatives tend to share mainly conspiracy-based videos, as well ones with a nationalistic content.

5 Insider Threat Prediction The Success Story

As presented in [33, 34], it is possible to use machine learning techniques to detect potential insider based on analysis of their generated content in YouTube. Similarly to the Panopticon methodology, to predict potential insiders we analyzed the collected dataset using machine learning techniques (i.e. comment classification) and classified comments into one of the predefined categories of attitude towards law enforcement. To perform such classification, training of an appropriate classifier is required, as we did in Panopticon. To develop the appropriate classifier we also decided to treat greeklish as a different language and formed two different classifiers, one for the Greek language and one for greeklish, which was finally merge into one classifier.

Forming the classifier requires two processes: The first is comment selection from the database and the second is proper label assignment to comments according to the category they belong. The later categorization was supported by a domain expert (i.e., Sociologist), who could assign and justify the chosen labels on the training sets. Thus, we developed a reliable classification mechanism. We chose 430 comments from category P and 470 from category N of the training set for each language. The expert contributed by assigning a category label to each comment. Apart from the training set, we also created a test set, which is required to evaluate the efficiency of the resulting classifier. The test set consists of prelabeled data that are fed to the machine to check if the initial assigned label of each comment is equal to the one predicted by the algorithms. The test set labels were also assigned by the domain expert.

We performed comment classification using: (a) Naïve Bayes Multinomial (NBM), (b) Support Vector Machines (SVM), and (c) Logistic Regression (LR), so as to compare the results and pick the most efficient classifier. We compared each classifier's efficiency based on the metrics of precision, recall, f-score, and accuracy. Table 6 presents each classifier's efficiency, based on accuracy, precision, recall, and f-score metrics. LR and SVM achieve the highest accuracy.

As noticed, SVM and LR achieve similar results regarding all metrics, so we chose LR because of the better f-score value achieved for each category. By choosing an algorithm based solely on the recall or precision metrics, we would favor one metric at the expense of another. A better f-score assessment indicates a balanced combination of false positive and false negative classifications. LR was, also, chosen because of its ability to provide us the probability of each category's membership instead of the purely dichotomous result of SVM. We utilized the probability of LR to determine a

Table 6. Metrics comparison of classification algorithms.

Metrics Classifier	NBM		SVM		LR	
Classes	P	N	P	N	P	N
Precision	71	70	83	77	86	76
Recall	72	68	75	82	74	88
F-Score	71	69	79	79.5	80	81
Accuracy	70		80		81	

threshold above which a comment is classified into Category P. We chose to apply a threshold solely on the comments characterized by negative attitude, in order to reduce false positive classifications and avoid classifying a comment into category P without strong confidence. The threshold we determined is 72 %, i.e., if a comment belongs to category P and its probability of category membership is lower than 72 %, it is classified as non-negative. We tested several threshold values, and after utilizing all information provided by the Social Scientist involved in the above mentioned procedure, we verified that the set of comments with probability of category membership lesser than 72 % included enough false positive classifications.

The processes of video, list and user classification are the same with the aforementioned political profiling conclusion extraction method. The differentiation spotted in this case is that we utilized two instead of three categories, namely category P (for those negatively predisposed) and N (for those without negative predisposition towards law enforcement and authorities).

5.1   User Common Characteristics

Based on the analysis we performed using the Logistic Regression algorithm classifier, the 0.6 % of all collected comments contain negative attitude towards law enforcement. Regarding videos, 3.7 % of them are classified as videos containing negative attitude towards law enforcement. The percentage of users that indicate negative predisposing towards law enforcement is 37 %. The users classified in category P have been automatically located and manually verified that express negative attitude towards law enforcement and authorities.

Regarding users classified as negatively predisposed towards law enforcement, we found that they tend to prefer the greeklish way of writing (i.e., 28 % of the comments expressing negative attitude are written in Greek, 52 % in greeklish, and 20 % use both Greek and Latin alphabet). In Table 7 we present the average number of characters that a comment consists of.

Manual analysis of the classified comments indicates that comments written in greeklish tend to be shorter and more aggressive. On the contrary, comments written in Greek tend to be larger, more explanatory, and polite. Another finding is that the aggressive comments often tend to be misspelled.

Furthermore, users predisposed negatively towards law enforcement tend to comment on the same videos and add some of these to their list of favorites. We detected

Table 7. Average number of characters in a comment.

Alphabet	Average no. of characters (P)	Average no. of characters (N)
Greek	186	108
Greeklish	173	105
Both	196	159

that these videos contain unequivocal political issues, such as political events, music, incidents of police brutality, sports, political music clips, and content regarding the recent Greek financial crisis.

Regarding the users' demographic characteristics, 75 % of the ones predisposed negatively towards law enforcement are males, 23 % females, and a 2 % has not declared its genre. 55 % of users are between 16 and 35 years old, and 13 % has not declared age.

6 Ethical and Legal Issues

The use of this kind of methods may result to problems that are actually inherent in every kind of profiling. In brief, these methods may be regarded as a kind of (behavioral) profiling on the Internet, in the meaning of collecting data (recording, storing, and tracking) and searching it for identifying patterns [35]. Such profiling methods interfere with the right to informational privacy and are associated with discrimination risks. A threat for privacy rights is due to the fact that profiling methods can generate sensitive information "out of seemingly trivial and/or even anonymous data" [36].

6.1 Horror Story and the Law

By studying user's uploads it is possible to extract information related to the content, especially when it refers to areas such as political affiliation. Furthermore, a user is possible to have a private profile, however her comments could be collected from crawling random videos. Thus, a limited profile can be build based on those comments. The predominant rationales for acquiring knowledge about the political opinions and the relative sentiments seems to be either (political) research purposes or the goal of reducing risks both in the private and the public sector. However, personal data that are, by their nature, particularly sensitive and vulnerable to abuse, deserve specific protection.

Collecting and processing data about political beliefs is regarded by law as a highly exceptional situation. Many international and national laws prohibit explicitly the processing of personal data revealing political opinions (e.g. Art. 8 of the European Data Protection Directive and Art. 6 of the Convention 108 of the Council of Europe). Derogating from the prohibition on processing this "sensitive category" of data is allowed if done by a law that lays down the specific purposes and subject to suitable safeguards. Such derogations rely on a manifest public interest or the explicit, informed and written consent of the person concerned.

However, in European data protection law derogation is sometimes allowed also in the cases that "the processing relates to data which are manifestly made public by the data subject" (Art. 8, Sect. 2e of the European Data Protection Directive), which is the case if people generate content or comment on other users' content in social networks or media using their real identity and aiming at expressing their opinions publicly. According to the American theory and jurisprudence there is no "reasonable expectation of privacy if data is voluntarily revealed to others" [37]. It is "apparent", according to this theory, that one cannot retain a reasonable expectation of privacy in the case of YouTube, videos, likes, and comments left open to the public [38].

By generating content in social media users are generating information flows and aggregations. Providers and Online Social Networks encourage also through the default settings - "producers" [39] to publish personal information and enable anyone accessing this information thus actively contributing to shaping social media as an attractive product [40]. Does self-exposure in social media amount to freely and consciously chosen privacy abandonment?

YouTube offers several privacy options to users. These privacy options encompass: (a) creation of private channel/profile, which disables access to user's channel where her profile is available, (b) creation of private videos, which enables users to share them with a limited number of viewers (up to 50 persons) after inviting them, (c) creation of private video lists, which applies to favorite videos and playlists and disable a playlist from being publicly available, and (d) potentially disclose user's activity, e.g., comments, subscriptions or favorite videos. These options may protect user's actions from being tracked in order to get information about the video she likes, comments on, or the users she is subscribed to. However, we should take into consideration individual's general inertia toward default terms [41]. Moreover, it seems that the majority of users choose to disclose their personal data to as many users as possible, although average users do not have a clear idea about the actual reach of information they reveal or they underestimate the possible reach of their profiles visibility [40].

Users are losing control over their data and the use thereof, as they are becoming detectable and "correlatable". The combination of all this information provides a powerful tool for the accurate profiling of users. Moreover, it is quite simple to identify a particular person, even after her key attributes (name, affiliation, and address) have been removed, based on her web history [35].

However, even if individuals are profiled in a pseudonimised way they may be adversely influenced [42]. Informational privacy protects individuals against practices that erode individual freedom, their capacity for self-determination, and their autonomy to engage in relationships and foster social appearance. If individuals fear that information pertaining to them might lead to false incrimination, reprisals or manipulation of their data, they would probably hesitate to engage in communication and participatory activities [43]. The autonomy fostered by informational privacy generates collective benefits because it promotes "reasoned participation in the governance of the community" [44].

Risks of misuse and errors arising out of the aggregation and data mining of a large amount of data made public for other purposes are manifest. According to the German Federal Constitutional Court the "cataloguing" of the personality through the connection of personal data for the purpose of creating profiles and patterns is not permitted (Judgment of the Bundesverfassungsgericht, 4 April 2006, 1 BvR 518/ 02, 23.05.2006). A mass profiling of persons on the base of their views expressed in social media could have intimidation effects with further impacts on their behavior, the conception of their identity and the exercise of fundamental rights and freedoms such as the freedom of speech [45]. Fear of discrimination and prejudice may result to self-censorship and self-oppression [46]. Indeed, while profiling risks are usually conceived as threats to informational privacy we should point out the - eventually more - significant and actual risk of discrimination [47]. The safeguards relating to the use of personal information aim -among others- at preventing discrimination against persons because of their opinions, beliefs, health or social status. Studies conveyed how profiling and the widespread collection and aggregation of personal information increase social injustice and generate even further discrimination against political or ethnical minorities or traditionally disadvantaged groups [43].

Individuals may be confronted with major problems both in their workplace and in their social environment. Employers or rigid micro-societies could demonstrate marginalizing behavior against persons because of their deviating political affiliation. There are a lot of historical examples of people who have been side-lined by the hegemonic attitude of society. One should not look for numerous examples in order to evaluate this thesis: Victor Hugo's "The Miserable" (Sect. X: The Bishop in the presence of an unknown light) is the most representative evidence towards this result.

If we may generalize the above mentioned consideration to a macro environment, consequences to the deviating from the average political affiliation could lead to mass social exclusion, prejudice and discriminations. Such minorities may even be considered de facto delinquent and face a social stigma. In the context of a totalitarian/ authoritarian regime, implementation of such methods could lead to massive violation of civil and human rights or even threat the life of specific individuals.

6.2   Success Story and the Law

It is true that if a person generates digital/online content about herself or comment on other users' content - especially if using her real identity - could hardly claim that others refrain from judging her based on information that is made publicly available by her [48]. If theory and jurisprudence in the US recognizes no "reasonable expectation of privacy if data is voluntarily revealed to others" [37, 38], also the European data protection law allows data processing even of sensible categories of personal data if this data "are manifestly made public by the data subject". In this context, employers that have a legitimate interest to protect their organization from threats and ensure a secure environment and organization are, in principle, not prohibited to consider information about a person, which is documented in YouTube, videos, "likes", and public comments.

However, major concerns have to be expressed in case a person is not revealing her identity but can be identified, detected, correlated, and profiled, even "after her key attributes (name, affiliation, address) have been removed, based on her web history" [35]. Especially in such a case we have to take into consideration that persons tailor their (digital) presence and behavior towards particular audiences and within specific contexts. Informational privacy lies in the capacity to be a multiple personality, to maintain a variety of social identities and roles and to share different information depending on context, on condition that they cause no harm to other legitimate rights and interests. Being detected and judged out of context and for entirely different and unintended purposes bears the risk of "oversimplification" [49] and in any case constitutes an interference with a person's life choices and the possibility to act and express freely in society.

Profiling may be a useful tool to identify risks and propose predictions but, on the other side, it carries far-reaching consequences in terms of privacy infringement and unjustified and often invisible discrimination. Studies conveyed how profiling and the widespread collection and aggregation of personal information may increase social injustice and generate even further discrimination. Furthermore, we should reflect on the effects of profiling methods on other democratic rights. Profiling of persons on the base of their comments and views expressed in social media and networks could lead to self-censorship and impede the exercise of fundamental rights such as the freedom of speech [45]. If individuals fear that information pertaining to them might lead to false incrimination or reprisals they would probably hesitate to engage in communication and to abstain from participation [50].

These rights and freedoms are not only essential components of persons' dignity but also, they correspond to fundamental constitutional values and principles in democratic societies. The use of such methods should be regarded as exceptional and be applied on the ground of the so called proportionality test. A proportionality test may include the possibility of deciding that a method could be deemed as unacceptable because it may harm the essence of a fundamental right or of the constitutional order (democracy test: "necessary in a democratic state" test), even if it can be shown that this method can effectively realize another legitimate interest. Another aspect of a proportionality test lies in the obligation to explore if there are alternative measures that allow for the realization of the legitimate interest in a way that does not affect the fundamental rights in the same way as the proposed method. Such a method as the proposed one can be justified on the basis of concrete identified risks and or/in specific endangered environments, such as the case of critical infrastructures or where common goods of major importance are at stake. In the final analysis, the challenge that have to be faced is if – and to what extent – security of an organization should be preserved at the expense of dignity and freedom.

7 Conclusions and Further Research

In this paper we dealt with how the multifaceted information shared/revealed in the (context of) social media can be utilized, in order to achieve a dual purpose: (a). Deal with the possibility of a social threat that is based on user generated content exploitation and leads to political affiliation profiling; namely a new Panopticon of the digital era. We focus on raising user awareness, as a user might want to protect personal information other than political affiliation, namely information related to sexual orientation, racial discrimination or even the health condition of the user regardless of the national scope. Raising user awareness [51] is considered as an important priority in the Information Age. (b). Deal with the insider threat prediction and prevention, as malevolent insiders and predisposition towards computer crime has been closely linked

286 M. Kandias et al.

to the negative attitude towards law enforcement. It is important to enhance security in critical infrastructures [52, 53] as they encounter several threats [54], that some of them may not be easily detected [54].

To demonstrate the efficiency of the aforementioned cases, we collected a vast amount of data from Social Media, i.e. 12.964 users, 207.377 videos and 2.043.362 comments from YouTube. In order to prove and highlight the possibility of a social threat we developed a Panopticon methodology that is able to materialize it. To deal with the insider threat we presented an extension of the Panopticon methodology that uses machine learning techniques to extract a conclusion over the user's attitude towards law enforcement and authorities as expressed in its content.

Afterwards, we conducted content and graph theoretic analysis of the dataset in order to verify that it is possible to extract conclusions over users' political affiliation and predisposition towards law enforcement. Our results confirmed the initial hypothesis that YouTube is a social medium that can support the study of users' political affiliation and attitude towards law enforcement, as the feeling of anonymity enables users to express even their extreme opinions and beliefs.

Both methodologies presented need the contribution of a field specialist in order to assign category labels to each comment of the training set. Then, a machine is trained in classifying YouTube comments to these categories. Comparison of each classifier's efficiency was based on the metrics of precision, recall, f-score and accuracy and indicated that for both cases, Logistic Regression algorithm is the most appropriate because of the better f-score value achieved. Classifying comments to these categories enables the classification of playlists, lists of favorites and uploads, thus it manages to classify users to the above mentioned categories.

Furthermore, we carried out a series of statistics regarding our dataset. In specific we quoted characteristics and demographics of the users of interest that we located in our data, for both of the stories presented. Together with these characteristics, we highlighted possible consequences of an alleged implementation of the described method. Regardless of the scope of the implementation, the resulting threats include working place discriminations, social prejudice or even stigma and marginalization of the victims We adopted a pro-privacy attitude and included a legal point of view in our analysis, along with the emergence of the demand for raising social awareness over this threat and the necessity for institutionalization of digital rights.

For future work we plan to further study the Panopticon and recognize more aspects of this social threat. We intend on spreading our research on other social media and study the phenomenon under the prism of different tools and methodologies along with optimization of our weight factors.

References

1. Tokunaga, R.: Social networking site or social surveillance site? Understanding the use of interpersonal electronic surveillance in romantic relationships. Comput. Human Behav. **27**, 705–713 (2011)
2. Brignall, T.: The new Panopticon: The internet viewed as a structure of social control. Theory Sci. **3**(1), 335–348 (2002)

3. Foucault, M., Surveiller et punir: Naissance de la prison, Paris: Gallimard. A. Sheridan (Trans.), Discipline and punish: The birth of the prison: Penguin (1975)

4. Allmer, T.: Towards a Critical Theory of Surveillance in Informational Capitalism. P. Lang, Frankfurt am Main (2012)

5. Jurgenson, N.: Review of Ondi Timoner's we live in public. Surveill. Soc. 8(3), 374–378 (2010)

6. Beyer, A., Kirchner, M., Kreuzberger, G., Schmeling, J.: Privacy im Social Web Zum kompetenten Umgang mit personlichen Daten im Web 2. Datenschutz und Datensicherung (DuD) 9(2008), 597–600 (2008)

7. Whitaker, R., 1999. The End of Privacy: How Total Surveillance Is Becoming a Reality

8. Fuchs, C.: New Media, Web 2.0 and Surveillance. In: Sociology Compass 5/2, pp. 134–147 (2011)

9. Gibson, S.: Open source intelligence. RUSI J. 149(1), 16–22 (2004)

10. Gritzalis, D.: A digital seal solution for deploying trust on commercial transactions. Inf. Manag. Comput. Secur. 9(2), 71–79 (2001)

11. Lambrinoudakis, C., Gritzalis, D., Tsoumas, V., Karyda, M., Ikonomopoulos, S.: Secure electronic voting: the current landscape. In: Gritzalis, D. (ed.) Secure Electronic Voting, pp. 101–122. Springer, New York (2003)

12. Marias, J., Dritsas, S., Theoharidou, M., Mallios, J. Gritzalis, D.: SIP vulnerabilities and anti-spit mechanisms assessment. In: Proceedings of the 16th IEEE International Conference on Computer Communications and Networks, pp. 597–604. IEEE (2007)

13. Mitrou, L., Gritzalis, D., Katsikas, S., Quirchmayr, G.: Electronic voting: Constitutional and legal requirements, and their technical implications. Secure Electron. Voting 7, 43–60 (2003)

14. Spinellis, D., Gritzalis, S., Iliadis, J., Gritzalis, D., Katsikas, S.: Trusted third party services for deploying secure telemedical applications over the web. Comput. Secur. 18(7), 627–639 (1999)

15. Shaw, E., Ruby, K., Post, J.: The insider threat to information systems: the psychology of the dangerous insider. Secur. Aware. Bull. 2(98), 1–10 (1998)

16. Pang, B., Lee, L.: Opinion mining and sentiment analysis. Found. Trends Inf. Retrieval 2(12), 11–35 (2008)

17. De Choudhury, M., Counts, S.: The nature of emotional expression in social media: measurement, inference and utility. In: Human Computer Interaction Consortium Workshop (2012)

18. Benevenuto, F., Rodrigues, T., Cha, M., Almeida, V.: Characterizing user behavior in online social networks. In: Proceedings of the 9th ACM Conference on Internet Measurement, pp. 49–62. ACM Press (2009)

19. Park, N., Kee, K., Valenzuela, S.: Being immersed in social networking environment: Facebook groups, uses and gratifications, and social outcomes. Cyber Psychol. Behav. 12(6), 729–733 (2009)

20. Balduzzi, M., Platzer, C., Holz, T., Kirda, E., Balzarotti, D., Kruegel, C.: Abusing social networks for automated user profiling. In: Jha, S., Sommer, R., Kreibich, C. (eds.) RAID 2010. LNCS, vol. 6307, pp. 422–441. Springer, Heidelberg (2010)

21. Kandias, M., Virvilis, N., Gritzalis, D.: The insider threat in cloud computing. In: Bologna, S., Hämmerli, B., Gritzalis, D., Wolthusen, S. (eds.) CRITIS 2011. LNCS, vol. 6983, pp. 93–103. Springer, Heidelberg (2013)

22. Kandias, M., Mylonas, A., Theoharidou, M., Gritzalis, D.: Exploitation of auctions for outsourcing security-critical projects. In: Proceedings of the 16th IEEE Symposium on Computers and Communications, pp. 646–651. IEEE (2011)

23. Magklaras, G., Furnell, S.: Insider threat prediction tool: evaluating the probability of IT misuse. Comput. Secur. **21**(1), 62–73 (2011)
24. Kandias, M., Mylonas, A., Virvilis, N., Theoharidou, M., Gritzalis, D.: An insider threat prediction model. In: Katsikas, S., Lopez, J., Soriano, M. (eds.) TrustBus 2010. LNCS, vol. 6264, pp. 26–37. Springer, Heidelberg (2010)
25. FBI, The Insider Threat: An introduction to detecting and deterring an insider spy (2012). http://www.fbi.gov/about-us/investigate/counterintelligence/the-insider-threat
26. Kandias, M., Galbogini, K., Mitrou, L., Gritzalis, D.: Insiders trapped in the mirror reveal themselves in social media. In: Lopez, J., Huang, X., Sandhu, R. (eds.) NSS 2013. LNCS, vol. 7873, pp. 220–235. Springer, Heidelberg (2013)
27. Kandias, M., Mitrou, L., Stavrou, V., Gritzalis, D.: Which side are you on? A new panopticon vs. privacy. In: Proceedings of the 10th International Conference on Security and Cryptography, SciTekPress, pp. 98–110 (2013)
28. Sebastiani, F.: Machine learning in automated text categorization. ACM Comput. Surv. **34**(1), 1–47 (2002)
29. McCallum, A., Nigam, K.: A comparison of event models for naive Bayes text classification. In: Work-shop on learning for text categorization, vol. 752, pp. 41–48 (1998)
30. Joachims, T.: Text categorization with support vector machines: Learning with many relevant features. In: Nédellec, C., Rouveirol, C. (eds.) ECML 1998. LNCS, vol. 1398. Springer, Heidelberg (1998)
31. Anderson, J.: Logistic regression. In: Handbook of Statistics. NorthHolland, Amsterdam, pp. 169–191 (1982)
32. Manning, C., Raghavan, P., Schütze, H.: Introduction to Information Retrieval. Cambridge University Press, New York (2008)
33. Kandias, M., Stavrou, V., Bosovic, N., Gritzalis, D.: Predicting the insider threat via social media: The YouTube case. In: Proceedings of the 12th ACM Workshop on Privacy in the Electronic Society, pp. 261–266. ACM Press (2013)
34. Kandias, M., Stavrou, V., Bozovic, N., Mitrou, L., Gritzalis, D.: Can we trust this user? Predicting insider's attitude via YouTube usage profiling. In: Proceedings of the 10th IEEE International Conference on Autonomic and Trusted Computing, pp. 347–354 (2013)
35. Castelluccia, C., Druschel, P., Hübner, S., Pasic, A., Preneel, B., Tschofenig, H.: Privacy, accountability and Trust-Challenges and opportunities, Technical report, ENISA (2011)
36. Hildebrandt, M.: Who is profiling who? Invisible visibility. In: Gutwirth, S., Poullet, Y., De Hert, P., de Terwangne, C., Nouwt, S. (eds.) Reinventing Data Protection, pp. 239–252. Springer, Netherlands (2009)
37. Solove, D.: A taxonomy of privacy. Univ. Pa. Law Rev. **154**(3), 477 (2006)
38. Henderson, S.: Expectations of Privacy in Social Media. Mississippi College L. Rev., 31 (2012). http://works.bepress.com/stephen_henderson/10
39. Bruns, A.: Towards produsage: Futures for user-led content production. In: Proceedings of Cultural Attitudes towards Communication and Technology Conference, pp. 275–284 (2006)
40. Ziegele, M., Quiring, O.: Privacy in social network sites. In: Trepte, S., Reinecke, L. (eds.) Privacy Online: Perspectives on Privacy and Self-Disclosure in the Social Web, pp. 175–189. Springer, Berlin (2011)
41. Mitrou, L.: The commodification of the individual in the internet era: informational self-determination or "self-alienation". In: Proceedings of the 8th International Conference of Computer Ethics Philosophical Enquiry, pp. 466–485 (2009)
42. Schermer, B.: The limits of privacy in automated profiling and data mining. Comput. Law Secur. Rev. **27**, 45–52 (2011)

43. Mitrou, L.: The impact of communications data retention on fundamental rights and democracy: The case of the EU Data Retention Directive. In: Haggerty/Samatas, pp. 127–147 (2010)
44. Cohen, J.: Examined lives: informational privacy and the subject as object. Stanf. Law Rev. **52**, 1373–1438 (2000)
45. Cas, I.: Ubiquitous computing, privacy and data protection: options and limitations to reconcile the unprecedented contradictions. In: Gutwirth, S., Poullet, Y., De Hert, P., Leenes, R. (eds.) Computers, Privacy and Data Protection: An Element of Choice, pp. 139–170. Springer, Netherlands (2011)
46. Fazekas, C.: 1984 is still fiction: electronic monitoring in the workplace and US privacy law. Duke L. Technol. Rev. 15–25 (2004)
47. Gutwirth, S., De Hert, P.: Regulating profiling in a democratic constitutional State. In: Hildebrandt, M., Gutwirth, S. (eds.) Profiling the European citizen: Cross-Disciplinary Perspectives, pp. 271–302. Springer, Netherlands (2008)
48. Abril-Sánchez, P., Levin, A., Del Riego, A.: Blurred boundaries: social media privacy and the 21st century employee. Am. Bus. Law J. **49**(1), 63–124 (2012)
49. Dumortier, F.: Facebook and Risks of "de-contextualization" of information. In: Gutwirth, S., Poullet, Y., De Hert, P. (eds.) Data Protection in a Profiled World, pp. 119–137. Springer, Netherlands (2010)
50. Mylonas, A., Tsoumas, B., Dritsas, S., Gritzalis, D.: A secure smartphone applications roll-out scheme. In: Furnell, S., Lambrinoudakis, C., Pernul, G. (eds.) TrustBus 2011. LNCS, vol. 6863, pp. 49–61. Springer, Heidelberg (2011)
51. Mylonas, A., Kastania, A., Gritzalis, D.: Delegate the smartphone user? Security awareness in smartphone platforms. Comput. Secur. **34**, 47–66 (2013)
52. Theoharidou, M., Tsalis, N., Gritzalis, D.: In cloud we trust: risk-assessment-as-a-service. In: Fernández-Gago, C., Martinelli, F., Pearson, S., Agudo, I. (eds.) Trust Management VII. IFIP AICT, vol. 401, pp. 100–110. Springer, Heidelberg (2013)
53. Kotzanikolaou, P., Theoharidou, M., Gritzalis, D.: Interdependencies between Critical Infrastructures: Analyzing the Risk of Cascading Effects. In: Bologna, S., Hämmerli, B., Gritzalis, D., Wolthusen, S. (eds.) CRITIS 2011. LNCS, vol. 6983, pp. 104–115. Springer, Heidelberg (2013)
54. Soupionis, Y., Basagiannis, S., Katsaros, P., Gritzalis, D.: A formally verified mechanism for countering SPIT. In: Xenakis, C., Wolthusen, S. (eds.) CRITIS 2010. LNCS, vol. 6712, pp. 128–139. Springer, Heidelberg (2011)
55. Virvilis, N., Gritzalis, D.: The big four what we did wrong in advanced persistent threat detection? In: Proceedings of the 8th International Conference on Availability, Reliability and Security, pp. 248–254. IEEE (2013)

Determining Cryptographic Distinguishers for eStream and SHA-3 Candidate Functions with Evolutionary Circuits

Petr Švenda[(✉)], Martin Ukrop, and Vashek Matyáš

Masaryk University, Brno, Czech Republic
{svenda,xukrop,matyas}@fi.muni.cz

Abstract. Cryptanalysis of a cryptographic function usually requires advanced cryptanalytical skills and extensive amount of human labor with an option of using randomness testing suites like STS NIST [1] or Dieharder [2]. These can be applied to test statistical properties of cryptographic function outputs. We propose a more open approach based on software circuit that acts as a testing function automatically evolved by a stochastic optimization algorithm. Information leaked during cryptographic function evaluation is used to find a distinguisher [4] of outputs produced by 25 candidate algorithms for eStream and SHA-3 competition from truly random sequences. We obtained similar results (with some exceptions) as those produced by STS NIST and Dieharder tests w.r.t. the number of rounds of the inspected algorithm.

Keywords: eStream · Genetic programming · Random distinguisher · Randomness statistical testing · Software circuit

1 Introduction

Typical cryptanalytical approach against a new cryptographic function is usually based on application of various statistical testing tools (e.g., STS NIST [1], Dieharder [2]) as the first step. Then follows application of established cryptanalytical procedures (algorithmic attacks, differential cryptanalysis, etc.) combined with an in-depth knowledge of the inspected function. This, however, usually requires extensive human cryptanalytical labor.

General statistical testing can be at least partly automated and easy to apply, but will detect only the most visible defects in the function design. Additionally, statistical testing tools are limited to a predefined set of statistical tests. That on one hand makes the follow-up analytical work easier if the function fails a certain test, yet on the other hand severely limits the potential to detect other defects.

This paper is significantly extended version of results presented in [3].

© Springer-Verlag Berlin Heidelberg 2014
M.S. Obaidat and J. Filipe (Eds.): ICETE 2013, CCIS 456, pp. 290–305, 2014.
DOI: 10.1007/978-3-662-44788-8_17

We propose a novel approach that can be used in a similar manner as general statistical testing suites, but additionally provides the possibility to automatically construct new tests. Every test is represented by an emulated hardware-like circuit. Evolutionary algorithms are used to design the circuit layout. Although such an automated tool will not (at least for the moment) outperform a skilled cryptographer, it brings two major advantages:

- It can be applied automatically against multiple cryptographic functions with no additional human labor – working implementation of the inspected function is sufficient. Cryptographic function competitions (e.g., SHA-3 [5], eStream [6]) are especially suitable due to standardized interface.
- Novel and/or unusual information leakage "side channels" may be used. The proposed approach requires no pre-selection of function parts, input/output bits or used statistics – these decisions are left for the evolutionary algorithm.

We tested our idea by evolving random distinguishers for several eStream and SHA-3 candidate functions. To assess the success of this method, we focused on functions with inner structure containing repeated rounds. By gradually increasing the number of rounds, one can identify the point where this approach still provides results (i.e., the function output can be distinguished with probability significantly better than random guessing). Results are very similar to those obtained from STS NIST and Dieharder statistical test suites w.r.t. the number of rounds of the inspected function. The implementation of the whole framework is available as an open-source project EACirc [7].

2   Previous Work

Numerous works tackled the problem of distinguisher construction between data produced by cryptographic functions and truly random data, both with reduced and full number of rounds. Usually, statistical testing with standard battery of tests or additional custom tailored statistical tests are performed.

In [8], detailed examination of eStream Phase 2 candidates (full and reduced round tests) with STS NIST battery and structural randomness tests was performed, finding six ciphers deviating from expected values. More recently, the same battery, but only a subset of tests, was applied to SHA-3 candidates with a reduced number of rounds as well as only to their compression functions [9].

A method to test statistical properties of short sequences typically obtained by block ciphers or hash algorithms for which some STS NIST tests can not be applied due to insufficient length was proposed in [10]. 256-bit versions of SHA-3 finalists were subjected to statistical tests using a GPU-accelerated evaluation [11]. Because of massive parallelization, superpoly tests introduced by [12] were possible to be performed, detecting some deviations in all but the Grøstl algorithm.

Stochastic algorithms were also applied in cryptography to some extent. A nice review of usage of genetic algorithms in cryptography up to year 2004 can be found in [13], a more recent review is provided by [14]. In [15] a comparison

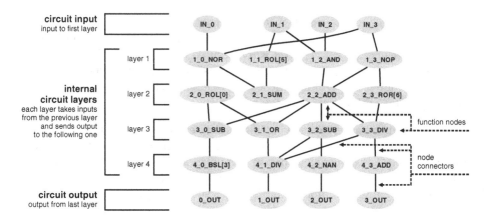

Fig. 1. Simple example of software-emulated circuit.

of genetic techniques is presented, with several suggestions which genetic techniques and parameters should be used to obtain better results. TEA algorithm [16] with a reduced number of rounds is a frequent target for cryptanalysis with genetic algorithms. In [17], a successful randomness distinguisher for XTEA limited to 4 rounds is evolved. The distinguisher generates a bit mask with high Hamming weight, which, when applied to function input, results in deviated χ^2 Goodness of Fit test of the output. However, no distinguisher for full number of rounds was found. Subsequent work [18] improves an earlier attack with quantum-inspired genetic algorithms, finding more efficient distinguishers for a reduced round TEA algorithm succeeding for 5 rounds.

We adopted the genetic programming [19] technique with steady-state replacement. An important difference of our approach is the production of a program (in the form of a software circuit) that provides different results depending on given inputs. Previous work produced a fixed result – e.g., a bit mask in [17,18] that is directly applied to all inputs.

3   Software Circuits Designed by Evolution

Software circuit is a software representation of a hardware-like circuit with nodes ("gates") responsible for computation of simple functions (e.g., AND, OR). Nodes are positioned in several layers with connectors ("wires") in between. A node may be connected to all nodes from the previous layer, to only some of them, or to none at all. A simple circuit overview can be seen in Fig. 1. Contrary to real single-layer hardware circuits, connectors may also cross each other.

Usage is versatile – from Boolean circuits where functions computed in nodes are limited to logical operators to artificial neural networks where nodes compute the weighted sum of the inputs. Besides studying complexity problems, these circuits were used in various applications like construction of a fully homomorphic

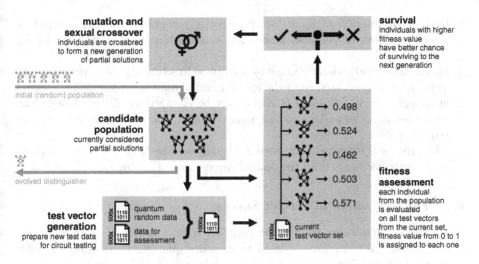

Fig. 2. Simplified work-flow of the evolution process in EACirc.

scheme or in design of efficient image filters. Circuit evaluation can be performed by a software emulator or possibly directly in hardware when FPGAs are used.

3.1 The Process of Evolution

The main goal is to find a circuit that will reveal an unwanted defect in the inspected cryptographic function. For example, if a circuit is able to correctly predict the nth bit generated by a stream cipher just by observing previous $(n-1)$ bits, then this circuit serves as a next-bit predictor [20], breaking the security of the given stream cipher. When a circuit is able to distinguish output of the tested function from a truly random sequence, it serves as a random distinguisher [4] providing a warning sign of function weakness. Note that a circuit does not provide correct answers for all inputs – it is sufficient if a correct answer is provided with a probability significantly better than random guessing.

The greatest challenge is the precise circuit design. It can be laid out by an experienced human analyst or created and further optimized automatically. We use the latter approach and combine a software circuit evaluated on a CPU/GPU with evolutionary algorithms. The whole process of circuit design, as also depicted in Fig. 2, is as follows:

1. Several circuits ("candidate solutions") are randomly initialized – both functions in nodes and connectors are chosen at random. Note that such a random circuit will, most probably, not provide any meaningful output for given inputs and can even have disconnected layers.
2. If necessary, new test vectors used for success evaluation are generated.
3. Every individual (circuit) in the population is emulated on all test inputs. The fitness function assigns each circuit a rating based on the obtained outputs

(e.g., what fraction of inputs were correctly recognized as being output of a stream cipher rather than a completely random sequence, see Sect. 3.2 for details).

4. Based on the evaluation provided by the fitness function, a potentially improved population is generated from the existing individuals by mutation and sexual crossover. Every individual (circuit) may be changed by altering operations computed in nodes and/or adding/removing connectors between nodes in subsequent layers.

5. The process is repeated from step 2. Usually hundreds of thousands or more repeats are necessary until the desired success rate of distinguisher is achieved.

3.2 The Evaluation of Circuit Success

Evolutionary algorithms need to be supplied with a metric of success – a so-called fitness function. This is used to measure quality of candidate circuits. Proper definition of fitness function is crucial for obtaining a working solution to the defined problem. In this work, we limit ourselves to randomness distinguishability as a target goal. Other goals like next-bit predictor [20] or defector of strict avalanche criterion [21] can be used.

A circuit input is a sequence of bytes produced either by the inspected function (first type) or generated completely randomly (second type). A circuit output is an encoding of the guessed source. Different encodings are possible: single bit (e.g., 0 meaning "random data" and 1 meaning "function output") or multiple bits (e.g., low versus high Hamming weight of whole output byte). Results in this work use only the byte's highest bit for easier interpretation, but Hamming weight seems to be a better choice for later experiments. Additionally, a circuit can be allowed to make multiple guesses by producing multiple output bytes. A circuit thus has the possibility to express its own certainty in the predicted result (e.g., by setting 2 out of 3 outputs to predict random data and remaining one to predict the function output) as well as to evolve more than one predictor inside a single circuit.

For evaluation of a circuit performance, we use supervised learning with test sets containing pairs of inputs and expected outputs generated prior to the evaluation. Corresponding circuit outputs are compared with expected values to see if the circuit predicted the input source correctly. The success rate (fitness) is then computed as a ratio of correctly predicted test vectors to the total number.

3.3 Evolution and Circuit Parameters

For our experiments, we used the following settings to maintain a good trade-off between the evaluation time (influenced mainly by the number of test vectors) and the ability to prevent over-learning (influenced by the test set change frequency).

– Every test set contains 1000 test vectors with exactly half taken from inspected function's output and second half taken from random data. Order of test vectors in the set is not important as test vectors are handled by circuit completely independently.

- Every test vector has the length of 16 bytes.
- Test set is periodically changed every 100th generation to prevent over-learning on a given test set.

Circuit and evolution parameters were fine-tuned empirically based on previous experiments. The settings for the presented experiments are as follows:

- 5 layers, 8 nodes in every internal layer, 16 input nodes (corresponding to 16 input bytes in every test vector) and 2 output nodes.
- Population consists of 20 individuals refreshed by the steady-state replacement strategy with two thirds of individuals replaced every generation.
- 30 000 generations were executed in a single evolution run with 30 separate evolution runs running in parallel.
- Mutation is applied with probability of 0.05 and changes function in a given node or connector mask by addition or removal of connector to a given node.
- Crossover is applied with a probability of 0.5 and performs single point crossover with the first i layers taken from the first parent and remaining layers from the second parent.

Reference experiments were performed using statistical batteries (Dieharder, STS NIST) as a more traditional approach of randomness distinguishing. Note that we will not discuss all results for Dieharder and STS NIST in details as such discussion was already done several times before [8,9]. We will focus only on the identification of the highest round where some defects are still detected and the significance of such detection – whether almost all tests fail or only a minority of them.

STS NIST was run on 100 sub-streams, each consisting of 1 000 000 bits. *Random Excursions* and *Random Excursions Variant* tests were omitted due to execution problems. All 15 available tests were run in all supported configurations. From the Dieharder suite, only the tests corresponding to the original Diehard collection were used (*Diehard sums test* was omitted due to implementation problems). Each of the chosen tests was run just once, but was allowed to process as much data as it required.

The total volume of data processed by EACirc varies greatly from the volume used by statistical batteries. As can be seen from (1), the results output by EACirc are based on a sample of about 2.3 MB of assessed data.

$$\Sigma = \frac{30000 \text{ generations}}{100 \; \frac{\text{generations}}{\text{test set}}} \cdot \frac{1}{2} \cdot 1000 \; \frac{\text{vector}}{\text{test set}} \cdot 16 \; \frac{\text{bytes}}{\text{vector}} \approx 2.29 \, \text{MB} \qquad (1)$$

When using STS NIST and Dieharder, we worked with an external file with 250 MB of the assessed stream. The usage of STS NIST amounts to about 11.92 MB while running the whole test set of Dieharder processed about 582 MB altogether with the smallest test consuming about 3 MB and the largest one about 127 MB. Furthermore, we would like to stress out that EACirc makes decisions on much smaller samples of 16 bytes at a time only.

3.4   Implementation Details

We used the following elementary operations for nodes: no operation (NOP), logical functions (AND, OR, XOR, NOR, NAND, NOT), bit manipulating functions (ROTR, ROTL, BITSELECTOR), arithmetic functions (ADD, SUBS, MULT, DIV, SUM), reading a specified input byte even from an internal layer (READX) and producing a constant value (CONST).

As the optimization process requires many evaluations of candidate circuits, we use our computation infrastructure to perform distributed computation with more than a thousand CPU cores. EACirc is implemented with the ability to recover computation based on logs and periodically saved internal state. This provides a possibility to perform evolution with unlimited number of generations even when a computation node itself lasts only a limited time before reboot.

Truly random data used for test vectors were produced by the Quantum Random Bit Generator Service [22] and High Bit Rate Quantum Random Number Generator Service [23].

To ease the analysis of the evolved circuits, we implemented an automatic removal of nodes and connectors not contributing to the resulting fitness value. Furthermore, circuits can be visualized using the Graphviz library.

To independently replicate results provided by a circuit emulator and to double check for possible implementation bugs, EACirc supports exporting circuits into the code of a plain C program. The resulting C program can be compiled separately and computes only the circuit from which it was generated, but completely circumvents the circuit emulator.

4   Application to eStream and SHA-3 Candidates

The testing methodology described in Sect. 3 was applied against several cryptographic functions in order to probe for unwanted properties of their output. We decided to analyze randomness of stream cipher outputs from the recent eStream competition [6] and candidate hash functions from SHA-3 competition [5]. Testing these implementations enabled us to utilize the unified function interface prescribed in the competitions. After this wide-testing, one can cherry-pick only such functions where a well-working circuit is found for further cryptanalysis.

Previous works evaluated statistical properties of candidate functions with the full number of rounds as well as with a reduced number of rounds [8]. Testing full number of rounds usually provides only limited information – either the function is very weak and exhibits weaknesses even in the full number of rounds or no defect at all is detected, even when an serious exploitable attack might exist for a limited number of rounds. In this work, we therefore inspected the functions in reduced-round versions trying to obtain at least the same results as with STS NIST/Dieharder batteries.

4.1 Reference Case

Before performing the experiments themselves, we needed to establish reference values corresponding to random guessing. We therefore let circuits distinguish between two groups of test vectors, which were both taken from truly random data. Intuitively, our approach should fail to find a working distinguisher and should behave as random guessing.

The predicted behavior was confirmed by an experiment with same settings as those used for testing functions. All statistical tests from Dieharder (20/20) and STS NIST (162/162) successfully passed on this random data, and no working distinguisher was found.

To express the success of evolution, we inspect the fitness of the best individual in the population just after the change of the test set (so as to suppress the influence of over-learning). We compute the average of these maximum fitness values over the whole run. Due to the probabilistic nature of evolutionary algorithms, we repeated every run 30 times and display the average of all runs. All in all, the success of EACirc is expressed by the average fitness value of the best individual in the population right after the change of test set, further averaged across 30 independent runs.

The evolution success for distinguishing two sets of random data, equivalent to random guessing, was 0.52 with independent runs differing in 3rd or 4th decimal place. We anticipated that the difference from the naive value of 0.50 was influenced by population size and the size of test set. As experimentally verified, decreasing the number of individuals in the population or increasing the number of vectors in a test set shifts the evolution success towards the naive value. We can thus conclude that, in our settings, the fitness value of 0.52 corresponds to indistinguishable streams.

4.2 Results for eStream Candidates

From 34 candidates in the eStream competition, 23 were potentially usable for testing (due to renamed or updated versions and problems with compilation). Out of these, we limited ourselves to only 7 (Decim, Grain, FUBUKI, Hermes, LEX, Salsa20 and TSC), since these had internal structure that allowed for a simple reduction of complexity by reducing a number of internal rounds. For all used ciphers, the implementation from the last successful phase of the competition was taken. The ciphers were tested in unlimited versions and then for all lower number of rounds until reaching indistinguishability from a random stream. We considered three scenarios with respect to the frequency of encryption key change:

1. The key is fixed for all generated test sets and vectors. Even when test sets change, new test vectors are generated using the same key.
2. Every test set was generated using a different key. All test vectors in a particular test set are generated with the same key.
3. Every test vector (16 bytes) was generated using a different key.

Table 1. Results for selected eStream candidates with both full and reduced number of internal rounds with respect to the key change frequency.

stream cipher	# of rounds	IV and key reinitialization								
		once for run			for each test set			for each test vector		
		Dieharder (x/20)	STS NIST (x/162)	EACirc	Dieharder (x/20)	STS NIST (x/162)	EACirc	Dieharder (x/20)	STS NIST (x/162)	EACirc
Decim	1	0.0	0	0.99	0.0	0	0.85	0.0	5	0.99
	2	0.5	0	0.54	1.0	0	0.54	15.5	146	0.52
	3	1.0	0	0.53	1.0	0	0.53	15.0	160	0.52
	4	3.5	79	0.52	3.0	78	0.52	20.0	160	0.52
	5	4.5	79	0.52	3.5	91	0.52	17.5	161	0.52
	6	19.0	158	0.52	19.0	159	0.52	18.0	162	0.52
	7	18.5	162	0.52	19.0	161	0.52	20.0	161	0.52
	8	20.0	162	0.52	20.0	159	0.52	19.0	161	0.52
FUBUKI	1	20.0	162	0.52	20.0	161	0.52	18.0	162	0.52
	4	20.0	162	0.52	20.0	162	0.52	20.0	162	0.52
Grain	1	0.0	0	1.00	0.0	0	0.67	18.5	162	0.52
	2	0.0	0	1.00	0.5	0	0.66	20.0	162	0.52
	3	19.5	160	0.52	20.0	162	0.52	20.0	162	0.52
	13	20.0	162	0.52	20.0	161	0.52	19.5	162	0.52
Hermes	1	20.0	162	0.52	20.0	162	0.52	20.0	162	0.52
	10	20.0	160	0.52	20.0	162	0.52	20.0	162	0.52
LEX	1	0.0	0	1.00	0.0	0	0.96	3.0	1	1.00
	2	4.0	1	1.00	4.0	1	1.00	3.5	1	1.00
	3	0.5	1	1.00	3.5	1	1.00	4.0	1	1.00
	4	20.0	162	0.52	19.5	162	0.52	20.0	161	0.52
	10	19.5	162	0.52	19.5	160	0.52	20.0	160	0.52
Salsa20	1	5.5	1	0.87	8.5	1	0.67	17.5	161	0.52
	2	5.5	1	0.87	7.0	1	0.67	19.5	162	0.52
	3	20.0	162	0.52	20.0	162	0.52	19.5	161	0.52
	12	20.0	162	0.52	19.5	161	0.52	19.0	161	0.52
TSC	1-8	0.0*	0	1.00	0.0*	0	1.00	0.0*	0	1.00
	9	1.0	1	1.00	1.5	1	1.00	2.0	1	1.00
	10	2.0	13	1.00	3.0	13	1.00	3.0	12	1.00
	11	10.0	157	0.52	11.5	157	0.52	14.0	159	0.52
	12	16.0	162	0.52	17.0	161	0.52	17.5	162	0.52
	13	20.0	162	0.52	20.0	162	0.52	19.0	162	0.52
	32	20.0	161	0.52	20.0	162	0.52	20.0	161	0.52

*During the first 8 rounds, TSC produces no output. This caused 4 Dieharder tests to get stuck, effectively reducing the number of tests to 16.

Table 1 summarizes results for the selected eStream candidates depending on a number of algorithm rounds and key change frequency. Interpretation of values in table is the following: Dieharder provides three levels of evaluation for a particular test: pass, weak and fail. Values 1, 0.5 and 0 were assigned to these levels respectively and sum over all tests is computed and displayed. For STS NIST, the number of all passed tests is displayed. This is deduced from the distribution of p-values across all 100 runs with respect to the significance level of $\alpha = 0.01$. The values for EACirc express the average maximum success rate, further averaged through multiple runs (for precise meaning see Sect. 4.1).

Cells representing a stream successfully distinguished from random are denoted by gray background for easier comprehension. Border cases (only a very small deviation found) are shaded in light gray.

The results indicate that, in this case, EACirc performs more or less the same as standard statistical batteries (Decim being the most prominent exception). Dieharder sometimes performed better than STS NIST, but it has to be taken into consideration that it is newer and made decision based on a much larger data sample. In general, both statistical batteries processed longer streams than EACirc (for detailed numbers see Sect. 3.3).

4.3   Results for SHA-3 Candidates

From 64 hash functions that entered the competition, 51 were selected to the first round. Out of these, 42 were potentially usable for testing (due to source code size, speed and compilation problems). The implementations were again taken from the last successful phase of the competition. In the end, 18 most promising candidates were chosen: ARIRANG, Aurora, Blake, Cheetah, CubeHash, DCH, Dynamic SHA, Dynamic SHA2, ECHO, Grøstl, Hamsi, JH, Lesamnta, Luffa, MD6, SIMD, Tangle, and Twister. These were the candidates fulfilling the following two requirements:

- The hash functions could be effortlessly limited in complexity by decreasing the number of internal rounds.
- While the unlimited version produced a random-looking output, their most limited version did not.

We generated continuous output stream by hashing a simple 4-byte counter starting from a randomly generated value. We obtained a 256-bit digest, which was cut in half to produce 2 independent test vector inputs of 16 bytes each. In case of generating a continuous stream (for statistical testing), we concatenated the digests.

The results, summarized in Tables 2 and 3, indicate that in this case EACirc performs slightly worse than standard statistical batteries. Although in most of the cases it found a statistically significant variation from a neutral success rate of 0.52, it can be seen that it often failed in the last round successfully distinguished by statistical batteries. Once again, when interpreting these results, we must be aware of the imbalance of test data available to statistical batteries and EACirc (for detailed numbers see Sect. 3.3).

Table 2. Results for selected SHA-3 candidates with both full and reduced number of internal rounds.

hash function	# of rounds	Dieharder (x/20)	STS NIST (x/162)	EACirc
ARIRANG	0	0.0	0	1.00
	1	0.0	0	1.00
	2	0.0	0	1.00
	3	0.0	0	1.00
	4	20.0	161	0.52
Aurora	0	0.0	1	0.99
	1	0.0	1	0.75
	2	0.5	132	0.78
	3	0.5	132	0.52
	4	20.0	160	0.52
	17	19.5	161	0.52
Blake	0	0.0	0	1.00
	1	0.0	0	0.52
	2	20.0	162	0.52
	14	20.0	159	0.52
Cheetah	0	0.0	1	1.00
	1	0.0	1	1.00
	2	0.0	0	1.00
	3	0.0	0	0.90
	4	0.0	1	0.86
	5	0.0	1	0.52
	6	20.0	161	0.52
	16	20.0	162	0.52
CubeHash	0	0.0	0	1.00
	1	0.0	0	0.52
	2	20.0	161	0.52
	8	20.0	162	0.52
DCH	0	0.0*	0	1.00
	1	0.0*	0	0.73
	2	19.5	162	0.52
	4	20.0	162	0.52
Dynamic SHA	0	0.0	0	1.00
	1	0.0	0	1.00
	2	0.0	1	0.99

hash function	# of rounds	Dieharder (x/20)	STS NIST (x/162)	EACirc
Dynamic SHA (continued)	3	0.0	1	0.95
	4	0.0	18	0.74
	5	0.5	18	0.61
	6	3.0	16	0.59
	7	3.0	17	0.59
	8	20.0	162	0.52
	16	20.0	160	0.52
Dynamic SHA2	1	1.0	1	0.94
	2	1.0	1	0.74
	3	0.0	1	0.75
	4	0.0	1	0.57
	5	3.5	1	0.60
	6	3.5	1	0.60
	7	4.0	2	0.61
	8	4.0	2	0.60
	9	3.5	5	0.61
	10	3.5	5	0.61
	11	11.5	46	0.52
	12	11.5	46	0.52
	13	20.0	161	0.52
	17	20.0	161	0.52
ECHO	1	9.0	24	0.73
	2	9.0	24	0.52
	3	20.0	161	0.52
	8	20.0	161	0.52
Grøstl	0	0.0	0	0.98
	1	0.0	0	0.58
	2	12.5	52	0.58
	3	12.5	52	0.52
	4	20.0	162	0.52
	10	20.0	162	0.52
Hamsi	0	2.5	1	0.98
	1	2.5	1	0.52
	2	19.5	161	0.52
	3	20.0	162	0.52

*Only 16 Dieharder tests were performed, due to execution problems in some cases.

Table 3. Results for selected SHA-3 candidates with both full and reduced number of internal rounds (continued).

hash function	# of rounds	Dieharder (x/20)	STS NIST (x/162)	EACirc
JH	0	0.0	0	1.00
	1	0.0	0	0.99
	2	0.0	1	0.99
	3	0.0	1	0.99
	4	0.0	1	1.00
	5	0.0	3	1.00
	6	0.0	3	0.98
	7	20.0	161	0.52
	42	20.0	162	0.52
Lesamnta	0	0.0	0	1.00
	1	0.0	0	1.00
	2	0.0	0	1.00
	3	0.0	0	0.52
	4	20.0	162	0.52
	32	20.0	162	0.52
Luffa	0	0.0	0	1.00
	1	0.0	0	1.00
	2	0.0	1	0.99
	3	0.0	1	0.99
	4	0.0	4	0.75
	5	0.0	3	0.75
	6	0.0	10	0.74
	7	6.0	11	0.74
	8	20.0	161	0.52
MD6	0	0.0*	0	1.00
	1	0.0*	0	1.00
	2	0.0	0	1.00
	3	0.0	0	1.00
	4	0.0	0	1.00
	5	0.0	0	0.98
	6	0.0	1	0.88
	7	0.0	1	0.65
	8	17.5	18	0.53
	9	17.5	18	0.52
	10	20.0	160	0.52
	104	20.0	162	0.52

hash function	# of rounds	Dieharder (x/20)	STS NIST (x/162)	EACirc
SIMD	0	0.0	1	0.99
	1	0.0	1	0.52
	2	19.5	162	0.52
	4	19.5	161	0.52
Tangle	0	0.0	0	1.00
	1	0.0	0	0.99
	2	0.0	1	0.99
	3	0.0	1	0.85
	4	1.0	2	0.84
	5	1.0	2	0.80
	10	3.5	4	0.64
	11	3.0	4	0.63
	12	3.0	4	0.64
	13	4.0	4	0.64
	14	4.0	4	0.64
	15	3.0	5	0.64
	16	3.0	5	0.64
	17	4.5	27	0.60
	18	4.5	27	0.60
	19	6.0	36	0.60
	20	5.5	39	0.60
	21	10.5	91	0.54
	22	10.5	90	0.54
	23	19.0	161	0.52
	24	20.0	161	0.52
	80	20.0	161	0.52
Twister	0	0.0	0	1.00
	1	0.0	0	1.00
	2	0.0	0	1.00
	3	0.0	0	1.00
	4	0.0	0	1.00
	5	0.0	0	1.00
	6	0.0	0	1.00
	7	0.0	0	0.52
	8	20.0	161	0.52
	9	20.0	162	0.52

*Only 16 Dieharder tests were performed, due to execution problems in some cases.

5   Analysis of Evolved Distinguisher

After performing a wide range of experiments, we analyzed one selected case in a more detailed manner. We studied the dependence of distinguisher success rate on the number of generations already computed. Further attention was paid to the evolved circuit and the statistical properties it uses to draw the final verdict (random vs. non-random).

5.1   Achieved Success Rate

The general relationship between fitness value and the number of evolved generations in evolutionary algorithms is very specific – the success rate rises, during the period when the test vector set remains unchanged (100 generations in our setting), and then suddenly drops after the set change. This is caused by the circuit over-learning on a specific test vector set (circuits are learning to distinguish this particular set instead of general characteristics of the streams). However, even with over-learning, the success rate of distinguishing two sets of random data only rarely exceeded the value of 0.55.

The phenomenon of over-learning can be easily suppressed by changing the test vectors more frequently or increasing the number of vectors in a set. On the other hand, higher test set change frequency or more vectors would increase computational complexity. Therefore a reasonable trade-off is used.

In Fig. 3 we see similar relationship for circuit distinguishing Salsa20 cipher limited to 2 rounds. The over-learning tendency (repeating continual rise and sudden drop) is partly present as well, but in contrast to the previous case the circuits success rate reaches much higher values. Even if not evolving a universal distinguisher, this would be a sufficient evidence for non-randomness of Salsa20 output stream. Also, the circuit is (over-)learning very quickly to a particular data set. Such a behavior led us to inspect the over-learning speed as another potential metric of success instead of how well the circuit is working after a test vector change.

We can further notice that, after initial fluctuations, the circuit success rate shows another periodic behavior about every 4000 generations. The circuit stabilizes at distinguishing the Salsa20 output and then suddenly drops back to about a success of random guessing. It than gets better again and after about 4,000 generations (equivalent to about 450 KB of data) drops again. This behavior is specific to Salsa20 and its source probably comes from the cipher design. A detailed analysis will be the part of our future work.

5.2   Detailed Distinguisher Inspection

Other type of detailed study of Salsa20 limited to 2 rounds included the evolved distinguishers. We took an evolved distinguisher circuit, pruned it (removing all nodes not participating in computing the final fitness), generated 1 000 000 random input sequences for the circuit and inspected the distribution of values coming from every node.

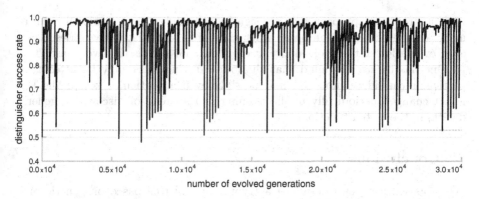

Fig. 3. Circuit success rate for distinguishing Salsa20 limited to 2 rounds from quantum random data (note the shifted scale on y-axis). The dotted line represents the value of 0.52 (stream indistinguishable from random).

Circuits evolved in parallel runs exhibited very similar behavior – in many of them, the output bytes (and thus the final verdict) depended only on the 7th input byte. It is difficult to tell what is the exact form of this weakness, but it draws our attention to the ever-mentioned byte 7. It definitely implies a possible design flaw in Salsa20 limited to 2 rounds influencing the randomness of every 7th output byte. More details can be found in [24].

6 Discussion

Based on results obtained with the proposed software circuits designed by genetic programming, a comparison to statistical batteries like STS NIST and Dieharder can be undertaken.

On one hand, the proposed method is based on a completely different approach than statistical tests used in batteries, opening space for detecting dependencies between tested function output bits not covered by tests from batteries. It offers a possibility to construct a distinguisher based on a dynamically constructed algorithm, rather than a predefined one from batteries. Once a working distinguisher is found, it requires extremely short sequences (tested on 16 bytes only) to detect function output. Statistical batteries require at least several megabytes of data. Lower amount of data extracted from a given function is necessary to provide a working distinguisher (at maximum, we used 2.2 MB). Data required by STS NIST and Dieharder were much larger. Note that some tests may provide indication of failure even when less data is available.

On the other hand, subtle statistical defects may not be detected because of very short sequences the circuit is working on. However, several modifications to the proposed approach might enable the processing of larger sequences (e.g., circuit with iterative memory processing data in chunks). Furthermore, the resulting distinguisher may be hard to analyze – what is the weakness detected and what should be fixed in the function design?

The proposed approach requires significantly higher computational requirements during the evolution phase when compared to statistical batteries. However, evaluation of the evolved circuit on additional data is then very fast.

One has to keep in mind that the found distinguisher may be fitted to a particular candidate function (and possibly even a particular key, if the key is not changed periodically in the training set), instead of discovering generic defects in the tested function.

7   Conclusions

We proposed a general design of a cryptanalytical tool based on genetic programming and applied it to the problem of finding a random distinguisher for 25 cryptographic functions taken from eStream and SHA-3 competitions. In general, the proposed approach proved to be capable of closely matching the performance of STS NIST and Dieharder battery. A robust evaluation of various scenarios was performed w.r.t. the key change frequency as well as the number of internal rounds.

The proposed approach provides a novel way of inspecting statistical defects in cryptographic functions and may provide a significant advantage when working with very short sequences once the learning phase of evolution is completed. Our future work will cover techniques that will enable processing significantly more data to provide more fair comparison to STS NIST and Dieharder batteries, as these are making statistical analysis on tens (STS NIST) up to hundreds (Dieharder) of megabytes of data.

Acknowledgments. This work was supported by the GAP202/11/0422 project of the Czech Science Foundation. The access to computing and storage facilities owned by parties and projects contributing to the National Grid Infrastructure MetaCentrum, provided under the program Projects of Large Infrastructure for Research, Development, and Innovations (LM2010005) is highly appreciated.

References

1. Rukhin, A.: A statistical test suite for the validation of random number generators and pseudo random number generators for cryptographic applications, version STS-2.1. NIST Special Publication 800–22rev1a (2010)
2. Brown, R.G.: Dieharder: A random number test suite, version 3.31.1 (2004)
3. Svenda, P., Ukrop, M., Matyas, V.: Towards cryptographic function distinguishers with evolutionary circuits. In: SECRYPT, pp. 135–146 (2013)
4. Englund, H., Hell, M., Johansson, T.: A note on distinguishing attacks. In: 2007 IEEE Information Theory Workshop on Information Theory for Wireless Networks, pp. 1–4. IEEE (2007)
5. SHA-3 competition, announced 2.11.2007 (2007)
6. ECRYPT: Ecrypt estream competition, announced November 2004 (2004)
7. EACirc project (2013). https://github.com/petrs/eacirc

8. Turan, M.S., Doğanaksoy, A., Çalik, Ç.: Detailed statistical analysis of synchronous stream ciphers. In: ECRYPT Workshop on the State of the Art of Stream Ciphers (SASC'06) (2006)
9. Doganaksoy, A., Ege, B., Koçak, O., Sulak, F.: Statistical analysis of reduced round compression functions of SHA-3 second round candidates. Technical report, Institute of Applied Mathematics, Middle East Technical University, Turkey (2010)
10. Sulak, F., Doğanaksoy, A., Ege, B., Koçak, O.: Evaluation of randomness test results for short sequences. In: Carlet, C., Pott, A. (eds.) SETA 2010. LNCS, vol. 6338, pp. 309–319. Springer, Heidelberg (2010)
11. Kaminsky, A.: GPU parallel statistical and cube test analysis of the SHA-3 finalist candidate hash functions. In: 15th SIAM Conference on Parallel Processing for Scientific Computing (PP12), SIAM (2012)
12. Dinur, I., Shamir, A.: Cube attacks on tweakable black box polynomials. In: Joux, A. (ed.) EUROCRYPT 2009. LNCS, vol. 5479, pp. 278–299. Springer, Heidelberg (2009)
13. Delman, B.: Genetic algorithms in cryptography. Ph.D. thesis, Rochester Institute of Technology (2004)
14. Picek, S., Golub, M.: On evolutionary computation methods in cryptography. In: MIPRO, 2011 Proceedings of the 34th International Convention, pp. 1496–1501 (2011)
15. Garrett, A., Hamilton, J., Dozier, G.: A comparison of genetic algorithm techniques for the cryptanalysis of tea. Int. J. Intell. Control Syst. **12**, 325–330 (2007)
16. Wheeler, D., Needham, R.: TEA, a tiny encryption algorithm. In: Preneel, B. (ed.) FSE 1994. LNCS, vol. 1008, pp. 363–366. Springer, Heidelberg (1995)
17. Castro, J.C.H., Viñuela, P.I.: New results on the genetic cryptanalysis of TEA and reduced-round versions of XTEA. New Gen. Comput. **23**, 233–243 (2005)
18. Hu, W.: Cryptanalysis of TEA using quantum-inspired genetic algorithms. J. Softw. Eng. Appl. **3**, 50–57 (2010)
19. Banzhaf, W., Nordin, P., Keller, R.E., Francone, F.D.: Genetic programming: an introduction: on the automatic evolution of computer programs and its applications (1997)
20. Yao, A.C.: Theory and application of trapdoor functions. In: Proceedings of the 23rd Annual Symposium on Foundations of Computer Science, SFCS '82, pp. 80–91. IEEE Computer Society, Washington, DC (1982)
21. Webster, A.F., Tavares, S.E.: On the design of S-boxes. In: Williams, H.C. (ed.) CRYPTO 1985. LNCS, vol. 218, pp. 523–534. Springer, Heidelberg (1986)
22. Stevanović, R., Topić, G., Skala, K., Stipčević, M., Rogina, B.M.: Quantum random bit generator service for Monte Carlo and other stochastic simulations. In: Lirkov, I., Margenov, S., Waśniewski, J. (eds.) LSSC 2007. LNCS, vol. 4818, pp. 508–515. Springer, Heidelberg (2008)
23. EQRNG Service, H.u. (2014). http://qrng.physik.hu-berlin.de/
24. Ukrop, M.: Usage of evolvable circuit for statistical testing of randomness. Bachelor thesis, Masaryk university (2013)

Self-contained Data Protection Scheme Based on CP-ABE

Bo Lang$^{(\boxtimes)}$, Runhua Xu, and Yawei Duan

State Key Laboratory of Software Development Environment,
School of Computer Science and Engineering, Beihang University,
Beijing 100191, China
langbo@buaa.edu.cn, {xurunhua,duanyawei}@nlsde.buaa.edu.cn

Abstract. Self-protection capabilities of outsourced data become note-worthily important in cloud computing. Ciphertext-Policy Attribute Based Encryption (CP-ABE) can dynamically control the user group of the encrypted data by defining decryption attributes; hence has certain ability of access control. Although there are different schemes of CP-ABE, as far as we know, most of these schemes can only express simple policies with *AND*, *OR* and *threshold* attribute operations, which cannot support traditional access control policies. In order to effectively integrate access control with encryption to build a self-contained data protection mechanism, this paper proposed an Extended CP-ABE (ECP-ABE) scheme based on the existing CP-ABE scheme. The ECP-ABE scheme can express any Attribute Based Access Control (ABAC) policies represented by arithmetic comparison and logical expressions that involve $NOT, <, \leq, >, \geq, [\,], (\,), (\,]$ and $[\,)$ operators in addition to *AND*, *OR* and *threshold* operators. We prove the Chosen-plaintext Attack (CPA) security of our scheme under the Decisional Bilinear Diffie-Hellman (DBDH) assumption in the standard model, and also discuss the experimental results of the efficiency of ECP-ABE.

Keywords: Self-contained data protection · Ciphertext-policy attribute based encryption (CP-ABE) · Extended CP-ABE · Attribute based access control · Cloud computing

1 Introduction

In open computing environment such as cloud computing, the protection mechanism of outsourced data (sometimes just simply called data) attracts much more attentions [1,2]. These data departs from the control domain of its owner and is stored and managed by unreliable service providers. Hence, the self-protection capabilities of data become very important. Traditionally, access control and encryption are the two basic protection mechanisms for achieving data integrity and confidentiality. Self-contained protection of data means that data itself can ensure its integrity and confidentiality without depending on other parties.

© Springer-Verlag Berlin Heidelberg 2014
M.S. Obaidat and J. Filipe (Eds.): ICETE 2013, CCIS 456, pp. 306–321, 2014.
DOI: 10.1007/978-3-662-44788-8_18

Data encryption is the primary data self-protection means at present. Traditional Public-Key encryption and Identity Based Encryption schemes [3] are designed for one-to-one communication, which means the information encrypted by a public key or identity can only be decrypted by the specific private key. This situation has been changed since Sahai and Waters proposed the Attribute Based Encryption scheme [4], where ciphertexts are not necessarily encrypted to one particular user. Both users private keys and ciphertexts are associated with a set of attributes or a policy over attributes. When the attributes of a users private key can match the attributes of the ciphertext in a certain extent, the user can be able to decrypt the ciphertext. By defining decryption attributes, ABE can dynamically control the user group of the encrypted data.

Goyal et al. further developed this idea and introduced two variants of ABE, namely key-policy attribute based encryption (KP-ABE) and ciphertext-policy attribute based encryption (CP-ABE). In KP-ABE, whose first construction is given by [5], ciphertext is associated with a set of attributes and the secret key is associated with the access tree. A user will be able to decrypt if and only if the attributes in the ciphertext satisfy his access tree. In CP-ABE, the idea is reversed. The ciphertext is associated with the access tree and the secret key is associated with a set of attributes, and the encrypting party determines the decryption policy.

Bethencourt et al. [6] gave the initial structure of CP-ABE. We refer to this scheme as BSW07 in this paper. BSW07 is relatively expressive and efficient, but the security argument is based on generic group model, an artificial model which assumes the attacker needs to access an oracle in order to perform any group operation. After that, many researchers have presented different schemes for the less ideal security argument, trying to prove the security based on a well-studied complexity-theoretic problem. And also there are many people worked at improving the efficiency or the flexibility of access policy for the CP-ABE scheme. These schemes mainly support three kinds of access policy structures: AND-gates, tree structure and Linear Secret Share Scheme (LSSS) matrix. Among them, the tree structure and LSSS matrix are relatively flexible, which supports *AND, OR* and *threshold* operation. BSW07 uses bag of bits to express policies containing $<, \leq, >, \geq$. However, this approach is much complex and has poor scalability, and is hard to be used in practical applications. For *NOT* operator, BSW07 has no solution. To the best of our knowledge, there is no efficient way to express an access policy that contains operators such as $NOT, <, \leq, >$ and $\geq$ in present CP-ABE schemes, which makes CP-ABE only support simple attribute policies.

Access control and encryption are the two key techniques in data-centric protection, and CP-ABE makes it possible to integrate these two techniques seamlessly. However, the limited access policy expression in CP-ABE restricts its access control capability.

Our Contribution. In the area of access control, Attribute-based Access Control (ABAC) model [7–9] makes access control decisions based on user attributes. The policies in ABAC are defined as attribute expressions that contain attributes, constants, and $AND, OR, NOT, <, \leq, >, \geq, [\,], (\,), (\,]$ and $[\,)$ operators, and can express complex access control rules. If the access policy structure of CP-ABE can be enhanced to express complex attribute policies as ABAC, CP-ABE will become an ideal scheme for implementing data self-protection in open computing environments. Following this idea, we proposed the Extended CP-ABE scheme (ECP-ABE). In ECP-ABE, by introducing extended leaf nodes, the access tree of CP-ABE is enhanced to support all kinds of logical and arithmetic comparison operators, including $<, \leq, >, \geq, NOT, [\,], (\,), (\,]$ and $[\,)$. Therefore, ECP-ABE can realize powerful access control as well as encryption, and data processed by ECP-ABE will have strong self-protection capabilities. Our scheme is proven to be chosen plaintext attack (CPA) secure under the decisional Bilinear Diffie-Hellman (DBDH) assumption in the standard model.

Organization. The remaining sections are organized as follows. In Sect. 2, we introduce related work. In Sect. 3, we review the preliminaries. We present our extended CP-ABE (ECP-ABE) scheme in Sect. 4, and give an implementation framework of ECP-ABE in Sect. 5. We then discuss the performance of ECP-ABE from aspects of security and efficiency in Sect. 6. Finally, we conclude this paper in Sect. 7.

2 Related Work

BSW07 expresses the access policy by a tree structure which supports *AND, OR* and *threshold* operations. At the same time, the length of the ciphertext and the encryption or decryption time are linearly related with the number of attributes of the access structure tree. However, the security proof of BSW07 is based on generic group model, rather than the standard numerical theoretical assumptions. In addition, as a result of using polynomial interpolation to resume secret during the decryption phase, BSW07 needs greater number of bilinear mapping and exponentiation operation, and costs of these operations are relatively high.

After that many scholars have proposed different schemes [10]. Cheung and Newport first gave the CP-ABE scheme (CN07) [11] under CPA security based on DBDH assumption. However, the scheme only have the *AND* and *NOT* operator in the access policy structure, and the ability of policy expression is poor. Moreover, the length of the ciphertext and the key, and the time of encryption or decryption are linearly related with the number of attributes, which lead to the lower efficiency. Goyal et al. raised the Bounded Ciphertext Policy Attribute Based Encryption scheme [12] based on DBDH assumption, which supported the *AND, OR* and *threshold* operations.

Nishide gave an Attribute-Based encryption scheme [13] with partially hidden encryptor-specified access structures, which only supported the *AND* operation and attributes have more than one candidate value. Emura et al. first raised the CP-ABE with constant ciphertext length based on Nishide's scheme [14], which improved the efficiency of the algorithm. But it also just supported the *AND* operation. Ibraimi et al. gave an efficient and provable secure CP-ABE scheme [15] based on DBDH assumption using the threshold secret share technology [16], which supported *AND, OR* and *threshold* operations. Its access structure was an n-tree and the costs of key generation, encryption and decryption are lower than the BSW07 scheme. Waters has used the LSSS matrix to express the access control policy and pointed out that the ability of expression is not lower than the tree structure [17].

In order to support complex Boolean access policies, Junod and Karlov [18] proposed an efficient public-key ABBE scheme allowing arbitrary access policies, which is based on a modification of the Boneh-Gentry-Waters broadcast encryption scheme. Chen et al. [19] presented two new CP-ABE schemes, which have both constant-size and constant computation costs for a non-monotone AND gate policy. Jin et al. [20] enhanced the attribute-based encryption with attribute hierarchy and obtain a provable secure HABE under tree hierarchy. Attrapadung et al. [21,22] proposed the first KP-ABE schemes allowing for non-monotonic access structures and with constant ciphertext size. Wan et al. [23] proposed a hierarchical attribute-set-based encryption (HASBE) scheme which extended the ciphertext-policy attribute-set-based encryption for access control in cloud computing.

From the view of security and expressive ability of access policy, only the W08 and ITHJ09 scheme supported the AND, OR and threshold operation under the theoretical assumptions of the standard numerical. And the computation cost of encryption and decryption of ITHJ09 is lower than W08's. Therefore, we choose ITHJ09 as the basic CP-ABE scheme, and further expand the access policy tree of ITHJ09 to construct an Extended CP-ABE scheme.

3 Preliminaries

3.1 Access Tree

Definition 1 *(Access Tree [6]). Let τ be a tree representing a kind of **Access Structure** [24]. Each non-leaf node of the tree represents a threshold gate, described by its children and a threshold value. If num_x is the number of children of a node x and k_x is its threshold value, then $0 < k_x < num_x$. When $k_x = 1$, the threshold gate is an OR gate and when $k_x = num_x$, it is an AND gate. Each leaf node x of the tree is described by an attribute and a threshold value $k_x = 1$.*

We define tree functions over the tree. The function **parent**(x) represents the parent of node x. If x is a leaf node, we define the function **attr**(x) to denote the attribute with the leaf node. As the access tree has an ordering between the children of every node, the function **index**(x) represents the index number of each child node.

Definition 2 *(Satisfied Access Tree [6]). Let τ be an access tree with root r. Denote by τ_x the subtree of τ rooted at the node x. Thus, τ is the same as τ_r. If a set of attributes γ satisfies the access tree τ_x, we denote it as $\tau_x(\gamma) = 1$. We compute $\tau_x(\gamma)$ recursively as follows. If x is a non-leaf node, evaluate $\tau_{x'}(\gamma)$ for all children x' of node x. $\tau_x(\gamma)$ returns 1 if and only if at least k_x children return 1. If x is a leaf node, then $\tau_x(\gamma)$ returns 1 if and only if **att**$(x) \in \gamma$.*

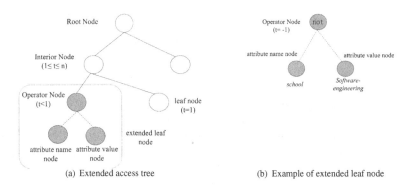

(a) Extended access tree   (b) Example of extended leaf node

Fig. 1. Extend access tree.

3.2 CP-ABE Algorithms

The ciphertext-policy attribute based encryption scheme consists of four fundamental algorithms [6]: Setup, Encrypt, Key Generation, and Decrypt.

- **Setup** (k). The setup algorithm takes no input other than the security parameter k. It outputs the public parameters PK and a master key MK.
- **Key-Generation** (MK, S). The key generation algorithm takes as input the master key MK and a set of attributes S that describe the key. It outputs a private key SK.
- **Encrypt** (PK, M, A). The encryption algorithm takes as input the public parameters PK, a message M, and an access structure A over the universe of attributes. The algorithm will encrypt M and produce a ciphertext C_T such that only a user that possesses a set of attributes that satisfies the access structure will be able to decrypt the message. We will assume that the ciphertext implicitly contains A.
- **Decrypt** (PK, C_T, SK). The decryption algorithm takes as input the public parameters PK, a ciphertext C_T which contains an access policy A, and a private key SK. If the set S of attributes satisfies the access structure A then the algorithm will decrypt the ciphertext and return a message M, otherwise return the error symbol $\bot$.

4   ECP-ABE Scheme

The ITHJ09 used Shamir secret sharing technique to support *AND, OR* and *of* (threshold) nodes based on CP-ABE scheme. The access policy tree is n-ary tree. Each node has two attributes: the number of child nodes n and threshold value $t(1 \leq t \leq n)$. When $t = 1$, it's an *OR* gate; when $t = n$, it's an *AND* gate; when $1 < t < n$, it's an *of* gate. The leaf node associates policy properties and its value t is 1. The ECP-ABE scheme we proposed is based on the ITHJ09 scheme and we extend the access tree to make it be able to express the complex policies that contain arithmetic and logical expressions.

4.1   Extended Leaf Node

The universal attribute set U is published by the Trusted Authority. Each user has his or her attribute set w which is used for key generation and we refer to it as the basic attribute set. In Attribute Based Access Control system, user's access right could be dynamically calculated according to his security character and the resource which he applies for. Inspired by this, we extend the leaf node of the access policy tree.

We replace the original leaf node with the *operator node* and give it two children, which we refer to as the *attribute name node* and the *attribute value node*, as shown in Fig. 1(a). The *operator node*, the *attribute name node* and the *attribute value node* compose an *extended leaf node*, and the attribute expression described by an extended leaf node is called an extended attribute, for instance, the attribute "age > 18" is an extended attribute. Meanwhile, the range of threshold value t of the extended leaf node is less than 0 from the original value 1.

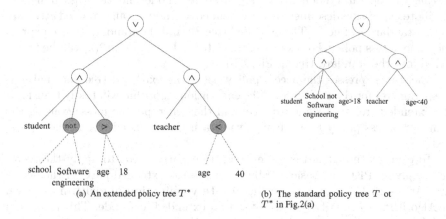

(a) An extended policy tree T^* (b) The standard policy tree T of T^* in Fig.2(a)

Fig. 2. Examples of extended and standard access policy tree.

The operator node only has the threshold value $t(t < 0)$. Different value of t denotes specific operator, for instance, $t = -1$ for NOT operator, $t = -2$ for > operator. The attribute name/value node denotes the attribute name and the attribute value respectively that are associated with the operator. With this structure, we can express policy attributes using operators of $NOT, <, \leq, >,$ $\geq, [\,], (\,), (\,]$ and $[\,)$. Figure 1(b) is an example of this structure, which express the policy attribute school not software-engineering.

ECP-ABE scheme augments two kinds of operators: comparison operators and logic operators.

- Comparison operators: $<, \leq, >, \geq$.
- Interval operators: $[\,], (\,), (\,], [\,)$.
- Logic operators: *not*.

The values of t and the corresponding operator that each value represents are defined in Table 1.

Table 1. Values of t and its corresponding operator.

Value t	-1	-2	-3	-4	-5	-6	-7	-8	-9
Operator	not	$<$	$>$	$\leq$	$\geq$	$[\,]$	$(\,)$	$(\,]$	$[\,)$

4.2 Transforming an Extended Policy Tree to a Standard Tree

Now we define the extended policy tree as the *extended tree* T^* and the original tree is called the *standard tree* T. An extended tree can be transformed to an equivalent standard tree by removing the attribute name/value node, converting the operator node to the standard leaf node and then assigning the attribute expression described by the extended leaf node as an extended attribute to the standard leaf node. The extended tree T^* and the standard tree T express the same access policy. For example, the extended tree in Fig. 2(a) can be transferred into the standard tree in Fig. 2(b).

The user expresses the access policy using the extended tree and makes it the parameter for the encryption. The encryption algorithm will firstly transform the extended tree to a standard tree, and then encrypts the message using the standard access policy tree. Finally, we attach the extended tree in the ciphertext.

To decrypt the ciphertext, the decryption party needs to apply the secret key by giving PKG his basic attribute set and the extended parts of the access tree. At the PKG side, we use the **attribute verification algorithm** as shown in Algorithm 1 to verify and transform an extended leaf node. This algorithm will first get user's basic attribute set and then traverse the attribute set to check whether or not the attribute N satisfies the expression $exp(N.O.V)$. If the answer is yes, it returns the string form of $exp(N.O.V)$, i.e. "*attribute name operator attribute value*" which is regarded as an *extended attribute* of the user. Otherwise it will return null.

Here is an example of the transformation.

There is a file F in a campus network system and the file has an access policy: "It can be accessed if and only if the user is a teacher under age of 40 or an older than 18-year-old student who is not in school of software-engineering". So, we can give the policy "$T^* = (student \land school not software-engineering \land age > 18) \lor (teacher \land age < 40)$", and the extended access tree for this policy is shown in Fig. 2(a). Figure 2(b) is the standard access tree which converts from the extended tree in Fig. 2(a). The encryption party encrypts the file F with T and attaches T^* in the ciphertext.

Suppose user A and user B wants to decrypt the file F. The basic attributes of A is {*student, school=computer science, age=20*}, and the basic attributes of

---

Algorithm 1. Attribute Verification.

1   Get the expression $exp(N.O.V)$ of the extended leaf node, where N,O and V denote
     the basic attribute name, the operator array and the attribute value array respectively;
2   Traverse the basic attribute set A' to find the basic attribute N and its value V';
3   Let O_{size} be the size of the array O, V_{size} be the size of the array V;
4   **if** $O_{size} == 1$ & & $V_{size} == 1$
5   Let $N=V$', calculate the boolean expression N.O[1].V[1];
6   **if** the value of the expression is true
7   Convert $exp(N.O.V)$ to string S=N.O[1].V[1];
8   return S;
9   **else**
10   return null;
11   **end if**
12   **else if** $O_{size} == 2$ & & $V_{size} == 2$
13   Let $N=V$', calculate the boolean expression V[1].O[1].N.O[2].V[2];
14   **if** the value of the expression is true
15   Convert $exp(N.O.V)$ to string S=V[1].O[1].N.O[2].V[2];
16   return S;
17   **else**
18   return null;
19   **end if**
20   **else**
21   return null;
22   **end if**

B is {*student, school=computer science, age=17*}. Firstly, Both A and B need
to extract the extended parts of T^* from the ciphertext and send them with
their basic attribute set to PKG. Then, PKG verifies and generates the new
attribute set {*student, school not software-engineering, age<18*} for A, and the
new attribute set {*student,school not software-engineering, age=17*} for B. The
corresponding private keys are generated using these new attribute sets by PGK
concurrently. Obviously, the attribute set of user B doesn't satisfy the access
policy, hence user A can decrypt the file F while user B can't.

4.3   Encryption and Decryption Process of ECP-ABE

The encryption party expresses the access policy with an extended tree and the
tree in the ciphertext is also in the extended structure. However, when encrypts
a message, the encryption algorithm will first transform the extend tree to an
equivalent standard tree and encrypt the message using the standard one. So in
the encryption phase, we can use the algorithm of ITHJ09 scheme. For ciphertexts that encrypted under different extended access trees, users have to apply for
different secret keys, since PKG need to verify and generate extended attributes
according to the extended tree and user's basic attributes. Detailed encryption
and decryption processes are described as follows.

a. **Initialize:** the system initializes and generates public parameter pk and master key mk. It gives pk to the encryption party. The description of initialization
   algorithm *Setup (k)* is as follow.

    i. Generate a bilinear group G of prime order p with a generator g and a bilinear map $e : G \times G \to G_T$.

    ii. Generate the attribute set $U = \{a_1, a_2, \ldots, a_m\}$, for some integer m, and random elements $\alpha, t_1, t_2, \ldots, t_m \in Z_p^*$. Let $y = e(g, g)^\alpha, T_j = g^{t_j} (1 \leq j \leq m)$. The public key is $pk = \{e, g, y, T_j (1 \leq j \leq m)\}$, and the master key is $mk = (\alpha, t_j (1 \leq j \leq m))$.

b. **Specify the Access Policy:** the encryption party specifies access policy, which is expressed by an extended tree T^*.

c. **Encryption:** the encryption party calls the encryption algorithm *Encrypt (m, T*, pk)* with plaintext m, the extended tree T^* and the public parameter pk. The encryption algorithm will first transform T^* to the equivalent standard tree T, and then encrypt m under T using Shamir's secret sharing technique. Finally it returns the ciphertext C_T which contains T^*, such that only users who have the secret key generated from the attributes that satisfy T^* will be able to decrypt the message. The detail description is as follows:

    i. Convert the T^* to the standard tree T;

    ii. Select a random element $s \in Z_p^*$ and compute $c_0 = g^s$ and $c_1 = M \cdot y^s = M \cdot e(g, g)^{\alpha s}$;

    iii. Set the value of the root node of T to be s, mark all child nodes as un-assigned, and mark the root node assigned. Recursively, for each un-assigned non-leaf node, do the following:

If its child nodes are un-assigned the secret s is divided using *(t,n)*-Shamir secret sharing technique. The relation of n and t is: if the symbol is *of* then $1 \leq t \leq n$; if the symbol is *AND*, then $t = n$; if the symbol is *OR*, then $t = 1$. To each child node a share secret $s_i = f(i)$ is assigned. Mark this node assigned. The function $f(x)$ is the random polynomial over Z_p: $f(x) = \sum_{j=0}^{t-1} a_j x^j$.

    iv. For each leaf attribute $a_{j,i} \in T$, compute $c_{j,i} = T_j^{s_i}$, where i denote the index of the attribute in the access tree.

    v. Return the ciphertext: $C_T = (T, c_0, c_1, \forall a_{j,i} \in T : c_{j,i})$.

d. **Secret Key Request:** when a user gets C_T and wants to decrypt, he first needs to analyze the structure of T^* and find the extended parts, then apply for the secret key by giving PKG his basic attribute set w and the extended parts of the access tree.

e. **Secret Key Generation:** PKG first verify the user's basic attribute. If the basic attributes of the user are authenticated, PKG will extract the attribute name, the attribute value and the operator, and run Algorithm 1. Attributes in w that satisfy the extended leaf node will be replaced by the returned extended attributes. Finally PKG gets the new attribute set w^* and generates the secret key sk_{w^*} corresponds to w^* and sends it back to the user. The detailed description is as follows:

    i. Select a random value $r \in Z_p^*, d_0 = g^{\alpha-r}$.

    ii. For each attribute a_j in w, compute $d_j = g^{rt_j^{-1}}$.

    iii. Return the secret key $sk_w = (d_0, \forall a_j \in w : d_j)$.

f. **Decryption:** the user calls the decryption algorithm $Decrypt(C_T, sk_{w^*})$. The algorithm returns message m if the smallest attribute set $w \in w^*$ that corresponds to sk_{w^*} satisfies T. Otherwise it returns an error symbol $\perp$. More details are as follows:

For every attribute $a_j \in w'$, computing:

$$m = \frac{c_1}{e(c_0, d_0) \cdot \prod_{a_j \in w'} e(c_{j,i}, d_j)^{l_i(0)}} \tag{1}$$

$l_i(0)$ is a Lagrange coefficient and can be computed by everyone who knows the index of the attribute in the access tree.

Proof. Correctness.

$$
\begin{aligned}
m' &= \frac{c_1}{e(c_0, d_0) \cdot \prod_{a_j \in w'} e(c_{j,i}, d_j)^{l_i(0)}} \\
&= \frac{m \cdot e(g,g)^{\alpha s}}{e(g^s, g^{\alpha-r}) \cdot e(T_j^{s_i}, g^{rt_i^{-1}})^{l_i(0)}} \\
&= \frac{m \cdot e(g,g)^{\alpha s}}{e(g^s, g^{\alpha-r}) \cdot \prod_{a_j \in w'} e(g^{t_j s_i}, g^{rt_i^{-1}})^{l_i(0)}} \\
&= \frac{m \cdot e(g,g)^{\alpha s}}{e(g^s, g^{\alpha-r}) \cdot e(g,g)^{rs}} \\
&= \frac{m \cdot e(g,g)^{\alpha s}}{e(g^s, g^{\alpha})} = m
\end{aligned}
\tag{2}
$$

5 ECP-ABE Implementation Framework

The ECP-ABE scheme can be used to protect data which is owned by enterprises and collaborative groups and is stored in a cloud. Building a practical and efficient ECP-ABE implementation mechanism is meaningful for these applications. The typical CP-ABE scheme has three basic components, which are PKG Server, Encryption party and Decryption party. In our proposed ECP-ABE implementation framework, we introduce the Attribute Authority (AA) to relieve the burdens of PKG and avoid the efficiency bottlenecks. Our ECP-ABE implementation framework is shown in Fig. 3, and the framework has four main components:

- PKG, which generates ABE private keys for users based on the attributes submitted.
- AA, which authenticates user's identity and verify the user's attribute set.
- Encrypt party, which encrypts a file.
- Decrypt party, which decrypts a ciphertext to get the original file.

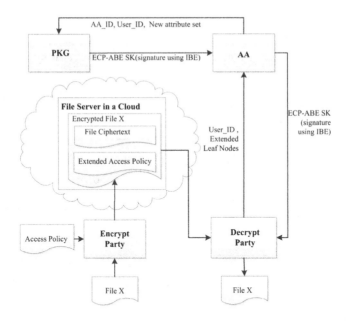

Fig. 3. The implementation framework of ECP-ABE.

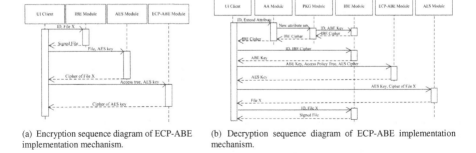

(a) Encryption sequence diagram of ECP-ABE implementation mechanism.

(b) Decryption sequence diagram of ECP-ABE implementation mechanism.

Fig. 4. Encryption/decryption process in ECP-ABE implementation framework.

In order to realize the integral data protection, the framework synthetically uses ECP-ABE, IBE and AES scheme. Among the three schemes, the AES symmetric encryption algorithm is used to encrypt the data file, and the key of AES is encrypted by ECP-ABE, while IBE provides the signature verification for the communications in the process of ECP-ABE private key distribution.

The file encryption process is achieved in the Encrypt Party of the framework, as shown in Fig. 4(a). Firstly, the user signs the file by IBE module to ensure data integrity. And then, it uses the AES symmetric encryption algorithm to encrypt the data file. The AES key is encrypted by ECP-ABE module with the extended access policy tree. At last, the Encrypt party puts the signature file, the ECP-ABE ciphertext, the data file ciphertext and the access policy file together and forms a final ciphertext.

The file decryption process is achieved in the Decrypt Party of the framework, as shown in Fig. 4(b). Firstly, the decrypt party parses the ciphertext and gets every part of the ciphertext. Then, it extracts the extended leaf nodes from the access policy tree and sends them to the AA with the ID of the user. The AA authenticates the user and verifies the extended leaf nodes using user ID and sends the new attribute set to PKG. PKG generates the ECP-ABE private key and sign it using IBE and returns it back. The decrypt party decrypts and verifies the IBE ciphertext, gets the ECP-ABE private key. Then, the AES key can be decrypted from the ECP-ABE ciphertext and the original data file is decrypted. At last, the decrypt party signed the data file using IBE and then compare signature with the original signature to verify if the file has been tampered.

6 ECP-ABE Performance Analysis

6.1 Security

The major contribution of ECP-ABE scheme is the extension of the access tree. The core encryption/decryption algorithm of ECP-ABE is based on ITHJ09 scheme. In ITHJ09 scheme semantic security under chosen-plaintext attack (CPA) is modeled by IND-sAtt-CPA game. The security model of ECP-ABE will still be based on IND-sAtt-CPA game, but the challenging access tree provided by the adversary in **Init** phase will be an extended tree instead of a standard tree. IND-sAtt-CPA game of ECP-ABE security model is as follows:

- **Init.** The adversary A chooses the challenge access tree T^* and gives it to the challenger, T^* is an extended tree.
- **Setup.** The challenger runs *Setup* to generate (pk, mk) and gives the public key pk to adversary A. The challenger also transforms T^* to the equivalent standard tree T.
- **Phase1.** Adversary A makes a secret key request to the *Keygen* oracle for any attribute set $w = \{a_j | a_j \in U\}$, with the restriction $a_j \in T^*$ and a_j does not satisfy the policy attribute requirement expressed by the extend part of T^*. The challenger runs Algorithm 1 to generate extended attribute set w^* and then returns $Keygen(w^*, mk)$.
- **Challenge.** Adversary A sends to the challenger two equal length messages m_0, m_1. The challenger picks a random bit $b \in 0, 1$ and returns $c_b = Encrypt(m_b, T^*, pk)$.
- **Phase2.** Adversary A can continue querying *Keygen* oracle with the same restriction as in **Phase1**.
- **Guess.** Adversary A outputs a guess $b' \in 0, 1$.

The advantage of A winning this game is defined as:

$$\epsilon = |Pr[b' = b] - 1/2|. \tag{3}$$

Definition 3. *We say that the* (t, ϵ)-*DBDH assumption [4, 25] holds if no t-time algorithm has advantage at least* ϵ *in solving the DBDH problem in* G_0.

Definition 4. *ECP-ABE scheme is said to be secure against an adaptive chosenplaintext attack(CPA) in the standard model if any polynomial-time adversary has only a negligible advantage in the above IND-sAtt-CPA game.*

In the above game, adversary A uses an extended tree to challenge instead of a standard tree. We have the following analyse:

- The limitation for the basic attribute set $w = \{a_j | a_j \in U\}$ provided by adversary A in **Phase1** is $a_j \notin T^*$ and a_j does not satisfy the policy attribute requirement expressed by the extended part of T^*. According to this limitation, we can infer that $\forall b_j^* \in w^*, b_j^* \notin T$. So in **Phase1**, changes of access tree will not introduce any new security problem, i.e. the secret key that A gets could not decrypt the ciphertext c_b.

- Although adversary A submits the extended tree T^* in **Init** phase, message m_b is encrypted under standard tree T. Transformation between T^* and T is public. In **Phase1**, Challenge and **Phase2**, adversary A could design the query and challenge against T^*. So the attacking ability of A keeps the same.

Hence, we can conclude that in ECP-ABE scheme the advantage of A in the IND-sAtt-CPA game equals to the advantage of A in ITHJ09 scheme, i.e. in ECP-ABE scheme any polynomial-time adversary has only a negligible advantage in the IND-sAtt-CPA game.

So ECP-ABE scheme is secure against an adaptive CPA in the standard model. Our extension for the access tree will not lower the system security compared with ITHJ09.

6.2   Efficiency

In ITHJ09 scheme, encryption requires $|T| + 1$ exponentiations in G and one exponentiation in G_T and $|T|$ is the number of attributes in the access tree T. Key generation requires $|w| + 1$ exponentiations in G, w is the attribute set the user has. Decryption requires $|w'| + 1$ pairing operations, $|w'|$ multiplications, w' is the set of attributes satisfying the access tree, $w' \in w$.

ECP-ABE uses the encryption and decryption algorithms of ITHJ09 scheme, so the calculation expenses and the length of ciphertext are the same as ITHJ09. The ECP-ABE scheme has two main differences compared with ITHJ09 scheme: the ECP-ABE has the conversion from an extended tree to a standard tree during the encryption; it also has the verification and transformation of extended attributes during the key generation. Meanwhile, in ECP-ABE, the attribute set used to generate the private key will be expanded after the extended leaf node transformation. Therefore, the added calculation expense comes from the following two factors:

- The transformation from the extended tree to the standard tree during the encryption phase.

- The verification and transformation of the extended attributes during the key generation phase.

The following experiments illustrate the impact of the above factors on the actual efficiency.

We use two groups of policy files as the test samples. One group only contains policies with the standard attributes which are used as the policies of the ITHJ09 scheme, and the other only contains policies with the extended attributes which are used as the policies of our ECP-ABE scheme. Each group has 10 test policy files to test the efficiency and the number of attribute node varies from 1 to 10. The access tree is a two-tier structure when there are 1–4 attribute nodes, a three-tier structure when there are 5–7 attribute nodes, and a four-tier structure when there are 8–10 attribute nodes.

We run three times for each test policy file and get the average cost as the result. Figure 5 is the result of the tests.

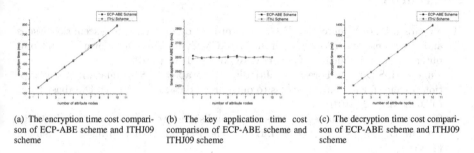

(a) The encryption time cost comparison of ECP-ABE scheme and ITHJ09 scheme

(b) The key application time cost comparison of ECP-ABE scheme and ITHJ09 scheme

(c) The decryption time cost comparison of ECP-ABE scheme and ITHJ09 scheme

Fig. 5. The efficiency comparison of ECP-ABE and ITHJ09 scheme.

Discussion: the verification of the extended leaf nodes and the transformation from the extended tree to the standard tree nearly have no effect on the performance during the encryption and key application phase. However, the ECP-ABE scheme has greatly enhanced the access policy expression capability.

7 Conclusions

The paper proposed an ECP-ABE scheme, which introduces the extended leaf nodes into the access policy tree to support access policy formulas involving operators including $NOT, <, \leq, >, \geq, [\,], (\,), (\,]$ and $[\,)$ in addition to AND, OR and $threshold$ operators. Hence the scheme enhanced access control ability of CP-ABE prominently, and achieved self-contained protection for outsourced data in open computing environments.

ECP-ABE adopts the same implementation mechanism as other CP-ABE schemes. Basing on the experiments analysis, we can see that our scheme has nearly the same expense compared with ITHJ09 scheme, and ECP-ABE scheme is proven chosen plaintext attack (CPA) secure under the decisional Bilinear Diffie-Hellman assumption in the standard model. Hence, ECP-ABE can keep the security and efficiency properties of the CP-ABE scheme which it based on, but prominently improves the access capability of the baseline scheme. Also, the policy extension method used in ECP-ABE is not limited to the ITHJ09 scheme; it can be used on other CP-ABE schemes that utilize tree-based access policy structures.

For future work, it would be interesting to probe other more efficient way to enhance the access control capability of CP-ABE schemes, such as working on other access policy structures like LSSS.

Acknowledgments. This work was supported by the National Natural Science Foundation of China (Grant No.61170088) and Foundation of the State Key Laboratory of Software Development Environment (Grant No. SKLSDE-2013ZX-05).

References

1. Samarati, P., di Vimercati, S.D.C.: Data protection in outsourcing scenarios: issues and directions. In: Proceedings of the 5th ACM Symposium on Informational Computer and Communications Security, ACM, pp. 1–14 (2010)
2. Vimercati, S.D.C.D., Foresti, S., Jajodia, S., Paraboschi, S., Samarati, P.: Encryption policies for regulating access to outsourced data. ACM Trans. Database Syst. (TODS) **35**, 12 (2010)
3. Shamir, A.: Identity-based cryptosystems and signature schemes. In: Blakely, G.R., Chaum, D. (eds.) CRYPTO 1984. LNCS, vol. 196, pp. 47–53. Springer, Heidelberg (1985)
4. Sahai, A., Waters, B.: Fuzzy Identity-Based Encryption. In: Cramer, R. (ed.) EUROCRYPT 2005. LNCS, vol. 3494, pp. 457–473. Springer, Heidelberg (2005)
5. Goyal, V., Pandey, O., Sahai, A., Waters, B.: Attribute-based encryption for fine-grained access control of encrypted data. In: Proceedings of the 13th ACM Conference on Computer and Communications Security, ACM, pp. 89–98 (2006)
6. Bethencourt, J., Sahai, A., Waters, B.: Ciphertext-policy attribute-based encryption. In: 2007 IEEE Symposium on Security and Privacy, SP'07, IEEE, pp. 321–334 (2007)
7. Hur, J., Noh, D.K.: Attribute-based access control with efficient revocation in data outsourcing systems. IEEE Trans. Parallel Distrib. Syst. **22**, 1214–1221 (2011)
8. Lang, B., Foster, I., Siebenlist, F., Ananthakrishnan, R., Freeman, T.: A flexible attribute based access control method for grid computing. J. Grid Comput. **7**, 169–180 (2009)
9. Wang, G., Liu, Q., Wu, J.: Hierarchical attribute-based encryption for fine-grained access control in cloud storage services. In: Proceedings of the 17th ACM Conference on Computer and Communications Security, ACM, pp. 735–737 (2010)
10. Su, J.S., Cao, D., Wang, X.F., Sun, Y.P., Hu, Q.L.: Attribute based encryption schemes. J. Softw. **22**, 1299–1315 (2011)
11. Cheung, L., Newport, C.: Provably secure ciphertext policy ABE. In: Proceedings of the 14th ACM Conference on Computer and Communications Security, ACM, pp. 456–465 (2007)

12. Goyal, V., Jain, A., Pandey, O., Sahai, A.: Bounded ciphertext policy attribute based encryption. In: Aceto, L., Damgård, I., Goldberg, L.A., Halldórsson, M.M., Ingólfsdóttir, A., Walukiewicz, I. (eds.) ICALP 2008, Part II. LNCS, vol. 5126, pp. 579–591. Springer, Heidelberg (2008)
13. Nishide, T., Yoneyama, K., Ohta, K.: Attribute-based encryption with partially hidden encryptor-specified access structures. In: Bellovin, S.M., Gennaro, R., Keromytis, A.D., Yung, M. (eds.) ACNS 2008. LNCS, vol. 5037, pp. 111–129. Springer, Heidelberg (2008)
14. Emura, K., Miyaji, A., Nomura, A., Omote, K., Soshi, M.: A ciphertext-policy attribute-based encryption scheme with constant ciphertext length. In: Bao, F., Li, H., Wang, G. (eds.) ISPEC 2009. LNCS, vol. 5451, pp. 13–23. Springer, Heidelberg (2009)
15. Ibraimi, L., Tang, Q., Hartel, P., Jonker, W.: Efficient and provable secure ciphertext-policy attribute-based encryption schemes. In: Bao, F., Li, H., Wang, G. (eds.) ISPEC 2009. LNCS, vol. 5451, pp. 1–12. Springer, Heidelberg (2009)
16. Shamir, A.: How to share a secret. Commun. ACM 22, 612–613 (1979)
17. Waters, B.: Ciphertext-policy attribute-based encryption: an expressive, efficient, and provably secure realization. In: Catalano, D., Fazio, N., Gennaro, R., Nicolosi, A. (eds.) PKC 2011. LNCS, vol. 6571, pp. 53–70. Springer, Heidelberg (2011)
18. Junod, P., Karlov, A.: An efficient public-key attribute-based broadcast encryption scheme allowing arbitrary access policies. In: Proceedings of the Tenth Annual ACM Workshop on Digital Rights Management, ACM, pp. 13–24 (2010)
19. Chen, C., Zhang, Z., Feng, D.: Efficient ciphertext policy attribute-based encryption with constant-size ciphertext and constant computation-cost. In: Boyen, X., Chen, X. (eds.) ProvSec 2011. LNCS, vol. 6980, pp. 84–101. Springer, Heidelberg (2011)
20. Li, J., Wang, Q., Wang, C., Ren, K.: Enhancing attribute-based encryption with attribute hierarchy. Mob. Netw. Appl. 16, 553–561 (2011)
21. Attrapadung, N., Libert, B., de Panafieu, E.: Expressive key-policy attribute-based encryption with constant-size ciphertexts. In: Catalano, D., Fazio, N., Gennaro, R., Nicolosi, A. (eds.) PKC 2011. LNCS, vol. 6571, pp. 90–108. Springer, Heidelberg (2011)
22. Attrapadung, N., Herranz, J., Laguillaumie, F., Libert, B., De Panafieu, E., Ràfols, C.: Attribute-based encryption schemes with constant-size ciphertexts. Theor. Comput. Sci. 422, 15–38 (2012)
23. Wan, Z., Liu, J., Deng, R.H.: Hasbe: a hierarchical attribute-based solution for flexible and scalable access control in cloud computing. IEEE Trans. Inf. Forensics Secur. 7, 743–754 (2012)
24. Beimel, A.: Secure schemes for secret sharing and key distribution. Ph.D. thesis. Israel Institute of Technology, Technion, Haifa, Israel (1996)
25. Boneh, D., Boyen, X.: Efficient selective-ID secure identity-based encryption without random oracles. In: Cachin, C., Camenisch, J.L. (eds.) EUROCRYPT 2004. LNCS, vol. 3027, pp. 223–238. Springer, Heidelberg (2004)

An Efficient Framework for Evaluating the Risk of Zero-Day Vulnerabilities

Massimiliano Albanese[1], Sushil Jajodia[1,2(✉)],
Anoop Singhal[3], and Lingyu Wang[4]

[1] Center for Secure Information Systems, George Mason University,
4400 University Dr, Fairfax, VA 22030, USA
jaodia@gmu.edu
[2] The MITRE Corporation, 7515 Colshire Dr, McLean, VA 22102, USA
[3] Computer Security Division, NIST, 100 Bureau Dr, Gaithersburg, MD 20899, USA
[4] Concordia Institute for Information Systems Engineering, Concordia University,
1515 Sainte-Catherine St W, Montreal, QC H3G 2W1, Canada

Abstract. Computer systems are vulnerable to both known and zero-day attacks. Although known attack patterns can be easily modeled, thus enabling the definition of suitable hardening strategies, handling zero-day vulnerabilities is inherently difficult due to their unpredictable nature. Previous research has attempted to assess the risk associated with unknown attack patterns, and a metric to quantify such risk, the k-zero-day safety metric, has been defined. However, existing algorithms for computing this metric are not scalable, and assume that complete zero-day attack graphs have been generated, which may be unfeasible in practice for large networks. In this paper, we propose a framework comprising a suite of polynomial algorithms for estimating the k-zero-day safety of possibly large networks efficiently, without pre-computing the entire attack graph. We validate our approach experimentally, and show that the proposed solution is computationally efficient and accurate.

Keywords: Zero-day attacks · Vulnerability analysis · Attack graphs

1 Introduction

In today's networked systems, attackers can leverage complex interdependencies among network configurations and vulnerabilities to penetrate seemingly well-guarded networks. Besides well-known weaknesses, attackers may leverage unknown (zero-day) vulnerabilities, which developers are not aware of. In-depth analysis of network vulnerabilities must consider attacker exploits not merely

The work presented in this paper is supported in part by the National Institutes of Standard and Technology under grant number 70NANB12H236, by the Army Research Office under MURI award number W911NF-09-1-0525, and by the Office of Naval Research under award number N00014-12-1-0461. The work of Sushil Jajodia was also supported by the MITRE Sponsored Research Program.

© Springer-Verlag Berlin Heidelberg 2014
M.S. Obaidat and J. Filipe (Eds.): ICETE 2013, CCIS 456, pp. 322–340, 2014.
DOI: 10.1007/978-3-662-44788-8_19

in isolation, but in combination. Attack graphs reveal such threats by enumerating potential paths that attackers can take to penetrate networks [1,2]. This helps determine whether a given set of network hardening measures provides safety of given critical assets. However, attack graphs can only provide qualitative results, and this renders resulting hardening recommendations ineffective or far from optimal, as illustrated by the example discussed in Sect. 3.1.

To address these limitations, traditional efforts on network security metrics typically assign numeric scores to vulnerabilities as their relative exploitability or likelihood, based on known facts about each vulnerability. However, this approach is clearly not applicable to zero-day vulnerabilities due to the lack of prior knowledge or experience. In fact, a major criticism of existing efforts on security metrics is that zero-day vulnerabilities are unmeasurable due to the less predictable nature of both the process of introducing software flaws and that of discovering and exploiting vulnerabilities [3]. Recent work addresses the above limitations by proposing a security metric for zero-day vulnerabilities, namely, k-zero-day safety [4]. Intuitively, the metric is based on the number of distinct zero-day vulnerabilities that are needed to compromise a given network asset. A larger such number indicates relatively more security, because it will be less likely to have a larger number of different unknown vulnerabilities all available at the same time, applicable to the same network, and exploitable by the same attacker. However, as shown in [4], the problem of computing the exact value of k is intractable. Moreover, [4] assumes the existence of a complete attack graph, but generating attack graphs for large networks is usually infeasible in practice [5]. These facts comprise a major limitation in applying this metric or any other similar metric based on attack graphs.

In this paper, we propose a suite of efficient algorithms to address this limitation and thus enable zero-day analysis of practical importance to be applied to networks of realistic sizes. Therefore, the major contribution of this work is to provide a practical solution to a problem which was previously considered intractable. We start from the problem of deciding whether a given network asset is at least k-zero-day safe for a given value of k [4], but then we go beyond this basic problem and provide a more complete analysis. First, we drop the assumption that the zero-day vulnerability graph has been precomputed, and combine on-demand attack graph generation with the evaluation of k-zero-day safety. Second, we identify an upper bound on the value of k using a heuristic algorithm that integrates attack graph generation and zero-day analysis. Third, when the upper bound on k is below an admissible threshold, we compute the exact value of k by reusing the computed partial attack graph. Section 4 formally states the three related problems we are addressing in this paper, and shows their role within the framework. To the best of our knowledge, this is the first attempt to define a comprehensive and efficient approach to zero-day analysis.

The paper is organized as follows. Section 2 discusses related work. Section 3 recalls some preliminary definitions and provides a motivating example. Then Sect. 4 discusses the limitations of previous approaches and provides a formal statement of the problems addressed in our work. Section 5 describes our approach to efficient evaluation of k zero-day safety. Finally, Sect. 6 reports experimental results, and Sect. 7 gives some concluding remarks.

2 Related Work

Existing standardization efforts, such as the Common Vulnerability Scoring System (CVSS) [6] and the Common Weakness Scoring System (CWSS) [7], provide standard ways for security analysts and vendors to rank known vulnerabilities or software weaknesses using numerical scores. These efforts provide a practical foundation for research on security metrics, but are designed for individual vulnerabilities and do not address the combined effect of multiple vulnerabilities. Early work on security metrics include a Markov model-based metric for estimating the time and efforts required by adversaries [8], and a metric based on lengths of shortest attack paths [9]. The main limitation of these approaches is that they do not consider the relative severity or likelihood of different vulnerabilities. Another line of work adapts the PageRank algorithm to rank states in an attack graph based on the relative likelihood of attackers' reaching these states when they progress along different paths in a random fashion [10]. Other recent work uses specially marked attack trees [11] or more expressive attack graphs [12] in order to find the easiest attack paths. A Mean Time-to-Compromise metric based on the predator state-space model (SSM) captures the average time required to compromise network assets [13]. A probabilistic approach defines a network security metric as attack probabilities and derives such probabilities from CVSS scores [14]. Several important issues in calculating probabilistic security metrics, such as dependencies between attack sequences and cyclic structures, are addressed in [15].

Most existing work on network security metrics has focused on previously known vulnerabilities [3]. A few exceptions include an empirical study on the total number of zero-day vulnerabilities available on a single day [16], a study on the popularity of zero-day vulnerabilities [17], and an empirical study on software vulnerabilities' life cycles [18]. Another recent effort ranks different applications by the relative severity of having one zero-day vulnerability in each application [19], which has a different focus than our work. Closest to our work, recent work on k-zero-day safety defines a metric based on the number of potential unknown vulnerabilities in a network [4].

In this paper, we address the complexity issues associated with the metric proposed in [4], and propose a set of polynomial algorithms for estimating the k-zero-day safety of possibly large networks efficiently. The proposed zero-day attack graph model borrows the compact model given in [2] – based on the *monotonicity assumption* – while incorporating zero-day vulnerabilities.

3 Preliminaries

Attack graphs represent prior knowledge about vulnerabilities, their dependencies, and network connectivity. With a *monotonicity* assumption, an attack graph can record the dependencies among vulnerabilities and keep attack paths implicitly without losing any information. The resulting attack graph has no duplicate vertices and hence has a polynomial size in the number of vulnerabilities multiplied by the number of connected pairs of hosts.

Definition 1 (Attack Graph). *Given a set of exploits E, a set of security conditions C, a require relation $R_r \subseteq C \times E$, and an imply relation $R_i \subseteq E \times C$, an attack graph G is the directed graph $G = (E \cup C, R_r \cup R_i)$, where $E \cup C$ is the vertex set and $R_r \cup R_i$ the edge set. For an exploit e, we call the conditions related to e by R_r and R_i as its pre- and post-conditions, denoted using functions $pre : E \to 2^C$ and $post : E \to 2^C$, respectively.*

We denote an exploit as a triple $\langle v, h_s, h_d \rangle$, indicating an exploitation of vulnerability v on the destination host h_d, initiated from the source host h_s. A security condition is a pair $\langle c, h_d \rangle$ – that indicates a satisfied security-related condition c on host h_d, such as the existence of a vulnerability – or a pair $\langle h_s, h_d \rangle$ – that indicates connectivity between hosts h_s and h_d. Initial conditions are a special subset of security conditions that are initially satisfied, whereas intermediate conditions are those that can only be satisfied as post-conditions of some exploits.

Definition 2 (Initial Conditions). *Given an attack graph $G = (E \cup C, R_r \cup R_i)$, initial conditions refer to the subset of conditions $C_i = \{c \in C | \nexists e \in E \text{ s.t. } (e, c) \in R_i\}$, whereas intermediate conditions refer to the subset $C \backslash C_i$.*

3.1 Zero-Day Attack Model

The very notion of *unknown* zero-day vulnerability means we cannot assume any vulnerability-specific property, such as the likelihood or severity. Therefore, our zero-day vulnerability model is based on following generic properties that are common to most vulnerabilities. Specifically, a zero-day vulnerability is a vulnerability whose details are unknown except that its exploitation requires a network connection between the source and destination hosts, a remotely accessible service on the destination host, and that the attacker already has a privilege on the source host. In addition, we assume that the exploitation can potentially yield any privilege on the destination host. These assumptions intend to depict a worst-case scenario about the pre- and post-conditions of a zero-day exploit, and are formalized as the first type of zero-day exploit in Definition 3, whereas the second type represents subsequent privilege escalation.

Definition 3 (Zero-day Exploit). *We define two types of zero-day exploits,*

– *for each remote service s, we define a zero-day vulnerability v_s such that the zero-day exploit $\langle v_s, h, h' \rangle$ has three pre-conditions, $\langle s, h' \rangle$ (existence of service), $\langle h, h' \rangle$ (connectivity), and $\langle p, h \rangle$ (attacker's existing privilege); this zero-day exploit has one post-condition $\langle p', h' \rangle$ where p' is the privilege of service s on h'.*

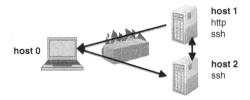

Fig. 1. Example of network configuration.

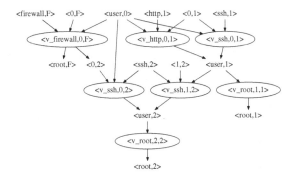

Fig. 2. Example of zero-day attack graph.

– *for each privilege p, we define a zero-day vulnerability v_p such that the zero-day exploit $\langle v_p, h, h \rangle$ has its pre-conditions to include all privileges of remote services on h, and its post-condition to be p on h.*

We use E_0 and C_0 to denote the set of all zero-day exploits and the set of all their pre- and post-conditions respectively, and we extend the functions pre() and post() accordingly.

We are now ready to assemble all known and zero-day exploits via their common pre- and post-conditions into a zero-day attack graph.

Definition 4 (Zero-Day Attack Graph). *Given an attack graph $G = (E \cup C, R_r \cup R_i)$, a set E_0 of zero-day exploits, a set C_0 of pre and post-conditions of exploits in E_0, a zero-day attack graph G^* is the directed graph $G^* = (E^* \cup C^*, R_r^* \cup R_i^*)$, where $E^* = E \cup E_0$, $C^* = C \cup C_0$, $R_r^* = R_r \cup \{(c, e) \mid e \in E_0 \wedge c \in pre(e)\}$, and $R_i^* = R_i \cup \{(e, c) \mid e \in E_0 \wedge c \in post(e)\}$.*

Figure 1 shows a simple network configuration including three hosts. Host 0 is the user's machine used to launch attacks, whereas host 1 and host 2 are machines within the perimeter of the enterprise network we are seeking to protect. Host 1 provides an HTTP service (http) and a secure shell service (ssh), whereas host 2 provides only ssh. The firewall allows traffic to and from host 1, but only connections originated from host 2. In this example, we assume the main security concern is over the root privilege on host 2. Clearly, if all the services are free of known vulnerabilities, a vulnerability scanner or attack graph will both lead to the same conclusion, that is, the network is secure (an attacker on host 0 can never obtain the root privilege on host 2), and no additional network hardening effort is necessary. However, we may reach a different conclusion by hypothesizing the presence of zero-day vulnerabilities and considering how many distinct zero-day exploits the network can resist.

Specifically, the zero-day attack graph of this example is depicted in Fig. 2, where each triple inside an oval denotes a zero-day exploit and a pair denotes a condition. In this attack graph, we can observe three sequences of zero-day exploits leading to $root(2)$. First, an attacker on host 0 can exploit a zero-day vulnerability in the firewall (e.g., a weak password in its Web-base remote administration interface) to re-establish the blocked connection to host 2 and then exploit ssh on host 2, or the attacker can exploit a zero-day vulnerability in either http or ssh on host 1 to obtain the user privilege and then, using host 1 as a stepping stone, the attacker can further exploit a zero-day vulnerability in ssh on host 2 to reach $root(2)$. Since this last sequence (ssh on host 1 and then ssh on host 2) involves one zero-day vulnerability in the ssh service on both hosts, this network can resist at most one zero-day attack. Contrary to the previous belief that further hardening this network is not necessary, this zero-day attack graph shows that further hardening may indeed improve the security. For example, suppose we limit accesses to the ssh service on host 1 using a personal firewall or iptables rules, such that an arbitrary host 0 cannot reach this service from the Internet. We can then imagine that the new attack graph will only include sequences of at least two different zero-day vulnerabilities (e.g., the attacker must first exploit the personal firewall or iptables rules before exploiting ssh on host 1). This seemingly unnecessary hardening effort thus can help the network resist one more zero-day attack.

4   Problem Statement

The exact algorithm for computing the k-zero-day safety metric presented in [4] first derives a logic proposition of each asset in terms of exploits by traversing the attack graph backwards. Each conjunctive clause in the disjunctive normal form (DNF) of the derived proposition corresponds to a minimal set of exploits that jointly compromise the asset. The value of k can then be decided by applying the metric $k0d()$ – which counts the number of distinct zero-day vulnerabilities – to each such conjunctive clause. Although the logic proposition can be derived efficiently, converting it to its DNF may incur an exponential explosion. In fact, the authors of [4] show that the problem of computing the k-zero day safety metrics is NP-hard in general, and then focus on the solution of a more practical problem. They claim that, for many practical purposes, it may suffice to know that every asset in a network is k-zero-day safe for a given value of k, even though the network may in reality be k'-zero-day safe for some unknown $k' > k$ (note that determining k' is intractable). Then, they describe a solution whose complexity is polynomial in the size of a zero-day attack graph if k is a constant compared to this size. However, there are cases in which it is not satisfactory to just know $k' > k$, but more accurate estimations or exact calculation of the value of k is desired. Moreover, those analyses are all based on complete zero-day attack graphs, but for really large networks, it may even be infeasible to generate the zero-day attack graph in the first place. The metric then becomes impractical in such cases since there is little we can say about the value of k.

The aforementioned intractability result means no polynomial algorithm will likely exist for computing the exact value of k. However, in this section we show that a decision process may still allow security administrators to obtain good estimations about k, and to calculate the exact value of k when it is practically feasible. Our main objectives are three-fold. First, all the algorithms involved in the decision process will be efficient and have polynomial complexity. Second, all the algorithms will adopt an on-demand approach to attack graph generation, which will only generate partial attack graphs necessary for the analysis. Third, subsequent algorithms will reuse the partial attack graph already generated earlier in the decision process, thus further improving the overall efficiency. With those optimizations, we can provide a better understanding of zero-day vulnerabilities even for relatively large networks. Specifically, in most practical scenarios, security administrators may simply want to assess *whether the network or specific assets are secure enough*. In such cases, knowing that k is larger than or equal to a given lower bound l may be sufficient. However, once it has been confirmed that $k > l$, a security administrator may want to know *whether it is possible to compute the exact value of k*. Since the problem of computing the exact value of k is intractable, this may only be possible for relatively small values of k. Therefore, we need to estimate whether k is less than a practical upper bound that represents available computational power. Finally, if this is true, then we can proceed to *calculate the actual value of k in an efficient way*. In the following, we formalize the three related problems that form the basis of the above decision process. We describe a solution to each of these problem in the next section.

Problem 1 (Lower Bound). Given a network N, a goal condition c_g, and a small integer l, determine whether $k \geq l$ is true for N with respect to c_g.

Our goal is to identify a lower bound on the value of k. This problem is analogous to the practical problem addressed in [4], but we do not assume the entire attack graph is available. We simply assume that the network is defined in terms of initial conditions C_i and known and unknown exploits E^*.

Problem 2 (Upper Bound). Given a network N, a goal condition c_g, and an integer u, find an upper bound u on the value of k with respect to c_g.

Our goal is to identify an upper bound on the value of k. We show that, using a heuristic approach, it is feasible to compute a good upper bound in polynomial time. If the value of u is below a threshold u^*, it may then be feasible to compute the exact value of k.

Problem 3 (Exact Value). Given a network N, and a goal condition c_g such that $l \leq k \leq u \leq u^*$ is true for N with respect to c_g, find the exact value of k.

In other words, when the value of k is known to be bounded and the upper bound is small enough, we will compute the exact value of k, leveraging the upper bound u for pruning, and reusing the partial attack graph generated during previous steps of the decision process. Figure 3 shows the role of these three problems in the overall decision process.

5 Proposed Solution

5.1 Solution for Problem 1

The existing solution for this problem assumes that the entire zero-day attack graph is available [4], which is impractical since generating such an attack graph may be infeasible for large networks. Paths with up to l zero-day vulnerabilities are generated and evaluated using the metric. The idea behind our solution is to combine an exhaustive forward search of limited depth with partial attack graph generation, so that only attack

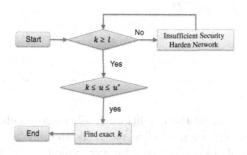

Fig. 3. Flowchart of the decision process.

We use connectivity information to hypothesize zero-day exploits (see Definition 3) and guide the generation of the graph.

Algorithm $k0dLowerBound$ (Algorithm 1) takes as input a set C_i of initial conditions on hosts, the set E^* of known and zero-day exploits, an integer $l \in \mathbb{N}$ representing the desired lower bound on the value of k, and a goal condition $c_g \in C^*$. It returns a partial zero-day attack graph $G = (E \cup C, R_r \cup R_i)$, and a truth value indicating whether $k \geq l$.

For ease of presentation, we consider problems with a single goal condition. The generalization to the case where multiple target conditions need to be considered at the same time is straightforward and is discussed below. Given a set C_g of goal conditions, we can add a dummy exploit e_g, such that e_g has each $c_i \in C_g$ as a precondition. Then, we can add a dummy goal condition c_g as the only postcondition of e_g. It is clear that the minimum number of zero-day

Algorithm 1. $k0dLowerBound(C_i, E^*, l, c_g)$.

Input: Set C_i of initial conditions, set E^* of known and zero-day exploits, integer $l \in \mathbb{N}$ representing the desired lower bound on k, and goal condition $c_g \in C^*$.
Output: Partial zero-day attack graph $G = (E \cup C, R_r \cup R_i)$, and a truth value indicating whether $k \geq l$.

```
 1: C ← Cᵢ
 2: E ← ∅
 3: Cₙₑw ← Cᵢ
 4: for all c ∈ Cᵢ do
 5:     π(c) ← ∅
 6: end for
 7: while Cₙₑw ≠ ∅ do
 8:     Eₙₑw ← {e ∈ E | pre(e) ⊆ C ∧ pre(e) ∩ Cₙₑw ≠ ∅}    // Unvisited exploits reachable from C
 9:     for all e ∈ Eₙₑw do
10:         for all c ∈ pre(e) do
11:             Rᵣ ← Rᵣ ∪ {(c,e)}    // Add an edge from c to e
12:         end for
13:         {c₁,...,cₘ} ← {c ∈ C | (c,e) ∈ Rᵣ}
14:         π(e) ← {P₁ ∪ ... ∪ Pₘ ∪ {e} | Pᵢ ∈ π(cᵢ)}
15:         π(e) ← {P ∈ π(e) | k0d(P) < l}    // Prune paths with l or more zero-day vulnerabilities
16:     end for
17:     Cₙₑw ← ∅
18:     for all e ∈ Eₙₑw s.t. π(e) ≠ ∅  do
19:         for all c ∈ post(e) do
20:             Rᵢ ← Rᵢ ∪ {(e,c)}    // Add an edge from e to c
21:             Cₙₑw ← Cₙₑw ∪ {c}
22:             if c ≡ cg then
23:                 return G, false
24:             end if
25:             π(c) ← ⋃ₑ∈E|(e,c)∈Rᵢ π(e)
26:         end for
27:     end for
28:     C ← C ∪ Cₙₑw
29:     E ← E ∪ Eₙₑw
30: end while
31: return G, true
```

exploits needed to reach all the conditions in C_g corresponds to the minimum number of zero-day exploits needed to reach the dummy goal condition c_g. In fact, as c_g is reachable only from the dummy exploit e_g, all the preconditions of e_g must be satisfied, therefore all the actual goal conditions in C_g must be reached.

Lines 1–6 of algorithm $k0dLowerBound$ simply initialize the sets of conditions and exploits in the partial attack graph, the set C_{new} of newly satisfied conditions, and the mapping $\pi : E \cup C \rightarrow 2^{2^E}$ which associates each exploit or condition with a set of attack paths leading to it, where an attack path is a set of exploits. By default, $\pi(c) = \emptyset$ for all $c \in C_i$. The set C_{new} will initially contain all the initial conditions, whereas in each subsequent iteration of the algorithm it will contain the conditions implied by exploit visited in that iteration. The main loop at Lines 7–30 iterates until the goal condition is reached (Lines 22–24) or the set of newly satisfied conditions becomes empty – which means that no path with fewer than l distinct zero-day vulnerabilities can reach the goal condition. In the first case the algorithm returns $false$ (i.e., $k < l$), otherwise it returns $true$ (i.e., $k \geq l$).

Line 8 defines the set E_{new} of unvisited exploits reachable from C. An exploit is *unvisited* if at least one of its preconditions is in C_{new}. For each $e \in E_{new}$, Lines 10–12 add edges from all preconditions of e to e itself, and Lines 13–14 compute partial attack paths leading to and including e. Finally, Line 15 prunes all attack paths with l or more distinct zero-day vulnerabilities. As an exploit needs all the preconditions to be satisfied, an attack path for e is constructed by combining an attack path to each precondition.

Once all the newly visited exploits have been processed and added to the attack graph, the algorithm considers the new conditions that are implied by such exploits. For each $e \in E_{new}$ such that at least one partial path reaching e has $k0d(P) < l$, and each condition c in $post(e)$, Lines 20–21 add an edge from e to c to the graph and update C_{new} (which was reset on Line 17), and Line 25 computes the set $\pi(c)$ of attack paths leading to c as the union of the sets of attack paths leading to each of the exploit implying c, unless c is the goal condition, in which case the algorithm terminates.

Example 1. When applied to the graph in Fig. 2, Algorithm *k0dLowerBound* (Algorithm 1) will proceed by each horizontal level of conditions and exploits, from top to bottom, until it reaches the second level of exploits (i.e., $\langle v_{ssh}, 0, 2 \rangle$, $\langle v_{ssh}, 1, 2 \rangle$, and $\langle v_{root}, 1, 1 \rangle$). Suppose l is given to be 2, then obviously all the paths up to now will be pruned by Line 15 (since each of them includes two distinct zero-day vulnerabilities, failing the condition $k0d(P) < l$), except the path $\langle v_{ssh}, 0, 1 \rangle$, $\langle v_{ssh}, 1, 2 \rangle$ (which includes only one vulnerability v_{ssh}). Therefore, the next loop on Lines 18–27 will be skipped for exploit $\langle v_{ssh}, 0, 2 \rangle$ and $\langle v_{root}, 1, 1 \rangle$ (meaning the partial attack graph generation stops at those exploits), but it continues from exploit $\langle v_{ssh}, 1, 2 \rangle$ (the final result will depend on whether we assume $\langle v_{ssh}, 1, 2 \rangle$ directly yields $\langle root, 2 \rangle$).

The complexity of Algorithm *k0dLowerBound* (Algorithm 1) is clearly dominated by the steps for extending the paths on Lines 13–15. Specifically, the loop at Line 7 will run at most $\mid C \mid$ times; the nested loop at Line 9 will run $\mid E \mid$ times; steps 13–15 will involve at most $\mid E \mid^l$ paths each of which has maximum possible length of $\mid E \mid$. Therefore, the overall complexity is $O(\mid C \mid \cdot \mid E \mid \cdot \mid E \mid^l \cdot \mid E \mid) = O(\mid C \mid \cdot \mid E \mid^l)$, which is polynomial when l is given as a constant (compared to attack graph size).

5.2   Solution for Problem 2

In this section, we propose a solution to Problem 2. As we did for the previous algorithm, instead of building the entire attack graph, we only build the portions of the attack graph that are most promising for finding an upper bound on the value of k. In order to avoid the exponential explosion of the search space – which includes all the sets of exploits leading to the goal condition – we design an heuristic algorithm that maintains only the best partial paths with respect to the $k0d$ metric.

Algorithm *k0dUpperBound* (Algorithm 2) builds the attack graph forward, starting from initial conditions. A key advantage of building the attack graph

---

Algorithm 2. $k0dUpperBound(C_i, E^*, c_g)$.

Input: Set C_i of initial conditions, set E^* of known and zero-day exploits, and goal condition
$c_g \in C^*$.
Output: Partial zero-day attack graph $G = (E \cup C, R_r \cup R_i)$, mapping $\pi : C \cup E \to 2^{2^E}$, mapping
$zdu : C \to \mathbb{N}$, and upper bound u on the value of k.
1: $C \leftarrow C_i$
2: $R_r \leftarrow \emptyset$
3: $R_i \leftarrow \emptyset$
4: **for all** $c \in C_i$ **do**
5:   $\pi(c) \leftarrow \emptyset$
6:   $zdu(c) \leftarrow 0$
7: **end for**
8: $E \leftarrow \{e \in E^* \,|\, pre(e) \subseteq C\}$
9: **for all** $e \in E$ **do**
10:   **for all** $c \in pre(e)$ **do**
11:     $R_r \leftarrow R_r \cup \{(c, e)\}$
12:   **end for**
13:   $\pi(e) \leftarrow \{\{e\}\}$
14:   $zdu(e) \leftarrow k0d(\{e\})$
15: **end for**
16: $\langle E_1, \ldots, E_n \rangle \leftarrow rankedPartition(E)$
17: $i \leftarrow 0$
18: **while** $c_g \notin C \wedge i \leq n$ **do**
19:   $i \leftarrow i + 1$
20:   $u \leftarrow DFS(E_i)$
21: **end while**
22: **return** $G, \pi(), zdu(), u$

---

forward is that intermediate solutions are indeed estimates of the upper bound on
k for intermediate conditions. In fact, in a single pass, algorithm $k0dUpperBound$
can estimate an upper bound on k with respect to any condition in C. To limit
the exponential explosion of the search space, intermediate solutions can be
pruned – based on some pruning strategy – whereas this would not be possible
for an algorithm building the attack graph backwards.

The algorithm takes as input the set C_i of initial conditions on hosts, the set
E^* of known and zero-day exploits, and a goal condition $c_g \in C^*$. The algorithm
returns an upper bound u on the value of k, and also computes a partial zero-day
attack graph $G = (E \cup C, R_r \cup R_i)$, a mapping $\pi : C \cup E \to 2^{2^E}$ which associates
each node in the partial attack graph with attack paths leading to it, and a mapping $zdu : C \to \mathbb{N}$ which associates each node in the partial attack graph with an
estimate of the upper bound on k. In this section, we assume that Algorithm 2
starts from initial conditions, but modifying the algorithm to reuse partial attack
graphs generated by previous execution of Algorithm 1 is straightforward, and
can be done as shown for algorithm $k0dValue$ (Algorithm 5).

Lines 1–8 simply initialize all the components of the partial attack graph.
Line 1 adds the initial conditions to the set C of security conditions in the
partial attack graph. As the algorithm builds the attack graph, new conditions
will be added to C. Lines 2–3 initialize the *require* and *imply* relationships as
empty sets. For each $c \in C_i$, Lines 5–6 set $\pi(c)$ to $\emptyset$ – meaning that no exploit is
needed to reach initial conditions, as they are satisfied by default – and $zdu(c)$
to 0 – meaning that no zero-day exploit is needed to reach initial conditions.
Finally, Line 8 sets E to the set of exploits reachable from conditions in C.

For each exploit $e \in E$, Lines 10–12 add edges to e from each of its preconditions, Line 13 associates e with the only set of exploits leading to it, that is $\{e\}$, and Line 14 computes $zdu(e)$ as the number of distinct zero-day vulnerabilities in $\{e\}$, that is $k0d(\{e\})$[1].

Line 16–21 try to find an attack path reaching the goal condition with the lowest possible number of distinct zero-day vulnerabilities. Since we use an heuristic approach to prune the search space, the number of distinct zero-day vulnerabilities in such path is naturally an upper bound on the minimum number k of zero-day vulnerabilities needed to reach the goal. Line 16 uses Algorithm *rankedPartition* (Algorithm 3) to rank exploits in E by increasing value of $zdu(e)$ and partition the set into ranked subsets. Then, Lines 18–21 iteratively explore the partial attack graph in a depth-first manner, by using the recursive algorithm DFS (Algorithm 4), starting from the set of exploits E_1 with the smallest values of $zdu()$.

Algorithm 3. *rankedPartition*(E').

Input: Set E' of exploits.
Output: Partition P_E of E
1: $E_r \leftarrow \langle e_1, \ldots, e_{|E'|} \rangle$ s.t. $(\forall i, j \in [1, |E'|])(i \leq j \Rightarrow zdu(e_i) \leq zdu(e_j))$
2: $P_E \leftarrow \langle E_1, \ldots, E_n \rangle$ s.t. $(\forall i, j \in [1, n])(i \leq j \Rightarrow (\forall e' \in E_i, e'' \in E_j)(zdu(e') \leq zdu(e'')))$
3: **return** P_E

Algorithm *rankedPartition* (Algorithm 3) takes as input a set of exploits E' and returns a partition P_E of E. Line 1 sorts exploits in E by increasing value of $zdu(e)$. Then, Line 2 partitions E into an ordered set of sets $E_1, \ldots, E_n$, such that for each $i \leq j \leq n$ all exploits in E_i have smaller values of $zdu()$ than any exploit in E_j.

Algorithm DFS (Algorithm 4) takes as input a set E_{start} of exploits and a goal condition $c_g \in C^*$, and returns an upper bound u on the value of k. We assume that the partial attack graph and the two mappings $\pi()$ and $zdu()$ are global variables.

For each $e \in E_{start}$ and each $c \in post(e)$, (i) Lines 4–5 add an edge from e to c, and update the set C_{new} of newly reached conditions, (ii) Line 6 computes the set $\pi(c)$ of attack paths leading to c as the union of the sets of attack paths leading to each exploit implying it, and (iii) Line 7 computes an estimate $zdu(c)$ of the upper bound on k with respect to c as the smallest $zdu(P)$ over all paths P in $\pi(c)$. If c is the goal condition, then the algorithm returns $zdu(c)$.

If none of the conditions in C_{new} is the goal condition, then Line 14 defines a new set E_{new} of unvisited exploits reachable from C, which has been updated to include all conditions reached from E_{start}. An exploit is *unvisited* if at least one of its preconditions is in C_{new}. If no new exploit is enabled, then the algorithm return $+\infty$ (Line 16), meaning that the goal condition cannot be reached from

---

[1] For exploits directly reachable from initial conditions, $zdu(e)$ is either 1, if e is a zero-day exploit, or 0, otherwise.

Algorithm 4. $DFS(E_{start}, c_g)$.

Input: Set E_{start} of exploits and goal condition $c_g \in C^*$
Output: Upper bound u on the value of k.
```
 1:  C_new ← ∅
 2:  for all e ∈ E_start do
 3:      for all c ∈ post(e) do
 4:          R_i ← R_i ∪ {(e, c)}
 5:          C_new ← C_new ∪ {c}
 6:          π(c) ← ⋃_{e∈E|(e,c)∈R_i} π(e)
 7:          zdu(c) ← min_{P∈π(c)} k0d(P)
 8:          if c = c_g then
 9:              return zdu(c)
10:          end if
11:      end for
12:  end for
13:  C ← C ∪ C_new
14:  E_new ← {e ∈ E | pre(e) ⊆ C ∧ pre(e) ∩ C_new ≠ ∅}
15:  if E_new = ∅ then
16:      return +∞
17:  end if
18:  for all e ∈ E_new do
19:      E ← E ∪ {e}
20:      for all c ∈ pre(e) do
21:          R_r ← R_r ∪ {(c, e)}
22:      end for
23:      {c_1, ..., c_m} ← {c ∈ C | (c, e) ∈ R_r}
24:      π(e) ← {P_1 ∪ ... ∪ P_m ∪ {e} | P_i ∈ π(c_i)}
25:      π(e) ← top(π(e), t)
26:      zdu(e) ← min_{P∈π(e)} k0d(P)
27:  end for
28:  ⟨E_1, ..., E_n⟩ ← rankedPartition(E_new)
29:  i ← 0
30:  while c_g ∉ C ∧ i ≤ n do
31:      i ← i + 1
32:      u ← DFS(E_i)
33:  end while
34:  return u
```

the branch of the attack graph explored in the current iteration of the algorithm. Otherwise, for each $e \in E_{new}$, (i) Lines 19–22 add e and edges to e from each of its preconditions to the partial attack graph, (ii) Lines 23–24 compute the set $\pi(e)$ of partial attack paths ending with e in the same way we have described for algorithm $k0dLowerBound$, (iii) Line 25 prunes $\pi(e)$ by maintaining only the top b partial attack paths with respect to the $k0d()$ metric, and (iv) Line 26 computes an estimate $zdu(e)$ of the upper bound on k with respect to e as the smallest $zdu(P)$ over all paths P in $\pi(e)$.

Finally, Line 28 uses algorithm $rankedPartition$ (Algorithm 3) to rank exploits in E by increasing value of $zdu(e)$ and partition the set. Then, Lines 30–33 iteratively explore the partial attack graph in a depth-first manner, by recursively calling algorithm DFS, starting from the set of exploits E_1 with the smallest values of $zdu()$.

Example 2. When applied to the graph of Fig. 2, algorithm $k0dUpperBound$ (Algorithm 2) will first consider exploits E reachable from the initial conditions (i.e., the first level of exploits, namely $\langle v_{firewall}, 0, F\rangle$, $\langle v_{http}, 0, 1\rangle$, $\langle v_{ssh}, 0, 1\rangle$), and will rank them by increasing value of $zdu()$. Then, assume that algorithm

$rankedPartition$ (Algorithm 3) partitions the set of exploits into subsets of size 1. As each exploit e on the first level has $zdu(e) = 1$, algorithm $k0dUpperBound$ will continue building the graph starting from any such exploit. If we assume it will start from $\langle v_{firewall}, 0, F \rangle$, then its post-condition $\langle 0, 2 \rangle$ will be added to the graph. Subsequent recursive calls of algorithm DFS will add $\langle v_{ssh}, 0, 1 \rangle$, $\langle user, 2 \rangle$, $\langle v_{root}, 2, 2 \rangle$, and $\langle root, 2 \rangle$, thus reaching the goal condition and returning $u = 2$. As seen in the previous example, the actual value of k in this scenario is 1, so $u = 2$ is a reasonable upper bound, which we were able to compute efficiently by building only a partial attack graph.

The complexity of Algorithm $k0dUpperBound$ (Algorithm 2) is clearly dominated by the recursive execution of algorithm DFS (Algorithm 4), which in the worst case – due to the adopted pruning strategy – has to process t partial attack paths for each node in the partial attack graph. Therefore, the complexity is $O(t \cdot (|C| + |E|))$, which is linear in the size of the graph when t is constant.

5.3   Solution for Problem 3

When the upper bound on the value of k is below a practical threshold u^*, we would like to compute the exact value of k, which is intractable in general. Our solution consists in performing a forward search, similarly to algorithm $k0dLowerBound$, starting from the partial attack graphs computed in previous steps of the decision process discussed in Sect. 4. To limit the search space, compared to a traditional forward search, and avoid the generation of the entire attack graph, we leverage the upper bound computed by algorithm $k0dUpperBound$ to prune paths not leading to the solution. In fact, although the value of k is known to be no larger than u, there still may be many paths with more the u distinct zero-day vulnerabilities, and we want to avoid adding such paths to the attack graph. Algorithm $k0dValue$ (Algorithm 5) is indeed very similar to algorithm $k0dLowerBound$. Therefore, for reasons of space, we only highlight the main differences in our discussion. First, the algorithm takes as input partial attack graphs, instead of starting from initial conditions. Thus, Line 1 computes C_{new} as the set of pre-conditions of unvisited exploits (i.e., exploits not added yet to the attack graph). Second, Line 10 prunes all attack paths with more than u distinct zero-day vulnerabilities. Finally, when the goal condition is reached, the algorithm computes the exact value of k as the smallest $k0d(P)$ over all paths P in $\pi(c_g)$.

6   Experimental Results

In this section, we present the results of experiments we conducted to validate our approach. Specifically, our objective is three-fold. First, we evaluated the performance of the proposed algorithms in terms of processing time in order to confirm that they are efficient enough to be practical. Second, we evaluated the percentage of nodes included in the generated partial attack graph compared to the full attack graph, which shows the degree of savings, in terms of both

time and storage, that may be achieved through our on-demand generation of
attack graphs. Third, we also evaluated the accuracy of estimations made using
algorithm $k0dUpperBound$ compared to the real results obtained using a brute
force approach.

Algorithm 5. $k0dValue(G, E^*, u, c_g)$.

Input: Partial zero-day attack graph $G = (E \cup C, R_r \cup R_i)$, set E^* of known and zero-day
exploits, integer $u \in \mathbb{N}$ representing the upper bound on the value of k computed by algorithm
$k0dUpperBound$, and goal condition $c_g \in C^*$.
Output: Updated Partial zero-day attack graph $G = (E \cup C, R_r \cup R_i)$, and the exact value of k.
1:   $C_{new} \leftarrow \{c \in C \mid \nexists e \in E, (c, e) \in R_r\}$
2:   **while** $C_{new} \neq \emptyset$ **do**
3:     $E_{new} \leftarrow \{e \in E \mid pre(e) \subseteq C \wedge pre(e) \cap C_{new} \neq \emptyset\}$ // Unvisited exploits reachable from
     C
4:     **for all** $e \in E_{new}$ **do**
5:       **for all** $c \in pre(e)$ **do**
6:        $R_r \leftarrow R_r \cup \{(c, e)\}$ // Add an edge from c to e
7:       **end for**
8:       $\{c_1, \ldots, c_m\} \leftarrow \{c \in C \mid (c, e) \in R_r\}$
9:       $\pi(e) \leftarrow \{P_1 \cup \ldots \cup P_m \cup \{e\} \mid P_i \in \pi(c_i)\}$
10:      $\pi(e) \leftarrow \{P \in \pi(e) \mid k0d(P) \le u\}$ // Prune paths with more than u zero-day vulnera-
      bilities
11:     **end for**
12:     $C_{new} \leftarrow \emptyset$
13:     **for all** $e \in E_{new}$ s.t. $\pi(e) \neq \emptyset$ **do**
14:       **for all** $c \in post(e)$ **do**
15:        $R_i \leftarrow R_i \cup \{(e, c)\}$ // Add an edge from e to c
16:        $C_{new} \leftarrow C_{new} \cup \{c\}$
17:        $\pi(c) \leftarrow \bigcup_{e \in E \mid (e,c) \in R_i} \pi(e)$
18:        **if** $c \equiv c_g$ **then**
19:         **return** $G, min_{P \in \pi(c)} k0d(P)$
20:        **end if**
21:       **end for**
22:     **end for**
23:     $C \leftarrow C \cup C_{new}$
24:     $E \leftarrow E \cup E_{new}$
25: **end while**

First, we show that, as expected, algorithm $k0dLowerBound$ is polynomial
for given small values of l. Specifically, Fig. 4(a) shows that the running time
of algorithm $k0dLowerBound$ grows almost quadratically in the size of attack
graphs. It is also clear that the actual running time is quite reasonable even
for relatively large graphs (e.g., it only takes about 20 s to determine $k > 3$ for
a graph with 80,000 nodes). We can also observe that, although the value of l
affects the average running time of the algorithm, such effect is not dramatic
for such small values of l (which may be sufficient in most practical cases).
This experiment confirms that algorithm $k0dLowerBound$ is efficient enough
for realistic applications. Next, we show how generating partial attack graphs
may lead to savings in both time and storage cost. Specifically, Fig. 4(b) shows
the percentage of nodes that are generated by algorithm $k0dLowerBound$ in
performing the analysis. We can see that such a percentage will decrease while
the size of attack graphs increases, which is desirable since this reflects higher
amount of savings for larger graphs. It is also clear that although a higher value

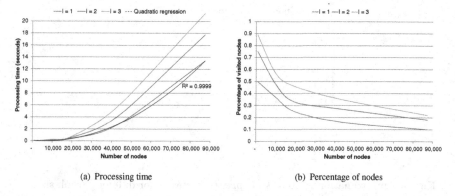

(a) Processing time

(b) Percentage of nodes

Fig. 4. Processing time and percentage of nodes for algorithm $k0dLowerBound$ vs. number of nodes in the full attack graph for different values of l.

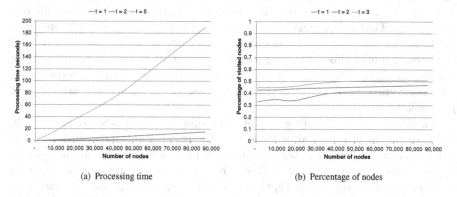

(a) Processing time

(b) Percentage of nodes

Fig. 5. Processing time and percentage of nodes for algorithm $k0dUpperBound$ vs. number of nodes in the full attack graph for different values of t.

of l will imply less savings (more nodes need to be generated), in most cases the savings are significant (e.g., less than half of the nodes are generated in most cases). This experiment confirms the effectiveness of our on-demand approach to generating attack graphs.

Similarly, we now show that algorithm $k0dUpperBound$ is polynomial for given small parameters. Specifically, Fig. 5(a) shows that the running time of algorithm $k0dUpperBound$ grows linearly in the size of attack graphs. The value of t represents the number of partial solutions maintained at each step (i.e., the degree of approximation). It is clear that the actual running time is very reasonable even for large graphs (e.g., it only takes less than 20 s for a graph with almost 90,000 nodes). However, we can also observe that the degree of approximation (the value of t) will significantly affect the growth of the average running time of the algorithm, which shows a natural trade-off between accuracy and cost. Next, we also show how generating partial attack graphs may lead to savings for this algorithm. Specifically, Fig. 5(b) shows the percentage of nodes

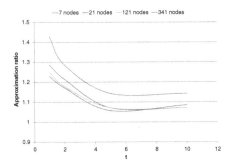

Fig. 6. Approximation ratio of $k0dUpperBound$ vs. t for different graph sizes.

that are generated by algorithm $k0dUpperBound$ in performing the analysis. We can see that such a percentage remains relatively stable across different graph sizes. That is, although the absolute number of generated nodes increases for larger graphs, the ratio remains almost constant, which partially justifies the linear running time of the algorithm. It is also clear that in most cases the savings are significant (less than half of the nodes are generated in most cases). This experiment again confirms the effectiveness of our on-demand attack graph generation.

Finally, we show the accuracy of algorithm $k0dUpperBound$. Specifically, Fig. 6 shows the approximation ratio (i.e., the result u obtained using the algorithm divided by the real value of k obtained using a brute force method) in the approximation parameter t. We can see that, as expected, such a ratio decreases when more partial results are kept at each step, resulting in higher accuracy (and higher cost as well). Overall, the approximation ratio is acceptably low even for a small t (e.g., the result is only about 1.4 times the real value of k when $t = 1$). We can also observe that larger graphs tend to have more accurate results, which is desirable since the analysis actually becomes relevant for larger graphs. Since algorithm $k0dValue(G, E^*, u, c_g)$ is similar to algorithm $k0dLowerBound$ except that it reuses, instead of generating, attack graphs, we expect its running time to be similar to (lower than) that of the latter and thus experiments are omitted here for reasons of space.

7   Conclusions

In this paper, we have studied the problem of efficiently estimating and calculating the k-zero-day safety of large networks. We presented a decision framework comprising three polynomial algorithms for establishing lower and upper bounds of k and for calculating the actual value of k, while generating only partial attack graphs in an on-demand manner. Experimental results confirm the efficiency and effectiveness of our algorithms. Although we have focused on the k-zero-day safety metric in this paper, we believe our techniques can be easily extended to other useful analyses related to attack graphs. Other future work include fine-tuning the approximation algorithm through various ways for ranking the partial solutions and evaluating the solution on diverse network scenarios.

References

1. Sheyner, O., Haines, J., Jha, S., Lippmann, R., Wing, J.M.: Automated generation and analysis of attack graphs. In: Proceedings of the 2002 IEEE Symposium on Security and Privacy (S&P 2002), Berkeley, CA, USA, pp. 273–284 (2002)
2. Ammann, P., Wijesekera, D., Kaushik, S.: Scalable, graph-based network vulnerability analysis. In: Proceedings of the 9th ACM Conference on Computer and Communications Security (CCS 2002), Washington, DC, USA, pp. 217–224 (2002)
3. McHugh, J.: Quality of protection: Measuring the unmeasurable? In: Proceedings of the 2nd ACM Workshop on Quality of Protection (QoP 2006), Alexandria, VA, USA, ACM, pp. 1–2 (2006)
4. Wang, L., Jajodia, S., Singhal, A., Noel, S.: k-zero day safety: measuring the security risk of networks against unknown attacks. In: Gritzalis, D., Preneel, B., Theoharidou, M. (eds.) ESORICS 2010. LNCS, vol. 6345, pp. 573–587. Springer, Heidelberg (2010)
5. Noel, S., Jajodia, S.: Managing attack graph complexity through visual hierarchical aggregation. In: Proceedings of the ACM CCS Workshop on Visualization and Data Mining for Computer Security (VizSEC/DMSEC 2004), Fairfax, VA, USA, ACM, pp. 109–118 (2004)
6. Mell, P., Scarfone, K., Romanosky, S.: Common vulnerability scoring system. IEEE Secur. Priv. **4**, 85–89 (2006)
7. The MITRE Corporation: Common Weakness Scoring System (CWSS^{TM}) Version 0.8 (2011). http://cwe.mitre.org/cwss/
8. Dacier, M.: Towards quantitative evaluation of computer security. Ph.D. thesis. Institut National Polytechnique de Toulouse (1994)
9. Phillips, C., Swiler, L.P.: A graph-based system for network-vulnerability analysis. In: Proceedings of the New Security Paradigms Workshop (NSPW 1998), Charlottesville, VA, USA, pp. 71–79 (1998)
10. Mehta, V., Bartzis, C., Zhu, H., Clarke, E.: Ranking attack graphs. In: Zamboni, D., Kruegel, C. (eds.) RAID 2006. LNCS, vol. 4219, pp. 127–144. Springer, Heidelberg (2006)
11. Balzarotti, D., Monga, M., Sicari, S.: Assessing the risk of using vulnerable components. In: Gollmann, D., Massacci, F., Yautsiukhin, A. (eds.) Quality of Protection. Advances in Information Security, vol. 23, pp. 65–77. Springer, Heidelberg (2006)
12. Pamula, J., Jajodia, S., Ammann, P., Swarup, V.: A weakest-adversary security metric for network configuration security analysis. In: Proceedings of the 2nd ACM Workshop on Quality of Protection (QoP 2006). Advances in Information Security, Alexandria, VA, USA, Springer, vol. 23, pp. 31–68 (2006)
13. Leversage, D.J., Byres, E.J.: Estimating a system's mean time-to-compromise. IEEE Secur. Priv. **6**, 52–60 (2008)
14. Wang, L., Islam, T., Long, T., Singhal, A., Jajodia, S.: An attack graph-based probabilistic security metric. In: Atluri, V. (ed.) DAS 2008. LNCS, vol. 5094, pp. 283–296. Springer, Heidelberg (2008)
15. Homer, J., Ou, X., Schmidt, D.: A sound and practical approach to quantifying security risk in enterprise networks, Technical report. Kansas State University (2009)

16. McQueen, M.A., McQueen, T.A., Boyer, W.F., Chaffin, M.R.: Empirical estimates and observations of 0day vulnerabilities. In: Proceedings of the 42nd Hawaii International Conference on System Sciences (HICSS 2009), Waikoloa, Big Island, HI, USA (2009)

17. Greenberg, A.: Shopping for Zero-Days: A Price List for Hackers' Secret Software Exploits. Forbes, New York (2012)

18. Shahzad, M., Shafiq, M.Z., Liu, A.X.: A large scale exploratory analysis of software vulnerability life cycles. In: Proceedings of the 34th International Conference on Software Engineering (ICSE 2012), Zurich, Switzerland, pp. 771–781 (2012)

19. Ingols, K., Chu, M., Lippmann, R., Webster, S., Boyer, S.: Modeling modern network attacks and countermeasures using attack graphs. In: Proceedings of the Annual Computer Security Applications Conference (ACSAC 2009), Honolulu, HI, USA, pp. 117–126 (2009)

Signal Processing and Multimedia Applications

Optimal Distribution of Computational Power in Free Viewpoint Interpolation by Depth Hypothesis Density Adaptation in Plane Sweeping

Patrik Goorts$^{(\boxtimes)}$, Steven Maesen, Maarten Dumont, Sammy Rogmans, and Philippe Bekaert

Expertise Centre for Digital Media, Hasselt University - tUL - iMinds,
Wetenschapspark 2, 3590 Diepenbeek, Belgium
patrik.goorts@uhasselt.be

Abstract. In this paper, we present a system to redistribute computational power in plane sweeping. Plane sweeping allows the generation of novel viewpoints of a scene by testing different depth hypotheses across input cameras. Typical plane sweeping approaches incorporate a uniform depth plane distribution to investigate different depth hypotheses to generate a depth map. When the scene consists of a sparse number of objects, some depth hypotheses do not contain objects and can cause noise and wasted computational power. Therefore, we propose a method to adapt the plane distribution to increase the quality of the depth map around objects and to reduce computational power waste by reducing the number of planes in empty spaces in the scene. First, we generate the cumulative histogram of the depth map of the scene. This depth map can be obtained from the previous frame in a temporal sequence of images, or from a depth camera with lower resolution or quality. Next, we determine a new normalized depth for every depth plane by analyzing the cumulative histogram. Steep sections of the cumulative histogram will result in a dense local distribution of planes; a flat section will result in a sparse distribution. The results, performed on controlled and on real images, demonstrate the effectiveness of the method over a uniform distribution and the possibility of using a lower number of depth planes, and thus a more performant processing, for the same quality.

Keywords: Plane sweep · Free viewpoint interpolation · Cumulative histogram · Optimization · Non-uniform distribution

1 Introduction

View interpolation is an important technique for computational video and photography, allowing the generation of novel viewpoints from a scene. A number of real cameras are capturing a scene. Using view interpolation, it is possible to

© Springer-Verlag Berlin Heidelberg 2014
M.S. Obaidat and J. Filipe (Eds.): ICETE 2013, CCIS 456, pp. 343–358, 2014.
DOI: 10.1007/978-3-662-44788-8_20

generate images from non-existing camera views using the images from the real cameras. This can increase the user experience, for example in sports broadcasting [1,2] and video conferencing [3].

View interpolation is typically achieved by using 3D reconstruction or by image-based rendering. 3D reconstruction estimates the geometry of the scene and can choose the novel viewpoint accordingly. The most notable methods are visual hull [4,5], photo hull [6] and space carving [7]. While 3D reconstruction allows a large range of novel viewpoints, the reconstruction is typically slow and the quality is limited to the quality of the reconstructed 3D models.

Image-based rendering, on the other hand, does not use geometry-based models of the scene. Instead, only the images are used to generate the novel image directly. The most known approach is the generation of depth maps for small baseline setups using stereo matching [8,9] and plane sweeping [3,10], including depth-selective plane sweeping for two views [11] or for large scenes [2].

In the plane sweep approach, the scene is divided in planes, all representing a depth hypothesis. The input cameras are projected to a plane, and backprojected to the virtual image plane. By comparing the photoconsistency of every depth plane for every pixel of the virtual image, an optimal virtual image with a depth map can be created. We propose a system to reduce the waste of computational power for the plane sweep approach.

Typically, the planes for the depth hypotheses are distributed evenly in the scene space, thus allocating uniform computational power to all depth hypotheses. Because the scene typically does not have a uniform distribution of objects, wasted performance can be perceived by considering depth values where no objects are present. Therefore, we present a system where the distribution of the planes is adapted to the scene. A histogram is calculated of the resulting depth map to determine the plane distribution for the next temporal frame. This will redistribute computational power to the more dense regions of the scene, and consequently increase the quality of the interpolation by reducing mismatches and noise.

The used histogram is obtained from the depth map of the previous frame, or from the depth map generated by an active depth camera. When using the depth map from the previous frame, no extra hardware is required. However, the depth hypotheses adaptation lags one frame. When using an active depth camera, no lag is present, but hardware considerations may limit the working range of the setup. We used the Microsoft Kinect [12] as active depth camera, limiting the depth range to 5 meters. Furthermore, the resolution and the image quality are low, such that the depth map cannot be used directly for view interpolation. However, the depth map is adequate to be used in our plane redistribution method, thus effectively creating a hybrid method between low resolution active depth cameras and high resolution multi camera depth methods.

Multiple methods have been proposed to reduce plane sweep complexity, reduce required computational power and increase quality. The method of Rogmans et al. [11] also uses a histogram to select applicable depth ranges, but without redistributing or changing the plane density. Gallup et al. [13] propose a histogram-based method to determine the optimal orientation of the planes to increase quality and reduce computational complexity, but also without optimizing for sparse scene regions.

The view interpolation system is achieved using commodity GPU hardware to acquire real-time processing. By redistributing computational power to significant parts of the scene, less power is wasted and more is available to other image processing stages, such as demosaicing [14], segmentation or depth filtering [2].

2   View Interpolation Using Plane Sweeping

View interpolation allows the generation of novel views of a scene. We accomplish this by using the well-known plane sweep approach [15], implemented using traditional GPU paradigms to acquire real-time processing by leveraging the projective texturing capabilities of Cg shaders. We place a number of cameras directed at the scene and calibrate them to acquire the projection matrices P_i using the Multicamera Calibration Toolbox of Svoboda et al. [16]. Using those cameras, we can construct a novel viewpoint and generate the image thereof using a plane sweeping approach.

First, we divide the space in front of the virtual camera C_v into M planes on different depths D_i with $D_{min} \leq D_i \leq D_{max}$, parallel to the image plane of the virtual camera. Then, for every plane, we project the input camera images C_i to the plane, reproject them to the image plane of the virtual camera I_v and calculate the photoconsistency of every pixel on the virtual plane. This process is demonstrated in Fig. 1.

To acquire a metric for the photoconsistency, we use a cost function, aggregated over a window to improve quality. The cost function is defined as the sum of squared differences (SSD):

$$\sigma(x,y) = \sum_{i=1}^{N} \frac{\|\gamma - C_i(x,y)\|^2}{3N} \text{ with } \gamma = \sum_{i=1}^{N} \frac{C_i(x,y)}{N} \tag{1}$$

where γ is the average of the reprojected pixels and C_i is the ith input image of total N. The final photoconsistency error is acquired by aggregating the SSD for the pixels in a fixed-size window, weighted by a (separable) Gauss filter:

$$\epsilon(x,y) = \sum_{u,v} w(u,v)\sigma(x+u, y+v) \tag{2}$$

for a window with coordinates u and v, centered at (x,y), and Gauss weights $w(u,v)$.

The depth plane with the lowest error value ϵ is chosen, thus selecting the depth value with the highest photoconsistency using a winner-takes-all approach. This will result in a simultaneous generation of the depth map and the final color, γ.

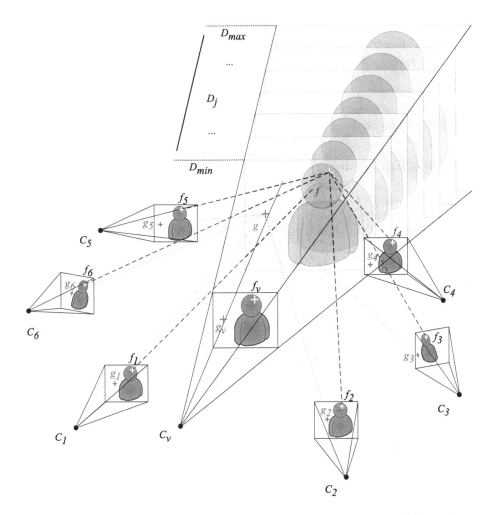

Fig. 1. Plane sweeping. The space in front of the virtual camera is divided in planes on different depths. The photoconsistency of every pixel for every plane is considered in the selection of the optimal depth plane, thus selecting the optimal depth and color for the virtual image.

Quality is increased by using a foreground/background segmentation applied to the input images. $\epsilon(x, y)$ is set to infinity when the projected pixels contains a background pixel. This will reduce mismatches caused by noise in the background and will reduce disappearance of foreground objects on a uniform background. This is due to the similarity of every pixel on a uniform background, thus obtaining a low error value ϵ for incorrectly matched background pixels. This will result in the destruction of the foreground objects. These artifacts are greatly reduced by processing the foreground and the background independently.

In the traditional approach [15], the planes are distributed uniformly in the sweeping space. However, this will allocate computational resources to depth planes where no scene information is available. Therefore, we propose a method to reduce wasted computational power and increase quality in important regions of the scene.

3 Adaptive Non-uniform Plane Distribution

When the scene consists of a limited range of depths between D_{min} and D_{max}, some processing resources are allocated to depth planes where no scene is available. This is demonstrated in Fig. 2(a). Here, a lot of planes are placed in the scene where no objects are positioned. This will waste resources and introduce more noise due to mismatches between the cameras. Therefore, we rearrange the distribution of the depth planes to provide fewer planes in depth ranges with less object, and more, dense planes in scene regions with more objects. We determine the interest of a depth by analyzing the previous frame in a temporal sequence, or use the depth map of a depth camera.

When using the depth map of the previous frame, we generate the histogram of the depth map using the well-known occlusion querying method [17] on GPU, allowing fast processing. The histogram can be seen in Fig. 2(b). The occurrence of every depth value, as determined by the depth of the depth planes, in the depth map is counted. The histogram will have discrete depth values between D_{min} and D_{max}, represented by the depth plane numbers, because there is a limited number of planes. Scene depths of high interest will contain more depth values than depths of low interest. If there are depths in the scene where no objects are present, few of this depth values will be available in the depth map and this will be reflected in the histogram. In the next frame, we want to provide

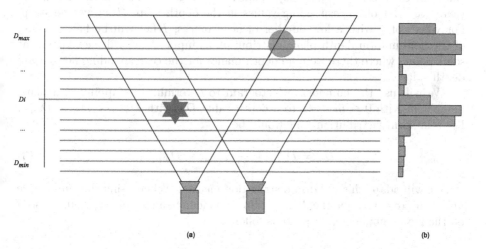

(a)   (b)

Fig. 2. (a) Uniform plane distribution (b) Histogram of the depth values.

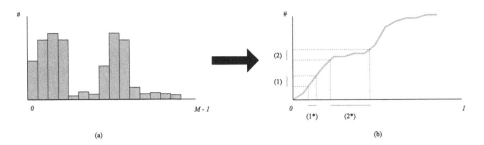

Fig. 3. (a) Resulting histogram (b) Corresponding cumulative histogram $H(x)$.

more planes in depth ranges where a lot of depth values can be found, thus where there are large values in the depth histogram. The depth planes are not necessary uniformly distributed, thus the histogram uses the depth plane number as the bin value, instead of the depth directly. When using the depth camera, the depth map is used directly. All depth values are converted to the corresponding depth values in the coordinate space of the color cameras before using them in the histogram creation. These depth values correspond to plane depths, thus creating an analogous histogram as the previously discussed method.

To use the depth distribution information, we convert the histogram to its cumulative version, as shown in Fig. 3. Here, we do not count the number of occurrences per depth value, but we also include the number of occurrences lower than this depth. Furthermore, we rescale the depth values from $[D_{min}, D_{max}]$, as represented by the depth plane numbers, to $[0, 1]$. This will transform the non-uniform distribution of the depth planes to actual normalized depth values between 0 and 1. This transformation will generate an increasing function $H(x) = y$, where $x \in [0, 1]$ is a normalized depth value and y is the number of values in the rescaled depth map smaller or equal to x. For values of x where there are a lot of corresponding values in the depth map, $H(x)$ will be steep. For values of x with a low number of occurrences, $H(x)$ will be flat. Because of the non-uniform depth plane distribution as input, $H(x)$ will be constant at some points where there were no depth planes for the corresponding normalized depth value.

We will use the cumulative histogram to determine a mapping of a plane number m with $0 \leq m < M$ to a depth value D_m with $D_{min} \leq D_m \leq D_{max}$. For a uniform distribution, this would be:

$$D_m = D_{min} + \frac{m}{M}(D_{max} - D_{min}) \tag{3}$$

We will adapt this uniform distribution method. When using the cumulative histogram to determine the distribution, we calculate a fraction $\tau_m \in [0, 1]$ based on the plane number m, applied as follows:

$$D_m = D_{min} + \tau_m(D_{max} - D_{min}) \tag{4}$$

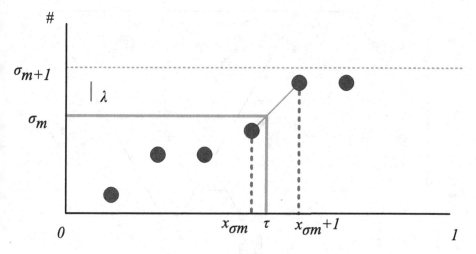

Fig. 4. Detail of the cumulative histogram with discrete values. τ is calculated by determining $x_{\sigma m}$ and $x_{\sigma m} + 1$, such that $H(x_{\sigma m}) \leq \sigma_m$ and $H(x_{\sigma m} + 1) > \sigma_m$, where σ_m represents a depth plane number.

The fraction τ_m is determined by the cumulative histogram. The Y axis is divided in M cross sections, with a distance λ from each other, where $\lambda = max(H)/M$. Each cross section represents a depth plane m. The actual depth fraction τ_m for each cross section σ_m, i.e. a depth plane, is calculated by first determining the depth value $x_{\sigma m}$ where $H(x_{\sigma m}) \leq \sigma_m$ and $H(x_{\sigma m} + 1) > \sigma_m$. This is demonstrated in Fig. 4. Because the depth values x in the cumulative histogram are discrete, finding a value $x_{\sigma m}$ where $H(x_{\sigma m}) = \sigma_m$ is unlikely, and not desirable when generating planes that are dense, i.e. closer together, than the depth values provided in the cumulative histogram.

Once $x_{\sigma m}$ is determined, τ_m is calculated as follows:

$$\phi = \frac{m\lambda - H(x_{\sigma m})}{H(x_{\sigma m} + 1) - H(x_{\sigma m})} \tag{5}$$

$$\tau_m = \phi(x_{\sigma m} + 1) + (1 - \phi)(x_{\sigma m}) \tag{6}$$

Figure 3(b) shows the transformation from a uniform depth plane distribution to a non-uniform distribution based on the cumulative histogram. In point (1), where the cumulative histogram is steep, there will be a dense plane distribution, as can be seen at (1*). When the cumulative histogram is flat, a sparse plane distribution is acquired, as can be seen at (2*).

Using τ_m, an actual depth for every plane m ($0 \leq m < M$) is determined and used in the plane sweeping step:

$$D_m = D_{min} + \tau_m(D_{max} - D_{min}) \tag{7}$$

This can be seen in Fig. 5. Here, the planes are redistributed using the cumulative histogram of Fig. 3(b). As can be seen, more planes are available for determining the depth of the objects, and fewer planes are available in empty space.

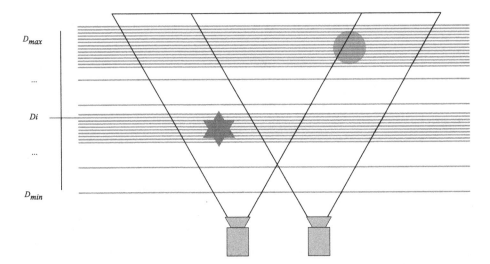

Fig. 5. Redistributed depth planes.

It is desirable to include some planes in the empty spaces between objects to allow the appearance of objects in dynamic scenes. To allow this, all the values in the histogram are increased with a fixed number, based on the number of pixels. This way, the cumulative histogram will be less flat in less interesting regions, allowing some planes here. In our tests, 0.1 % of the total amount of pixels demonstrated to be a correct value.

4   Results

We tested the proposed method on different scenes and compared image quality and planes required.

The first experiment shows the quality increase when a low number of planes is available. To increase overall quality in both methods, foreground and background segmentation is used. Figure 6(a) shows the result for a uniform depth plane distribution. Artifacts caused by the sparse plane distribution can be clearly seen; the depth map shows clear outliers. The depth map when using a non-uniform plane distribution, based on the histogram of the first depth map, can be seen in Fig. 6(b). Less noise and outliers in the depth values can be perceived. Furthermore, the silhouette is more distinct and the features of the persons are clearer. Using the non-uniform plane distribution increased the quality of the depth map using a low number of planes, thus increasing overall performance.

(a)   (b)   (c)

Fig. 6. Comparison of the depth map with: (a) a uniform depth plane distribution (only 50 planes used), (b) a non-uniform depth plane distribution (only 50 planes used), and (c) a uniform depth plane distribution (with 256 planes used).

Figure 6(c) shows the result for a high number of planes. Here, some noise and unclear edges can be perceived. These artifacts are effectively filtered out using the non-uniform plane distribution. The depth planes generating vague edges and noise are not used and can not contribute to the depth map, and thus to the noise and artifacts.

To demonstrate the effect of the cumulative histograms, Figs. 7 and 8 show an input image of a video sequence (a), the corresponding cumulative histogram of the depth map of the preceding frame (b) and the corresponding fraction τ from Eq. 6 (c). When only one dominant depth can be perceived, such as in Fig. 7, one steep section in the cumulative histogram is visible. This part will be transformed to a flat value of τ, thus increasing the density of the planes in the corresponding region in the sweeping space. Flat sections of the cumulative histogram will correspond to steep values in the graph of τ, resulting in a sparse plane distribution. When multiple dominant depths are available in the scene, the cumulative histogram will show multiple steep sections (see Fig. 8). This will result in multiple dense regions in the plane distribution, as reflected by the values of τ in Fig. 8(c).

The second experiment shows the results for the interpolation for soccer games. The video streams used are from a live game. We placed 8 cameras at one side of the scene and performed real-time interpolation between the cameras. To increase overall quality in both methods, foreground and background segmentation is used. High-quality interpolation for soccer scenes consists of different steps, apart from the plane sweeping, such as debayering and depth filtering. Therefore, the interpolation step should be as fast as possible to reduce execution time and allow real-time processing. By reducing the number of depth planes, the performance can be greatly increased. By incorporating an adaptive plane distribution system, such as described in Sect. 3, fewer depth planes are required while preserving high quality.

The results can be seen in Fig. 11. The quality is increased compared with the uniform plane distribution, as seen in Fig. 10. Details of the quality difference can be seen in Fig. 9. In the uniform plane distribution in Fig. 9(a), missing

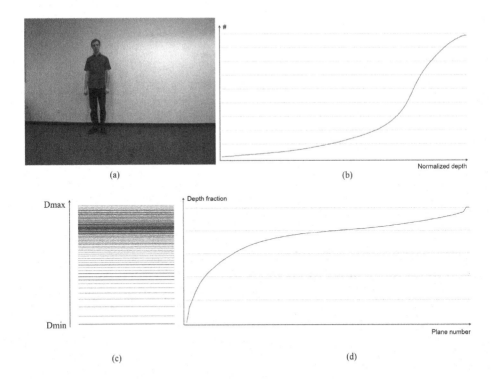

Fig. 7. (a) Input image with one person. (b) Cumulative histogram of the depth map. (c) New depth plane distribution. (d) Corresponding fraction τ for a given plane number.

heads and limbs can be perceived, caused by the low number of planes used to determine the interpolated view of the players. By redistributing the depth planes to the position of the players, as can be seen in Figs. 9(b) and 11, artifacts are seriously reduced. The non-uniform plane distribution method is especially applicable to soccer scenes due to the sparse location of players on the field and the multiple open spaces in the scene. Redistributing the depth planes will thus increase performance by reducing the number of wasted planes. The quality is not reduced by the movement of the scene due to the inclusion of depth planes in empty space. By including a few number of depth planes in empty space, players moving in these spaces are detected and the plane distribution is adapted accordingly.

To demonstrate the high quality of our results, we increased the number of depth planes to 5000. The quality of the result is high, as shown in Fig. 12, but real-time processing is no longer possible due to the high computational requirements. Comparing Figs. 11 and 12, we see little difference, proving the effectiveness of our method.

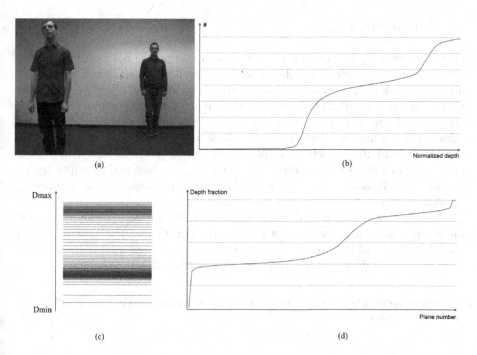

Fig. 8. (a) Input image with two persons on different depths. (b) Cumulative histogram of the depth map. (c) New depth plane distribution. (d) Corresponding fraction τ for a given plane number.

The last experiment demonstrates the results when using a lower quality depth camera to obtain the histogram used for the determination of the plane distribution. We used the Kinect [12] as the depth camera. The Kinect image can be seen in Fig. 13(a), together with the corresponding color image. As can be seen in the depth map, the quality is not sufficient for view interpolation, but can be used for our method. The depth map is relatively complete, so we can use fewer planes than when using the depth from the previous frame. We need fewer planes for empty spaces to compensate for moving objects; the depth map will contain these objects nonetheless. The resulting depth plane distribution and corresponding cumulative histogram can be seen in Fig. 13.

Figure 14(a) shows the result for a uniform depth plane distribution using 10 planes. As can be seen, the depth map contains lots of errors, noise and artifacts; many parts are missing or are incorrect. Figure 14(b) shows the result for a non-uniform depth plane distribution using 10 planes, based on the depth map of the Kinect. The depth map is complete, and noise and artifacts are seriously reduced, while maintaining high performance. This demonstrates the usefulness of a lower quality depth camera for our method. However, due to the limited range of the Kinect, only small scale scenes can be used.

5 Conclusions

In this paper, we presented a method to reduce computational requirements for view interpolation. When the depth of the scene is not distributed evenly, the plane sweeping method can search in depth ranges where no objects are present, thus reducing computational power and increasing the opportunity for noise. Our method uses the cumulative histogram of the previous temporal frame or from the depth map of a low quality depth camera to determine a more suitable depth plane distribution where the planes are more dense in regions with objects and sparse in regions with no objects. Some planes are assigned to empty spaces to cope with dynamic scenes. All algorithms are implemented using commodity graphics hardware to achieve real-time processing.

We tested the method on different kinds of input sequences, including a scene under controlled conditions and a scene of a live soccer game. Both results proved the effectiveness of the proposed method by providing high quality results with a low number of depth planes, thus reducing computational requirements.

Acknowledgements. Patrik Goorts would like to thank the IWT for its PhD specialization bursary.

Appendix

(a)   (b)

Fig. 9. Details of the quality differences between (a) Fig. 10 and (b) Fig. 11 (our method).

Fig. 10. Plane sweeping of a soccer scene with a low number of depth planes (40) and a uniform plane distribution. Many artifacts and missing people can be perceived.

Fig. 11. Plane sweeping of a soccer scene with a low number of depth planes (40) and an adaptive plane distribution. The quality is greatly increased in comparison with Fig. 10.

Fig. 12. Plane sweeping of a soccer scene with a high number of depth planes (5000) and a uniform plane distribution. The quality is comparable with Fig. 11, which proves the effectiveness of the method.

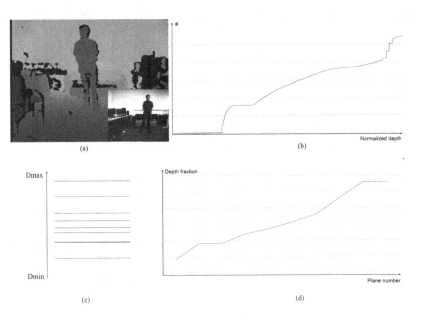

Fig. 13. (a) Kinect input image with one person, with the color image in the bottomright corner. (b) Cumulative histogram of the depth map. (c) New depth plane distribution for 10 planes. (d) Corresponding fraction τ for a given plane number.

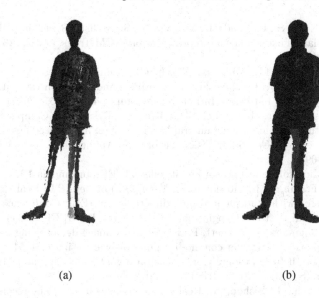

(a)   (b)

Fig. 14. Comparison of the depth map with: (a) a uniform depth plane distribution (only 10 planes used), and (b) a non-uniform depth plane distribution using kinect (only 10 planes used).

References

1. Goorts, P., Dumont, M., Rogmans, S., Bekaert, P.: An end-to-end system for free viewpoint video for smooth camera transitions. In: Proceedings of the Second International Conference on 3D Imaging (IC3D 2012), 3D Stereo Media (2012)
2. Goorts, P., Ancuti, C., Dumont, M., Bekaert, P.: Real-time video-based view interpolation of soccer events using depth-selective plane sweeping. In: Proceedings of the Eight International Conference on Computer Vision Theory and Applications (VISAPP 2013), INSTICC (2013)
3. Dumont, M., Rogmans, S., Maesen, S., Bekaert, P.: Optimized two-party video chat with restored eye contact using graphics hardware. In: Filipe, J., Obaidat, M.S. (eds.) ICETE 2008. CCIS, vol. 48, pp. 358–372. Springer, Heidelberg (2009)
4. Matusik, W., Buehler, C., Raskar, R., Gortler, S., McMillan, L.: Image-based visual hulls. In: Proceedings of the 27th Annual Conference on Computer Graphics and Interactive Techniques, pp. 369–374. ACM Press/Addison-Wesley Publishing Co. (2000)
5. Miller, G., Hilton, A., Starck, J.: Interactive free-viewpoint video. In: IEE European Conference on Visual Media Production, Citeseer, pp. 50–59 (2005)
6. Kutulakos, K., Seitz, S.: A theory of shape by space carving. Intl. J. Comput. Vis. **38**, 199–218 (2000)
7. Seitz, S., Dyer, C.: Photorealistic scene reconstruction by voxel coloring. Intl. J. Comput. Vis. **35**, 151–173 (1999)
8. Seitz, S., Curless, B., Diebel, J., Scharstein, D., Szeliski, R.: A comparison and evaluation of multi-view stereo reconstruction algorithms. In: 2006 IEEE Computer Society Conference on Computer Vision and Pattern Recognition, vol. 1, pp. 519–528. IEEE (2006)

9. Zitnick, C., Kang, S., Uyttendaele, M., Winder, S., Szeliski, R.: High-quality video view interpolation using a layered representation. ACM Trans. Graph. **23**, 600–608 (2004). ACM

10. Yang, R., Pollefeys, M., Yang, H., Welch, G.: A unified approach to real-time, multi-resolution, multi-baseline 2d view synthesis and 3d depth estimation using commodity graphics hardware. Intl. J. Image Graph. **4**, 627–651 (2004)

11. Rogmans, S., Dumont, M., Cuypers, T., Lafruit, G., Bekaert, P.: Complexity reduction of real-time depth scanning on graphics hardware. In: Proceedings of International Conference on Computer Vision Theory and Applications, Lisbon, Portugal, February 2009

12. Zhang, Z.: Microsoft kinect sensor and its effect. IEEE Multimedia **19**, 4–10 (2012)

13. Gallup, D., Frahm, J.M., Mordohai, P., Yang, Q., Pollefeys, M.: Real-time plane-sweeping stereo with multiple sweeping directions. In: IEEE Conference on Computer Vision and Pattern Recognition, CVPR'07, pp. 1–8. IEEE (2007)

14. Goorts, P., Rogmans, S., Bekaert, P.: Raw camera image demosaicing using finite impulse response filtering on commodity gpu hardware using cuda. In: Proceedings of the Tenth International Conference on Signal Processing and Multimedia Applications (SIGMAP 2012), INSTICC (2012)

15. Yang, R., Welch, G., Bishop, G.: Real-time consensus-based scene reconstruction using commodity graphics hardware. Comput. Graph. Forum **22**, 207–216 (2003). Wiley Online Library

16. Svoboda, T., Martinec, D., Pajdla, T.: A convenient multicamera self-calibration for virtual environments. Presence: Teleoperators Virtual Environ. **14**, 407–422 (2005)

17. Green, S.: Image processing tricks in opengl. Presentation GDC 2005, p. 2 (2005)

Effect of the Front-End Processing on Speaker Verification Performance Using PCA and Scores Level Fusion

Nassim Asbai[1,2(✉)], Messaoud Bengherabi[1], Farid Harizi[1], and Abderrahmane Amrouche[2]

[1] Center for Development of Advanced Technologies, Algiers, Algeria
{nasbai,mbengherabi,fharizi}@cdta.dz
[2] Speech Communication and Signal Processing Laboratory,
Faculty of Electronics and Computer Sciences, USTHB, Bab Ezzouar,
16 111 Algiers, Algeria
{nasbai,namrouche}@usthb.dz

Abstract. This paper evaluates the impact of low-level features on speaker verification performance, with an emphasis on the recently proposed MFCC variant based on asymmetric tapers (MFCC asymmetric from now on) standalone as features or followed by PCA as linear projection technique applied before the GMM-UBM back-end classifier in clean and noisy environments. The performances of the MFCC-asymmetric features are compared with: the standard Mel-Frequency Cepstral Coefficients (MFCC) that extracted from TIMIT corpus, under clean and noisy conditions. A score level fusion framework based on simples linear methods such as min, max, sum, ..., etc. and training methods like SVM is proposed to improve performance and to mitigate noise degradation. The obtained results on corrupted TIMIT database confirm the superiority of fused system in noisy environments against each system alone, and the drastic degradation of the performances of PCA based systems in the presence of environmental noise.

Keywords: MFCCs · Asymmetric tapers · Score fusion · Noises · GMM-UBM · TIMIT corpus

1 Introduction

Over the last two decades, speaker verification has been the subject of considerable research due to its various applications in such areas as telephone banking, remote access control and surveillance. One of the main challenges associated with the deployment of speaker verification in practice is that of undesired variations in speech characteristics caused by environmental noise. Such variations can in turn lead to a mismatch between the corresponding test and reference model from the same speaker [1], who can be modeled by various modeling techniques used in speaker verification system such as Gaussian Mixture Model-Universal Background Model (GMM-UBM) [2, 3], HMM [4] and SVM [5]. This mismatch existing between training and testing data is found to adversely affect the performance of speaker verification in terms of

© Springer-Verlag Berlin Heidelberg 2014
M.S. Obaidat and J. Filipe (Eds.): ICETE 2013, CCIS 456, pp. 359–368, 2014.
DOI: 10.1007/978-3-662-44788-8_21

accuracy. So, to address the above problem, one research direction focuses on new features or variants of MFCCs namely MFCCs based on asymmetric tapers [6, 7]. Another promising direction is the fusion at different levels mainly at the score or confidence level to mitigate noise degradation. Performance improvement can be attained through score fusion of systems with different frontends or back-ends. This can be achieved by the use of different voice activity detectors (VADs) [8, 9] and/or feature extraction techniques across systems; and in back-ends includes the use of different classifiers and/or compensation techniques across systems [10].

As a speaker verification systems typically use acoustic parameters calculated from short-term spectrum characteristics of the speech signal and the envelope of the spectrum [11], in this paper, the performance of MFCC-asymmetric is compared with: the standard Mel-Frequency Cepstral Coefficients (MFCC) [12] stand-alone as features or followed by Principal Component Analysis (PCA) [13] that interests to inter-speaker variability under clean and noisy environments. The focus of this work is to evaluate the effect of front-end on the performance of our speaker verification system based on GMM-UBM, as a baseline classifier under clean and noisy environments. The Gaussian mixture model (GMM) with universal background model UBM, has proven to be extremely efficient for characterizing speaker identity at the acoustic level. In this approach, speaker models are obtained from the normalization of a universal background model (UBM) [3]. The UBM is usually trained by means of the Expectation-Maximization (EM) algorithm from a background dataset, which includes a wide range of speakers, languages (for Multilanguage application), communication channels, recording devices, and environments. The GMM-UBM [2] becomes a standard technique for text-independent speaker verification due to its reliable performance, especially after the introduction of the Maximum a Posteriori (MAP) adaptation [2] coupling the client and the UBM model.

The outline of paper is as follows. In Sect. 2, we describe the different feature vectors used in this work. At Sect. 3, we present the theoretical principles of PCA, and we describe the experimental protocol adopted in this work at Sect. 4. in Sect. 5, we discuss the results that found. Finally, a conclusion is given in Sect. 6.

2   Feature Extraction Overview

The speech signal continuously changes due to articulatory movements and therefore, the signal must be analyzed within short frames of about 20–30 ms duration. Within this interval, the signal is assumed to remain stationary and a spectral feature vector is provided for each frame.

2.1   Mel-Frequency Cepstral Coefficients (MFCCs)

The mel-frequency cepstral coefficients (MFCCs) [12] were introduced in early 1980s for speech recognition applications and since then have also been adopted for speaker identification applications. A sample of speech signal is first extracted through a window. Typically, two parameters are important for the windowing procedure: the duration of the window (ranges from 20 to 30 ms) and the shift between two consecutive windows (ranges from 10 to 15 ms) [12]. The values correspond to the average duration for which the speech signal can be assumed to be stationary or its statistical and spectral information does not change significantly. The speech samples are then weighed by a suitable windowing function, such as, Hamming or Hanning window [12], that are extensively used in speaker verification. The weighing reduces the artifacts (such as side lobes and signal leakage) due to the use of a finite duration window size for analysis. The magnitude spectrum of the speech sample is then computed using a fast Fourier transform (FFT). For a discrete signal $\{x[n]\}$ with $0 < n < N$, where N is the number of samples of an analysis window, is the sampling frequency, the discrete Fourier transform (DFT) is used and is given by equation below:

$$S(f) = \left| \sum_{t=0}^{N-1} w(t)x(t)e^{-i2\pi tf/N} \right|^2 \tag{1}$$

where $i = \sqrt{-1}$ is the imaginary unit and $f = 0, 1, ..., N - 1$ denotes the discrete frequency index. Here, $w = [w(0) ... w(N - 1)]^T$ is a time-domain window function which usually is symmetric and decreases towards the frame boundaries. Then, $S(f)$ is processed by a bank of band-pass filters. The filters that are generally used in MFCC computation are triangular filters [14], and their center frequencies are chosen according a logarithmic frequency scale, also known as Mel-frequency scale. The filter bank is then used to transform the frequency bins to Mel-scale bins by the following equations:

$$m_y[b] = \sum_f w_b[f] |S[f]^2| \tag{2}$$

where w_b is the bth Mel-scale filter's weight for the frequency f and $S[f]$ is the FFT of the windowed speech signal. The rationale for choosing a logarithmic frequency scale conforms to the response observed in the human auditory system that has been validated through several biophysical experiments [14]. The Mel-frequency weighted magnitude spectrum is processed by a compressive non-linearity (typically a logarithmic function) which also models the observed response in a human auditory system. The last step in MFCC computation is a discrete cosine transform (DCT) which is used to de-correlate the Mel-scale filter outputs. A subset of the DCT coefficients are chosen (typically the first and the last few coefficients are ignored) and represent the MFCC features used in the enrollment and the verification phases.

2.2   MFCCs Based on Asymmetric Tapers

Usually, speaker/speech recognition systems for short-time analysis of a speech signal use standard symmetric-tapers such as Hamming, Hann, etc. These tapers have a poor magnitude response under mismatched conditions and a larger time delay [15]. One elegant technique for reducing the time delay and enhancing the magnitude response under noisy conditions is to replace symmetric tapers by asymmetric tapers [6, 7, 15].

The method based on asymmetric tapers is an extension of the conventional windowed using symmetric tapers. From a symmetric taper $w_s(n)$ of length N, the instantaneous phase $\theta(n)$ computed by applying a Hilbert transform to the symmetric taper. Then, the asymmetric taper is $w_{at}(n)$ obtained as:

$$w_{at}(n) = cw_s(n)e^{k\theta(n)}, \quad 0 \leq n \leq N - 1 \tag{3}$$

where n is the time index, $w_s(n)$ is the symmetric taper of length N, $e^{k\theta(n)}$ is an asymmetric function, k is a parameter that controls the degree of asymmetry, and c is the normalizing constant given by (Fig. 1)

$$c = \frac{\max(w_s(n))}{\max(w_s(n)e^{k\theta(n)})}, \quad 0 \leq n \leq N - 1 \tag{4}$$

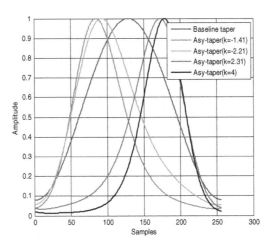

Fig. 1. Comparison between symmetric hamming taper and asymmetric tapers in time domain.

3 Principal Component Analysis (PCA)

The PCA algorithm is introduced for the first time in the work of Turk [16]. It is also known under the eigenfaces name because it uses eigenvectors and eigenvalues. The main idea of PCA is to represent a data set in terms of a minimum of variables and correlation between features while preserving most of the information present in the data set [17]. In mathematical terms, PCA calculates a projection matrix made up of m vectors which are the eigenvectors of the covariance matrix of data set associated with the m eigenvalues. So, the eigenvectors containing information are independent from a vector to another [16, 17].

Assume that we have M Speakers, and each speaker i is represented by a matrix A_i of size ($n_i \times m$, $i = 1, \ldots, M$) of feature vectors (MFCCs) (n_i is the number of rows and m is the number of columns). After having concatenated our M matrices into a single matrix, we obtain a global matrix $A(N \times m, N = \sum_{i}^{M} n_i)$ of all speakers. Then we calculate the mean vector of the global matrix A:

$$\psi = \frac{1}{N} \sum_{i}^{N} a_i, \quad N = \sum_{i}^{M} n_i \tag{5}$$

Where a_i is the ith row vector of the global matrix A.
Then the mean vector is subtracted from each row vector of the matrix A which expression is given by the following formula:

$$\phi_i = a_i - \psi, \quad i = 1,\ldots,N \tag{6}$$

Then, we calculate the covariance matrix C of ϕ as follow:

$$C = \phi^T \phi \quad \phi = [\phi_1 \phi_2 \ldots \phi_N] \tag{7}$$

Considering the matrix of eigenvectors $e(m \times m)$ of $C = \phi^T \phi$ associated with the vector of eigenvalues $\lambda(1 \times m)$. We have:

$$Ce = \lambda e \tag{8}$$

So, the orthonormal projection of A into the orthogonal space is a simple multiplication between $A(N \times m)$ and $e(m \times m)$ as follow:

$$A' = Ae \tag{9}$$

4 Speaker Verification Protocol

Speaker verification experiments are carried out on the TIMIT corpus which consists of read speech sampled at 16 kHz. It involves 168 target speakers (100 males and 68 females) with 168 client scores and 28056 impostor scores. For each target speaker, approximately 15 s of training data is available whereas duration of the test utterances is 9 s. Gaussian mixture model with the universal background model (GMM-UBM) [1] is used as classifier. Each enrolment utterance is adapted to UBM data using MAP adaptation [3]. Our UBM (42 min of speech) is a GMM with 128 components trained via Expectation Maximization (EM) [3]. PCA [13] is used as dimensionality reduction technique to project the features that characterized our speakers into principal directions and Fisher space before they are modeled by GMM-UBM. In parameterization phase, we specified the feature space used. Indeed, as the speech signal is dynamic and variable, we presented the observation sequences of various sizes by vectors of fixed size. Each vector is given by the coefficients Mel cepstrum MFCC (23 coefficients) extracted from the middle window every 10 ms. In asymmetric taper MFCCs extraction (23 coefficients), we used different values of the parameter k (k = −2.21, −1.41, 2.31

and 4). Hence, we have conducted verification tests with added noises (Babble and factory) extracted from the database Noisex-92 [18] (NATO: AC 243/RSG 10) at different SNR levels (0, 5, 10 and 15 dB). We used Equal Error Rate (EER) [1, 11] as the evaluation metrics.

5 Experimental Results

5.1 Speaker Verification Performances in Clean Conditions

In this section, a performances comparison between GMM-MAP and PCA-GMM-MAP in terms of EER, in clean environment when using two types of feature vectors: MFCCs and MFCCs based on asymmetric tapers are presented.

Firstly, our feature vectors are used without PCA projection as input for our model GMM-MAP. Secondly, the same feature vectors are projected into one projection space using PCA technique, before being modeled by GMM-UBM. Figure 2 illustrates the DET curves of the 10 verification systems in clean environment.

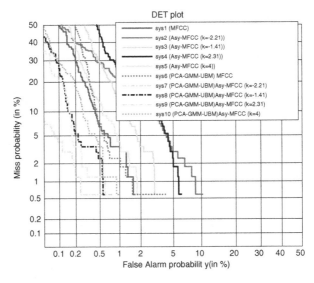

Fig. 2. DET curves of all systems under clean conditions.

From Fig. 2, when using PCA in front-end processing it observed that, MFCCs based on asymmetric taper outperforms MFCC with Hamming taper in terms of EER, especially when the asymmetric windows are considered as low-pass filter (k = −2.21), because in clean conditions, the useful information in the speech exists in the lower frequencies (in this case low frequencies can reach 4 kHz). Also, it can be noticed from the same figure that, when we projected the feature vectors into PCA space, an important improvement of EER is observed, especially when MFCCs based on asymmetric tapers is used. This improvement can be explained by the fact that, GMM-UBM that is used as a baseline classifier in this work, is based on diagonal covariance matrix for each Gaussian, and this assumption is satisfied by the clusters obtained by the projection of feature vectors in the PCA subspace. By cons, if the features are projected into PCA, the covariance matrix of new features becomes diagonal and including all information contained in the new features. Because this technique (PCA) decorrelate the features in the projection space by diagonalizing their covariance matrix. So in this case. For this reason, the performance of GMM-MAP appears best when the features are projected in projection subspace than before.

5.2   Speaker Verification Performances in Noisy Conditions

To test the performances of all feature methods with and without PCA in real noise, we used some of the noise samples babble-speech and factory extracted from the NOISEX-92 database shown by Fig. 3. These noises were added to test speech data after being scaled. The results obtained are given by Table 1.

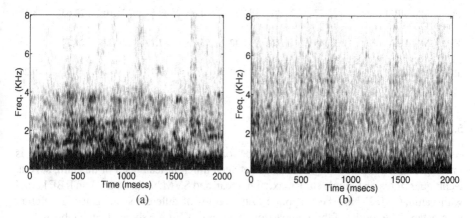

(a)   (b)

Fig. 3. Spectrograms of (a) babble noise, (b) factory noise.

From the results given in Table 1, it is observed that, there is a drop in accuracy of all methods as SNR decreases and the MFCCs based on asymmetric tapers (high-pass filter) brings an improvement in terms of EER, under both noises. This demonstrates that asymmetric windows (k = 2.31, k = 4) capture better the useful frequencies that are not significantly corrupted by the noise (Babble for example) in high frequencies region (sometimes, there is some phonemes in speech like fricatives that existing in high frequencies region especially for female speakers) than symmetric hamming tapers. However, a significant degradation of performances of all methods when PCA is applied to the features is observed.

This can be explained by the fact that, PCA projection is learnt from clean speech and according to recent studies [19], the mean and the variances of the corrupted testing speech (even high order statistics) changes drastically under noise compared to the ones estimated in clean environment. This is why; PCA do not provide good results in noisy environment.

Table 1. Comparative Equal Error Rate (EER%) of all systems under noisy environments.

Systems	Babble noise				Factory noise			
	SNR (dB)				SNR (dB)			
	0	5	10	15	0	5	10	15
GMM-UBM (MFCC)	36.13	26.47	16.15	8.35	42.59	36.13	23.40	12.88
GMM-UBM (Asy-MFCC, k = −2.21)	33.25	20.63	8.31	3.12	42.46	35.04	22.80	10.25
GMM-UBM (Asy-MFCC, k = −1.41)	34.86	23.86	12.68	5.52	43.47	36.49	24.56	9.09
GMM-UBM (Asy-MFCC, k = 2.31)	**30.93**	19.12	8.59	3.13	**40.37**	35.16	19.08	**6.61**
GMM-UBM (Asy-MFCC, k = 4)	31.06	**17.56**	**5.44**	**1.86**	41.96	**31.46**	**16.93**	7.57
PCA-GMM-UBM (MFCC)	36.08	27.67	17.32	6.94	44.03	35.17	24.51	11.68
PCA-GMM-UBM (Asy-MFCC, k = −2.21)	37.89	31.35	22.67	13.42	43.03	35.78	26.46	15.64
PCA-GMM-UBM (Asy-MFCC, k = −1.41)	35.77	24.30	11.27	4.00	42.57	36.10	22.65	8.45
PCA-GMM-UBM (Asy-MFCC, k = 2.31)	35.45	23.92	11.42	3.99	43.79	36.22	21.37	9.15
PCA-GMM-UBM (Asy-MFCC, k = 4)	35.49	20.78	8.13	2.76	42.77	36.87	21.41	9.26

5.3   Scores Fusion

A further step toward improving of the performance of speaker verification system is investigating a possible complimentarily between different features. For this aim, several techniques of fusion (simple sum, max, min, mean and SVM bi-class based on RBF kernel with gamma = 0.2) have been applied to the scores of different systems using different parameters. The results of this comparison in terms of EER are shown by the table below:

As shown in Table 2, there is an improvement in terms of ERR when a scores fusion is applied to the different feature vectors (MFCCs, and asymmetric MFCCs with

Table 2. Comparative Equal Error Rate (EER%) between different fusion systems under noisy environments.

Fusion systems	Babble noise				Factory noise			
	SNR (dB)				SNR (dB)			
	0	5	10	15	0	5	10	15
sum	33.81	22.88	11.36	2.97	42.11	33.69	18.50	**6.56**
min	36.33	28.00	17.45	9.52	43.09	36.14	22.63	13.17
max	31.23	17.83	**5.30**	**1.38**	41.23	31.36	**15.28**	8.36
mean	33.81	22.88	11.36	2.97	42.11	33.69	18.50	6.94
SVM	**19.04**	**15.64**	14.76	3.57	**19.64**	**17.85**	16.94	10.19

and without PCA), this validates our assumption about the complimentarily existing between these parameters. Also it is observed that, at level SNR = 10 dB and 15 dB, the simples methods (for example fusion with max: Babble noise: EER = 5.30 % at 10 dB and EER = 2.08 % at 15 dB. Factory noise: EER = 15.28 % at 10 dB and EER = 8.36 % at 15 dB) provide better results compared to SVM. By cons, in situations where the environment is very noisy (SNR = 0 dB and 5 dB), we see that, the SVM provides a significant improvement in term of ERR (Babble noise: EER = 19.04 % at 0 dB and EER = 15.64 % at 5 dB. Factory noise: EER = 19.64 % at 0 dB and EER = 17.85 % at 5 dB). This can be explained by the fact that in low-noisy environments (SNR > = 10 dB), the scores issued from different classifiers are linearly separable therefore a simple linear fusion can do the trick (good results). By cons, when environment becomes very noisy (SNR < 10 dB), data (scores) become non-linearly separable (overlapping data), so here SVM appears better than simple methods.

6 Conclusion

In this paper, different feature extraction methods were studied for speaker verification system based on GMM-UBM classifier in clean and noisy conditions. Also, we have demonstrated through different tests, the improvements in performances that the linear projection technique namely PCA brings in quiet environment and its non-robustness in the presence of noise. MFCC outperformed MFCC based on asymmetric tapers without PCA in calm conditions. However, under two different additive noise types, factory and babble noises, MFCC based on asymmetric tapers (k = 2.31, k = 4) gave the best performances than other. Via the linear score fusion based on the maximum (max) method, an interesting gain in performance is achieved when SNR is high (Babble speech for example). Whereas, in hard conditions (SNR < 10 dB), we showed that a score fusion based on a training method like SVM, gives better results in terms of accuracy error than a simple methods. The focus of our work, was to find the features which provide a good speaker verification performances in terms of equal error rate, especially under real world in goal to coupling them with advanced backend classifiers like JFA and I-Vector.

References

1. Reynolds, D. A.: An overview of automatic speaker recognition technology. ICASSP, pp. 4072–4075 (2002)
2. Bimbot, F., Bonastre, J.F., Fredouille, C., Gravier, G., Magrin-Chagnolleau, I., Meignier, S., Merlin, T., Ortega-Garcia, J., Petrovska-Delacretaz, D., Reynolds, D.A.: A tutorial on text-independent speaker verification. EURASIP J. Appl. Signal Process. 4(2), 430–451 (2004)
3. Reynolds, D.A., Quatieri, T.F., Dunn, R.: Speaker verification using adapted Gaussian mixture models. Dig. Signal Process. 10(1–3), 19–41 (2000)
4. Minh, N., Do, M.: Fast approximation of Kullback-Leibler distance for dependence trees and hidden Markov models. IEEE Signal Process. Lett. 10(4), 115–118 (2003)

5. Dong, X., Zhaohui, W.: Speaker Recognition using continuous density support vector machines. Electron. Lett. **37**(17), 1099–1101 (2001)
6. Morales-Cordovilla, J.A., Sánchez, V., Gómez, A.M., Peinado, A.M.,: On the use of asymmetric windows for robust speech recognition. Circ. Syst. Signal Process. **31**(2), 727–736 (2012)
7. Rozman, R., Kodek, D.M.: Using asymmetric windows in automatic speech recognition. Speech Commun. **49**, 268–276 (2007)
8. Kitaoka, N., Yamamoto, K., Kusamizu, T., Nakagawa, S., Yamada, T., Tsuge, S., Miyajima, C., Nishiura, T., Nakayama, M., Denda, Y., et al.: Development of VAD evaluation framework CENSREC-1-C and investigation of relationship between VAD and speech recognition performance. In: ASRU IEEE Workshop on Automatic Speech Recognition and Understanding, pp. 607–612 (2007)
9. Kinnunen, T., Rajan, P.: A practical, self-adaptive voice activity detector for speaker verification with noisy telephone and microphone data. In: Proceedings of the International Conference on Acoustics, Speech and Signal Processing (ICASSP 2013), pp. 7229–7233, Vancouver, Canada, May 2013
10. Kua, J.M., Epps, J.R., Ambikairajah, E., Nosratighods, M.H.: Front-end diversity in fused speaker recognition systems. In: The Proceedings of APSIPA ASC 2010, Asia-Pacific Signal Processing Association, Hong Kong, Presented at Asia-Pacific Signal Processing Association Conference, Singapore, 14–17 Dec 2010
11. Kinnunen, T., Li, H.: An overview of text independent speaker recognition: from features to supervectors. Speech Commun. **52,** 12–40, Science Direct (2009)
12. Harris, F.: On the use of windows for harmonic analysis with the discrete Fourier transform. Proc. IEEE **66**(1), 51–84 (1978)
13. Delac, K., Grgic, M., Grgic, S.: Independent comparative study of PCA, ICA, and LDA on the FERET data set. Technical report, University of Zagreb (2004)
14. Moore, B.: Hearing. Academic Press, San Diego, ISBN 0-12-505626-5 (1995)
15. Alam. J., Kenny, P., O Shaughnessy, D.: On the use of asymmetric-shaped tapers for speaker verification using I-Vectors. In: Proceedings of the Odyssey Speaker and Language Recognition Workshop, Singapore, June 2012
16. Turk, M., Pentland, A.: Eigenfaces for recognition. J. Cogn. Neurosci. **3**(1), 71–86 (1991)
17. Golub, G.H.: The generalized eigenvalue problem. Lectures on matrix computation, Ph.D. program of the Dipartimento di Matematica Istituto "Guido Castelnuovo". Lecture No. 11, Roma (2004)
18. Varga, A.P, et al.: The NOISEX-92 study on the effect of additive noise on automatic speech recognition. NOISEX92, CDROM (1992)
19. Toh, A.M.: Feature extraction for robust speech recognition in hostile environments. Ph.D. thesis, School of Electrical, Electronic and Computer Engineering, University of Western Australia (UWA) (2008)

Automatic Geographic Enrichment by Multi-modal Bike Sensing

Steven Verstockt[1(✉)], Viktor Slavkovikj[1], Pieterjan De Potter[1],
Olivier Janssens[1,2], Jürgen Slowack[3], and Rik Van de Walle[1]

[1] Multimedia Lab – ELIS Department, Ghent University - iMinds,
Gaston Crommenlaan 8, Bus 201, Ledeberg, Ghent, Belgium
{steven.verstockt,viktor.slavkovikj,pieterjan.
depotter,djansse.janssens,rik.vandewalle}@ugent.be
[2] Electronics and Information Technology Lab, ISP, Ghent University,
Graaf Karel de Goedelaan 5, 8500 Kortrijk, Belgium
[3] Barco NV, President Kennedypark 35, 8500 Kortrijk, Belgium
jurgen.slowack@barco.com

Abstract. This paper focuses on the automatic geo-annotation of road/terrain types by collaborative bike sensing. The proposed terrain classification system is mainly based on the analysis of volunteered geographic information gathered by cyclists. By using participatory accelerometer and GPS sensor data collected from the cyclists' smartphones, which is enriched with image data from geographic web services or the smartphone camera, the proposed system is able to distinguish between 6 different terrain types. For the classification of the multi-modal bike data, the system employs a random decision forest (RDF), which compared favorably for the geo-annotation task against different classification algorithms. The system classifies the features of every instance of road (over a 5 seconds interval) and maps the results onto the corresponding GPS coordinates. Finally, based on all the collected instances, we can annotate geographic maps with the terrain types, create more advanced route statistics and facilitate geo-based recommender systems. The accuracy of the bike sensing system is 92 % for 6-class terrain classification. For the 2-class on-road/off-road classification an accuracy of 97 % is achieved, almost six percent above the state-of-the-art in this domain.

Keywords: Multi-modal sensing · Image classification · Geo-annotation · Bike-sensing · Volunteered geographic information · Accelerometer analysis · Mobile vision · Machine learning

1 Introduction

Mobile phones have increasingly evolved in functionality, features and capability over the last decade. Nowadays, they are being used by many for more than just communication. With the continuous improvement in sensor technology built into these 'smartphones', and web services to aggregate and interpret the logged information, people are able to create, record, analyze and share information about their daily activities. As such, the mobile phone is well on its way to become a personal sensing platform [5].

© Springer-Verlag Berlin Heidelberg 2014
M.S. Obaidat and J. Filipe (Eds.): ICETE 2013, CCIS 456, pp. 369–384, 2014.
DOI: 10.1007/978-3-662-44788-8_22

Within this mobile sensing (r)evolution, phone users acts as sensor operators, i.e., they contribute sensor measurements about their activities or the places they visit as part of a larger-scale effort to collect data about a population or a geographical area [21]. This is the idea behind participatory or human-centric sensing. Recently, this tendency has also started to occur in the domain of geographic information systems (GIS). Where the process of mapping the Earth has been the task of a small group of people (surveyors, cartographers, and geographers) for many years, it starts to become possible now for everyone to participate in several types of collaborative geographic projects, such as OpenStreetMap and RouteYou [6]. These projects are built upon user generated geographic content, so called volunteered geographic information (VGI). VGI makes it easier to create, combine, and share maps and supports the rapid production of geographic information. One drawback, however, is that a lot of the work still involves manual labor. Within our work we focus on how mobile sensors can help to automate and facilitate the more labor-intensive VGI tasks.

A common task performed by recreational GPS-users is to find good routes in an area. From all the route characteristics, the road quality, i.e., the physical condition of the terrain, and the terrain surface showed to have a significant impact on how the users rank their routes [19]. Currently, however, this information is largely unavailable. In order to bridge this gap, there is need for automatic road classification. Within this paper, we investigate the ability to determine the current terrain type from 'onboard' mobile sensors, enriched with geographic web data from the GPS coordinates. Contrarily to manual VGI, our approach facilitates real-time updates/annotation, e.g. when road conditions change or new roads are found. Furthermore, it is not required to buy specialized sensing equipment, keeping costs very low.

A general overview of the proposed setup is shown in Fig. 1. Both bike data and web data can be used to extract geographic information of the terrain the user is traversing. The 'bike data' consists of accelerometer/vibration signals and GPS coordinates, which are collected using the 'onboard' smartphone of the cyclist. Furthermore, images of the mobile camera can be used as 'optional' bike data. Alternatively, visual information can also be extracted 'online' from geographic web services. This 'web data' consists of a set of geographic images and features centered at the location that corresponds to the bike GPS coordinates. In order to retrieve this information, we query the web APIs of online geo-services like Google Maps and OpenStreetMap (OSM). When available, it is also possible to use 'external' data sources.

Based on the bike data and corresponding web data, the terrain type is estimated using the novel multi-modal RDF-based classification algorithm, which is fed with a set of discriminative image and accelerometer features. Finally, using this road/terrain information, a geographic map can be annotated automatically and more advanced route statistics can be generated, which, for example, can facilitate geo-based recommender systems.

It is important to remark that when no visual bike data from the mobile camera is used, the device can be placed or stored as wanted by the user. Compared to the 'onboard' camera set-up, this gives more flexibility and freedom to the user. Our experimental results also show that this has no impact on the accuracy of the proposed multi-modal terrain classification algorithm.

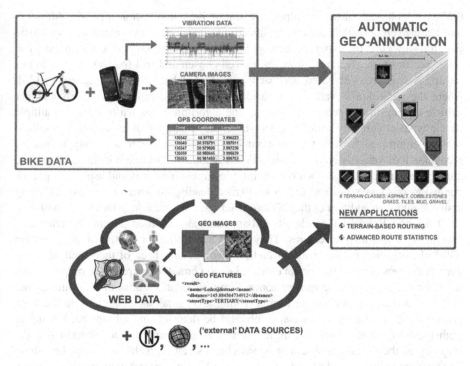

Fig. 1. General overview of the multi-modal bike sensing setup. Based on the bike data and corresponding web data, the terrain type is estimated using the novel multi-modal RDF-based classification algorithm.

The remainder of this paper is organized as follows. Section 2 presents the related work in mobile-sensing for GIS road/terrain classification and web-based enrichment. Subsequently, Sect. 3 proposes our novel terrain classification method, based on accelerometer and mobile and/or web-based visual features which are fed to the RDF. Next, Sect. 4 presents the experimental setup and discusses the data collection, ground truth (GT) creation and evaluation strategy/results. Finally, Sect. 5 ends this paper with conclusions and points out directions for future work.

2 Related Work

2.1 Mobile-Sensing: GIS Terrain Classification

Current mobile-sensing solutions for GIS road/terrain classification either use accelerometer data or visual images. Although they can easily (and successfully) be combined, the combination of both sensor types is not yet investigated.

Based on the observation that traversing different terrain types induces different vibration signals, Weiss et al. [27] use an accelerometer mounted on a vehicle (i.e., a robot) to perform vibration-based road classification. To train and classify the vibration signals they fed a set of distinctive accelerometer features to a Support Vector Machine

(SVM), which was shown to outperform alternative classification methods. Although they achieve around 80 % correct classifications, the speed of the vehicle is not realistic (i.e., too slow) and the experiments were performed in a 'controlled' environment. The set of accelerometer features, however, is well-chosen and will (partly) be used in our set-up. A similar SVM-based approach is presented by Ward and Iagnemma [26], where the algorithm is validated with experimental data collected with a passenger vehicle driving in real-world conditions. The algorithm is shown to classify multiple terrain types as correctly with 89 %. However, they make use of expensive, specialized sensing equipment to achieve this accuracy and the classifier was only trained to recognize four very distinctive classes. When the classes vibration behavior would be closer to each other, e.g., when comparing tiles to cobblestones and asphalt to gravel, confusion of classes is expected to be higher, leading to lower accuracy. By using visual features, in addition to the accelerometer data, we are able to tackle this problem.

Tang and Breckon [25] classify urban, rural and off-road terrains by analyzing several color and texture features. They report a performance of almost 90 % correct SVM classification on the road/off-road problem. A drawback of their method, however, is the genericity of the terrain classes, i.e., too broad for recreational purposes, and the strict positioning of the camera zones. Similar limitations arise in [17]. Interesting, however, is that these authors perform a 'voting' over small image regions. In this way, conflicting or confusing zones can (probably) be detected and eliminated, leading to higher classification accuracy. Furthermore, it is also important to mention that the majority of the visual classification approaches use an 'unrealistic' set-up, i.e., sharp images containing a single terrain type captured from a perpendicular camera angle. Our approach, on the opposite, uses images from real bike runs or online geo-queries, containing blurred images with non-sharp terrain boundaries. As such our accuracy of 92 % is a 'real-life' accuracy.

Although SVM has shown to perform best in the majority of the related work, Khan et al. [11] recently showed that Random Decision Forests (RDF) improve the SVM results in the context of road/terrain classification. This hypothesis was also confirmed by SVM-RDF comparisons performed on our experimental data. A gain of 7 % was achieved when using RDF instead of SVM for visual classification. For accelerometer classification, the gain was lower, however, still 2 %. As such, RDF, which is an ensemble classifier consisting of a collection of individual decision tree predictors, is used in our work.

2.2   Data Enrichment Using Web APIs

While the SOTA approaches discussed in the previous section only use their own sensor data to detect the terrain type, we expect it is beneficial to use publicly available geo-data from the Internet. With the growing availability of geo web services, it is possible to achieve a unique combination of geographic data of different origin coupled to the location's coordinates. The integration of geo-data from several providers yields new knowledge, mutual enrichment and benefit, improvement of information sharing and reuse. In this section, we briefly discuss the related work in this domain.

Hariharan et al. [7] describe several applications that take advantage of existing Web data combined with GPS location measurements. They show that web-enhanced

GPS can be easily used to create compelling location-aware applications with almost no deployment cost. In [14], a time and space aware information system for mobile phones is proposed based on geo-data mined from the web. The authors discuss several providers of location related web data and list the problems related to each of these services. The two main problems geo-spatial data may suffer from are the variable quality and the description conflicts [10]. The first one concerns updating, completeness and accuracy of the data. The second one concerns inconsistent descriptions provided by different sources for the same (latitude, longitude) pair. In order to cope with geo-data from different origin with different data models, resolution and types of geometric representations, we extract and weight the geographical features from each geo-service individually and do not merge the geo-data itself.

The works most closely related to our approach are [8] and [9]. Both approaches query OpenStreetMap (OSM) data to enrich a location-based mobile application. Hentschel and Wagner, on the one hand, improve autonomous robot navigation in urban environments using the free to use and globally available online geographic OSM data. Kaklanis et al., on the other hand, present a mobile application that enables location-based haptic exploration of OSM data for the visually impaired and blind users using mobile devices. Both OSM-based approaches show the feasibility of web-based geo-data enrichment. Instead of only focusing on OSM, our approach also uses other geographic data providers in order to improve the overall classification result.

3 Multi-sensor Terrain Classification

The multi-modal bike sensing system is built upon three (or four) sensing components: an accelerometer, a digital camera, a GPS and/or a location based querier of geographic web APIs. Each of these 'data providers' independently and concurrently captures terrain data. Based on this multi-modal data, the proposed terrain classification system estimates which type of terrain (asphalt, cobblestones, tiles, gravel, grass, and mud) the vehicle is currently traversing.

A general scheme of the classification system is shown in Fig. 2. First, the raw sensor data is pre-processed. The windowing groups the vibration data into overlapping data fragments of 5 seconds and aligns them onto the corresponding images and the GPS data. The images are also split into blocks in order to detect/eliminate conflicting or confusing zones, as in the work of Popescu et al. [17]. Subsequently, we further process/analyze the sensor data to create a set of training and test feature vectors (which is discussed in detail in Sect. 3.1). Next, the training vectors are used to construct a random forest of binary decision trees (as explained in Sect. 3.2). Finally, the test vectors are classified using the trained RDF. Based on the RDF class probabilities and the corresponding GPS data, geo-annotation of test data can be performed.

3.1 Feature Extraction

For each of the sensor data segments, i.e., for each 5 seconds of biking, we extract a set of discriminative visual and vibration features which best describe the road/terrain conditions. The selection of these features is based on the state-of-the-art (SOTA) study

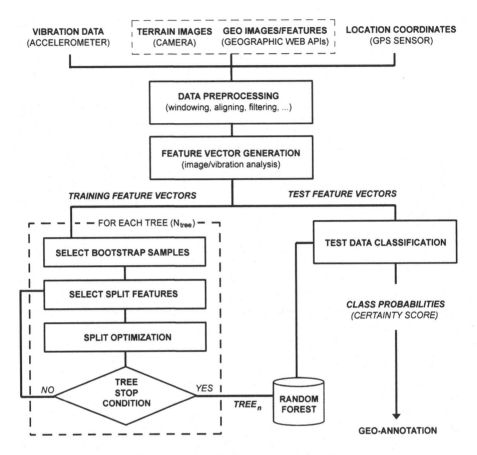

Fig. 2. Multi-sensor RDF-based terrain classification.

(discussed in Sect. 2), and on our test data evaluation (Sect. 4). When features show similar behavior, the feature with lowest computational cost is chosen.

Accelerometer/vibration Features. By inspection of the accelerometer readings for the different terrain types, it was found that not every road type has a distinct pattern. Similar 'feature equalities' occur when analyzing the geo web images, however, not between the same pairs of road/terrain types. As such, by performing a multi-modal analysis it is expected that the ambiguities in the vibration data can be compensated by visual data, and vice versa.

The accelerometer of our mobile device(s) detects the vibration along the X, Y and Z-axes. Important to remark is that, depending on the position of the device, $\{x,y,z\}$ coordinates will vary and will complicate the classification task. In order to overcome this obstacle, of forcing the user to place the device in a pre-defined position, the magnitude m of the acceleration is calculated:

$$m = \sqrt{x^2 + y^2 + z^2}. \tag{1}$$

Computing (and analyzing) the features on the vibration magnitude m, instead of on the individual accelerometer data along the X, Y and Z-axes, enables our system to assume an arbitrary and possibly changing orientation for the mobile device, i.e., increases the user's freedom. The set of features which were found to best describe the bike vibrations are a combination of the once proposed in [27] and [20], and are defined as follows:

- $\mu(m)$: mean of m - for flatter/smoother surfaces (e.g. asphalt and gravel), $\mu(m)$ is low (close to 0).
- $max(m)$: maximum of m - takes large values for terrain types that contain big bumps, e.g., cobblestones and grass/mud.
- $min(m)$: minimum of m - takes larger values for flat terrains (e.g., asphalt).
- $\sigma(m)$: standard deviation of m - is higher for coarse terrain types (e.g., gravel) than for smoother ones (such as tiles and asphalt).
- $\|m\|$: norm of m - is large if the acceleration is constantly high, as it is for cobblestones.
- $E(m)$: energy, i.e., squared FFT sum of m [18] - takes larger values for coarse terrain types, such as grass, mud and gravel.

It is important to remark that each of these vibration features is calculated over a sliding overlapping time window of 5 seconds, in order to align them with the visual features which are discussed hereafter. A similar windowing approach has demonstrated success in previous work [1].

Our experiments showed that some of the investigated terrain types are hard to recognize using an accelerometer (see evaluation results - Sect. 4). Since these terrains have similar vibration behavior, it is not always possible to distinguish between their feature values. Visual features can help to overcome these problems. The other way around, accelerometer features can help to cope with (possible) visual ambiguities. Multi-modal combination of visual and vibration features is, as such, a win-win. In the next subsections, visual features from both a mobile camera and online geo-queries are discussed in more detail.

Visual Features (of Mobile Camera). The set of visual features that has been found to be most appropriate for the terrain classification task, consists of color-, texture-, edge- and energy-based measures. In total, 8 features are used (each of them calculated on the mobile camera image I). They are defined as follows:

- $blue(I)$: percentage 'blue' pixels based on HSV-blue range – for cobblestones and asphalt, for example, $blue(I)$ is close to 1.
- $green(I)$: histogram spread of 'green' HSV pixels – has large values for grass.
- $mud(I)$: percentage low-saturated 'orange-red' HSV pixels – is large for mud and some types of brown colored gravel.
- $gray(I)$: percentage pixels that meet the gray RGB equality criteria $R \approx G \approx B$ - is higher for road types (e.g., asphalt and cobblestones) than for off-road ones (such as grass and gravel).

- $E(I)$: FFT energy spread of I – is large if the terrain image has a lot of high energy texture, as it is for grass and cobblestones.
- $Hough(I)$: Hough Transform based number of distinct edge directions in I – is only high for tiles and cobblestones.
- $EOH(I)$: MPEG-7 Edge Orientation Histogram based spread of edges in I [16] - takes large values for terrain types with random edge distribution, such as grass and gravel.
- $GLCM(I)$: Product of gray-level co-occurence matrix [3] statistics of local binary pattern [15] filtered image of I – is high for cobblestones and off-road terrains.

Map-Based Features (of Online Geo-queries). As an alternative (or complement) to the mobile camera images, we also generate map-based features of online geo-queries centered at the location that corresponds to the bike GPS coordinates. In order to select an appropriate set of map-based features, we have evaluated several geographic web services based on their ease of use, data type ($\sim$ mutual information) and accuracy. Most of the geographic web services allow to query images from the neighborhood of a (lat, long)-pair. Depending on the service, these images may differ in detail, colors and content or representation. As such, it is necessary to convert each of these image types individually into one or more features representing the image content. In the current set-up, we use images from OpenStreetMap (I_{OSM}), Google Maps (I_{GM}) & Street View (I_{SV}), and NGI (I_{NGI}), i.e., the Belgian National Geographic Institute. From these images, we extracted the following 8 features:

- $texture(I_{SV})$ number of strong Canny edge pixels of the Google Street View image I_{SV} (which pitch is set to -90 to face down the 'camera') – takes large values for cobblestones and tiles. Since no Street View images exist for off-road locations, texture (I_{SV}) is left blank, facilitating road/off-road classification.
- $streets(I_{OSM})/streets(I_{NGI})$: percentage street-colored pixels in the OSM and NGI image. The street pixels are filtered out using the specific OSM and NGI street color ranges - is higher for road types (e.g., asphalt and cobblestones) than for off-road ones (such as grass and gravel).
- $grass(I_{OSM})/grass(I_{GM})/grass(I_{NGI})$: percentage grass- or rural-colored pixels in the OSM, Google Maps and NGI image. Grass pixels are filtered out using the specific rural color ranges - takes large values for off-road terrain types. $grass(I_{GM})$ only takes large values for grass, and not for mud or gravel.
- $mud(I_{GM})$: percentage low-saturated 'orange-red' HSV pixels ($\sim$ mud-colored pixels) in the Google Maps image I_{GM} - is large for mud and some types of gravel.
- $urban(I_{OSM})$: percentage 'gray' pixels based on RGB- equality - is larger for road terrain types like asphalt, cobblestones and tiles.

3.2   RDF Classification

Random Decision Forests (RDF) is a very fast tool for classification and clustering, which has shown to be extremely flexible in the context of computer vision [4]. The most known application of RDF is the detection of human body parts from depth data in the Microsoft KINECT [23]. This commercial application demonstrates the practicability of RDF for large-scale real-world computer vision problems. The accuracy of RDF is comparable with other classifiers. Furthermore, Khan et al. [11] recently showed that RDF improves SVM in terrain classification tasks. Other advantages of RDF are its simple training and testing algorithms, and the fact that is can easily perform multi-class classifications.

Random forests are ensembles of randomized decision trees T_n, as illustrated in Fig. 3. Each of the N_{tree} trees consists of split nodes and leaves which map the multi-modal feature vector v to a distribution $P_i(c)$ stored at each leaf. The split nodes evaluate the arriving feature vector and depending on the feature values, pass it to the left or right child. Each leaf stores the statistics of the training vectors. For a classification task, it is the probability for each class c, denoted by $P(c|v)$:

$$P(c|v) = \sum_{n=1}^{N_{tree}} P_n(c|v). \tag{2}$$

For a more general discussion on random forests, we refer to the book of Breiman [2] and the tutorial of Shotton et al. [22].

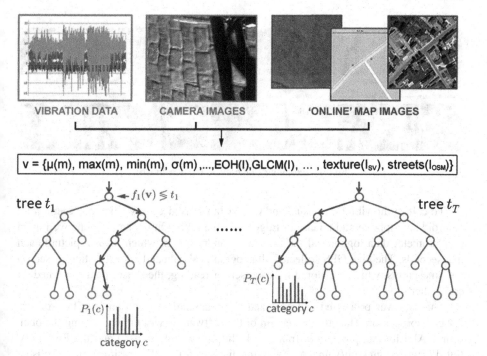

Fig. 3. The random forest consists of a set of trees that map the multi-modal feature vector v to a distribution $P_i(c)$ stored at each leaf. The disks indicate split nodes that evaluate one of the features of v and pass it to the right/left child until a leaf is reached [22].

4   Experimental Setup and Evaluation Results

In order to evaluate the proposed architecture we have performed several bike tours. During these tours we collected the training/test data and annotated them with the ground truth (GT). Based on this GT, we evaluated the test data while varying the number of trees (Ntree) and the sample ratio r (i.e., the percentage randomized training vectors used in each tree construction). Recently, we have also launched a bike app to extensively test the proposed set-up and collect more test data. Further development/ testing will be performed on the user collected field data.

4.1   Data Collection

The data collection was performed using standard 26" and 29" mountain bikes. Multiple cycles with varying terrain conditions (in type and frequency) were performed in several rural and (sub)urban regions all over Belgium. An exemplary run, in which all 6 terrain types occurred, is shown in Fig. 4. In order to have varying weather conditions, the cycle runs were spread over the year, both in winter and summer on sunny and rainy days. Furthermore, tyre pressure and tyre types were changed in between several runs in order to cope with the tyre-vibration dependency.

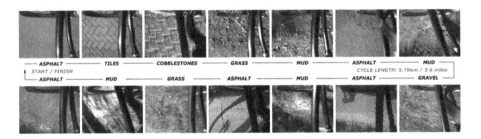

Fig. 4. Exemplary bike cycle (start = finish).

To collect the vibration, visual and GPS data we used a Sony Ericsson Xperia mini Android smartphone and a Garmin Edge 800 bike GPS. On the smartphone we ran an accelerometer data logger and the time lapse android app, which takes a picture each five seconds. The bike GPS collected all geographical data and bike statistics. Based on the timestamps, which are stored for each sensor reading, the sensor data is aligned on each other.

The data was processed and analyzed on a standard PC with an Intel Pentium IV 2.4 GHz processor. The current version of the software is written in C# using the open source AlgLib data processing framework (http://www.alglib.net/) and the Emgu CV (http://www.emgu.com/) image processing library (for RDF classification and visual analysis respectively).

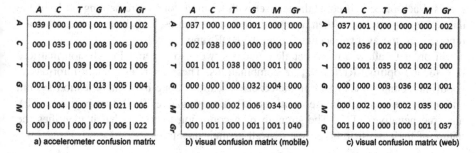

Fig. 5. Confusion matrices.

4.2 Ground Truth Creation

The ground truth creation is performed by visual analysis of the terrain images using a custom built ground-truth marking application. If no terrain images are available, the GT can also be created with the available geographic terrain data of online maps.

Important to remark is that it is not always clear/easy to distinguish between some of the off-road types, as can be seen in the cycle run in Fig. 4. Sometimes, the terrain consists of a combination of multiple terrain types, e.g., grass and mud, or gravel and mud. In these situations, ground truth annotation is difficult and can be error-prone. A similar kind of ground-truth inaccuracy was also reported in [24]. In order to cope with this GT issue, we will extend the GT concept to allow multi-annotation. Currently, one can also discard these misclassifications from the confusion matrices and other evaluation metrics, which are discussed hereafter.

4.3 Evaluation Strategy/Metrics

First of all, it is important to mention that both 6-class and 2-class road/off-road classifications are evaluated. This facilitates comparison with SOTA works, which mainly perform 2-class classification or not always use the same set of terrain types. Furthermore, depending the application in which the classification system is used, the degree of specificity will also differ, i.e., for some GIS tools a road/off-road discrimination is sufficient.

The accuracy of the proposed system is evaluated for increasing number of RDF trees (N_{tree}) and increasing sample ratio r (which is related to the number of bootstrap samples). We define the accuracy as the proportion of the total number of predictions that were correct, i.e., the ratio of the number of correctly classified test vectors and the total number of test vectors. This accuracy will be calculated for each of the sensors individually, i.e., the accelerometer and mobile/web-based image accuracy, and also for their combination, i.e., the multi-modal accuracy. When they are combined, we use a winner-take-all strategy, where the sensor with the highest class probability in $P(c\,|\,v)$ wins. Other 'merging' strategies were also investigated, however, not leading to better multi-modal accuracy results.

Like in the work of [12], the evaluation is performed using 10-fold cross-validation. The data collected during our bike cycles is randomly divided into ten equal-sized pieces. Each piece is used as the test set with training done on remaining 90 % of the data. The test results are then averaged over the ten cases, i.e., the accuracies that are reported are the average accuracy over 10 RDF runs.

In order to allow a more detailed analysis, we also generated confusion matrices [13] for the optimal RDF $N_{tree}-r$ combinations. These matrices contain information about the actual ($\sim GT$) and predicted classifications done by a classification system and report the number of false positives (FP), false negatives (FN), true positives (TP), and true negatives (TN). The strength of a confusion matrix is that it identifies the nature of the classification errors, as well as their quantities.

4.4   Results

First, we will present the accuracy results for each of the sensors individually, i.e., the accelerometer and mobile/web-based image accuracy. Subsequently, we will present their multi-modal accuracy, based on a simple merging strategy. The graphs (Graph 1–4) show the accuracy for increasing number of RDF trees (N_{tree}) and increasing sample ratio r. Both 6-class and road/off-road 2-class accuracy are shown.

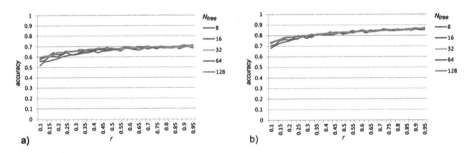

Graph 1. (a) Accuracy of 6-class terrain classification and (b) 2-class road/off-road terrain classification solely based on accelerometer data. Results are shown for increasing number of RDF trees (N_{tree}) and increasing sample ratio r.

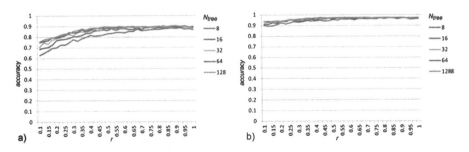

Graph 2. (a) Accuracy of 6-class terrain classification and (b) 2-class road/off-road terrain classification solely based on visual data of the mobile camera. Results are shown for increasing number of RDF trees (N_{tree}) and increasing sample ratio r.

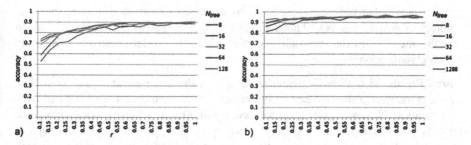

Graph 3. (a) Accuracy of 6-class terrain classification and (b) 2-class road/off-road terrain classification solely based on geographic map data of online geo-queries. Results are shown for increasing number of RDF trees (N_{tree}) and increasing sample ratio r.

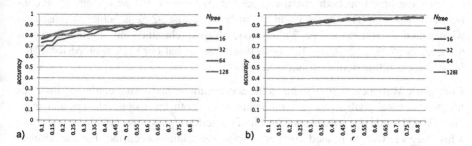

Graph 4. (a) Accuracy of 6-class terrain classification and (b) 2-class road/off-road terrain classification based on both visual and accelerometer data. Results are shown for increasing number of RDF trees (N_{tree}) and increasing sample ratio r.

In general, each of the terrain types were classified correctly to a high degree, but also some misclassifications occurred. From these misdetections, mud and grass were mostly confused with each other. As discussed in Sect. 4.2, however, this can also be caused due to some ground-truth inaccuracy in case of multi-class terrain images. Furthermore, it is also important to remark that the mobile image accuracy is based on an optimal positioning of the smartphone camera. It the camera is not placed facing down as in our setup, we expect the visual accuracy to be some percentages lower. A similar remark holds for the web-based accuracy, which assumes good GPS signals.

Accelerometer/Vibration Results. Graph 1a shows the accuracy for the 6-class terrain classification solely based on accelerometer data. For an optimal RDF configuration ($N_{tree} \approx 32$; $r \approx 0.65$), an accuracy of 71 % is achieved. For 2-class road/off-road classification, the accuracy is 87 %, as can be seen in Graph 1b.

Visual Results of Mobile Camera. Graph 2a shows the accuracy for the 6-class terrain classification solely based on visual data of the smartphone's mobile camera. For an optimal RDF configuration ($N_{tree} \approx 32$; $r \approx 0.60$), an accuracy of 90 % is achieved. For 2-class road/off-road classification, the 'visual-only' accuracy is 96 %, as can be seen in Graph 2b. Again we remark that this visual accuracy is based on an optimal positioning of the smartphone camera. Due to this optimal positioning, the gain of multi-modal analysis is not that big (less than 2 %), as discussed hereafter. However, since the accuracy of visual analysis will not always be so high in real-life conditions, it is safe to state that the multi-modal approach outperforms both the accelerometer and visual-only terrain classification.

Visual Results of Online Geo-queries. Graph 3a shows the accuracy for the 6-class terrain classification solely based on online geographic map data. For an optimal RDF configuration ($N_{tree} \approx 64$; $r \approx 0.60$), an accuracy of 90 % is achieved. For 2-class road/off-road classification, the 'GEO-only' accuracy is 95 %, as can be seen in Graph 4. Due to the 'big' online enrichment, the gain of multi-modal analysis is not that high (again less than 2 %). However, such an extensive enrichment will not always be possible, e.g. due to lack of geographic data or inaccurate GPS positioning.

Combined 'Multi-modal' Results. Graph 4a shows the accuracy for the 6-class terrain classification based on both visual and accelerometer data. For an optimal RDF configuration ($N_{tree} \approx 64$; $r \approx 0.55$), an accuracy of almost 92 % is achieved (based on winner-take-all strategy). For 2-class road/off-road classification, the multi-modal accuracy is 97 % (see Graph 4b). Both results show that our system outperforms the SOTA work in this domain (discussed in Sect. 2).

Confusion Matrices. Figure 5 shows the accelerometer and visual confusion matrices for their optimal RDF $N_{tree}-r$ combinations. As both the mobile camera and web-based visual confusion matrix show, each of the terrain types was classified correctly to a high degree. Only a limited number of misclassifications occurred. For the accelerometer classification, most misdetections occur on off-road terrain types.

Similar to [18], we also performed leave-one-out feature evaluation, in order to find out which features among the selected ones are less important than the others. We ran the RDF classification with one attribute removed at a time. For the accelerometer features, for example, $E(I)$ and $\|m\|$ turn out to be the least significant. Leaving them out, however, leads to a significant change of 2–3 % in accuracy, i.e., a trade-off between accuracy and computational complexity. A similar remark holds for the mobile and web-based visual features.

5 Conclusions

In this paper, we have presented the detailed design, implementation and evaluation of a novel road/terrain classification system. The proposed system shows how mobile sensors can help to automate and facilitate some of the more labor intensive VGI tasks. Based on the analysis of volunteered geographic information gathered by bikers, geographic maps can be annotated automatically with each of the 6 terrain types: asphalt, cobblestones, tiles, gravel, grass, and mud.

In order to perform the terrain classification task, the system employs a random decision forest (RDF), fed with a set of discriminative image and accelerometer features. The multi-sensor terrain classification achieves 92 % accuracy for the 6-class terrain classification problem, and 97 % accuracy for the on-/off-road classification. Since the evaluation is performed on data gathered during real bike runs, these are 'real-life' accuracies.

Future work will focus on the influence of bike conditions (e.g., speed and ascent/ descent) on the classification results. If someone is biking faster, for example, it is expected that the accelerometer will be more discriminative, while for slower bikers, visual features will (probably) be. Further research is needed to check these hypotheses and to incorporate these kinds of dependencies in our system.

References

1. Bao, L., Intille, S.S.: Activity recognition from user-annotated acceleration data. In: Ferscha, A., Mattern, F. (eds.) PERVASIVE 2004. LNCS, vol. 3001, pp. 1–17. Springer, Heidelberg (2004)
2. Breiman, L.: Random forests. Mach. Learn. **45**(1), 5–32 (2001)
3. Ershad, S.F.: Texture classification approach based on combination of edge and co-occurrence and local binary pattern. In: Proceedings of International Conference on Image Processing, Computer Vision, and Pattern Recognition, pp. 626–629 (2011)
4. Gall, J., Razavi, N., Van Gool, L.: An introduction to random forests for multi-class object detection. In: Dellaert, F., Frahm, J.-M., Pollefeys, M., Leal-Taixé, L., Rosenhahn, B. (eds.) Real-World Scene Analysis 2011. LNCS, vol. 7474, pp. 243–263. Springer, Heidelberg (2012)
5. Goldman, J., Shilton, K., Burke, J., Estrin, D., Hansen, M., Ramanathan, N., Reddy, S., Samanta, V., Srivastava, M., West, R.: Participatory sensing - a citizen-powered approach to illuminating the patterns that shape our world. In: White paper of Woodrow Wilson International Center for Scholars – Foresight and Governance project (2009)
6. Haklay, M., Weber, P.: OpenStreetMap: user-generated street maps. Pervasive Comput. **7** (4), 12–18 (2008)
7. Hariharan, R., Krumm, J., Horvitz, E.: Web-enhanced GPS. In: Strang, T., Linnhoff-Popien, C. (eds.) LoCA 2005. LNCS, vol. 3479, pp. 95–104. Springer, Heidelberg (2005)
8. Hentschel, M., Wagner, B.: Autonomous robot navigation based on OpenStreetMap geodata. In: Proceedings of 13th International IEEE Conference on Intelligent Transportation Systems, pp. 1645–1650 (2010)
9. Kaklanis, N., Votis, K., Tzovaras, D.: Touching OpenStreetMap data in mobile context for the visually impaired. In: Proceedings of the 3rd Workshop on Mobile Accessibility - ACM SIGCHI Conference on Human Factors in Computing Systems (2013)
10. Karam, R., Melchiori, M.: Improving geo-spatial linked data with the wisdom of the crowds. In: Proceedings of the Joint EDBT/ICDT 2013 Workshops, pp. 68–74 (2013)
11. Khan, Y.N., Komma, P., Bohlmann, K., Zell, A.: Grid-based visual terrain classification for outdoor robots using local features. In: IEEE Symposium on Computational Intelligence in Vehicles and Transportation Systems (CIVTS 2011), pp. 16–22 (2011)
12. Khan, Y.N., Masselli, A., Zell, A.: Visual terrain classification by flying robots. In: IEEE International Conference on Robotics and Automation, pp. 498–503 (2012)
13. Kohavi, R., Provost, F.: Glossary of terms. Mach. Learn. **30**, 271–274 (1998)
14. Pannevis, M., Marx, M.: Using web-sources for location based systems on mobile phones. In: Proceedings of Workshop on Mobile Information Retrieval (MobIR'08) (2008)
15. Pietikäinen, M., Hadid, A., Zhao, G., Ahonen, T.: Computer Vision Using Local Binary Patterns. Computational Imaging and Vision, vol. 40. Springer, London (2011)
16. Pinheiro, A.M.G.: Image descriptors based on the edge orientation. In: Proceedings of the 4th International Workshop on Semantic Media Adaptation and Personalization, pp. 73–78 (2009)

17. Popescu, D., Dobrescu, R., Merezeanu, D.: Road analysis based on texture similarity evaluation. In: Proceedings of the 7th WSEAS International Conference on Signal Processing (SIP'08), pp. 47–51 (2008)
18. Ravi, N., Dandekar, N., Mysore, P., Littman, M.L.: Activity recognition from accelerometer data. In: Proceedings of the 17th Conference on Innovative Applications of Artificial Intelligence, pp. 1541–1546 (2005)
19. Reddy, S., Shilton, K., Denisov, G., Cenizal, C., Estrin, D., Srivastava, M.: Biketastic: sensing and mapping for better biking. In: Proceedings of the SIGCHI Conference on Human Factors in Computing Systems (CHI'10), pp. 1817–1820 (2010)
20. Reddy, S., Mun, M., Burke, J., Estrin, D., Hansen, M., Srivastava, M.: Using mobile phones to determine transportation modes. Trans. Sens. Netw. 6(2), 13:1–27 (2010)
21. Srivastava, M., Abdelzaher, T., Szymanski, B.: Human-centric sensing. Philos. Trans. Roy. Soc. 370(1958), 176–197 (2012)
22. Shotton, J., Kim, T.-K., Stenger, B.: Boosting and randomized forests for visual recognition (tutorial). In: International Conference on Computer Vision (2009)
23. Shotton, J., Fitzgibbon, A., Cook, M., Sharp, T., Finocchio, M., Moore, R., Kipman, A., Blake, A.: Real-time human pose recognition in parts from single depth images. In: IEEE Conference on Computer Vision and Pattern Recognition, pp. 1–8 (2011)
24. Strazdins, G., Mednis, A., Zviedris, R., Kanonirs, G., Selavo, L.: Virtual ground truth in vehicular sensing experiments: how to mark it accurately. In: Proceedings of 5th International Conference on Sensor Technologies and Applications (SENSORCOMM 2011), pp. 295–300 (2011)
25. Tang, I., Breckon, T.P.: Automatic road environment classification. Trans. Intell. Transp. Syst. 12(2), 476–484 (2011)
26. Ward, C.C., Iagnemma, K.: Speed-independent vibration-based terrain classification for passenger vehicles. Veh. Syst. Dyn. 47(9), 1095–1113 (2009)
27. Weiss, C., Frohlich, H., Zell, A.: Vibration-based terrain classification using support vector machines. In: Proceedings of the 2006 IEEE/RSJ International Conference on Intelligent Robots and Systems (IROS), pp. 4429–4434 (2006)

Wireless Information Networks
and Systems

Reliability of Cooperative Vehicular Applications on Real Scenarios Over an IEEE 802.11p Communications Architecture

Unai Hernandez-Jayo and Idoia De-la-Iglesia[✉]

DeustoTech-Mobility Lab, Deusto Institute of Technology,
Av. Universidaddes 24, 48007 Bilbao, Spain
{unai.hernandez,idoia.delaiglesia}@deusto.es
http://www.deustotech.eu

Abstract. In this paper, the performance of the NEC LinkBird-MX communications gateways and three safety applications are tested. These communications modules allow developers to design and deploy cooperative vehicular applications over Vehicular Ad-hoc Networks. In this work, it is analyzed how the reliability of these applications depends mainly on the goodness of the V2V or I2V radio links. The results of the analysis of these three cooperative applications (intersection crossing warning, emergency vehicle warning and roadwork warning) are shown in this paper.

Keywords: Cooperative vehicular systems · Communications reliability · Active safety applications performance

1 Introduction

Vehicular Ad-Hoc Networks or VANETs have been of particular interest to the communication research area in order to develop a set of applications that could help the driver to avoid or prevent from risky situations. These services are based on the cooperation among vehicles and offer great potential in reducing road accidents and therefore in improving drivers' comfort and efficiency of highways from the traffic management point of view.

But first, to provide these cooperative services a stable and reliable wireless communication system must be deployed on the road infrastructure. For this propose, different technologies have been analyzed in the scenario of infrastructure-to-vehicle (I2V-V2I) and vehicle-to-vehicle (V2V) communications [1,2,16]. Table 1 shows selected characteristics and attributes of a few wireless systems that could be used in a vehicle cooperative scenario [3].

Once the communication link is stable then cooperative and warning services could be deployed with the security that all agents involved in a VANET will have the chance of sending and receiving information regarding road events.

According to ETSI TC on ITS a set of applications can be used as a reference for developing cooperative vehicular systems [4]. In the same way, the U.S.

© Springer-Verlag Berlin Heidelberg 2014
M.S. Obaidat and J. Filipe (Eds.): ICETE 2013, CCIS 456, pp. 387–401, 2014.
DOI: 10.1007/978-3-662-44788-8_23

Department of Transportation (USDOT) has identified similar applications to be deployed thanks to the potential of DSRC to support wireless data communications between vehicles, and between vehicles and infrastructure.

In this framework, this paper aims to determine if a set of applications based on the description provided by ETSI TC on TC can be deployed in a real VANET using two IEEE 802.11p compliant devices, namely LinkBird-MX communication modules provided by NEC Technologies. In order to determine the reliability of both the communication link and the applications, first the main characteristics of tested cooperative vehicle applications are described at Sects. 2 and 3 respectively, whereas the scenarios used during this validation process are described at Sect. 4. The results of this experiments and the analysis about how some safety applications can work in these scenarios are shown in Sect. 5. Finally the conclusions of the paper are presented at Sect. 6.

2   DSRC and IEEE 802.11p

Although all systems included at Table 1 provide specific solutions to different connectivity problems, in a mobile environment in which all the nodes must be able to send and receive reliable messages in real-time, DSRC is the only one system that:

- Is dedicated to wireless access in vehicular Ad-Hoc networks 1-hop and multihop communications.
- Provides active vehicle services with Line-Of-Sight (LOS) and Non-LOS (NLOS) link scenarios.
- Is ready to operate in a rapidly varying environment and to exchange messages without having to join a Basic Service Set (BSS), that is, without the management overhead.
- Makes possible low latency in communications among vehicles and infrastructure allowing sharing real-time information.
- Provides unicast, broadcast, real-time and bidirectional communications.

Table 1. Candidate wireless technologies and attributes.

	DSRC	3G	WLAN
Range	1 km	4–6 km	1 km
One-way to vehicle	X		
One-way from vehicle	X		
Two-way	X	X	X
Point-to-point	X	X	X
Point-to-multipoint	X		
Latency	200 us	1.5–3.5 s	3–4 s

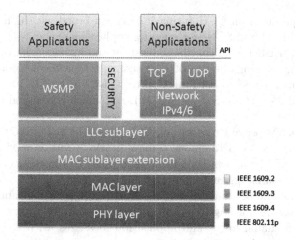

Fig. 1. IEEE WAVE/802.11p protocol stack.

IEEE 802.11p WAVE is only a part of a group of standards related to all layers of protocols of Dedicated Short Range Communications (DSRC) standard [5]. In the DSCR 5.9 GHz band, FCC (Federal Communications Commission) reserved seven channels (1 Control Channel -CCH-, 4 Service Channel -SCH-, 1 Critical Safety of life Channel and 1 Hi-Power Public Channel) of 10 MHz in a bandwidth of 75 MHz for ITS applications while in Europe, ETSI reserved five channel, 1 Control Channel and 4 Service Channel [6].

The IEEE 802.11p standard is limited by the scope of IEEE 802.11 which is the definition of MAC and PHY layers, as it is shown at Fig. 1 [7]. At PHY layer, IEEE 802.11p operates in the band of 5 GHz, reusing IEEE 802.11a OFDM (Orthogonal Frequency Division Multiplexing) modulation considering 52 subcarriers that can be modulated using BPSK, QPSK, 64-QAM or 16-QAM modulation schemas. Besides, IEEE 802.11p reduces inter symbol interference and the channel throughput (from 3 Mbps to 27 Mbps, instead of 6 Mbps to 54 Mbps commonly used in IEEE 802.11a). This setup allows theoretically a communication range over 1000 m (depending on the antennas configuration) and the establishment of communication among vehicles driving up to 200 km/h.

At MAC level, in order to speed up the exchange of messages among the vehicles (referenced as On-Board Units) and Road-Side-Units (RSU), IEEE 802.11p standard simplifies initial connection setup used in common IEEE 802.11 networks. The basic MAC layer is based on CSMA/CD improved with IEEE 802.11e EDCA protocol to provide services with priority levels.

Anyway, MAC layer of IEEE 802.11p is a trend research topic in which many alternatives and protocols are being developing [8-12].

IEEE 1609.4 defines a time-division scheme for DSRC radios to alternately switch within these channels to support different applications concurrently, that is, it supplements IEEE 802.11 features providing frequency band coordination and management within the MAC layer [13]. This is possible thanks to the coordinated operation on CCH (using it only for broadcast, high priority and single-use messages) and SCH (for ongoing applications).

Meanwhile, IEEE 1609.3 specifies operation and management of the communications stack, defining the use of UDP transport protocol, coordinating the IPv6 configuration and Logical Link Control (LLC) in VANETs. This standard also manages WAVE Basic Service Set (WBSS), which is required to handle the SCH transmission.

WAVE Short Message Protocol (WSMP) is used by IEEE 1609.3 networking services in CCH and SCH to enable communications with a maximum payload of 1400 bytes. WSMP allows WAVE-aware devices to directly control physical characteristics (channel number and transmitter power).

Finally, IEEE 1609.2 standard defines secure message formats and the processing of those secure messages in the WAVE system. It covers methods for securing WAVE management and application messages, with the exception of vehicle-originating safety messages.

To sum up, IEEE 802.11p WAVE is only a part of a group of standards related to all layers of protocols for DSRC based operations which concerns to physical and MAC layers. Therefore all the characteristics of the links V2X and the performance of the others DSRC layers depend on the efficiency of IEEE 802.11p standard. For this reason in this paper we will evaluate first the throughput of the IEEE 802.11p link and then the reliability of the applications based on it.

3   Cooperative Based Applications

In the field of cooperative ITS services, a huge variety of applications and use cases can be described. Taking into account strategic, economical and organizational requirements, system capabilities and performances as well as legal and standardization requirements, the ETSI TC on ITS has defined a Basic Set of Applications to be used as a reference for developers [4]. These applications are close similar to those described by the USDOT [3].

They found four different type of applications in the vehicular environment which are active road safety, cooperative traffic efficiency, cooperative local services and global internet services. In each type, different applications and use cases are defined.

Depending on the application and timing restrictions, data exchange among entities can be categorized as:

- Warning messages: these are defined as Decentralized environmental Notification Messages and they can be sent out to each vehicle or RSU.
- Heartbeat messages or beacons: these messages are used by OBUs to report their position, speed and ID to the RSUs. Moreover, these messages are also used to keep updated information about traffic situation. For this, WAVE defines Cooperative Awareness Messages (CAMs), which are broadcasting periodically by each vehicle.
- Non-safety messages: which are used to enhance driver information and comfort: tourism information, Internet access, navigation aid, and so on.

Based on the previously referenced works [3,4], only three active road safety use cases have been analyzed in this paper due to this relevance and likelihood of being deployed in a near future: Intersection Collision Warning, Emergency Vehicle Warning and Roadwork Warning.

4 Scenario Definition

For the purpose of deploying cooperative vehicle applications, a platform of vehicular communications has been designed, where different technologies are implemented to achieve the right exchange and management of data in the system. This platform is composed of the following agents:

- OBUs (On-Board Units) are the different vehicles travelling the roads. They are composed by a Communication Control Unit (CCU), which is the IEEE 802.11p communication router, and an Application Unit (AU), which is a PC which receives, analyses, saves and shows the different information which arrives by the IEEE 802.11p communication link.
- RSUs are different units distributed along the roadsides and they form the infrastructure with the TMC. Each RSU is composed, as OBUs, by a CCU which exchange information with vehicles, and an AU, which decides what received information is relevant and what to do with it. The RSU ask periodically to the TMC about new events in its coverage area, and it shows them in the RSU interface.
- TMC is the Traffic Management Centre and it receives from all the RSUs the information about events happening in their coverage area. Therefore, it manages a database where all the events which have taken place on the road are stored. Thanks to the TMC it is possible to obtain and see in a map the global situation of the roads in a certain time. The database of the TMC is updated with real time traffic issues of the Basque Autonomous Region which are obtained from the Open Data Euskadi initiative.
- HMI (Human Machine Interface) is the device used to show to the driver the information on the screen of a tablet.

4.1 Hardware Setup

In all tests described in this paper, a single omnidirectional radio link is evaluated, either between two OBUs or between a RSU and an OBU. In both entities, the same hardware has been deployed running as OBU or as RSU. The selected hardware is LinkBird-MX which embedded Linux machines based on a 64 bits MIPS processor working at 266 MHz. Besides an IEEE 802.11p interface, these modules are equipped with an Ethernet connector that is used to communicate with the Application Unit (the one that runs the applications in a regular PC), a GPS interface and other interfaces as CAN or RS-232. Figure 2 shows the hardware setup used in the tests that have been carried out in the described scenarios.

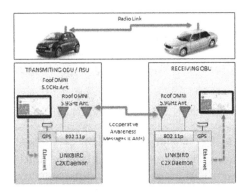

Fig. 2. Hardware setup.

Table 2. IEEE 802.11P hardware setup.

LinkBird-MX		Antenna	
Parameter	Values	Parameter	Values
Frequency	5725–5925 MHz	Model	ECO6-5500
Bandwidth	10 MHz	Frequency	5.0–6.0 GHz
Tx Power	21 dBm	Gain	6 dBi
Bitrates	3 Mbps	Radation	Omni-directional

Although LinkBird allows to select two channel bandwidth, in these tests 10 MHz bandwidth has been selected instead of the 20 MHz one usually used by 802.11a devices, in order to minimize multipath delay spread and Doppler effect that appears in mobility and highway scenarios. Moreover, in order to maintain sufficient reliability of the data transfer in a 1-hop scenario, the lowest bit rate has been used, that is 3 Mbps (bit rates from 3 to 27 Mbps are available at IEEE 802.11p standard), so also the lowest coding rate (1/2) with BPSK modulation has been used to transmit data packets.

Along with the communication modules, two antennas whose characteristics fit well with vehicular applications are provided. One antenna is tuned to the 178 CCH frequency (5.890 GHz) and the other one to the 180 SCH frequency (5.9 GHz) Technical characteristics of hardware setup are shown at Table 2.

4.2 Application Setup

As it has been mentioned in the introduction, one of the objectives of this paper is to check the reliability of three active road safety applications listed by the ETSI TC on ITS. The goal is to test if the links V2X that are deployed using previous hardware setup satisfy the requirement of these applications. According to [4], these requirements are summarized in Table 3.

Table 3. Requirements of applications under test.

	Intersection collision warning	Emergency vehicle warning	Roadwork warning
Application	Driving assistance co-operative awareness	Driving assistance co-operative awareness	Driving assistance road hazard warning
Latency	Less than 100 ms	Less than 100 ms	Less than 100 ms
Message frequency	10 Hz	10 Hz	2 Hz
Special needs	Accurate position of OBU	Triggered by vehicle	RSU broadcasts periodic message
Link	V2V	V2V	I2V

The SDK provided by NEC with the LinkBird-MX modules includes a set of Java API to interact with the IEEE 802.11p protocol stack. Thanks to these facilities, it is simple to develop applications that send Geographical Unicast, Topologically-Scoped Broadcast, Single-Hop Broadcast and Geographically-Scoped Broadcast or Unicast messages. In this way and according to the applications that we want to test (Table 3), all the packets that will be transmitted in our scenarios will be Single-Hop Broadcast.

To carry out these experiments a Java application which sends packets with 100 bytes of payload was developed. The sending frequency is also configurable, from 1 Hz to 10 Hz. This application also measures the delay of a packet from the source to the destination. Each packet is formed by a header, which contents vehicle identification, GPS position and speed, and a payload which contains different information depending on the type of application.

5   Experiments Results

As we mentioned before, the validation of application reliability is necessary to deploy cooperative applications. This reliability depends on the reached goodput of the IEEE 802.11p radio link in the different application defined: Intersection crossing warning, Emergency vehicle warning and Roadwork warning.

An essential characteristic to validate the IEEE 802.11p communications is the Packet Delivery Rate (PDR) at a target distance, since for these cooperative applications make sense messages must be received before the vehicle arrives at the event being reporting (an accident, a traffic jam, etc.).

This distance is Ds and is defined as the distance needed by a driver to stop the vehicle. To calculate this distance is necessary to take into account the driver's reaction time and the braking distance. Using Eq. 1, where V is the velocity expressed in Km/h, f represents the friction coefficient and i the slope of the road in %, we calculate the braking distance.

$$D_s = \frac{V^2}{254(f + i)} \tag{1}$$

As the PDR is not always 1, the Cooperative Awareness Message (CAM) should not be exchanged between vehicles only once, so it is send repeated times. The easiest way would be to send it repeatedly until reach the cross-road, although this is not viable since they could overload the radio link. Then we have to define the ideal number of times, N_T, that the message must be resent for the application to be reliable. N_T depends on two different values, which are the message sending frequency, Tf, and the Twindow [17] which is a concept proposed to evaluate the applications reliability.

$$N_T = Tf * Twindow \tag{2}$$

Twindow is related with Dwindow, which is the distance that the vehicle travels during the time defined by Twindow. At the same time, Dwindow is related with the application reliability because it needs to be defined to quantify the probability of successfully communicating the two vehicles before the target distance Ds.

$$Dwindow = Twindow * Vvehicle \tag{3}$$

The application reliability (p_{app}) is defined as the probability of receiving at least one packet before Ds in a given time Twindow.

$$p_{app} = 1 - \prod_{k=1}^{k=N_T} (1 - p_i) \tag{4}$$

5.1   Intersection Crossing Warning

Chosen scenario is shown at Fig. 3, where there are two vehicles approaching to the intersection. Although tested scenario is placed at an industrial area, this is a typical situation in urban scenarios where buildings create closed intersections with Non-Line-Of-Sight between vehicles. Therefore intersection crossing warning messages is created in order to warn drivers of potential impact when entering an intersection.

The tested scenario recreated the situation where both vehicles approach to the intersection at 50 km/h (13.88 m/s). While in this scenario a stop bar is in the lane of red vehicle, we consider the worst scenario where this vehicle enters the intersection without stopping and could collision with green vehicle.

In order to determinate how the IEEE 802.11p system can be used to avoid the collision, first we work backwards from the worst scenario, that is, the collision occurs. Applying Eq. 1, at 50 km/h each vehicle requires at least 24 m to stop in a flat road. According to [14,15], drive's reaction time can be from 1.26 s to 3 s. If we consider an average value of 2.5 s, in this time car travels 34 m, so in total driver needs 57 m to stop the car.

Hence, in order to avoid the collision and warm the drivers about the presence of each other, the communication link must be reliable and make possible the

Fig. 3. Intersection crossing warning scenario.

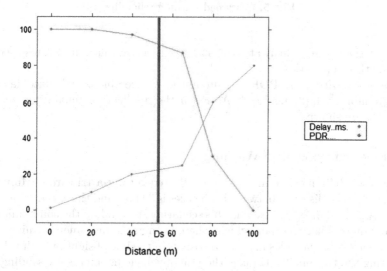

Fig. 4. Intersection crossing warning test results.

messages interchange among vehicles before they enter within 57 m range, refer-enced as '*unavoidable collision area*' (in red) at Fig. 3. For this type of advisor application the Twindow is 2.0 s [17].

In this scenario, the results obtained using LinkBirds communication modules are shown at Fig. 4. It exposes that in this NLOS scenario, these modules can provide a reliable communication link between both vehicles (speed@50km/h) with a Package Delivery Rate of 95 % at a distance of 60 m from the collision point. Hence the vehicles will be able to interchange awareness messages to inform about their presence near the intersection in order to avoid a collision.

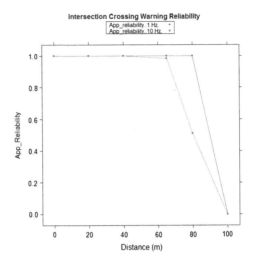

Fig. 5. Crossroad warning reliability.

Moreover, the measure delay at 60 m is 5 ms, that is less than the 100 ms specified at [4] for this application.

Therefore, with these PDR measurements we are able to calculate de application reliability applying Eq. 4. At Fig. 5 the application reliabilities at 1 Hz and 10 Hz are shown.

5.2 Emergency Vehicle Warning

In this test, PDR measurements were collected during a trip from Mungia to Portugalete. The distance between both cities is 34 kms and the speed limit of the motorway is 100 km/h. The goal in this scenario is to validate the communication link from one vehicle to other vehicle where both are in movement at high speed and there are other vehicles like cars or trucks in the line of sight of both vehicles.

During the trip one OBU plays the role of vehicle in emergency sending continuously warning messages to the surrounding vehicles with a period of 1 Hz. The other OBU is the receiver and it analyzes the received message. Different situations were recreated (Fig. 6): V2V link with direct and reflected paths (ground reflections) and different distances and relative speed between transmitter and receiver and V2V link with vehicle blockage (other cars and trucks) between the OBUs, so it is a NLOS and that it includes a diffracted signal path to the receiver, creating the worst-case performance in this scenario.

Figure 7(a) gives the results of motorway experiment to measure the PDR for V2V communication link test using packages with a payload of 100 bytes. The results can be analyzed in sections according to the events recorder during the test:

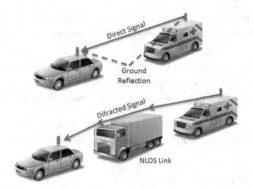

Fig. 6. Emergency vehicle warning scenario.

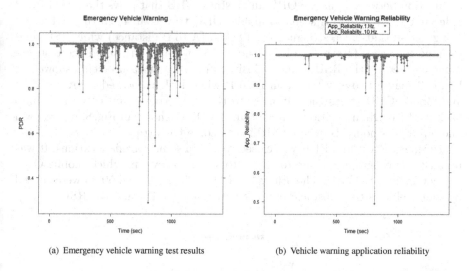

(a) Emergency vehicle warning test results   (b) Vehicle warning application reliability

Fig. 7. Emergency vehicle warning application test.

- Events 'A': in both time slots a LOS situation is shown. Both vehicles' speed was the same, first 80 km/h and then 100 km/h and their relative distance was 45 and 60 m respectively. In both situations PDR is close to 100 % being in the worst cases 98–96 %.
- Event 'B': in this time slot, vehicles' speed was 90 km/h and the relative distance was 177 m because 3 cars were located between OBUs under test. In this NLOS situation the worst PDR is 78 %.
- Event 'C': it reflects the same previous NLOS link but the distance between OBUs was bigger due to the 5 vehicles that were in the middle of the communication link. In this case, the number of low PDR measures is bigger due to the number of obstacles and distance between the OBUs.
- Events 'D' and 'E': these events represent the scenario when a truck blocked the link between OBUs. Here the worst PDR values were obtained being the

event 'E' the time slot in which the lowest PDR (29 %) was measured. It happened when the distance between OBUs where close to 200 m and truck blocked the communication link.

– Event 'F': during this time slot, only 4 vehicles were between OBUs but it happened at the motorway output ramp, where there is u-shaped bend so it was NLOS link. In this case values of PDR lower than 80 % were measured.

Once we have the PDR measurements we can calculate the Emergency Vehicle Warning application reliability applying Eq. 4 as it can be seen at Fig. 7(b).

5.3 Roadwork Warning

To test this safety application, we have recreated a vehicle-to-infrastructure communication between a mobile OBU and a static OBU that plays the role of Road Side Unit (RSU). In this scenario mobile OBU travels at 40 km/h (11,12 m/s) along a road that has a straight line of 860 m (A to B distance) while RSU send warning messages (100 bytes of payload). First we have measured the distance range covered by the RSU using LinkBirds units. The measurements showed at Fig. 7 display a two-way trip from A to B when RSU is located at 'A' location and mobile OBU starts the trip close to the RSU, travels until 'B' and comes back to the original position. The obtained PDR is shown in Fig. 8, where dash line represents point 'B' where OBU starts come back trip.

During the test link PDR was closed to 0 % in some specific locations. It was because the orography of the road due to some 'valleys' in which mobile OBU has not LOS to the RSU. The others low PDR values (around 50 %) were caused by some vehicles that obstacle the link between the OBU and the RSU.

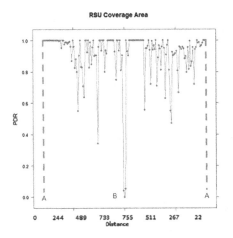

Fig. 8. I2V scenario PDR measurements.

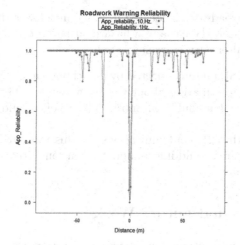

Fig. 9. Roadwork warning reliability.

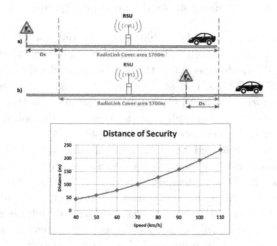

Fig. 10. Roadwork warning scenario.

Based on the previous results, the roadwork warning reliability is show at Fig. 9. According to these results and considering that RSU is equipped with an isotropic antenna, RSU's radio link cover area can be close to 1700 m. In this situation the success of a Roadwork Working safety application depends on two factors: vehicle speed and distance from the end of the covered area by the RSU and the location of roadwork. The limiting cases happen when the OBU receives the warning message at the end of the RSU's covered area and the distance to the roadwork is equal to the distance that the drivers needs to stop the vehicle. Both situations are shown at Fig. 10 with the calculations of the security distance according to Eq. 1.

In case that the roadwork is located in a distance lower than Ds, the driver will not manage to stop the car and a hazard situation could happen. To avoid this situation, two alternatives are suggested:

- Deploy a net of RSUs interconnected by a backbone in order to keep updated all of them with information about the traffic events. Then the whole road (or specific section that could concentrate blackspots) could be covered by the IEEE 802.11p net.
- Combine I2V with V2V communications. In this way OBUs that are inside the RSU covered area could inform about hazardous situations to OBUs that come near to them.

6 Conclusions and Future Work

According to the results obtained in the previous section, we can conclude that a communications architecture based on the NEC-Linkbirds can be used to deploy cooperative awareness applications as the previous explained, in both LOS and NLOS scenarios.

Therefore, we can also conclude that using the proposed hardware configuration, there are no problems in LOS scenarios because high values of PDR are obtained and the delay obtained in all the measures is behind the threshold delay specified by the ETSI TC on ITS [4]. However, this configuration presents poor IEEE 802.11p performance in NLOS conditions, so in order to provide full coverage of a given area, the orography and building distribution must be studied and maybe a fixed RSUs network should be deployed [1].

It must also be considered that the application reliability depends on the CAM transmission frequency. As it is has been evalualed, the p_{app} changes its probability of success if the transmission frequency changes from 10 Hz to 1 Hz. In a NLOS scenario where the transmission frequency is setup to 10 Hz, the application reliability is 100 %, but in a scenario with a high density of vehicles, the communications link will be overload due to the huge amount of sending messages. In this situation, techniques of MAC must be deployed in order to allow every vehicle to exchange information with the maximum application reliability.

Before concluding this paper, we want to express that more measurement campaigns should be performed in a near future to complete this study, but it could be considered as a starting point towards better design of active safety applications. Higher distances among vehicles and RSUs should be tested and in these situations problems as handover, beacons delay or channel congestions issued will be tackled.

Acknowledgments. The authors would like to thank the EU Intelligent Cooperative Sensing for Improved traffic efficiency (ICSI) project (FP7-ICT-2011-8) for its support in the development of this work.

References

1. Bazzi, A., Masini, B.: Real time traffic updates via UMTS: unicast versus multicast transmissions. In: 2011 IEEE Vehicular Technology Conference (VTC Fall), pp. 1–6, September 2011
2. Wewetzer, C., Caliskan, M., Meier, K., Luebke, A.: Experimental evaluation of UMTS and wireless LAN for inter-vehicle communication. In: 7th International Conference on ITS Telecommunications 2007, ITST'07, pp. 1–6 (2007)
3. USDOT: Vehicle Safety Communications Project: Task 3 Final Report: Identify Intelligent Vehicle Safety Applications Enabled by DSRC. National Highway Traffic Safety Administration, Office of Research and Development, Washington, DC (2004)
4. ETSI (2009-06). Intelligent Transport Systems (ITS) and Vehicular communications and Basic set of applications and Definitions. ETSI TR 102 638 V1.1.1
5. Uzcategui, R., Acosta-Marum, G.: Wave: a tutorial. IEEE Commun. Mag. **47**(5), 126–133 (2009)
6. ETSI (2010-01). Intelligent Transport Systems (ITS) and European profile standard for the physical and medium access control layer of Intelligent Transport Systems operating in the 5 GHz frequency band. ETSI ES 202 663 V1.1.0
7. Jiang, D., Delgrossi, L.: IEEE 802.11p: towards an international standard for wireless access in vehicular environments. In: 2008 IEEE Vehicular Technology Conference, VTC Spring 2008, pp. 2036–2040 (2008)
8. Saeed, R.A., Naemat, A.B.H., Aris, A.B., Khamis, I.M., Awang, M.K.B.: Evaluation of the IEEE 802.11p-based TDMA MAC. Int. J. Netw. Mob. Technol. **1**(2) (2010–11)
9. Bhm, A., Jonsson, M.: Real-time communication support for cooperative, infrastructure-based traffic safety applications. Int. J. Veh. Technol. **17** (2011)
10. Bilstrup, K., Uhlemann, E., Strom, E., Bilstrup, U.: Evaluation of the IEEE 802.11p MAC method for vehicle-to-vehicle communication. In: 2008 IEEE 68th Vehicular Technology Conference, VTC 2008-Fall, pp. 1–5 (2008)
11. Han, C., Dianati, M., Tafazolli, R., Kernchen, R., Shen, X.: Analytical study of the IEEE 802.11p MAC sublayer in vehicular networks. IEEE Trans. Intell. Transp. Syst. **13**(2), 873–886 (2012)
12. Bilstrup, K., Uhlemann, E., Strm, E.G., Bilstrup, U.: On the ability of the 802.11p MAC method and STDMA to support real-time vehicle-to-vehicle communication. EURASIP J. Wirel. Commun. Netw. Spec. Issue Wirel. Access Veh. Environ. (5) (2009)
13. Chen, Q., Jiang, D., Delgrossi, L.: IEEE 1609.4 DSRC multi-channel operations and its implications on vehicle safety communications. In: 2009 IEEE Vehicular Networking Conference (VNC), pp. 1–8 (2009)
14. Triggs, T., Harris, W.G.: Reaction time of drivers to road stimuli. Human factors report. Human Factors Group, Department of Psychology, Monash University (1982)
15. American Association of State Highway and Transportation Officials (AASHTO). A Policy on Geometric Design of Highways and Streets (The Green Book) (2001)
16. Chou, C.-M., Li, C.-Y., Chien, W.-M., Chan Lan, K.: A feasibility study on vehicle-to infrastructure communication: Wifi vs. Wimax. In: 2009 Tenth International Conference on Mobile Data Management: Systems, Services and Middleware, MDM'09, pp. 397–398 (2009)
17. Bai, F., et al.: Reliability analysis of DSRC wireless communication for vehicle safety applications. In: Proceedings of the IEEE ITSC, pp. 355–362 (2006)

Transmitter-Side Antennas Correlation in SVD-assisted MIMO Systems

Andreas Ahrens[1]([⊠]), Francisco Cano-Broncano[2],
and César Benavente-Peces[2]

[1] Department of Electrical Engineering and Computer Science,
Communications Signal Processing Group, Hochschule Wismar,
University of Technology, Business and Design, Philipp-Müller-Straße 14,
23966 Wismar, Germany
andreas.ahrens@hs-wismar.de
http://www.hs-wismar.de
[2] E.T.S. de Ingeniería y Sistemas de Telecomunicación,
Universidad Politécnica de Madrid, Ctra. Valencia. km. 7, 28031 Madrid, Spain
fcbroncano@gpss.euitt.upm.es, cesar.benavente@upm.es
http://www.upm.es

Abstract. MIMO techniques allow increasing wireless channel performance by decreasing the BER and increasing the channel throughput and in consequence are included in current mobile communication standards. MIMO techniques are based on benefiting the existence of multipath in wireless communications and the application of appropriate signal processing techniques. The singular value decomposition (SVD) is a popular signal processing technique which, based on the perfect channel state information (PCSI) knowledge at both the transmitter and receiver sides, removes inter-antenna interferences and improves channel performance. Nevertheless, the proximity of the multiple antennas at each front-end produces the so called antennas correlation effect due to the similarity of the various physical paths. In consequence, antennas correlation drops the MIMO channel performance. This investigation focuses on the analysis of a MIMO channel under transmitter-side antennas correlation conditions. First, antennas correlation is analyzed and characterized by the correlation coefficients. The analysis describes the relation between antennas correlation and the appearance of predominant layers which significantly affect the channel performance. Then, based on the SVD, pre- and post-processing is applied to remove inter-antenna interferences. Finally, bit- and power allocation strategies are applied to reach the best performance. The resulting BER reveals that antennas correlation effect diminishes the channel performance and that not necessarily all MIMO layers must be activated to obtain the best performance.

Keywords: Multiple-Input Multiple-Output (MIMO) System · Wireless transmission · Singular value decomposition (SVD) · Bit allocation · Power allocation · Antennas correlation

© Springer-Verlag Berlin Heidelberg 2014
M.S. Obaidat and J. Filipe (Eds.): ICETE 2013, CCIS 456, pp. 402–417, 2014.
DOI: 10.1007/978-3-662-44788-8_24

1   Introduction

MIMO communication systems have been studied along the last two decades because their ability to improve wireless channel performance by decreasing the BER and increasing the channel capacity (data rate) without requiring either additional transmit power neither extra bandwidth. In consequence MIMO techniques are incorporated in communication standards. MIMO systems benefits from scattered environments where multipath is present and in order to obtain the full advantages promised by MIMO techniques additional appropriate signal processing techniques are applied to take advantage of the multipath effect [5].

The singular value decomposition (SVD) is a popular technique which allows removing the inter-antenna interferences due to the multiple antennas arrangements at both the transmitter and the receiver sides [3]. The SVD transforms the multipath MIMO channel into multiple independent layers (single-input single-output channels, SISO). In order to get the full benefits of using the SVD and obtain the best performance, perfect channel state information (PCSI) should be available at both the transmitter and receiver front-ends. Once the SVD has been applied each resulting layer path is affected by a different gain factor given by the corresponding singular value resulting in layers with different performance. The ideal set-up is that in which after applying the SVD all the layers behave in the same way, i.e., all the singular values take the same value. Unfortunately this is not the common situation and the various layers have different performance.

MIMO wireless channels are affected by the various disturbances influencing regular wireless communication systems. Additionally, due to the use of multiple antennas at both the transmitter and receiver sides, and the typical close spacing of the antennas due to physical limitations, the so called antennas correlation effect arises [6,10,11] affecting the MIMO channel performance.

MIMO channels where antennas are uncorrelated have been largely studied and have reached a state of maturity. In contrast, antennas-correlated MIMO channels require substantial further research in order to characterize the antennas correlation effect and its influence on the channel performance which allows the application of appropriate strategies to optimize the MIMO channel performance.

Antennas correlation diminishes multipath richness, which is essential to MIMO techniques. Due to that effect the various paths established from each transmitter-side antenna to each receiver-side antenna become similar. Under this condition applying the SVD deals to singular values which are quite different and the ratio between the largest and smallest singular values becomes high. In consequence predominant layers arise, some with large singular values which have a pretty good performance and others with quite low singular values which have a poor performance. The overall effect is the drop of the channel performance.

In consequence this paper analyzes and characterizes the antennas correlation effect focusing the attention on the transmitter-side. The analysis remarks the parameters affecting the correlation effect and their influence on the overall system performance in order to seek for appropriate strategies to improve the overall channel performance.

Based on independent layers resulting from the application of the pre- and post- processing by using the SVD to the antennas correlated MIMO channel, bit and power allocation techniques can be applied to improve the MIMO system performance [7,13]. Given the MIMO channel decomposition into various independent layers with different performance, various transmission modes are defined and investigating by allocating a different number of bits per transmit symbol along the various layers while maintaining the overall data rate. Through the analysis of some exemplary transmission modes this paper shows that not all the layers should be activated in order to obtain the best results.

Power allocation techniques distribute the available transmit power along the different transmit antennas. One of the most popular techniques is the so called water-filling. Based on the layers quality (mainly determined by the corresponding singular value), the layers which should be activated are indentified and hence the total available transmit power is appropriately distributed.

Against the aforementioned background, the novel contribution of this paper is that we demonstrate the benefits of amalgamating a suitable choice of activated MIMO layers and number of bits per symbol together with the appropriate allocation of the transmit power under the constraint of a given fixed data throughput and under the antennas correlation effect. Our results show that under the constraint of correlation only a few number of layers should be used for the data transmission when minimizing the overall bit-error rate.

The remaining part of this paper is organized as follows. Section 2 describes the MIMO system model including the antennas correlation characterization. The bit- and power assignment in correlated channel situation is discussed in Sect. 3. The obtained results are presented and interpreted in Sect. 4. Finally Sect. 5 remarks the main results obtained in this investigation.

2   MIMO System Model

This section is aimed to establish the MIMO channel model under the transmitter-side antennas correlation effect. First, the correlation coefficients are defined and mathematically deduced from the physical set-up in order to characterize the overall MIMO system model.

2.1   Transmitter-Side Correlation Coefficients Characterization

The correlation effect is described by the correlation coefficients. Transmitter-side antennas correlation coefficients describe the similitude between paths corresponding to a pair of antennas (at the transmitter side) with respect to a reference antenna (at the receiver side). Figure 1 describes the basic set-up for obtaining the correlation coefficient, where d is the transmitter-side antennas spacing, d_1 is the distance between transmit antenna #1 and the receiver-side antenna (taken as reference) and d_2 is the distance from transmit antenna #2 to the reference receive antenna (it is assumed $d << d_1, d_2$); ϕ is the departure

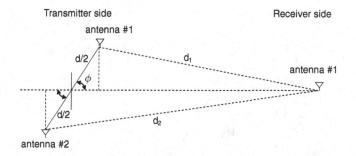

Fig. 1. Antennas' physical disposition: two transmit and one receive antennas.

angle. In consequence two paths are described and the correlation coefficient describes how like they are.

When analyzing the system configuration, presented in Fig. 1, the correlation between the signal $s_{\mathrm{r}\,1}(t)$, i.e. the signal arriving at the receive antenna from transmit antenna #1, and the signal $s_{\mathrm{r}\,2}(t)$, i.e. the signal arriving at the receive antenna from transmit antenna #2, is given by

$$\rho_{1,2}^{(\mathrm{TX})} = \frac{\mathbf{E}\left\{s_{\mathrm{r}\,1}(t) \cdot s_{\mathrm{r}\,2}^{*}(t)\right\} - \mathbf{E}\left\{s_{\mathrm{r}\,1}(t)\right\} \cdot \mathbf{E}\left\{s_{\mathrm{r}\,2}(t)\right\}}{\sqrt{\mathbf{E}\left\{s_{\mathrm{r}\,1}(t) \cdot s_{\mathrm{r}\,1}^{*}(t)\right\}} \cdot \sqrt{\mathbf{E}\left\{s_{\mathrm{r}\,2}(t) \cdot s_{\mathrm{r}\,2}^{*}(t)\right\}}} \,, \tag{1}$$

and simplifies as shown in [2] to

$$\rho_{1,2}^{(\mathrm{TX})} = \mathrm{e}^{-\,\mathrm{j}\,2\,\pi\,\frac{(d_1 - d_2)}{\lambda}} \,. \tag{2}$$

The transmit antenna separation $d_\lambda = d/\lambda$ given in wavelengths units can be expressed as

$$\frac{d_2 - d_1}{\lambda} = d_\lambda \cdot \cos(\phi) \,. \tag{3}$$

Inserting (3) in (2), the transmitter-side correlation coefficient is given by

$$\rho_{1,2}^{(\mathrm{TX})} = \mathrm{e}^{\mathrm{j}\,2\,\pi\,d_\lambda\,\cos(\phi)} \,. \tag{4}$$

The antennas path correlation coefficient for line of sight (LOS) trajectories depends on the antennas separation d_λ and the transmit antennas reference axis rotation angle ϕ (or *signals angle of departure*). By taking the scattered environment of wireless channels into consideration, the transmit antennas reference axis rotation angle ϕ becomes time-variant and (4) results in:

$$\rho_{1,2}^{(\mathrm{TX})} = \mathbf{E}\left\{\mathrm{e}^{\mathrm{j}\,2\,\pi\,d_\lambda\,\cos(\phi+\xi_i)}\right\} \,. \tag{5}$$

The parameter ξ_i in (5) expresses the randomness of the angles for the various scatters and is described by a Gaussian distribution with zero mean and variance σ_ξ^2. Calculating the expectation under this assumption leads to the following equation:

$$\rho_{1,2}^{(\mathrm{TX})}(\phi, \sigma_\xi) = \mathrm{e}^{\mathrm{j}\,2\,\pi\,d_\lambda\,\cos(\phi)}\,\mathrm{e}^{-\frac{1}{2}(2\,\pi\,d_\lambda\,\sin(\phi)\,\sigma_\xi)^2} \,. \tag{6}$$

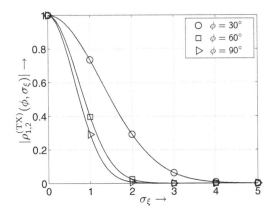

Fig. 2. Variation of the correlation coefficient $|\rho_{1,2}^{(\mathrm{TX})}(\phi, \sigma_\xi)|$ as a function of σ_ξ and ϕ assuming an antennas separation in wavelengths of $d_\lambda = 1/4$.

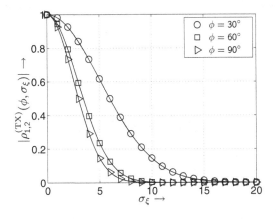

Fig. 3. Variation of the correlation coefficient $|\rho_{1,2}^{(\mathrm{TX})}(\phi, \sigma_\xi)|$ as a function of σ_ξ and ϕ assuming a wavelength specific antenna separation of $d_\lambda = 1/16$.

When analysing Figs. 2 and 3, high valued correlation coefficients appear for small values of ϕ and σ_ξ parameters. Additionally, in case of a small antenna separation, i.e. reducing d_λ, the received signals $s_{\mathrm{r}\,1}(t)$ and $s_{\mathrm{r}\,2}(t)$ become even more similar.

2.2   Correlated MIMO System Model

The $(n_{\mathrm{R}} \times n_{\mathrm{T}})$ system matrix $\mathbf{H}$ of a correlated MIMO system model is given by

$$\mathrm{vec}(\mathbf{H}) = \mathbf{R}_{\mathrm{HH}}^{\frac{1}{2}} \cdot \mathrm{vec}(\mathbf{G}), \tag{7}$$

where $\mathbf{G}$ is a $(n_R \times n_T)$ uncorrelated channel matrix with independent, identically distributed complex-valued Rayleigh elements and $\text{vec}(\cdot)$ is the operator stacking the matrix $\mathbf{G}$ into a vector column-wise [8]. Based on the quite common assumption that the correlation between the antenna elements at the transmitter side is independent from the correlation between the antenna elements at the receiver side, the correlation matrix $\mathbf{R}_{HH}$ can be decomposed into a transmitter side correlation matrix $\mathbf{R}_{TX}$ and a receiver side correlation matrix $\mathbf{R}_{RX}$ following the Kronecker product $\otimes$. Under this assumption the matrix $\mathbf{R}_{HH}$ is formulated as

$$\mathbf{R}_{HH} = \mathbf{R}_{TX} \otimes \mathbf{R}_{RX} \,. \tag{8}$$

In this paper, no correlation at the receiver side is assumed. Therefore, the $(n_R \times n_R)$ receiver-side correlation matrix $\mathbf{R}_{RX}$ simplifies to

$$\mathbf{R}_{RX} = \mathbf{I} \,, \tag{9}$$

with the matrix $\mathbf{I}$ describing the identity matrix. The $(n_R \times n_R)$ correlation matrix $\mathbf{R}_{TX}$ for the investigated (4×4) MIMO system is finally given by:

$$\mathbf{R}_{TX}^{(4 \times 4)} = \begin{pmatrix} 1 & \rho_{1,2}^{(TX)} & \rho_{1,3}^{(TX)} & \rho_{1,4}^{(TX)} \\ \rho_{2,1}^{(TX)} & 1 & \rho_{2,3}^{(TX)} & \rho_{2,4}^{(TX)} \\ \rho_{3,1}^{(TX)} & \rho_{3,2}^{(TX)} & 1 & \rho_{3,4}^{(TX)} \\ \rho_{4,1}^{(TX)} & \rho_{4,2}^{(TX)} & \rho_{4,3}^{(TX)} & 1 \end{pmatrix} \,. \tag{10}$$

Therein, the correlation coefficient $\rho_{k,\ell}^{(TX)}$ describes the transmitter side correlation between the transmit antenna k and ℓ. Taking line-of-sight conditions into account, the correlation coefficient results according to (4) in

$$\rho_{k,\ell}^{(TX)} = e^{-j\,2\,\pi\,(k-\ell)\,d_\lambda\,\cos(\phi)} \quad \text{for} \quad k < \ell \,. \tag{11}$$

Extending these results to scattered conditions, the transmitter side correlation coefficient results according to (5) for $k < \ell$ in

$$\rho_{k,\ell}^{(TX)}(\phi, \sigma_\xi) = e^{-j\,2\,\pi(k-\ell)d_\lambda\,\cos(\phi)}\, e^{-\frac{1}{2}(2\,\pi\,(k-\ell)\,d_\lambda\,\sin(\phi)\,\sigma_\xi)^2} \,. \tag{12}$$

For the calculation of the transmitter-side correlation coefficient for values of $k > \ell$ it can be exploited that the values of the correlation coefficients are complex conjugated. This is due to the sign change when computing the distance difference between antennas with different antenna reference (see Fig. 4). Finally, the following equation can be used to calculate the correlation coefficient for values of $k > \ell$

$$\rho_{\ell,k}^{(TX)} = \rho_{k,\ell}^{*(TX)} \,. \tag{13}$$

Having frequency non-selective MIMO channels, the whole MIMO system can be decomposed into a number of independent, non-interfering layers. Figure 5 depicts the layer system model resulting after applying the singular value decomposition, where the weighting factors $\sqrt{\xi_{\ell,k}}$ represent the positive square roots

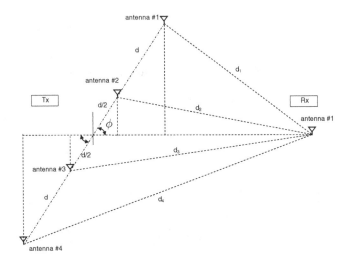

Fig. 4. Antennas' physical disposition: four transmit and one receive antennas.

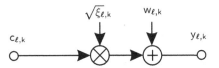

Fig. 5. Resulting system model per MIMO layer ℓ and transmitted data block k.

Table 1. Parameters of the of the investigated channel constellations

Description	ϕ	σ_ξ	d_λ
Weak correlation	30°	1	1
Strong correlation	30°	1	0,25

of the eigenvalues of the system matrix per MIMO layer ℓ and per transmitted data block k. The transmitted complex input symbol per MIMO layer ℓ is described by $c_{\ell,k}$ and the additive white Gaussian noise (AWGN) by $w_{\ell,k}$, respectively. In general, correlation influenced the unequal weighting of the different layers. In order to carefully study the influence of the correlation, two channel constellations are chosen as highlighted in Table 1. The corresponding unequal weighting of the different layers is shown in Figs. 6 and 7 for an exemplarily studied (4×4) MIMO system. Therein, the difference in the layer-specific fluctuations is described by the probability density function (pdf) of the parameter $\vartheta = \sqrt{\xi_{\ell=4,k}}/\sqrt{\xi_{\ell=1,k}}$, which shows the unequal weighting of the different layers within the MIMO system.

The ratio between the smallest and the largest singular values is an appropriate way to infer the antennas correlation effects. When this parameter ϑ

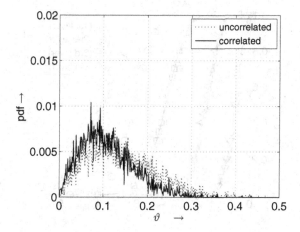

Fig. 6. PDF (probability density function) of the ratio ϑ between the smallest and the largest singular value for weakly correlated (solid line) as well as uncorrelated (dotted line) frequency non-selective (4×4) MIMO channels $(d_\lambda = 1$, $\phi = 30°$ and $\sigma_\xi = 1,0)$.

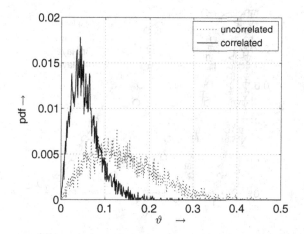

Fig. 7. PDF (probability density function) of the ratio ϑ between the smallest and the largest singular value for strongly correlated (solid line) as well as uncorrelated (dotted line) frequency non-selective (4×4) MIMO channels $(d_\lambda = 1/4$, $\phi = 30°$ and $\sigma_\xi = 1,0)$.

approaches the unity the MIMO channel is close to the best performance which is reached when all the layers have the same performance (assuming the same noise power at the receiver-side). In this particular case the layer-specific weighting factors, i.e., the singular values, are very similar. For weak antennas correlation, as depicted in Fig. 6, this parameter decreases which means some layers performs better than others and the overall MIMO channel performance

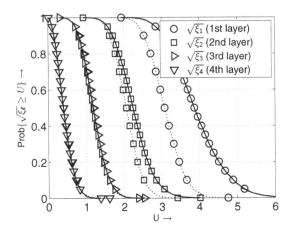

Fig. 8. CCDF of the layer-specific distribution for weakly correlated (solid line) as well as uncorrelated (dotted line) frequency non-selective (4×4) MIMO channels $(d_\lambda = 1$, $\phi = 30°$ and $\sigma_\xi = 1{,}0)$.

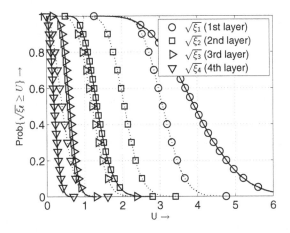

Fig. 9. CCDF of the layer-specific distribution for strongly correlated (solid line) as well as uncorrelated (dotted line) frequency non-selective (4×4) MIMO channels $(d_\lambda = 1/4$, $\phi = 30°$ and $\sigma_\xi = 1{,}0)$.

drops. When antennas correlation is significantly high, the parameter ϑ becomes smaller, meaning a noticeable difference in the performance of the various layer. Now, predominant strong and weak layers appear which decreases the overall channel performance (by increasing the BER).

The distribution of the layer-specific characteristic can be studied when analyzing the CCDF (complementary cumulative distribution function) for the different degrees of correlation as shown in Figs. 8 and 9. The antennas correlation increases the probability of having layers with larger values (see layers $\sqrt{\xi_1}$ and $\sqrt{\xi_2}$) and increases for weak layers the probability of having lower values (see layers $\sqrt{\xi_3}$ and $\sqrt{\xi_4}$).

The inspection of the CCDF also provides relevant information to predict the MIMO channel performance. Increasing antennas correlation spreads the singular values CCDF curves. For the non-correlated case, the various layers CCDF seem to be more concentrated. In the ideal case all of them overlap and the best performance is obtained. Weak correlation spreads the curves by right shifting those corresponding to the highest singular values increasing the probability of getting large values in contrast to the smallest singular values. Under strong antennas correlation the CCDF curve for the largest singular values are indeed more right shifted while the smallest ones are left shifted. In consequence, in this case the probability of the largest singular value to obtain a high value increases while the probability of taking the smallest singular values a lower value also increases dealing to the MIMO channel worse performance.

3   Bit- and Power Assignment

Assuming M-ary Quadrature Amplitude Modulation (QAM), the argument $\varrho = U_{\mathrm{A}}^2/U_{\mathrm{R}}^2$ of the complementary error function [4,9] can be used to optimize the quality of a data communication system by taking the half-vertical eye-opening U_{A} and the noise power per quadrature component U_{R}^2 at the detector input into account [1]. The half-vertical eye-opening per MIMO layer ℓ and per transmitted symbol block k results in

$$U_{\mathrm{A}}^{(\ell,k)} = \sqrt{\xi_{\ell,k}} \cdot U_{\mathrm{s}\ell}, \tag{14}$$

where $U_{\mathrm{s}\ell}$ denotes the half-level transmit amplitude assuming M_ℓ-ary QAM and $\sqrt{\xi_{\ell,k}}$ represents the positive square roots of the eigenvalues of the matrix $\mathbf{H}^{\mathrm{H}}\,\mathbf{H}$. The average transmit power $P_{\mathrm{s}\ell}$ per MIMO layer ℓ determines the half-level transmit amplitude $U_{\mathrm{s}\ell}$ and is given by

$$P_{\mathrm{s}\ell} = \frac{2}{3} U_{\mathrm{s}\ell}^2 (M_\ell - 1). \tag{15}$$

Activating $L \leq \min(n_{\mathrm{T}}, n_{\mathrm{R}})$ MIMO layers, the overall transmit power $P_{\mathrm{s}} = \sum_{\ell=1}^{L} P_{\mathrm{s}\ell}$ can be calculated.

Power Allocation (PA) can be used to balance the BER in the different numbers of activated MIMO layers [1]. The resulting layer-specific system model including power allocation is highlighted in Fig. 10. The layer-specific power allocation factors $\sqrt{p_{\ell,k}}$ adjust the half-vertical eye opening according to

$$U_{\mathrm{A\,PA}}^{(\ell,k)} = \sqrt{p_{\ell,k}} \cdot \sqrt{\xi_{\ell,k}} \cdot U_{\mathrm{s}\ell}. \tag{16}$$

This results in the layer-specific transmit power per symbol block k

$$P_{\mathrm{s\,PA}}^{(\ell,k)} = p_{\ell,k}\, P_{\mathrm{s}\ell}. \tag{17}$$

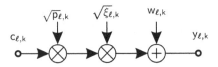

Fig. 10. Resulting layer-specific system model including MIMO-layer PA.

Taking all activated MIMO layers into account, the overall transmit power per symbol block k is obtained as

$$P_{s\,PA}^{(k)} = \sum_{\ell=1}^{L} P_{s\,PA}^{(\ell,k)} = P_s \,. \tag{18}$$

In order to balance the BER in the different numbers of activated MIMO layers, solutions for the so far unknown PA parameters are needed.

A simplified PA solution can be found when guaranteeing that the signal-to-noise-ratio at the detector input is the same for all activated MIMO layers per data block k. In this particular case, the following condition should be ensured for the signal-to-noise ratio at the detector input

$$\varrho_{PA}^{(\ell,k)} = \frac{\left(U_{A\,PA}^{(\ell,k)}\right)^2}{U_R^2} = \text{constant} \quad \ell = 1, 2, \ldots, L \,. \tag{19}$$

When assuming an identical detector input noise variance U_R^2 for each channel output symbol the beforehand introduces Equal-SNR criteria requires the same half vertical eye opening of each channel output symbol

$$U_{A\,PA}^{(\ell,k)} = \text{constant} \quad \ell = 1, 2, \ldots, L \,. \tag{20}$$

The power to be allocated to each activated MIMO layer ℓ and transmitted data block k can be shown to be calculated as follows:

$$p_{\ell,k} = \frac{1}{U_{s\,\ell}^2 \cdot \xi_{\ell,k}} \cdot \frac{L}{\sum_{\nu=1}^{L} \frac{1}{U_{s\,\nu}^2 \cdot \xi_{\nu,k}}} \,, \tag{21}$$

and guarantees for each channel output symbol $(\ell = 1, \ldots, L)$ the same half vertical eye opening of

$$U_{A\,PA}^{(\ell,k)} = \sqrt{p_{\ell,k}} \cdot \sqrt{\xi_{\ell,k}} \cdot U_{s\,\ell} = \sqrt{\frac{L}{\sum_{\nu=1}^{L} \frac{1}{U_{s\,\nu}^2 \, \xi_{\nu,k}}}} \,. \tag{22}$$

Together with the identical detector input noise variance for each channel output symbol, the above-mentioned equal quality scenario is encountered.

4 Results

In this work a (4×4) MIMO system with transmitter-side antennas correlation is studied.

In order to transmit at a fixed data rate while maintaining the best possible integrity, i. e., bit-error rate, an appropriate number of MIMO layers has to be used, which depends on the specific transmission mode, as detailed in Table 2.

The choice of fixed transmission modes regardless of the channel quality can be justified when analyzing the probability of choosing a specific transmission mode by using optimal bit loading [12]. As highlighted in Table 3 for uncorrelated MIMO channels, it turns out that only an appropriate number of MIMO layers has to be activated, e. g., the $(16, 4, 4, 0)$ QAM configuration. However, when the correlation effect appears as illustrated in Table 4 for weakly correlated as well as in Table 5 for highly correlated MIMO channels, the importance of using layers with large singular values increases.

Table 2. Investigated QAM transmission modes.

Throughput	Layer 1	Layer 2	Layer 3	Layer 4
8 bit/s/Hz	256	0	0	0
8 bit/s/Hz	**64**	**4**	**0**	**0**
8 bit/s/Hz	**16**	**16**	**0**	**0**
8 bit/s/Hz	**16**	**4**	**4**	**0**
8 bit/s/Hz	4	4	4	4

Table 3. Probability of choosing specific transmission modes at a fixed data rate by using optimal bitloading $(10 \cdot \log_{10}(E_s/N_0) = 10\,\text{dB})$.

mode	$(64,4,0,0)$	$(16,16,0,0)$	$(16,4,4,0)$	$(4,4,4,4)$
pdf	0.0116	0.2504	0.7373	0.0008

Table 4. Probability of choosing specific transmission modes in weakly correlated MIMO channels at a fixed data rate by using optimal bitloading $(10 \cdot \log_{10}(E_s/N_0) = 10\,\text{dB})$.

mode	$(64,4,0,0)$	$(16,16,0,0)$	$(16,4,4,0)$	$(4,4,4,4)$
pdf	0.1274	0.3360	0.5366	0.0

Table 5. Probability of choosing specific transmission modes in strongly correlated MIMO channels at a fixed data rate by using optimal bitloading $(10 \cdot \log_{10}(E_s/N_0) = 10\,\text{dB})$.

mode	$(64,4,0,0)$	$(16,16,0,0)$	$(16,4,4,0)$	$(4,4,4,4)$
pdf	0.8252	0.1087	0.0605	0.0

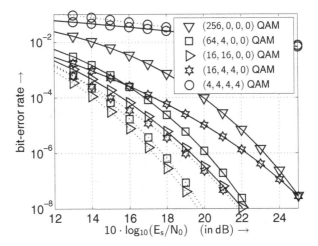

Fig. 11. BER with optimal PA (dotted line) and without PA (solid line) when using the transmission modes introduced in Table 2 and transmitting 8 bit/s/Hz over frequency non-selective (4 × 4) MIMO channels ($d_\lambda = 1$, $\phi = 30°$ and $\sigma_\xi = 1{,}0$) with weak transmitter-side correlation.

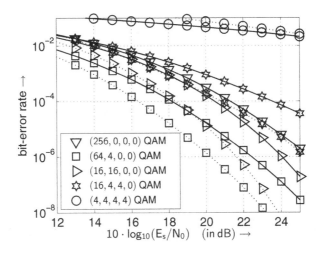

Fig. 12. BER with optimal PA (dotted line) and without PA (solid line) when using the transmission modes introduced in Table 2 and transmitting 8 bit/s/Hz over frequency non-selective (4 × 4) MIMO channels ($d_\lambda = 1/4$, $\phi = 30°$ and $\sigma_\xi = 1{,}0$) with strong transmitter-side correlation.

The optimal performance results when using PA are shown in Figs. 11 and 12: The BER becomes minimal in case of an optimized bit loading with highest bit loading in the layer with largest singular values.

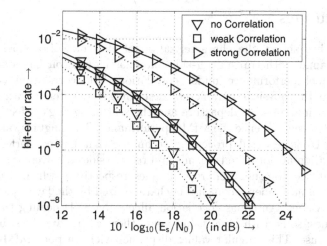

Fig. 13. BER with optimal PA (dotted line) and without PA (solid line) when using the $(16, 16, 0, 0$ QAM transmission mode and transmitting 8 bit/s/Hz over frequency non-selective (4×4) MIMO channels with different degrees of correlation.

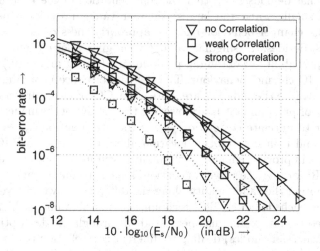

Fig. 14. BER with optimal PA (dotted line) and without PA (solid line) when using the $(64, 4, 0, 0$ QAM transmission mode and transmitting 8 bit/s/Hz over frequency non-selective (4×4) MIMO channels with different degrees of correlation.

Figures 13 and 14 show the MIMO system performance when using fixed transmission modes and having different degrees of correlation. As highlighted by the BER curves, in case of high correlation only the layers with the largest singular values should be used for the data transmission.

5   Conclusions

This paper has shown the characterization of the correlation coefficients in a MIMO channel with transmitter-side antennas correlation has analyzed the MIMO channel performance under correlation. The correlation coefficients depend on paths physical parameters describing the antennas arrangement. Antennas spacing, angle of departure and the scattering angle affect the paths correlation degree and hence the MIMO performance. The singular value decomposition (SVD) is a signal processing technique that having perfect channel state information at both the transmit and receive sides involves pre- and post-processing at the transmit and receive sides respectively which converts the MIMO channel into independent layers characterized by the layer gain given by the singular values. Antennas correlation affects the SVD dealing to dispersed singular values: some with large values and others with low values, in contrast to the ideal case. This singular values dispersion yields a poor MIMO channel performance due to those layers with low singular values which present a low reliability. The overall antennas correlation effect is described by the correlation matrix which relates the channel uncorrelated matrix to the correlated one. The analysis has demonstrated that the representation of the PDF of the ratio between the smallest and the largest singular values provides a useful mean to predict the channel behavior and the appropriateness of activating all the MIMO layers. Besides, the singular values CCDF gives relevant information concerning the probability of obtaining predominant (strong and weak) layers and infer the MIMO channel behaviour. The best performance is obtained when all CCDF coincide (are the same) or are quite close. CCDF curve dispersion reveals the existence of predominant layer lowering the MIMO performance. Additionally, in order to mitigate correlation effects the investigation has analyzed the effect of bit and transmit power allocation along the various MIMO layers as techniques for improving channel performance even in the presence of antennas correlation. Regarding the power allocation, a basic technique has been applied in order to obtain the same quality along the different activated layers, i.e., the same SNR at each detector. This technique allows obtaining a higher performance. Moreover, bit loading has been studied through the description of some profiles (transmission modes) dealing to different constellation per layer (bit per symbol interval) but maintaining the overall transmission rate. A remarkable conclusion is that activating all the MIMO layers not necessarily provides the best performance as highlighted in the results where the transmission modes $(64, 4, 0, 0)$ and $(16, 16, 0, 0)$ present the best performance. In order to highlight the importance of this fact the probability of using each transmission mode was analyzed and the previous conclusion was remarked.

References

1. Ahrens, A., Lange, C.: Modulation-mode and power assignment in SVD-equalized MIMO systems. Facta Univ. (Series Electronics and Energetics) **21**(2), 167–181 (2008)

2. Cano-Broncano, F., Benavente-Peces, C., Ahrens, A., Ortega-Gonzalez, F.J., Pardo-Martin, J.M.: Analysis of MIMO systems with transmitter-side antennas correlation. In: International Conference on Pervasive and Embedded Computing and Communication Systems (PECCS), Barcelona, Spain (2013)
3. Haykin, S.S.: Adaptive Filter Theory. Prentice Hall, New Jersey (2002)
4. Kalet, I.: Optimization of linearly equalized QAM. IEEE Trans. Commun. **35**(11), 1234–1236 (1987)
5. Kühn, V.: Wireless Communications over MIMO Channels - Applications to CDMA and Multiple Antenna Systems. Wiley, Chichester (2006)
6. Lee, W.-Y.: Effects on correlation between two mobile radio base-station antennas. IEEE Trans. Veh. Technol. **22**(4), 130–140 (1973)
7. Mutti, C., Dahlhaus, P.: Adaptive power loading for multiple-input multiple-output ofdm systems with perfect channel state information. In: Joint COST 273/284 Workshop on Antennas and Related System Aspects in Wireless Communications, pp. 93–98, Gothenburg (2004)
8. Oestges, C.: Validity of the kronocker model for MIMO correlated channels. In: Vehicular Technology Conference, Melbourne, vol. 6, pp. 2818–2822 (2006)
9. Proakis, J.G.: Digital Communications. McGraw-Hill, Boston (2000)
10. Salz, J., Winters, J.H.: Effect of fading correlation on adaptive arrays in digital mobile radio. IEEE Trans. Veh. Technol. **43**(4), 1049–1057 (1994)
11. Shiu, D., Foschini, G., Gans, M., Kahn, J.: Fading correlation and its effect on the capacity of multielement antenna systems. IEEE Trans. Commun. **48**(3), 502–513 (2000)
12. Wong, C.Y., Cheng, R.S., Letaief, K.B., Murch, R.D.: Multiuser OFDM with adaptive subcarrier, bit, and power allocation. IEEE J. Sel. Areas Commun. **17**(10), 1747–1758 (1999)
13. Zhou, Z., Vucetic, B., Dohler, M., Li, Y.: MIMO systems with adaptive modulation. IEEE Trans. Veh. Technol. **54**(5), 1073–1096 (2005)

Author Index